Rebel women
between the wars

Manchester University Press

Rebel women between the wars

Fearless writers and adventurers

Sarah Lonsdale

Manchester University Press

Copyright © Sarah Lonsdale 2020

The right of Sarah Lonsdale to be identified as the author of this work has been asserted by her in accordance with the Copyright, Designs and Patents Act 1988.

Published by Manchester University Press
Altrincham Street, Manchester M1 7JA
www.manchesteruniversitypress.co.uk

British Library Cataloguing-in-Publication Data
A catalogue record for this book is available from the British Library

ISBN 978 1 5261 3711 1 hardback

First published 2020

The publisher has no responsibility for the persistence or accuracy of URLs for any external or third-party internet websites referred to in this book, and does not guarantee that any content on such websites is, or will remain, accurate or appropriate.

Typeset by
Servis Filmsetting Ltd, Stockport, Cheshire
Printed in Great Britain by
Bell and Bain Ltd, Glasgow

For my parents, Moya and John

Enough of pulling off high heels to run
...
Let us want none of what anchored our mothers
Let us never evolve to be good or beautiful
Let us spit and snarl and rattle the hatches

...

You
Are a mighty thing

From 'Daughters' by Phoebe Stuckes

Contents

List of figures	viii
Acknowledgements	x
List of abbreviations	xiii
Introduction: 'The women at the gate'	1
1 Female friendship, work and collaboration	19
2 Alternative channels	62
3 Parallel platforms and safe havens	97
4 Risk-takers	136
5 Parental influence and family networks	175
6 Rejecting the feminine	211
7 Formal networks	249
8 Explosive engagement	297
9 Hiding in plain sight	332
Conclusion	358
Appendix: The Second World War and beyond	368
Bibliography	380
Index	405

Figures

1. Alison Settle as editor of *Vogue*, 1929, Alison Settle Archive, University of Brighton Design Archives/Howard and Joan Coster — 39
2. Alison Settle, *Observer* war correspondent, 1944, Alison Settle Archive, University of Brighton Design Archives/Tricolor — 44
3. Francesca Wilson, early 1900s, with thanks to Josephine Horder — 67
4. Dorothy Pilley, c. 1926, with thanks to the Alpine Club Library — 104
5. Ladies' Alpine Club annual report cover, with thanks to the Alpine Club Library — 123
6. *Pinnacle Club Journal* cover, with thanks to the Pinnacle Club — 124
7. Shiela Grant Duff, 1939, copyright National Portrait Gallery — 138
8. Margaret Lane, c. 1930s, with thanks to Selina Hastings — 178

Figures

9 Stanhope Forbes, *The Munition Girls* (1918), courtesy of the Science Museum/Science and Society Picture Library — 215
10 Claudia Parsons, c. 1920s, with thanks to Loughborough University and Heather Cullity — 224
11 Leah Manning, c. 1920s, with thanks to the Essex County Record Office — 259
12 Una Marson at the BBC, 1941, copyright BBC (reproduced courtesy of the British Broadcasting Corporation, all rights reserved) — 273
13 Kylie Tennant, c. 1930, 'Buchner Portrait' (photograph by Rudolph Buchner), MS 10043 Box 44, National Library of Australia — 306
14 Stella Martin, c. 1920s, with thanks to James Currey — 346

Acknowledgements

This book was partly written while I was on sabbatical from my post at City University, and I would like to thank City for giving me the time to think and write. I would also like to thank my friend and colleague Professor Jan Montefiore, for reading early chapters and for giving me encouragement at critical times. Thanks, too, to my editor, Emma Brennan at Manchester University Press, for being so enthusiastic and for believing in this project right from the start, and without whom this book would never have seen the light of day. Also huge thanks to Andrew Kirk, for his fine, patient and careful copy-editing.

I have been helped in many generous ways by the surviving relatives of the women in this book, without whom I would not have had access to some of the more intimate aspects of their lives, including diaries, letters and personal reminiscences; and I also thank them for giving me permission to quote from their relatives' material. I would particularly like to thank Alison Settle's grandsons, Mark Settle and Charles Wakefield; Francesca Wilson's great nephew and niece John and Josephine Horder; Dan Richards, great great nephew of Dorothy Pilley;

Acknowledgements

Penelope Newsome, daughter of Shiela Grant Duff; Selina Hastings, daughter of Margaret Lane; Heather Cullity, niece of Claudia Parsons; and James Currey, son of Stella Martin Currey.

In addition, I would like to thank the Society of Authors as the Literary Representative of the Estate of Rose Macaulay for permission to quote extracts from Macaulay's poems and letters; the Library of the Society of Friends for permission to quote from *Reconstruction*, the *Friends Quarterly Examiner* and Friends' Committee documents; Fred Wolsey, literary executor for Francesca Wilson, for permission to quote from Wilson's books, letters and journalism, published and unpublished; Richard Luckett, literary executor for Dorothy Pilley Richards, for permission to quote from *Climbing Days* as well as unpublished letters and diary extracts. Thanks to the Alpine Club Library for permission to quote from their records of Dorothy Pilley and also for permission to reproduce the front cover of the *Ladies Alpine Club Journal*. Thanks to the Pinnacle Club for permission to reproduce the front cover of the *Pinnacle Journal* and to the Master and Fellows of Magdalene College, Cambridge, for permission to quote from the I. A. Richards and Dorothea Pilley Richards material.

Thank you also to the poet Phoebe Stuckes for permission to quote from her poem 'Daughters' (2013) for this book's epigraph. Though written decades after the interwar period, its words sum up perfectly the spirit of the women studied here and remind us how freedoms, once gained, must be nurtured and protected.

For published work, all extracts fall under the Society of Authors 'Fair Dealing' guidelines and all extracts are referenced, with author, publisher and title listed in the bibliography at the

Acknowledgements

end of the book. While every effort has been made to contact the literary executors of unpublished texts still in copyright, there may, inevitably, have been some lacunae, and I would be grateful to hear from anyone not contacted for permission.

I would also like to thank the army of archivists, curators and librarians who dug out such a treasure trove of material for me: the Alpine Club Library staff, who showed me Dorothy Pilley's ice axes; Catherine Sutherland, Deputy Librarian at the Pepys Library and Special Collections, Magdalene College, Cambridge, for finding Dorothy Pilley's newspaper cuttings books; John Cable, archivist at the Institution of Engineering and Technology; and the wonderful staff of the British Library newsroom, who brought me volume after volume of historical newspapers and periodicals, some very heavy. Special thanks to Lucy McCann at the Bodleian Library, Oxford, for providing references to the Shiela Grant Duff archive, which on my visit was still a work in progress; and to Lois Roemer, volunteer curator at Steyning Museum, who helped me find Edith Shackleton's grave in Steyning churchyard. A full list of archives consulted, every one of which was extremely helpful, is found in the bibliography.

Finally, I would like to acknowledge Dr Elizabeth June Horder, Francesca Wilson's niece, who gave me two interviews despite being 96 and very frail at the time. She took great interest in this project and it is terribly sad that she did not live to see this book in print. A generous and strong woman, she admonished me, somewhat fiercely, at the end of our interviews: 'Whatever you do, make it readable.' I hope I have, at least, carried out her wishes.

Abbreviations

ABPP	Archive of British Printing and Publishing, University of Reading
BBK	Beaverbrook Papers, House of Commons
BDA	Brighton Design Archives
Bodl.	Bodleian Library
ECRO	Essex County Records Office
FL	Friends Library, London
HRC	Harry Ransom Center, University of Texas
IAWSEC	International Alliance of Women for Suffrage and Equal Citizenship
IET	Institution of Engineering and Technology, London
LCP	League of Coloured Peoples
MLSH	Margaret Lane Papers, St Hugh's College, Oxford
MML	Marx Memorial Library, London
NAA	National Archives of Australia
NLA	National Library of Australia
NUSEC	National Union of Societies for Equal Citizenship
PFVH	Prix Femina-Vie Heureuse archives, Cambridge University Library

Abbreviations

RCM — I. A. Richards collection, Magdalene College, Cambridge
WILPF — Women's International League for Peace and Freedom

Introduction:
'The women at the gate'

In the summer of 1921, three Englishwomen travelled across Switzerland by train, dressed in skirts adorned at the hem, as was the fashion, with feminine 'frills and furbelows'.[1] Having arrived at the Alpine station of Stalden, they opened their travelling trunks and underwent a strange transformation. Off came the skirts and ladies' soft gloves; 'out came tins of herrings in tomato sauce, worn corduroys, woolly mufflers, battered aluminium saucepans and spirit stoves, a box of Keating's and mud-stained leather gloves'.[2] Now in breeches and hobnail boots, with cotton bandanas around their heads, the women slung knapsacks over their backs and walked 20 kilometres to the village of Saas Fee from where they would complete a remarkable feat: the first Alpine *cordée féminine*, up the Mittaghorn, and a traverse of the Egginergrat ridge: rope climbing above 3,000 metres, including a difficult 100-metre 'chimney', bodies suspended over the abyss, without a male guide or escort. 'Manless climbing', as it was then known, was a highly subversive act and expression of modernity, encompassing subterfuge, transvestism, gender disruption, physical exertion, danger and a 'joyous release of body' as they dangled over the void.[3] It may seem like a commonplace thing today for a woman to rope-climb without a man to help her, but in 1921 this was an extreme act of rebellion against the 'masculine outdoors' which decreed that women were not sufficiently strong, skilled or experienced to be trusted to mountaineer alone.[4] The pre-eminent climbing journal of the day, the *Alpine Club Journal*, indeed described 'lady mountaineers' as both 'foolish' and 'insane'.

When, three years later, two of the trio, Dorothy Pilley and Lilian Bray, launched the *Pinnacle Club Journal*, a 'little' magazine for women climbers, Bray wrote an article on that 'manless' ascent, and 'Three Pinnaclers in the Alps' was published in the first issue.[5] In writing down, editing, typesetting, printing and disseminating their account of this rebellious climb, they were acknowledging the indivisibility of women's activism and writing. During the years of suffrage campaigning, women, denied their rights as citizens to vote or stand for Parliament, and mostly unable to raise their voices at public meetings, created a rich ecosystem of advocacy newspapers and journals as the basis of a powerful extra-parliamentary political culture. This alternative print culture, connecting activists and social reformers with an increasingly literate female reading public, maintained a strong hold on women's activism through the 1930s.[6] They were outsiders, so they wrote, advocating for change, persuading, challenging and celebrating the inch-by-inch gains they made in print. With the caveat that writing and publishing magazines required literacy and economic agency, and therefore favoured the middle classes, print's central role in helping women, before 1928, to 'construct their own identity' as citizen subjects cannot be underestimated.[7] While voting in parliamentary elections, legislating and practising law (until 1919) was forbidden to women, writing, at least, was not. Virginia

Introduction

Woolf, in her feminist tract *Three Guineas* (1938), acknowledged that of all the professions and activities contested by women because they were barred from participating in them by patriarchal structures, only writing was not fought over:

> There has been no battle of Grub Street. That profession has never been shut to the daughters of educated men. This was due of course to the extreme cheapness of its professional requirements. Books, pens and paper are so cheap, reading and writing have been, since the eighteenth century, so universally taught in our class.[8]

When she launched the *Pinnacle Club Journal*, Dorothy Pilley was 29 and thus unable to enjoy full rights as a citizen.[9] So she turned the magazine into a public platform where women could assert their rights to participate in and write about the wild, and yes, celebrate wearing breeches, eating sardines with muddy fingers and swinging from ropes. While 'manless climbing' is of a different order of activism to campaigning for employment rights, the right to control one's own fertility, or the right to participate in international disarmament conferences, as other women were doing, it was still, in 1921, a boldly political act, completed when written down and published, and part of the wide-ranging and vast line of battle on which women in their thousands were contesting the masculine hegemony of the 1920s and 1930s. This book will show how, beneath the well-turned surface of such familiar names as Virginia Woolf, Beatrice Webb, the Pankhursts, Nancy Astor, Ellen Wilkinson, Marie Stopes, Helena Swanwick and Winifred Holtby, 'ordinary' women were daily chipping away at patriarchal power, making inroads in all walks of life, from engineering, to humanitarian activism, to foreign correspondence, and how their writing, in diaries, letters, newspapers and periodicals, was axiomatic to the construction of these new public selves. This volume will also show the wide range of strategies – many ingenious and courageous – that women employed to overcome the enormous social and political obstacles in their way, so that we can better understand how change and progress can be achieved.

The women's movement after the First World War

The First World War had, in many countries, radically disrupted gender roles and enabled women to break out of the domestic sphere and assert their right to work in traditional masculine occupations, and generally to be more active, productive and visible.[10] After the war, various legislative and social pressures curtailed to an extent women's continued advancement, such as the Restoration of Pre-War Practices Act (1919) and male-dominated unions blocking equal pay and challenging women's ability to work on an equal footing with men.[11] On a more personal level, fathers and elder brothers returning from extended absence due to the war reasserted their patriarchal control over their wives, sisters and daughters. Newspapers and women's magazines also exerted some 'back to home and duty' pressure, encouraging women, through news pieces and features, to be dutiful wives and mothers and demonising the bachelor woman.[12] However, this kind of article was liberally leavened, particularly in the popular press, by others celebrating women's successes and female 'firsts', from motor racing, flying and swimming the Channel, to becoming magistrates and police officers, although it must be stressed that not all women found this emphasis on the tabloid 'superwoman' helpful.[13] Dorothy Pilley herself became a fleeting newspaper celebrity

Introduction

when the *Daily Mail* reported: 'Englishwoman Climber: First to Perform Alpine Feat', after she made the first ascent of the Dent Blanche (4,300 m), one of the most difficult peaks in the Alps, in July 1928.[14]

It is now generally agreed that although the women's movement fragmented after the 1918 and 1928 suffrage victories, women continued to seek equality in all parts of their lives, despite Ray Strachey's triumphant signing off, in her classic feminist history, that 'the main fight is over and the main victory is won'.[15] There is still disagreement, however, over the strength, focus, direction and achievements of women's activism in the interwar years. Some scholars continue to argue that the feminist movement declined, lacked direction and suffered deepening divisions as organisations such as the National Union of Societies for Equal Citizenship (NUSEC) fought over what their priorities should be.[16] Others argue that women turned from overtly feminist goals and embraced domesticity while still working for social reform from within non-feminist organisations such as the Mothers' Union and Women's Institute; others claim that the movement simply morphed into equally forceful campaigns for peace, welfare and children's rights.[17] Of course there is no easy generalisation to be made, either of the 'backlash' model or of the 'surprising vibrancy' argument. As with all periods there is a messy, unfocused and kaleidoscopic picture, and scholars who work on this basis probably get closer to the truth of how events unravelled.[18] My contention is that the movement simply altered its cellular chemistry, as it were, and the fight was joined not just by large, single-issue organisations but by thousands of smaller groups and individual women enacting multiple assaults upon the fortress of the masculine public sphere, often in intensely private and personal ways – rejecting proposals of marriage, standing up to sexual harassment, or insisting on seeking employment and living outside the family home.

What is certainly clear is that by the end of the two decades, women's opportunities and employment were utterly transformed. They may still have suffered unfair discrimination, unequal pay, sexual harassment in the workplace and a lack of promotion prospects, but compared to 1919, by 1939 the field of opportunity had widened enormously for the educated woman. One only has to examine the pages of *The Lady*, that bastion of aspirational domesticity, to see how the employment sections changed over the two decades. Early post-war issues simply carried classified advertisements matching the magazine's readers with less fortunate women seeking employment as 'half-cooks' and 'ladies' companions'; in May 1932, the magazine began a new regular 'Earning a Living' feature, this time for its readers' benefit, presenting, every fortnight, employment opportunities in the worlds of dancing, architecture, accountancy and dentistry, among other professions. Many of the women who pioneered to take their place in the world of work and public life have flown below the radar, and to see them we need to refocus our field of vision, to catch the single-cell structures, as well as the larger organisms, a process of 'rethinking the political'.[19] As Maria DiCenzo and Claire Eustance have recently argued, in order to understand better the direction and energy of the women's movement during the interwar years, we need to look beyond traditional concepts of political activism, which 'have not been able to account adequately for the range of spaces in which not just women generally, but an individual woman might take political action'.[20]

Introduction

This book is a contribution to the ongoing interpretive quest, and foregrounds the struggles of individual women in their efforts to participate in public life. Recognising that listening to women's voices is central to the task of writing women back into history, I recover here many of their overlooked texts in poems, novels, memoirs and journalism.[21] We can read in their own words their ideas, passions, and their unique interpretation of this rapidly changing, brilliantly modern and at times terrifying two decades. My focus is twofold: to fill in some of the gaps where individual struggles are concerned with a rich layer of detail about women's lives, motivations and personal dispositions, and also to identify a range of participation strategies employed by women seeking to leave the domestic sphere and to engage with the public world. In doing so, I contend, as other scholars have done, that because of their legal, social and political subjugation, women during the interwar years must be seen as a minority or marginalised group, even though in numerical terms they outnumbered men.[22] Studies of activism among marginalised groups or populations have established that even within minorities facing apparently insuperable obstacles, there is always a 'culture of resistance' which fosters endless renewal in strategies to oppose and overcome, just as the elite or dominant culture practises continuous strategies of defence and exclusion.[23]

Feminist critics argue that early concepts of the public sphere, while useful in describing the world of politics, economics and public action, have been 'gender blind', and as originally conceived, having its roots in a period before women were allowed to be citizens, would better be described as the 'masculine public sphere'. Public sphere theory simply replicates age-old patterns of male dominance and female subordination

Rebel women between the wars

as it classifies production in terms of the male/active/public/ economic and the female/passive/private/unpaid and thus legitimates the confinement of women to a 'separate sphere.'[24] Neither do public sphere theories recognise the fact that in the paid workplace, women have traditionally been assigned to subordinate, low-paid, service-oriented and often sexualised occupations which enable and serve the masculine world of power and money without benefiting equally from it.[25] What this means in essence is that to break out of the domestic, private world and participate in the masculine, public one, women, particularly in the interwar years, needed to be disruptors.

Storming the fortress

As a useful conceptual device, I have envisaged the masculine public sphere as it was configured in the 1920s and 1930s as a well-defended fortress designed to protect its occupants from challenge but also active in repelling potential invaders. Around this fortress is a complex system of defensive rings: these are many and varied, and include the denial of the vote to women (and then after 1928 the painfully slow increase in the number of women MPs) and restrictive employment practices, both enshrined in law but also imposed by individual employers, such as marriage bars in various workplaces, or the ban on women working at night 'for their own safety'. A particularly powerful defensive ring was the poor quality of women's education compared to that of men. This applies both to middle-class women (Virginia Woolf's famous 'Arthur's Education Fund' of *Three Guineas*) and ordinary elementary school education, which devoted less of girls' time at school to literacy and numeracy than boys.[26] To schooling we can also add the resistance of

Introduction

universities to admitting women on some degree courses, particularly in science and medicine, and some not conferring full degrees on women even after they had passed their exams.[27] Further legislative rings in the area of rights over property, children and divorce also existed in 1918, although through the 1920s much legislation was enacted to amend these long-standing inequalities.[28]

Other rings of defence relied on assumptions and traditions, the most potent being that women were expected to put their husbands' and families' wishes before their own. Others were the social pressure to marry and start a family, prejudices against the 'spinster', the 'new woman', the 'business woman' or the 'surplus woman' who did not fit into conventional social patterns, prejudices that extended to suspicions over female friendships, and the general assumption that women were simply inferior, both intellectually and physically, to men. How then to mount an attack on this fastness, when knocking at the gate and asking for entry seemed so hopeless a task, if even one could reach the gate unscathed? Is it possible to identify a set of assets and dispositions, and then a strategy for undermining the fortress's defences, that made it more likely that a particular woman might succeed in creating a breach through which others might follow?

For each chapter a different participation strategy is identified. Studies of other kinds of female activism identify various strategies such as 'direct action', putting one's head over the parapet, including running for public office and union work. There is also 'intellectual activism', which includes writing as resistance, journalism and filing lawsuits. Then there are acts of 'everyday resistance', such as dressing or cutting one's hair in a certain way and resisting being stereotyped, but these are often easy generalisations.[29] This book aims to identify and assess a range of strategies that women of the past employed, which include the use of formal and informal networks and friendships to increase one's ability to mount an attack; other kinds of individual direct action; and more subtle methods including subterfuge and what I call 'hiding in plain sight'. Different strategies depended on individual women's dispositions, motivations and targets. Some, such as the MP Leah Manning, aimed for high public office, and social networks at the group, organisational and international level helped her to pursue this goal successfully.[30] Others, such as the engineer and chauffeur Claudia Parsons, simply wanted to study engineering, in overalls, alongside men, and obtain the same qualifications that a man could; for her, rejecting a series of powerful figures' and organisations' socially conservative views of what constituted acceptable feminine behaviour was a long and weary battle throughout her life. Shiela Grant Duff wanted to be a foreign correspondent, and when the 'safe' option of taking a job in a newspaper foreign department was closed to her on account of her gender, she chose to take the riskier freelance route. Francesca Wilson, a humanitarian aid worker, found, like Grant Duff, conventional channels of engagement closed because of her youth and perceived unserious temperament, but she opted for subterfuge as a way of getting around the obstacles before her.

In order to identify the strategies, motivations and dispositions of this 'baker's dozen' of women, this study adopts a multidisciplinary approach, employing cultural, literary and historical analysis, newspaper and periodical history, feminist theory and other sociological, behavioural and philosophical concepts. In embedding each chapter in its social context, the book adds to our understanding of the interwar years in areas

Introduction

from motoring and leisure, to mountaineering and the wild, to education and journalism, to humanitarian activism and race relations in the imperial metropolis. While most of the subjects here are British, I have included two major international case studies in order to connect British feminist activism at this time with international movements. The first is the poet and activist Una Marson, who left Jamaica to seek literary engagement only to encounter a bewildering and exclusionary racism in 'the mother country'. The second is the Australian novelist Kylie Tennant, who used her documentary fiction to expose the hypocrisy of the White Australia Policy and to chronicle the lives of both rural and urban workers in Depression-era Australia. Other minor international case studies also help add to our understanding of how women across the globe became galvanised by successive suffrage victories and how they interpreted and fashioned their own new identities as active citizens. Sustained by links to the original women's movements, women's activism remained vibrant, looking forward to 'a future based on true equality with men'.[31]

Recent work on the interwar period has shed light on women's achievements in a number of areas, from the literary world to the rise of female civil servants, women in the colonial and diplomatic services, women humanitarians, scientists and political theorists.[32] However, scholarship tends to focus either on 'extraordinary' women such as Virginia Woolf, Nancy Astor, the feminist pacifist Helena Swanwick, or the Labour MP Margaret Bondfield, in great detail, or to look at groups of women in organisations such as the Women's International League for Peace and Freedom, the Labour Party or the Women's Institutes. The former method, while providing a richly detailed narrative of one brilliant life, does not always help us understand how the vast ranks of women began to make individual advances towards participation in public life. The latter method, although giving enlightening overviews into the culture and achievements of such groups, fails to answer one of my central questions which asks how individual women became energised into choosing the strategies and participation goals that they did. This book takes the form of a multiple biography, its subjects comprising a large enough group to be valuable in identifying what the historian E. P. Thompson called the 'nodal points of conflict', the tensions between the private life and the sociopolitical world that provoke action.[33] The accumulation of new and illuminating historical 'facts' and psychological insights, it is hoped, will help us read societal change through the individual life, 'providing a different path into the past'.[34]

Biography as method

Much of this study employs the biographical method, often used by historians of interwar feminism, illustrating that that the 'personal is political'.[35] There are, however, drawbacks that need to be addressed. Biography, one eminent historian (and biographer) recently wrote, 'remains the profession's unloved stepchild, occasionally but grudgingly let in the door, more often shut outside with the riffraff'.[36] Another has called it an 'abject form of history ... a kind of history lite', because it often relies less on empirical facts and more on creative interpretation.[37] The problems of biography as a way of investigating the past are numerous: leading journals often refuse to review biographical studies; the traditional 'cradle-to-grave' approach tends to ignore greater moments of periodisation, outside the birth and death of the subject; and biography

Introduction

is necessarily highly selective: among all the letters, diaries, newspaper articles and other sources, how does one distil the essence of a life in convenient chapters? Another weakness is that biographical study from a historical period such as the interwar years necessarily limits the subject matter to those who had the education and resources to write and keep letters and diaries and other private mementoes, to pay subscriptions to join organisations, to travel, and to have the confidence to write and speak in public. Ultimately, also, they needed relatives or interested parties: libraries and record offices to store and catalogue their private papers, so that one day a biographer or historian could unearth their lives. These requirements naturally limit the available subjects to women from the middle classes, and while I have made strenuous efforts to seek out subjects who have been overlooked, they are, without exception, middle class.

What, then, of a multiple biography such as this, with only a chapter, or in some cases half or a quarter of a chapter, devoted to a particular woman? What chance of capturing anything except a superficial and fleeting glimpse? Added to this problem is the inconsistency in the range of sources available. At one end of the scale, Dorothy Pilley kept a diary every year of her life from the age of 19 until her death. There are rows and rows of small, ruled notebooks, covered in her dense and at times barely legible inked script, recording not only activities, impressions and appointments, but books read and journals ordered, all stored carefully in the Old Library at Magdalene College, Cambridge. There also are her meticulously kept newspaper cuttings books and her heartrending letters to her future husband, the literary critic I. A. Richards, including a beautiful, closely argued, 60-page letter of rejection to his marriage proposal (and it was not that she did not love him). At this abundant end of the scale also is Shiela Grant Duff, who not only wrote a detailed memoir of her work in the 1930s but also kept almost all of her letters, diaries and much other memorabilia, including calling cards, dance cards, dinner menus, medical prescriptions and a card index system of political and journalistic contacts annotated with her hilariously spiky notes ('Bayer, Dr Frantisek, Bratislava (September 1936): Small, beady-eyed ... said to know about the Germans, might help but doesn't look very intelligent or special'). In her papers at the Bodleian there is also one small, brown, leather diary, locked with a little key hanging off a faded ribbon, dating back to when she was about 12, brought to me, as a waiter might bring a dish of Beluga caviar, by a white-gloved librarian, and revealing the character of a courageous little girl who clearly felt that she was special.

At the other end of the scale, Margaret Lane – rather irritatingly, as she was a biographer herself – tore up every letter and threw it in the bin or fire as soon as she had read it, ritually destroying her own archive as it formed.[38] At least Lane's daughter, Selina Hastings, gave much of her time to tell me about her mother, and directed me to various caches of information, including her old school magazine and a small collection of material at St Hugh's College, Oxford. The novelist Kylie Tennant has a small collection of her letters and first drafts of manuscripts in the National Library of Australia, with more material in the National Archives of Australia (including a partial file of the record kept on her by the Australian Security Intelligence Organisation when she was suspected of being a communist agent from 1935 to 1957). However, a sharp note at the beginning of her memoir – 'to the academic, whose name I have forgotten, who visited us when my husband was dying'

Introduction

and took away valuable records of book reviews and other material, but who never returned them, despite 'promising to post them back' – points to a tantalising quantity of disappeared 'evidence'.[39] Perhaps the most evasive of the subjects in this book, having apparently left no diary and only a few letters in the archive of English PEN at the Harry Ransom Center in Texas, is the journalist Edith Shackleton. For Shackleton I have relied mainly on her prodigious journalistic output and some staff records of her time at the *Daily Express* and *Evening Standard* in the Beaverbrook papers in the House of Commons. Biographical details, too, are pieced together from press cuttings on her kept in the Steyning Museum, Sussex, close to where she lived for her last thirty years.

The proper aim of biography should not be to try to capture the complete person, but, as historian Oscar Handlin wrote, to capture 'the point at which [the person and society] interact. There the situation and the individual illuminate each other.'[40] In addition, the biographical approach enables the author to answer questions about personality and character that the historian usually does not ask. Life stories can help us understand 'women's work in negotiating an identity apart from the domestic self' and thus go some way to answer how the transition from passivism to activism works.[41] The individual political journeys of women who, as Karen Hunt put it, have slipped through the net of many of the histories of the twentieth century, if taken together, can help to reveal the individual circumstances and choices that women made to move from the domestic towards the public sphere.[42]

Finally, employing the biographical approach enables us to recover the power of these women's words, in their letters, diaries, fiction, poetry and memoirs, and thus to finish what they so hopefully started, by writing them (back) into history. For readers curious about these women's lives after the Second World War, an Appendix at the end of this volume provides brief accounts of what they did in later life, and provides details of where their archives may be found.

Notes

1 The title of this chapter is taken from the Evelyn Sharp short story of the same name (1910), in which the narrator sees suffragist women trying to gain entry to the House of Commons and is energised to fight for her own equality.
2 Pilley 1965: 131; Keating's powder was an insecticide used to kill fleas and lice, which at that time spread typhus.
3 The climber Nan Shepherd was the original creator of this lovely phrase (see Chapter 3).
4 For a more detailed discussion of the 'masculine outdoors' versus feminine nature, see Chapter 3.
5 Bray 1924.
6 Tusan 2005: 2.
7 Tusan 2005: 7–8.
8 Woolf 2006: 107.
9 Women under 30 were not allowed to vote until 1928.
10 For a good account of the emergence of 'New Public Woman' 1880–1930, see Evans 2019.
11 See Chapter 6, particularly, where I discuss the multiple legal cases brought under the Restoration of Pre-War Practices Act by men's industrial unions. This Act was partially balanced by the Sex Disqualification (Removal) Act of 1919, which removed barriers to women entering the professions such as architecture, medicine and the law.
12 See Chapter 1 for examples. For women's magazines' role in encouraging the 'back to home and duty' theme, see Briganti and Mezei 2006. Bingham (2004a and 2004b) is particularly persuasive on the counter-argument.
13 In Chapter 6 I discuss the limitations of how helpful these kinds of 'superwoman' articles were to ordinary women.

Introduction

14 *Daily Mail*, 25 July 1928, p. 13.
15 DiCenzo and Delap 2008: 52; Strachey 1978: 385.
16 For example, Gottlieb 2014: 443–4; Beddoe 1989; Clay 2018: 32–4.
17 For example, Beaumont 2013; Theobald 2000; Thane 2001; Law 1997.
18 For example, Bingham 2004b; Hunt 2009; Glew 2016; McCarthy 2014.
19 Tusan 2005: 7–8.
20 DiCenzo and Eustance 2018: 328.
21 Barclay 2010: 338; this method also recognises the value of the so-called 'linguistic' or 'narrative turn' in historiography, which places high value on the texts of the past and challenges 'objective knowing' (Archibald 2012: 9; Munslow 2003: 1).
22 Beetham 1996: 1–14.
23 Guy-Sheftall 1999: xxi. In this context the author is discussing the resistance strategies of African-American women.
24 Fraser 1987: 34.
25 Fraser 1987: 37.
26 'Arthur's Education Fund', Woolf contends, is the system in middle-class families of saving up money to be able to send sons to boarding school and then university, to the detriment of expenditure on the 'daughters of educated men' who not only did without equivalent education but also had to go without travel and other opportunities. Woolf 2006: 7; Holloway 2005: 9.
27 Oxford University began conferring full degrees on women in 1921. Women graduates from Cambridge had to wait until 1947.
28 These included the Matrimonial Causes Act 1923, the Guardianship of Infants Act 1925 and the Law of Property Act 1922.
29 Springer 1999: 2–3; Springer's work studies black female activists in the United States.
30 See Westaby 2012 on how social networks can help individuals and groups attain their goals and shape their aspirations.
31 Theobald 2000: 67.
32 For example, Glew 2016, 2018 (civil servants); McCarthy 2014 (diplomats); Sloane 2018 (Labour party activists); Davies 2007 (international disarmament campaigners); Beaumont 2013 (organisations such as the Mothers' Union and Women's Institutes); Stockman 2017 (a fascinating look at political theorists in international relations, including Marjory Perham, Lucy Mair and Agnes Headlam-Morley).

33 Thompson 1993: xii.
34 Kessler-Harris 2009: 626.
35 Gottlieb 2014: 444.
36 Nasaw 2009: 573.
37 Munslow 2003: 2.
38 Interview with Selina Hastings, Margaret Lane's daughter.
39 Tennant 2012, 'Author's Note'.
40 Handlin 1979: 276.
41 Ward 2019: 31–3.
42 Hunt 2009: 212.

1
Female friendship, work and collaboration

> In fields you tread the thistle shall bear a fig;
> To walk with you is to travel a wizard land;
> You would come to Australia, or Hell, were you to dig.
> Curious stones twist slipping about your hand –
> Cat's eye, lapis, onyx, chalcedony,
> Winking with shadowy lights, or beaming bland,
> Or blue as night, or green as the rock-green sea,
> Or pink like a rose, or mild as the moon's rays –
> I cannot tell the curious stones they be.
> The lovely and witty earth before you lays
> (Seeking to snare your laughter or your praise)
> Rich jests, strange stones, and all things that amaze.[1]

Rose Macaulay was on the cusp of breaking through both as an author and as a witty participant in post-First World War London literary society when she wrote 'Dedicatory' for her friend Naomi Royde-Smith. Placed prominently at the front of her book of poems *Three Days* (1919), 'Dedicatory' evokes an exotic, mythically nurturing persona who conjures rich fertility from the most unpromising sources and who can find the delightfully unexpected, magic even, wherever she turns. The abundant natural imagery of the poem – precious stones, the sea, the moon, cuckoos, peacocks and figs – are all symbols associated with the 'queen' of goddesses, Juno, who was also the protector of women.[2] It was an appropriate tribute from the 'thistle' Macaulay, who owed much to her influential friend. Nearly 40 years old in 1919, Macaulay's had been a long apprenticeship. Her first novel, *Abbots Verney*, was published in 1906, but she would not find widespread critical success and the rewards of being a best-selling author until the 1920s. Naomi Royde-Smith was an astute literary editor of the *Saturday Westminster* and brought Macaulay, an awkward 'innocent from the Cam' as she described herself, into her circle of friends, who seemed to Macaulay 'to be more sparklingly alive than any in my home world'.[3] For more than a decade, before a rather dramatic falling out, Macaulay and Royde-Smith were 'inseparable'.[4] Macaulay would often stay in her friend's Knightsbridge home where they held soirées for authors and journalists to bolster each other's standing and forge mutually supportive networks. Royde-Smith used her position, first at the *Saturday Westminster* and then as editor of *The Queen*, to promote Macaulay and her work.

This was a heady and rivalrous time for writers, as successive literary cliques from the Bloomsbury group through to the Leavises and the Auden group sought to redefine writing and audience in response to mass literacy and the mass media of cinema, newspapers and cheap paperbacks.[5] Often linked to 'little' magazines such as the *Criterion*, *Adelphi* and *Scrutiny*, writers scrambled to claim the high ground. In her diary Virginia Woolf was scornful of her 'foe' Royde-Smith, and while Rose Macaulay's perceptive intellect appealed, she was still dangerously 'professional'.[6]

The interwar period also saw middlebrow writers, including E. M. Delafield, Ethel Mannin, Henrietta Leslie, Mary

Female friendship, work and collaboration

Agnes Hamilton and Naomi Royde-Smith herself, emphasising the pleasures of reading. Linked through writers' informal networks and through reviewing books for women's magazines such as *The Queen* and *Good Housekeeping* as well as the feminist weekly review *Time and Tide*, their novels foregrounded issues concerning women such as divorce, living independently and inequalities in the workplace, and many were stunningly successful in terms of sales and influence.[7] They represented not so much 'another Bloomsbury' as an 'alternative Bloomsbury' with their own magazines and friendships.[8] Some of these women represented energetic nodes of exchange, such as Royde-Smith and, as we will see later, Edith Shackleton, both of whom straddled the literary and the mainstream newspaper worlds. In response, highbrow writers and their groups worked assiduously to delimit the market for 'elite literary works' by occupying editors' chairs and reviewing books for influential journals.[9] Middlebrow women authors thus needed to be equally forceful in their search for publicity and readers to avoid being marginalised and dismissed as that most derided of cultural producers, the 'Lady Novelist'.[10] Hence we have Rose Macaulay writing articles for the *Daily Mail* on subjects such as 'Why I dislike cats, clothes and visits' at around the time of the publication of her novel *Keeping Up Appearances* (1928), to generate publicity and to fashion her persona as a down-to-earth, honest and unpretentious woman writer in direct opposition to the producers of more highbrow fiction.[11]

At a time when strong and mutually supportive networks counted for much, Macaulay and Royde-Smith undoubtedly found their friendship professionally beneficial.[12] Macaulay, six years Royde-Smith's junior, enjoyed the introductions and promotion through the pages of *Saturday Westminster*;

Royde-Smith, who astutely spotted Macaulay's talent long before many others did, reaped the cultural capital associated with the patronage of struggling artists – she also helped 'launch' Aldous Huxley, and gave Graham Greene his first big break, publishing his poem 'Paint and Wood' in the *Weekly Westminster Gazette* when he was only 18, and then a longer piece, 'Impressions of Dublin', a few weeks later.[13] Royde-Smith was also, in 1919, part of the committee to inaugurate the English version of the French Prix Femina-Vie Heureuse novel prize to celebrate and encourage early-career novelists, and which Macaulay won for her novel *Dangerous Ages* (1921).[14] The friendship between Macaulay and Royde-Smith, while it lasted, was also affectionate and sustaining and mirrors that of the writers Winifred Holtby and Vera Brittain, the most famous example of mutually beneficial literary female friendship of the interwar years.[15]

Friendship and the single woman

Vera Brittain and Winifred Holtby's friendship, combined with their talent, was a key element of their success as writers. During the early 1920s they shared the cost of London 'digs': they avoided the cleaning together, huddled round the feeble gas stove for warmth, worked over each other's manuscripts and swapped introductions with publishers and editors.[16] Despite the drawbacks of the chilly and cramped flat in Doughty Street, Brittain would later write: 'For the first time I knew the luxury of privacy, the tranquil happiness of being able to come and go just as I wished without interference or supervision.'[17] Their friendship was forged at a time, Brittain wrote, when 'the friendships of women ... have usually been not merely unsung,

Female friendship, work and collaboration

but mocked, belittled, and falsely interpreted'.[18] Friendship between educated, professional women became a site of contest during the interwar years as the Victorian model of the mutually supportive networks of a subjugated group transformed into a powerful force to challenge traditional power structures in the world of work.[19] Where women (outside elite aristocratic circles) had previously exerted influence, this was in predominantly female-only organisations such as boarding schools, suffrage organisations and convents, where they posed no threat to masculine hierarchies.[20] After the First World War, for the first time women were graduating in significant numbers from university and some were beginning to occupy positions of power in the public world of newspapers, politics and trades unions, and were able to help their more struggling friends. When Naomi Royde-Smith, for example, became editor of *The Queen*, she promoted the work of feminist writers Ray Strachey, Storm Jameson and Clemence Dane, modernists Dorothy Richardson and Eleanor Farjeon, as well as her friends Sylvia Lynd and Rose Macaulay, through reviews, features, commissions and profiles, bringing their work to a new, large and presumably surprised audience more used to reading about gun dogs and balls (for more on Royde-Smith's extraordinary editorship of *The Queen* in 1924, see Chapter 9).

Many of these professional, influential women were unmarried, and the phenomenon of the successful unmarried woman, who enjoyed close friendships with other women rather than marriage to a man, provoked ridicule and anxiety. Both during and after the war there were strong social pressures on women to do their patriotic duty, to become wives and mothers to help restore the population and thus avoid a 'biological crisis'.[21] After the war, cruel caricatures of single women and 'business' women appeared in newspapers, such as this from the London *Evening Standard* in 1923:

> Here is an advertisement from a morning paper of today, which would be significant of much to a thoughtful descendant: 'Furnished Bed-Sitting Room to let in business woman's flat, two minutes Earl's Court Station; lady (non-smoker) engaged during day preferred, accustomed to wait on self, gas fire, ring, slot meter, electric light.' Business Woman has evidently suffered … posterity will be … shocked at this evidence of the desiccated lives of emancipated woman in the early twentieth century.[22]

Another, more aggressive article, written by a male teacher in *The Woman Teacher*, quotes a marriage manual to support his argument against women teachers being paid the same as men: 'Those [spinsters] who can marry and do not are thus deliberately disregarding their biological duty to the race to which they belong. Those who would marry but cannot are supremely unfortunate. Both of them are a menace to the society in which they live …'[23]

Single and unaccompanied women encountered myriad forms of prejudice, described, for example, in Winifred Holtby's newspaper article about being refused service in a restaurant, for the simple reason that she and her middle-aged companion, despite being 'admirable and respectable', were not with a man.[24] The article, published in the *Manchester Guardian* in 1930, asks why two women of a certain age should be considered 'dangerous'. Other single, professional women, however, described the exhilarating freedom of living alone, earning enough to pay the rent, the chore of having to 'do' for oneself outweighed by a delicious independence, as in Eva Bretherton's short story 'The Eleventh Hour' in *The Quiver*. In the story, the heroine, Stella Hammond, who earns her own living through journalism, climbs out of her attic room on to the roofs of London late at night, enjoying a room of her own and multiple transgressions, both social and legal, under cover of darkness.[25] The author, a freelance writer, was deliberately playing with the common social theme of the 'dangerous' single woman, highlighted in Holtby's article. If such a woman combined with other single women in professional networks and friendships, they would together present a threat to centuries of social order by challenging the principle that women of every class must put their husband and children before their own desires for intellectual or professional fulfilment. If lucky enough to be born into the middle classes, such women would have advantages of education, mobility and friendship ties not enjoyed by working-class women, who were much more tied to a single location, early marriage and to close-knit family networks that excluded external friendships.[26]

Brittain and Holtby, Macaulay and Royde-Smith, and others, were developing models of professional friendship that, as well as being doubtless at times rivalrous, were fruitfully collaborative. Holtby, for example, took Brittain's first novel manuscript, *Dark Tide*, to the publisher John Lane after he had just accepted – but before he had published – her own first novel *Anderby Wold* (1923) – this despite Brittain's rather cruel and crude characterisation of her friend in the novel as the gawky and over-eager Daphne. Friendship enabled Holtby and Brittain to set a pattern for women 'to succeed in professional life like never before'.[27] They acknowledged the asymmetry of their friendship, energised on the one hand by Holtby's selfless generosity and possibly suppressed erotic feelings for Brittain, and on the other by Brittain's almost insatiable need for Holtby to boost her fragile ego.[28]

Emerging from the dreamy environment of post-First World War Oxford and cut short by Holtby's early death, this was just one of many models of female friendship. This chapter will examine two other interwar professional friendships to deepen our understanding of how these new forms of collaborative friendship did indeed boost women's participation in public life. I will first examine the friendship of the journalists Alison Settle and Edith Shackleton before turning to the more complex association between Rose Macaulay and Naomi Royde-Smith.

Alison Settle and Edith Shackleton: friendship and early professional struggles

Alison Settle and Edith Shackleton became friends in 1915 and remained so for sixty years until Shackleton's death in 1976. During the interwar years both were successful journalists, editors and taste-makers in the worlds of fashion and the arts. Settle was editor of British *Vogue* (1926–35) and Shackleton, after achieving fame in 1923 as the first female parliamentary correspondent for a major newspaper, became chief literary critic for the *Evening Standard* after Arnold Bennett's death, then reviewer for the *Observer*, *The Lady*, *The Queen* and *Time and Tide*. An active member of the National Union of Journalists, for a while she was the highest-paid woman journalist on Fleet Street, paid £2,700 a year in 1930, more than many senior men on the *Evening Standard*, and establishing an important precedent that talented women should be paid fairly for their work.[29] Like Winifred Holtby, Shackleton offered selfless help to Settle as she struggled to make it on Fleet Street, writing her fashion articles for her and introducing her to editors.[30]

Female friendship, work and collaboration

Alison Settle was born in London on 18 January 1891 to a Scottish army family on her mother's side, and minor German aristocracy on her father's (her full name was Alison Violet de Froideville Fuchs). Her father abandoned the family while she was still a baby and 'never contributed one penny towards the upkeep of his children', and much of her childhood was spent with her maternal grandparents 'in genteel poverty' on the Sussex coast, near Brighton.[31] She attended Brighton and Hove High School, and although she won a bursary to study history at Somerville College, Oxford, 'the little money [my] family had went to educate [my] brothers'.[32] After the outbreak of the First World War, she began working as secretary for the British Society for the Relief of the Belgian Wounded, earning 35 shillings a week, and was contacted by the women's page editor of the *Illustrated Sunday Herald*, who was looking for heart-warming human interest stories for her readers. The editor, Edith Shackleton, offered 7s 6d for a 71-word paragraph, one fifth of Settle's weekly wage for a few lines of text, and thereafter journalism became Settle's life.[33] Encouraged by Shackleton, she applied for a job as secretary to the editor of the new popular newspaper, the *Sunday Pictorial*.[34]

The war posed both challenges and opportunities to the press. In addition to censorship, shortages of newsprint, rising costs and loss of advertising revenue meant that many titles struggled financially, reducing pagination or having to raise their cover price.[35] On the other hand, the public's thirst for news and pictures of the war meant that popular, patriotic publications could thrive. In the first week of the war alone some ten new titles were launched, including *The War Budget* (3d), *War Pictures Weekly* (1d), *The War Weekly* (3d) and *The Graphic War Budget* (2d).[36] The *Illustrated Sunday Herald* and the *Sunday Pictorial* were launched in March 1915 within two weeks of each other, paying the country's leading writers, including H. G. Wells and Arnold Bennett, handsome sums to write weekly commentaries.[37] Edith Shackleton became editor of the *Sunday Herald*'s 'Through the Eyes of a Woman' page, and a few weeks later Alison de Froideville (the Germanic 'Fuchs' now dropped as an embarrassment) began editing 'Mainly for Women' on the rival *Sunday Pictorial* for a generous £6 a week. What neither newspaper editor knew was that the woman's page editor of the *Sunday Herald* was actually writing articles for the woman's page editor of the *Sunday Pictorial*. Alison Settle 'confessed' to this deception in an article for the Women's Press Club newsletter in 1947: 'the kind girl, talented far beyond what I could ever be, who ran the rival paper (the one we were to outshine) coached me in what I would have to do and helped me hold down that job until I learnt the ropes'.[38] She was more explicit in a later reminiscence: '[I] knew nothing about fashion, let alone duchesses ... so Edith Shackleton wrote my fashion pages for me, under my name, while I tried to learn what happened to my duchesses.'[39] Shackleton's generosity to her friends was well known on Fleet Street. The drama critic James Agate, who would often bump into her at theatrical first nights, described her as 'a tower of sympathy to people in trouble, and spends her quick and noble mind generously'.[40]

By February 1916 Alison de Froideville was writing 'op ed' articles alongside pieces by H. G. Wells and Austin Harrison, meditating on how the war was exerting profound changes on women's attitudes to work and gender imbalances. One article, 'Once a Woman Always a Woman', warns men that they must get used to their wives being interested in matters outside the domestic sphere including running a canteen,

Female friendship, work and collaboration

driving a 'motor-lorry' and working in a munitions factory. Another, 'The New Woman of the Grill Room', suggests that now women were doing other things than planning and cooking the family menu, they might actually become interested in food, rather than find it a daily drudgery.[41] She became Alison Settle after marrying Alfred Towers Settle, who was dying of tuberculosis, a week after Armistice Day. When their first child, Margaret, was born in 1920, she asked Shackleton to be godmother.[42] Her contract with the *Sunday Pictorial* appears to have come to an end at about the time of her marriage, but articles, now under the byline 'Alison Settle', can be found in the *Daily Herald*, a popular left-wing newspaper and sister to the *Sunday Herald*, where Shackleton now worked, from early 1919. In a memoir she also recorded that she worked for the *Daily Mirror* as a general reporter during this time.[43] On the *Daily Herald* Settle began a campaign for better nutrition for working-class children, a cause she would champion throughout her life.[44] A single mother from 1925, she grappled, unhappily, with the demands of having to earn money and her yearning to be with her children, while editing that icon of highbrow glamour, *Vogue*. Her diaries from this time reveal the extraordinary tensions that these competing stresses created.

Edith Heald was born on 12 September 1885 in Manchester, the youngest of four: a brother, Ivan, born in 1883, a sister, Nora, born in 1882, and another brother, Harry, about whom little is known.[45] Like Settle, she was also from a middle-class family, but they were not wealthy, and they, too, had been abandoned by their father, John Thomas Heald, a schoolteacher, when she was a child.[46] Their mother, Mary Shackleton, moved with her daughters to Stacksteads in rural Lancashire after she separated from their father. Ivan trained as a newspaper reporter on the

Ulster Gazette and after he was appointed assistant editor on the Manchester *Sunday Chronicle* he encouraged Edith to join him at the newspaper in 1909. In a short autobiographical piece she wrote:

> I had never seen a woman journalist until the day I accidentally caught sight of my own face in a mirror in a Manchester tea-shop not many minutes after the late Sir Edward Hulton had told me that he would allow me to start working on his papers at ten shillings a week for a trial month ... she was a stirring sight, that Woman Journalist – a little wan from the exertion of pretending that she was really quite grown up, that the Lancashire moor she had come from was the best possible place on which to have acquired a 'nose for news'.[47]

Hulton's gamble of employing the untrained young woman paid off. Almost as soon as she was hired, her pieces were being syndicated throughout the Hulton provincial newspaper empire. Controversial and with a strongly feminist stance, her journalism covered issues such as wages for housework and the 'intolerable' conditions of the general housemaid, often forced to live alone in basements or attics with no 'independent existence after working hours'.[48] It is worth noting that in these pre-First World War papers, before separate 'women's pages' had become a ubiquitous feature, Shackleton's articles, although almost always on women's issues, appeared in the main 'op ed' opinion pages and thus would have been seen by male as well as female readers.

The three elder Heald siblings were gifted writers and journalists, rising to the top of their profession despite financial constraints and a lack of university education. Ivan Heald became a leading columnist on the *Daily Express* from 1912, famous for his gently humorous pieces. At the outbreak of the war he joined the navy, and then in 1916 the Royal Flying Corps. He trained

Female friendship, work and collaboration

to take photographs of enemy troop movements, and was killed after being shot down over Germany on 4 December 1916.[49] Edith would place an 'In Memoriam' notice in *The Times* every year on the anniversary of his death, the last one appearing in 1975, just before her own death.[50] Nora Heald would become editor of *The Queen* and *The Lady* magazines, and the two sisters lived together with their mother at Waverley Place in St John's Wood until 1927, and then near Hyde Park, until they moved to Steyning in Sussex in 1934.[51]

It is not clear why Shackleton chose to use her mother's surname as her professional byline.[52] With its heroic associations with her distant relative, the polar explorer Ernest Shackleton, it was certainly more glamorous than Heald. It could also have been because of her father's desertion of the family, which left a profound impact on her – from an early age she would write articles defending a woman's right not to marry and urging young women not to accept the first proposal that came their way.[53] The absence of a father, through death or abandonment, will recur throughout this book as a common factor for many of the women discussed here. Shackleton's personal columns reveal the pain of her own childhood. During the mid to late 1920s she wrote a weekly column for the *Sunday Express*, commenting on a wide range of social and political issues, and particularly focusing on the status of women during the run-up to full enfranchisement in 1928. One such article chides a young woman who, in a celebrated court case, had just sued a man for breach of promise to marry, her complaint being that, at 24, her 'young life is wasted'. Shackleton argued that childhood and young adulthood can actually be miserable times and that 'there are other, and better bouquets than those we get at our first dances'.[54]

Shackleton was respected by her proprietor Lord Beaverbrook, who would send her congratulatory notes on her columns and leaders. He paid her well and sought her advice on literary matters, even though she was one of the few journalists on his papers who refused to work during the General Strike of 1926.[55] It is hugely to be regretted that in scholarship, Shackleton is only found as a footnote in biographies of W. B. Yeats as his 'last mistress': the two began a relationship in 1937.[56] This book is, in part, an attempt to correct the record.

Professional writing networks and the legacy of the suffrage press

During the First World War Settle and Shackleton were both young, single women with no family income, both abandoned by their fathers, and both, out of shame or hurt, abandoning their fathers' surnames, while trying to make it in London journalism at a time when Fleet Street was very much a masculine space. Although women were outsiders in this world, there were more women working as journalists than perhaps might be expected. In the 1911 Census, 1,756 women described themselves as belonging to the category 'Author, Editor, Journalist, Reporter, Shorthand Writer', as opposed to 12,030 men, meaning that women made up about 14 per cent of the journalistic workforce.[57] Almost all were precariously freelance, with very few enjoying the security of a staff job.[58] Until 1920, rates of pay for the same job were lower for women than for men, and a disparity between freelance rates for 'masculine' and 'feminine' journalism continued throughout the interwar period.[59] During the 1920s on the *Daily Mail*, for example, an article for the women's page paid between 10s 6d and 25s, whereas a standard 400-word article on the literary pages paid between £2 2s and £3 3s.[60] Nonetheless the opportunities for women on Fleet Street, which at the time was a hugely successful, dynamic and expanding world, were increasing, and by the 1931 Census the numbers of women describing themselves as journalists had nearly doubled from twenty years earlier to 3,213, and they now made up 17 per cent of the workforce.[61] Very few operated outside the women's pages, a feature now common to most newspapers, and they therefore occupied the strange position of having been brought into the public realm in order to help newspapers make money from fashion, health and nursery-ware advertising through being once again confined to domestic issues.[62]

If they did manage to escape the women's page, they did not necessarily manage to escape the 'woman' label. When Shackleton made history in becoming the first female parliamentary correspondent in February 1923, 'with all the usual press privileges', she was tasked with reporting on the Peeresses' parade as they entered the House of Lords during the state opening of Parliament. Her report, 'Brilliant Scenes in the Lords: Dignified and Magnificent Gowns of Peeresses', is bylined 'A woman correspondent'. She did her best to emphasise the 'dignity and magnificence' of the women, but it is clear that her brief was to describe the furs, jewels and velvet rather than make comment on women's new role in Parliament.[63]

Professional societies such as the Society of Women Journalists, which helped women make connections and strengthen their precarious status, were therefore supremely important, and anecdotal evidence suggests that women on newspapers did offer mutually supportive company.[64] In 1930 Shackleton wrote: 'in Fleet Street there is a sound fellowship among the women, and an ability for daily give or take friendship'.⁶⁵ Women journalists during the interwar years had grown up knowing the strength and organisation of the Edwardian suffrage groups and their newspapers, and many carried their campaigning zeal and their belief in the advocacy power of the press into their professional lives. They had seen how careful argumentation, organisation and communication through such papers as *The Vote* and *The Common Cause* had begun to legitimate women's presence in the public sphere and, in 1918, gain real results.⁶⁶ Shackleton read the suffragist newspaper *The Vote* – indeed she wrote a letter to it in 1909.⁶⁷ The suffrage press has been shown to have played a pivotal role during the First World War in representing women as 'ideal' citizens through its recording of women's war work, thus paving the way for the acceptance of women as voters.⁶⁸

Edith Shackleton, despite being confined to a popular newspaper women's page, also did her bit. Every week her *Illustrated Sunday Herald* page, 'Through the Eyes of a Woman', carried at least one and sometimes several stories about women doing war work, both in an organisational and a manual capacity. For example, 'Wonderful War Women' reported how Lady Henry Grosvenor was helping provide food and accommodation to 5,000 workers in Woolwich: 'Her detailed knowledge of the needs and difficulties of the workers in that district and of the housing and feeding capacity amazed even the experienced YMCA committeemen who sat with her.'⁶⁹ Another, 'Should Mayfair Supply Plough-Girls?', proposed that as women were now working on the land, other jobs previously only considered suitable for men should also be opened up to them.⁷⁰ She wrote positively about the women who sailed for Holland to attend the pacifist International Congress of Women at the Hague in April 1915, at a time when many suffrage groups and their newspapers marginalised pacifist views in favour of patriotically supporting the war effort.[71]

Other women journalists who wrote for the 'mainstream' press had also been influenced by or been members of the suffrage movement. Stella Wolfe Murray, another Fleet Street friend of Shackleton's, and the first woman Lobby correspondent (different from Shackleton's position as parliamentary correspondent), was a member of the Women's Freedom League and carried her feminism into the articles she wrote for the *Leeds Mercury* and other papers.[72] Another extraordinary and overlooked woman, though sadly there is no space here to discuss her more fully, Murray was a keen flier, wrote extensive travel articles on flight and edited the world's first published anthology of poetry on flying, *The Poetry of Flight* (1925).

Alison Settle joined the Society of Women Journalists, which provided members with a regular programme of lectures and teas as well as a bi-monthly magazine, *The Woman Journalist*, which declined during the First World War and finally closed in 1920. It was relaunched in 1923, revivified and full of useful information about job opportunities and training, and carrying interviews with newspaper editors and reports from women journalists across the globe.[73] Shackleton became the first woman chair of the central London branch of the National Union of Journalists in 1921. She was involved in helping the central London branch force employers to pay both men and women staff journalists a minimum of eight guineas a month.[74] During the 1920s Shackleton was also elected a member of the Critics' Circle, a group of mostly freelance drama critics formed in 1913 who believed that they were stronger as a group than as individuals. When she was elected a member of the council, she was the only woman ever to reach this position.[75]

Settle and both the Heald sisters became early members of English PEN (Poets, Essayists, Novelists). Nora Heald, at that time a theatre critic and feature writer on the *Daily Mail*, attended the inaugural dinner on 5 October 1921.[76] Although PEN became a prominent voice against the rise of fascism in Europe during the 1930s, and is known today for its campaigns for writers' freedoms throughout the world, it was originally formed as a sociable, mixed sex dining club for English writers and journalists.[77] However, freedom of expression became a central concern, and as early as 1928 the annual international congress passed motions promoting equality between the sexes and opposing the 'suppression of literature' under authoritarian regimes.[78] All three women were active within the organisation from its early years. Shackleton would co-host 'At Homes' for club members at the Garden Club in Chesterfield Gardens in the 1920s. Membership was good for their and other women's careers: Nora Heald became editor of *The Lady*, partly through contacts she made with the previous editor at a PEN club dinner in January 1930.[79]

Letters from Shackleton to the PEN administration show that she invited a number of up-and-coming writers to PEN dinners, including a then first-time novelist, J. B. Priestley, in 1928, and in 1929 Stella Gibbons, who later wrote the comic novel *Cold Comfort Farm* (1932). Gibbons and Shackleton met at the *Evening Standard* where Shackleton was a star feature writer and critic, and Gibbons was enduring a difficult and 'exhausting' apprenticeship and discovering that she was no good as a news reporter.[80] The letter inviting Gibbons reads: 'I would like Miss Gibbons to sit next to me but as she is a very attractive young poet, I hope you will put somebody nice on her other hand.'[81] Shackleton also introduced Gibbons to her sister,

Female friendship, work and collaboration

Nora, who became editor of *The Lady* in 1930 and Gibbons' reviews of country novels – many of them sources of parody for *Cold Comfort Farm* – begin to appear from this time.[82] This friendly help would be repaid when in 1933 Gibbons won the Prix Femina prize for her novel, and asked Edith and Nora Heald to be her guests of honour at the prize-giving ceremony.[83] Shackleton's letter inviting Priestley also asks that a Mr W. L. Wood of Rolls House Publishing be invited, and that he be placed next to Priestley, in what may have been an attempt to connect Priestley with a publisher. Shackleton also proposed the book illustrator Edmund Dulac for PEN membership.[84]

All three women's names appear regularly on lists of attendees of dinners, congresses and fundraising committees.[85] Settle served on the PEN council and while she was editor of *Vogue* she served on the executive committee. Shackleton and Settle gave generously to the fund established by English PEN in October 1938 to help Czech writers escape the country after the Munich crisis.[86] Like Shackleton, Settle would bring aspiring writers as guests to the monthly PEN dinners, but she would ask to be placed next to Shackleton, if her friend was attending.[87] A businesswoman as well as a journalist, Settle proposed speakers who might useful to writers to be invited to the PEN dinners. A letter dated 9 December 1935, for example, proposed that the advertising expert Sir Herbert Morgan be invited to speak about the possibilities for writers in the areas of film and radio: 'Many writers are so separated from the wider world or so closely linked in a world of other writers that they may not see changes taking place which will make a world of difference to them.'[88]

Aware of the importance of sustaining networks in journalism, a profession whose actors have very little agency, Settle would go on to be a founder member of the Women's Press

Club in 1943. The inaugural lunch, held on 14 October 1943, comprised 130 guests including the food writer Elizabeth Craig, the photographer Lee Miller and the founder and owner of *Time and Tide*, Viscountess Rhondda.[89] After being sacked from *Vogue*, Settle formed the 'Fashion Group of Great Britain', holding an inaugural lunch in December 1935.[90] This group of fashion writers and editors would push back against the power of the fashion houses and of male newspaper editors who saw everything in terms of a good story and therefore undervalued fashion editors' knowledge and expertise. Among the list of concerns Settle had were that big fashion houses pressurised editors into favouring them and would withdraw communications if they felt 'hurt'; that male editors didn't understand fashion and wanted 'some gimmick or vulgarity' over 'true news'; and that fashion journalists were often the least well-dressed people at a fashion show.[91] The 'hurt' of snubbed fashion houses impacted on Settle personally when she was 'kidnapped' by milliners from the fashion house Worth, and forcibly measured up for a hat.[92]

As leading journalists, Settle and Shackleton nurtured multiple informal networks that would help journalists in a world where the commercialisation of the press was making the role of the writer on mainstream newspapers and magazines fraught with strains, and with pressure to make compromises both with their employers and their sources.

Editor of *Vogue*, single mother, hitch-hiking war correspondent

Another strain for Alison Settle was that of being a single mother, performing a high-profile and demanding role while her children were still very young (her eldest child Margaret was

Female friendship, work and collaboration

only five years old when she took the *Vogue* editor's chair in May 1926, and was 14 when Settle was sacked due to a contractual dispute). Settle is one of only two women in this study who were mothers during the interwar years. The almost total absence of mothers in this study is, of course, no coincidence, as combining motherhood with working life was both arduous and, for many women, socially unacceptable; sometimes, in workplaces where a marriage bar was operating, it was impossible.[93]

Settle's diaries, written between 1930 and 1934 while she was both editor of *Vogue* and a mother of young children, shed fascinating light on what it was like to juggle family and work during

Figure 1 Alison Settle as editor of *Vogue*, 1929

this time. Rather than keeping it daily, she wrote long catch-up accounts at the end of each month, and sometimes over longer periods. The result is a distillation of the most important events and feelings, recalled after four or six weeks. Her children, and her long absences from them, are uppermost in her mind. Evening commitments and regular press trips, often extending over several days, meant that she was away from home for lengthy periods; often crucial moments, like helping her daughter prepare for a theatrical performance, had to be missed:

> Meg danced as a Greek archer at Mr Hoare's matinée at the Chelsea Palace. In all it was a busy day. I left instructions about Meg's make up, phoned Belle Harding [friend] to come, went to have a business talk with Watkins of John Lewis [the department store], to the office to see fresh pages, have a long talk to Nada [Nada Ruffer, fashion editor of *Vogue*], met Harry [brother], went to Brooke House for lunch, onto the Matinée with mum, Nance and Belle Harding: took them and the children to tea at Harrods.[94]

Another entry reads:

> Went to the PEN dinner ... met Gerald Slot who as my doctor had forbidden me to go to dinner ... went onto the Dorchester for supper ... Kiss Meg and John in sleep – Meg returns dear sleepy little kisses ... The children come to say goodbye in the morning before going to school ... Then I sleep until lunch, dream of missing trains and not finding seats and losing the children and losing my way and what not.[95]

Settle describes with relish occasions when she was able to spend extended periods of time with her children:

> Business worries and disappointments during this summer form an undercurrent, as they must this year [1930] to the lives of most wage slaves. I am more tired than I like to think, my eyes

wrong. But there are peaks of great happiness – a weekend at Sunt Farm [her grandparents' farm in Sussex] being one ... The farm spruced up, the garden planted and sweet with carnations and peonies – the hammock out in the really long orchard grass, the hay being cut in the field opposite the house, John being given a ride on the horses, Meg making hay nests and us having tea in them, scented nights, warm with a moon. Honeysuckle gathering and wild roses ... Meg and me painting.[96]

Although Settle was editor of British *Vogue*, editorial content was closely watched by the head office in New York, overseen by *Vogue*'s US editor-in-chief, Edna Woolman Chase, who was renowned for making exacting demands on her staff.[97] She insisted that Settle get rid of her Hampstead flat and buy a service flat in Maddox Street, Mayfair, as befitting the editor of *Vogue*. It pained her to leave the home she had made with her husband and children when they were little:

Mrs Chase was in England towards the end of July ... she just can't bear my minute flat – at first a weight settled on me whenever I thought of it, so close and with such a queer atmosphere ... Trying to dispose of beloved no. 17 East Heath Road with an ache in one's heart – and being unable to.[98]

Other diary entries record 'a rather awful conference' at the offices of *Vogue* in Paris, with Edna Woolman Chase and Michel de Brunhoff, the editor of *Vogue* Paris; and of taking a week off work to rest before the arrival of *Vogue*'s owner, Condé Nast.[99] Very often she records being exhausted.

There were, however, compensations. She met a wide array of interesting people, and visited grand country houses. Highlights of her diary include drinking champagne cocktails and playing shove ha'penny with the painter Augustus John; lunch with Rebecca West and Aldous Huxley; weekends with

Cecil Beaton, staying in his 'all-white four poster bed'; meeting the actor Charles Laughton, 'growing a Henry VIII beard and fatness'; and press trips all around the country, visiting castles and beauty spots with other journalists.[100] An unashamed *gourmande*, she describes beautiful furnishings and fabulous meals in great detail:

> Brooke House ... there was huge gold plate at the end of the room: three of the vastest bunches of sweet peas I've seen on the table, fine lace mats on the polished wood. We lunched off iced melon ... eggs fried with slices of thin tournedos with foie gras on top, very new peas and beans; quails cooked in pastry cases with salad; an Eton mess of strawberries, cherries and coffee.[101]

Other compensations were teas and lunches and weekend visits with family and friends: her mother and brother Harry feature most prominently, but the Heald sisters also crop up regularly. Many of her press trips, fashion shows and PEN events included Nora Heald, who, as editor of *The Queen* and then *The Lady*, would often be invited to the same functions. 'Godmother Edith' features in more informal family gatherings. Always the entries return to her children; she regrets the end of weekends at her rented cottage near Broadstairs in Kent ('Sunday so short, Monday comes so soon'), and while work is glossed over with mentions of dreaded board meetings, lunches and visits from the Nasts, the rich accounts of her time with her children are full of charming detail: 'John and I climb over the flint garden wall (and with bare legs onto nettles) and go tadpoling.'[102]

Ultimately, Settle was a cautious and conservative editor of *Vogue*. Her 'visionary' predecessor, Dorothy Todd (editor 1922–26), had initiated *Vogue*'s relationship with Bloomsbury highbrow culture and with the avant-garde, projecting the image of the *Vogue* reader as intelligent, chic and interested in modernity.[103] Settle continued this image, but initiated few innovations apart from expanding the magazine's travel coverage. Hemmed in by orders from New York and, as her diary shows, never totally enamoured of her job, it seems she saw it more a means of providing for her children than anything else. She did commission writers, including Aldous Huxley, Osbert Sitwell and Clive Bell, to write poems and essays (although they had written for *Vogue* before she took the chair), but she had no autonomy over the way the magazine looked and much of the editorial content emanated from New York. Notes for a possible book about her time at *Vogue* show this:

> How little our American bosses cared for the written word: how meticulous they were over layout, type, margins and all the visual arts. Virginia Woolf, Raymond Mortimer, [Marcel] Boulestin [the chef and food writer] all went fairly unnoticed by Condé Nast, Edna Chase and the others from New York. Yet let one number try out the slightest change of measure for, say, margins and a cable would arrive: 'NOT criticising but kindly explain reasoning behind change of margin measurements'.[104]

Her notes refer to the 'snobbishness' of the *Vogue* establishment, and how, having graduated from popular newspapers, she was considered as having 'no class'. She did, however, score minor victories. She hired a writer, Lesley Blanche, who sent in an unsolicited article 'which delighted me':

> telling how she tried to keep abreast with the dicta of *Vogue*'s fashion but how difficult she found, eg fox fur scarves, v. announced, were now demodé. She felt she must do her best to follow such guidance and so she had posted her long fox fur scarf, shoving it, bit by bit into the scarlet mouth of the post box outside *Vogue*'s door on New Bond Street.[105]

To be thrilled by what was in effect an act of wholesale subversion of everything *Vogue* stood for – fashion, newness, consumerism – suggests that Settle was never comfortable in her position. In a partial memoir, she described her best achievement in her professional life as the few months she spent as a war correspondent for the *Observer* in 1944, recording Dutch civilians trekking vast distances with their belongings tied up in sacks as the German army moved east. She

Figure 2 Alison Settle, *Observer* war correspondent, 1944

did, however, have to hitch-hike to the theatre of action, after arriving at a Belgian airfield only to discover that General Montgomery had reneged on a promise to facilitate female journalists.[106]

The diary peters out in the summer of 1934, so there is no record of Settle's reaction to being sacked from *Vogue*. A letter to PEN general secretary and friend Hermon Ould, however, describes her last few months at *Vogue* as a 'horrible situation' and 'pretty hellish. I had always been told American firms acted like that but I had never believed it. Anyway I am free now and what a difference it makes to my life.'[107] Less than two years later, Settle became editor of the *Observer*'s 'new page for women', where she remained until 1960.[108] In 1943 she would persuade the new *Observer* editor David Astor to give Edith Shackleton a job as book critic on the paper, finally repaying her friend's early generosity.

Naomi Royde-Smith and Rose Macaulay: professional friendship and rivalry

Naomi Royde-Smith and Rose Macaulay first met in 1911 and gradually became close friends. Between 1919 and 1926 the friendship was helpful to both of them during a pivotal time in their careers, covering Macaulay's breakthrough as a best-selling author and Royde-Smith's loss of the literary editorship at the *Weekly Westminster* and the publication of her first two novels. Royde-Smith's review of Macaulay's first big success, *Potterism* (1920), in the influential weekly review *Time and Tide* likened Macaulay to Jane Austen in her ability to mix social satire and intellectual bite with 'unmatched' readability:

> To be able to ... write of sociology, economics, revolutionary journalism and the Life and Liberty movement, and to make of them a book as easy to read, as hard to put down as the best detective story, is a feat so astonishing that the ordinary reader might be lost in wonder at it were it not so lightly done.[109]

The joint hosting, from 1919, of their weekly literary soirées, in particular, shows a shared enterprise in establishing a literary 'group'. Publishers would bring their newly signed novelists to these evenings in order to ingratiate them with critics and more established writers. Michael Sadleir, then an editor at the publisher Constable, brought a young Storm Jameson to one of these evenings, calling it 'your baptism into the literary world'.[110] Constable had just published Jameson's first novel, *The Pot Boils* (1919), and Jameson recorded seeing Arnold Bennett, Macaulay and Royde-Smith, whom she found 'a little formidable', at Prince's Gardens, in the days when 'cocktails, which have murdered conversation, were not yet the rule'.[111] Macaulay's letters to members of her family during the early 1920s thrill with accounts of these soirées and of what her friend thought and said about various literary characters. The frequent 'Naomi says ...' and 'Naomi told me ...' in her letters to her cousin Jean are clearly a way of presenting herself to her family as a writer who is making it and enjoying insider status in a literary milieu.[112]

Their falling out in 1926 was partly a result of unkind sketches of characters and descriptive details bearing too much truth in their novels: Royde-Smith's *The Housemaid* (1926) and Macaulay's *Crewe Train* (1926). While Macaulay's biographers blame Royde-Smith and her gossipy nature for the falling out, this is by no means the whole picture, as I will show later.[113] In fact the two continued a fertile epistolary relationship based on discussion of each other's literary output well into the 1940s, showing that their professional ties lasted beyond their emotional one.[114] After 1926 they went to the theatre together, went out on drives, had telephone conversations and, most importantly, continued a critical dialogue with each other about their published work. They thus present a different model of how women helped each other navigate the uncharted professional waters of the interwar years. Able and extensive biographies of both Macaulay and Royde-Smith are available, although their friendship and its decline are not analysed in much detail, and none describe their continued professional relationship after 1926.[115] This section will focus on a collection of unpublished letters and postcards from Macaulay to Royde-Smith between 1925 and 1947, which covers the period both before and after their falling out.

Before the publication of Royde-Smith's *The Housemaid* in 1926, Macaulay was an attentive friend. Royde-Smith was a regular visitor to Macaulay's mother's house in Hedgerley in south Buckinghamshire, where they would embark on hilarious and 'highly dramatic' tours in Mrs Macaulay's Ford.[116] Macaulay being a vague and distracted map reader, they would usually get lost, and once they drove across a village green and nearly plunged into the duck pond. Royde-Smith recorded the episode: 'I've never suppressed so much laughter, nor come nearer to death.'[117] Both were conducting illicit affairs with married men: Royde-Smith with the poet Walter de la Mare, and Macaulay with the novelist and former Irish priest Gerald O'Donovan.[118] Both alluded to their affairs in their fiction, Macaulay most notably in her novel *What Not* (1919) and Royde-Smith in her second novel, *The Housemaid*, although illicit love in all its myriad forms is a theme in many of her novels.[119] The women mixed socially with their lovers and their wives, were regular visitors to their family homes and were accepted as their fathers' friends by their lovers' children.[120] They thus enjoyed the comforts of family life and love, without having to submit to a husband, or to having children of their own at a time when both could have threatened their professional accomplishments.[121] This strange coincidence provided a unique bond: both writers risked – and indeed received – social opprobrium for their transgressive behaviour.[122]

Royde-Smith wrote her first novel, *The Tortoiseshell Cat* (dedicated to Walter de la Mare), in a feverish three-month period after she had been sacked from *The Queen* in September 1924. Finally, after years of commenting on other cultural producers' work, she produced one of her own, about an older woman's erotic fascination for a younger woman. Waiting for the reviews would have been a nerve-wracking experience, and she confessed to Walter de la Mare that she feared the novel was 'a little thin'.[123] During this period Macaulay was travelling across Mallorca, Spain and the Pyrenees with her lover Gerald O'Donovan. A postcard to Royde-Smith from Macaulay, dated 17 April 1925, reveals Macaulay's attentiveness to her friend's worries. Sent from Mallorca, the postcard depicts a shady, pillared and tiled Mallorcan patio. Macaulay writes: 'This island is heaven. Palma is a honey-pale town on a blue port, full of deep old streets and cave patios – in the middle of one patio (just like this) sat a tortoise-shell cat, licking its paws in the sun.' The reference to Royde-Smith's nascent novel shows that Macaulay was thinking of her friend even while she was on holiday with her lover, the illuminated image of feline contentment surely intended as a good omen.

Female friendship, work and collaboration

Royde-Smith, still a prolific reviewer for *Time and Tide* and *Outlook*, never missed chances to promote her friends' work while also alluding to her own central place in the world of witty women writers:

> These two delightful books [Sylvia Lynd's *The Mulberry Bush* and Rose Macaulay's *A Casual Commentary*] arrive for review in the same parcel, and as I cut their pages it seems as if the voices and laughter of two of my most amusing friends are joining together in another happy fireside hour, or shouting through the wind of a long day's walk on the Downs or across some heather covered common.[124]

Her second novel *The Housemaid* was published during the first months of 1926. One of the main characters in this story of love and deception is Michel Sherlock, an amateur archaeologist trying to unlock the mysteries of the Mayan calendar, and unhappily married to Beryl, a ghastly gold-digger. It is thought that Macaulay took exception to the use of the name Beryl, the name of Gerald O'Donovan's wife, and suspected that Royde-Smith was using her fiction to hint at the affair.[125] It was certainly a careless name to use, but another reading of the novel could be that it is a gender-switching confessional signalling the end of her own adulterous affair with de la Mare. Michel, the novel's protagonist, had rooms in Temple, where Royde-Smith was living when she wrote the novel, and the fictional adulterer reads the *Westminster Gazette*, the paper that made Royde-Smith famous in literary circles.

Whatever the real intention, Macaulay reacted with a vicious intensity in her own novel *Crewe Train*, which she was finishing as Royde-Smith's novel came out, in her portrait of the popular novelist Evelyn Gresham, who is accused of spreading 'vile nonsense'. A particularly telling line towards the end of the novel could be read as a direct message to Royde-Smith: 'Oh, why had Evelyn written that, invented all that ... It had been such a good friendship and now it was spoilt.'[126] It seems, however, that Macaulay repented of the attack almost immediately, writing in a letter to Royde-Smith just a month after the publication of *Crewe Train*: 'Darling, be a novelist and recognise one doesn't do whole portraits ... remember how one mixes and creates one's characters into little lines, or sprinklings, of actuality – often 2 or 3 people are in one, often a touch of one and the rest made up.'[127]

The cooling of relations could also have been influenced by Royde-Smith's marriage, at the end of 1926, to the American actor Ernest Milton, who was very protective against the slights he felt his wife had received from other writers. Milton described Macaulay as 'double' and 'unutterably false and dangerous', and suggested that she was continuing the pattern of other writers, including the poet Humbert Wolfe and the Sitwell siblings, who had used Royde-Smith on their way up but who then dropped her on finding fame.[128] In 1943 Royde-Smith herself wrote a pointed letter about the time when she was 'useful enough to Humbert [Wolfe, the poet] and Rose for them *to play at being friends*' (emphasis added).[129] Nonetheless the women continued to correspond, and meet. Macaulay's letters and postcards to Royde-Smith are warm, affectionate and at times plaintive. A postcard written in 1932, for example, tells Royde-Smith that she has bought tickets to see Milton in *Othello*: 'I hope E. is turning blacker all the time – I do look forward to it. I've seen no one for ages but family, and want to see you.'[130] Another, in 1933, asks whether she can sit with Royde-Smith if she is going to see Milton in the play *Night's Candles*: 'Is there any night you are going and I could come with you? That would be fun. If not

Female friendship, work and collaboration

I shall go alone one evening or bring someone else. But I would love to sit with you for it if you will be sitting.'[131] This message seems somewhat manipulative in suggesting either that she will go on her own, therefore hoping to gain sympathy, or that she will take another friend, thus intending to provoke jealousy.

Usually, however, the letters and postcards form part of a twenty-year ongoing dialogue about their work. For example, Macaulay sent a postcard after the publication of *The Double Heart* (1931), Royde-Smith's critically acclaimed study of the eighteenth-century French muse and salon hostess Julie de L'Espinasse. It is worth quoting at length:

> Being halfway through Julie (which I sent for from the Times B. C. [Book Club]) I feel I must burst into card about it – it is so well done, enthusiastic and interesting – a brilliant reconstruction and with lovely Naomi-ish bits that make me laugh. I don't think anyone before has set forth so well how it is possible ardently and simultaneously to love two or more – I am ½ through de Guibert [Jacque-Antoine Hippolyte, one of de L'Espinasse's two lovers], who is an adorable sketch. I do congratulate you on its brilliance and readableness. You make then all so tremendously alive. I only find one fault – you fell, on a page I was reading in bed last night, into the Bloomsbury myth, which I feel we should leave to those whom Harold Nicolson calls 'the softies' … I mean you seem to subscribe to it. Never mind, you shall do as you like, if you write a book like this one, and give me such an acute pleasure. It is quite the best thing you've done. I feel I must write a line to Hamish H [Hamilton, the publisher] about it and congratulate him … My love to E [Naomi's husband, Ernest Milton] and, with ardent wishes, to N.[132]

The tone is warm and affectionate, and full of praise for 'Julie'. Macaulay tries to conjure intimacy – 'lovely Naomi-ish bits' – and also a sense of their being in the same 'in' group, in opposition to Bloomsbury. There is also the generous suggestion that she will congratulate the publisher – although this is a double-edged gesture, underlining her own cultural capital. The repetition of 'ardently/ardent' is surely also intended to make the recipient feel that she is the object of a love as powerful as that of Julie de L'Espinasse.

Further letters and postcards seek to encourage the friendship and to flatter ('Rose Fyleman [a writer and poet] was enchanted to meet you: "so amusing, so nice to look at, such fun". I felt I had climbed up several steps in her esteem when I boasted how well I knew you. I like her, she is so genuine.')[133] Several letters refer to Royde-Smith's correspondence, which does not survive. The last in the collection is a justification of a fairly mixed and in parts rather damning review of Royde-Smith's biography of Mrs Sherwood, the Victorian author, which Macaulay wrote for the *Times Literary Supplement* in 1947.[134] The letter takes the trouble to send Royde-Smith the original proof of the article, which may have been slightly less critical, but which has not survived. Again, the tone is both appeasing and manipulative, and while justifying her criticism of *The State of Mind of Mrs Sherwood*, Macaulay also thanks Royde-Smith for her review of her own travelogue, *They Went to Portugal*. Whether intentional or not, the message is a transparent bid for a trade deal, underlining Macaulay's continued need for good notices and also her understanding that Royde-Smith still has the power to influence reception of her productions. Read as a whole, the letters and postcards do not show Macaulay in a good light, and suggest that she was rather a manipulative and at times disingenuous friend.

* * *

Female friendship, work and collaboration

In contrast to Macaulay and Royde-Smith, Alison Settle and Edith Shackleton would both eventually retire just yards from each other in the same street of the small Sussex village of Steyning. Shackleton lived with her sister Nora at Chantry House, a fine eighteenth-century red-brick and stone mansion, and Settle in a small rose-swathed terraced cottage up the road.[135] They were still helping and promoting each other in the pages of local and national newspapers in the 1960s and 1970s. By this time both women had faded from public view, and it appears that a number of the articles written by and about each other had at least in part the purpose of attempting to cement their reputations before their deaths, thus continuing six decades of professional collaboration.[136]

During the interwar years, women's status as public intellectuals and journalists was still highly contested and we have seen in this chapter how professional friendships could be beneficial in helping women overcome deep-seated obstacles. A critical mass of women occupying positions of influence on newspapers and in publishing was developing during this time, and we have seen how – whether genuinely based on deep love and affection, or whether more mercenary – friendships and professional networks were one way in which women could increase their agency and energy in achieving their aspirations. Social networks, from informal friendships and groups to more official bodies, have been shown to help individuals and organisations reach their goals, particularly if several people in the group or network are chasing the same target as 'partner goal strivers'.[137] We can count both the emotionally sustaining professional friendships of Shackleton and Settle, as well as the informal and semi-formal organisations they joined, as examples of this successful 'goal pursuit' in action.

Two other types of network that also bring positive results to members are those of the well-connected family, and the more formal national and international organisation, both of which will be examined in subsequent chapters. Before I turn to these, the next chapter examines a different strategy, employed by Francesca Wilson, the humanitarian activist. She was rejected by the influential organisation she tried to join and thus had to engage in a kind of subterfuge to bring her prodigious talent to the aid of the people who needed it most.

Notes

1 'Dedicatory' in Macaulay 1919 (frontispiece, n.p.); the dedication reads: 'To N. G. R. S. who is responsible for many of them.'
2 Earlier lines read: 'A sweet Gregorian chant the cuckoo sings;/ Peacocks flaunt the tails of a child's desire'.
3 The Cam is the river that runs through Cambridge. When Macaulay first started out in London her family was living in Great Shelford, just outside Cambridge. From 'Coming to London' (Macaulay 1957: 159).
4 Benton 2015: 125.
5 For more on the intellectual response to mass reading, see Carey 1992; Ayers 1999; LeMahieu 1988.
6 Woolf 1981: 236, 93.
7 There has recently been much scholarly backlash against the academy's neglect of so many interwar writers in favour of the modernist canon. Clay (2018: 75–101) has grounded this debate in her analysis of *Time and Tide*'s interwar book pages.
8 'Another Bloomsbury' is the term coined by Gillian Hanscombe and Virginia Smyers (1987) to describe those women writers of 1890–1940, who were less wealthy and less well-connected than the Woolfs and their set; many were bohemian and expatriate, and they included such writers and editors as May Sinclair, Harriet Monroe, Hilda Doolittle (H.D.) and Charlotte Mew.

Female friendship, work and collaboration

9 Jaffe 2005: 3.
10 Margaret Lane (see Chapter 5) delivered an impressive speech on the perils of being thus defined at a meeting of the Authors' Club in 1938.
11 Rose Macaulay, 'Why I Dislike Cats, Clothes and Visits', *Daily Mail*, 2 November, p. 19.
12 For more on interwar literary networks and culture, see Harding 2002; Clay 2018.
13 H. Graham Greene, 'Paint and Wood', *Weekly Westminster Gazette*, 4 August 1923, p. 15; 'Impressions of Dublin', *Weekly Westminster Gazette*, 25 August 1923, p. 7.
14 Royde-Smith attended the inaugural meeting of the English Prix Femina on 20 June 1919 at Bedford College (Prix Femina-Vie Heureuse archives, Cambridge University Library (PFVH)); she also promoted the prize in an article, 'Women Adjudicators', *Westminster Gazette*, 23 June 1919.
15 Gorham 1996: 163–9.
16 Much has been written about the friendship between Holtby and Brittain, and so I am simply providing a few details here. In my opinion, the most readable and plausible accounts of the friendship (both primary and secondary sources) are Brittain 1987; Shaw 1999; Gorham 1996; Holtby 1971; Kennard 1989.
17 Brittain 2004: 546.
18 Brittain 1987: 2.
19 Gorham 1992.
20 See, for example, Vicinus 1985.
21 See Beddoe 1989; while much of Beddoe's thesis has been challenged recently, the pressures on women to return to 'home and duty' after the war were nevertheless great and, for many, irresistible. Virginia Woolf quotes newspaper articles at length in *Three Guineas* (1938) giving examples of the strong trend in many papers in support of the idea that women who had worked during the war should now go home. See, for example, Austin Harrison, 'Motherhood the First Duty of Women: Biological Crisis of the Next Decade', *Sunday Pictorial*, 21 March 1915, p. 4.
22 *Evening Standard*, 1 January 1923, p. 4.
23 *The Woman Teacher*, 2 January 1920, p. 114.
24 Winifred Holtby, 'Ladies in Restaurants: Are We So Dangerous?', *Manchester Guardian*, 28 March 1930, p. 8.

25 Bretherton 1917: 885.
26 For early twentieth-century studies on working-class kinship ties, see, for example, Masterman 1980; Women's Co-operative Guild 1980; Young and Willmott 2011.
27 Clay 2006: 309.
28 Clay 2006: 323; scholars disagree over the nature of Holtby's feelings for Brittain; for an excellent analysis on whether or not Holtby desired sexual relations with Brittain, see Gorham 1996.
29 Staff salary details for the *Evening Standard* for 1930 show that Shackleton, a 'special writer', was paid £2,700 a year; this compares with £2,000 a year for the women's page editor, £2,210 for the news editor and £2,000 a year for the city editor. Her fellow male special writers, Harold Nicolson and Bruce Lockhart, were paid £3,000 a year. Beaverbrook Papers, House of Commons, BBK/H/19.
30 Settle 1973b.
31 Settle 1973a.
32 Settle 1973a. Settle's older brother, Harold Munro Fox (he changed his surname from Fuchs to Fox during the First World War), became a celebrated scientist and Professor of Zoology at Bedford College, London.
33 'Lady St Helier and the Belgian Wounded', *Illustrated Sunday Herald*, 11 April 1915, p. 19.
34 Interview with Alison Settle, 'The Editor Who Came in by the Back Door', *Worthing Herald*, 16 June 1961.
35 Tusan 2005: 191.
36 Full list published in *The Woman Journalist*, 23, September 1914, p. 2.
37 Lonsdale 2016: 93; Griffiths 2006: 193.
38 Settle 1947: 3–4.
39 Settle 1973b.
40 Agate 1935: 172.
41 *Sunday Pictorial*, 13 February 1916, p. 7, and 28 May 1916, p. 5, respectively.
42 Numerous references to 'Godmother Edith Heald' in Alison Settle's diaries, Charles Wakefield private collection.
43 Settle 1973b.
44 'The Age of Unrule', *Daily Herald*, 29 January 1920, p. 8.
45 Biographical details from an interview with Shackleton, 'A Stir in the Lords', *Shoreham Herald*, 28 September 1962.
46 Souhami 2013: 253–4.

Female friendship, work and collaboration

47 Shackleton 1930: 193.
48 See, for example, 'The Passing of the General', *Yarmouth Independent*, 30 January 1909, p. 6; 'Should Wives Be Paid Wages?', *Dundee Courier*, 8 December 1912.
49 Dark 1917: 1–12.
50 Various notices in *The Times* 'Deaths' column, 1917–75. The text was almost always the same: 'In proud and loving memory of Ivan Heald, Hood Battalion, R.N.D, attached R.F.C., killed in an air fight near Vimy 4 December 1916.' In later entries, his name was changed to Ivan Shackleton Heald.
51 Letterheads on letters written by Edith Shackleton to PEN administrators, Harry Ransom Center.
52 She occasionally used the double 'Edith Shackleton Heald' and also the initials 'E. S. H.' to sign her articles.
53 See, for example, 'Bachelor Fallacy', *Sunday Express*, 25 July 1925, p. 7.
54 'When a Girl's Ideals Crash', *Sunday Express*, 19 July 1925, p. 7.
55 Beaverbrook Papers, House of Commons, BBK/H/239 and BBK/H/45.
56 See, for example, Maddox 1999; Hassett 2010. Diana Souhami, in her biography of the painter Gluck (2013), makes a little more mention of Shackleton, though only scant and only in relation to her lover.
57 The proportion of women to men did, however, grow steadily, and by the outbreak of the Second World War about 20 per cent of journalists were female. This figure then plateaued until the 1970s.
58 Lonsdale 2018: 463–76.
59 The 'equal pay' victory won by the National Union of Journalists was recorded in the union's magazine, *The Journalist*, in June 1920, p. 34.
60 Lonsdale 2018: 464.
61 Census of England and Wales, via email.
62 Bingham 2004a: 232–3.
63 *Evening Standard*, 13 February 1923. The authorship is confirmed in an article in *The Woman Journalist*, March 1925, p. 14. This article corrects a previous article published in January 1925 which asserted that when Rebecca West became parliamentary representative for the *Daily News* that month, she was the first 'lady journalist' to be given that honour.

64 In her diary, Dorothy Pilley, also a young woman working on Fleet Street in the 1920s, describes taking cigarette breaks with a friend, 'Stella' (see Chapter 3).
65 Shackleton 1930: 199.
66 Tusan 2005.
67 'Another Disgusted Liberal', letters, *The Vote*, 2 April 1909, p. 502.
68 Tusan 2005.
69 *Illustrated Sunday Herald*, 29 August 1915, p. 15.
70 *Illustrated Sunday Herald*, 4 April 1915, p. 19.
71 *Illustrated Sunday Herald*, 18 April 1915, p. 19; for more on the women's movement and pacifism during the war, see Tusan 2005: 193–201.
72 Wolfe Murray became lobby correspondent for the *Leeds Mercury* in December 1924 (*Leeds Mercury*, 2 December 1924, p. 9); she also contributed to the women's page of the *Sheffield Daily Telegraph*. It is worth pointing out that although Rebecca West is often cited as the first woman parliamentary/lobby correspondent, Shackleton and Wolfe Murray were both appointed earlier. See also note 63 above.
73 For more on *The Woman Journalist*, see Lonsdale 2018.
74 An article on the meeting of the central London branch on 2 April 1921, reported in *The Journalist*, describes 'Miss Edith Heald presiding'. A year later, in an article Shackleton wrote for the second issue of *Good Housekeeping*, she was described as 'The first Woman Chairman of the Central London Branch of the National Union of Journalists', *Good Housekeeping*, April 1922, p. 16.
75 'A Stir in the Lords', *Shoreham Herald*, 28 September 1962.
76 Various membership lists in *The Woman Journalist*, 1923 onwards; membership index, English PEN Records 1912–2008; MS-03133, Harry Ransom Center (HRC).
77 Gearon 2012.
78 Report of the Sixth International Congress held in June 1928, write-up in *PEN News*, September 1928, pp. 2–3.
79 This serendipitous meeting was reported in *The Lady*, 16 January 1930, p. 62.
80 Oliver 1998: 63.
81 HRC Series 1, subseries A; 23-3 Edith Shackleton.
82 It is not clear exactly when Nora Heald became editor of *The Lady*. However, a letter to PEN dated 22 July 1931 is on *The Lady* notepaper, while a letter dated 24 January 1930 is on *Daily Herald* notepaper, so we can confidently put her appointment at some point during

these two dates (HRC). *The Lady* began to use initialled bylines in June 1932 when the initials 'S. G.' for Stella Gibbons appear under the book reviews (e.g. *The Lady*, 30 June 1932, p. 1078). Before this date book reviews were anonymous.
83 PFVH, Cambridge University Library.
84 PEN correspondence, HRC.
85 Various references in *PEN News*, 1927–37.
86 HRC.
87 Letters between Alison Settle and Hermon Ould, HRC series 1, subseries A; 62.6 Alison Settle.
88 Letter from Settle to Hermon Ould, 9 December 1935, HRC.
89 'W.P. 3' Lunch Guest List, Women's Press Club, Alison Settle archive, Brighton Design Archives (BDA).
90 Letter from Settle to Hermon Ould, 13 December 1935, HRC.
91 Typewritten notes, 'F.E. 1', Alison Settle archive, BDA.
92 Settle 1973a.
93 Marriage bars were 'nearly universal' in the clerical sector, operating in the civil service, Post Office, railways, libraries, schools, banks and insurance companies (Seltzer 2011); the BBC introduced a marriage bar in 1932; most newspapers operated informal ones (Lonsdale 2013).
94 Alison Settle diary, June 1930; Charles Wakefield private collection.
95 Ibid., May 1934.
96 Ibid., June 1930.
97 Coser 2017.
98 Alison Settle diary, September 1932.
99 Ibid., February 1930, July 1931.
100 Ibid., December 1930, October 1932, September 1933, July 1931, June 1930.
101 Ibid., July 1930; her *Who's Who* entry for 1931 lists her hobbies as 'eating and drinking' (cut out entry for *Who's Who* pasted into diary).
102 Ibid., May 1933.
103 Hankins 2004: 500.
104 Alison Settle notes, no date, Alison Settle archive, BDA.
105 Ibid.
106 Settle 1973b.
107 Letter from Settle to Hermon Ould, 13 December 1935, HRC.
108 Announcement, *Observer*, 11 April 1937, p. 19.
109 'Book Reviews', *Time and Tide*, 16 July 1920, pp. 209–10.

110 Jameson 1984: 160.
111 Jameson 1984: 160.
112 Various letters in Macaulay 2011, esp. pp. 39, 51, 55–8.
113 On Macaulay and Royde-Smith's falling out, see, for example, LeFanu 2003: 155.
114 Various letters and postcards from Macaulay to Royde-Smith, Naomi Royde-Smith papers, Temple University Libraries.
115 For example, LeFanu 2003; Benton 2015.
116 Letter from Royde-Smith to Walter de la Mare, 17 August 1920, quoted in Benton 2015: 126.
117 Benton 2015: 126.
118 LeFanu 2003; Benton 2015.
119 For a discussion of Macaulay's references to her own illicit love affair in *What Not*, see Lonsdale 2019: xxi–xxii.
120 LeFanu 2003: 156.
121 Royde-Smith in any case could not have children, having had gynaecological problems throughout her adulthood, and a hysterectomy in her early forties. When she did eventually marry, it was to a man fifteen years her junior, over whom it may have been easier to assert her own needs. Certainly the number of books she wrote after marriage suggests that she felt no pressure to retreat into domestic routine.
122 Benton 2015: 140; Le Fanu 2003: 155.
123 Letter from Royde-Smith to Walter de la Mare, November 1924, quoted in Benton 2015: 102.
124 Naomi Royde-Smith, 'Rolled Logs', *Time and Tide*, 13 November 1925, p. 1116.
125 Jill Benton takes this view (2015: 130).
126 Macaulay 2018: 240.
127 Letter from Macaulay to Royde-Smith, 28 October 1926, quoted in Benton 2015: 132.
128 Benton 2015: 135.
129 Letter from Royde-Smith to Viola Garvin, 20 September 1943, quoted in Benton 2015: 135.
130 Macaulay to Royde-Smith, 28 March 1932, Naomi Royde-Smith papers, Temple University Libraries.
131 Macaulay to Royde-Smith, 2 October 1933, ibid.
132 Macaulay to Royde-Smith, 8 September 1931, ibid.
133 Macaulay to Royde-Smith, 15 December 1937, ibid.

Female friendship, work and collaboration

134 Rose Macaulay, 'Mrs Sherwood's Doctrine', *Times Literary Supplement*, 18 January 1947, p. 36.
135 Nora temporarily moved out after Gluck and Shackleton became lovers and Gluck moved in in 1944.
136 For example, Shackleton's article about Settle in the *Birmingham Post*, 30 June 1960, p. 4, 'She Has Truly Earned her Place of Honour', explicitly encourages the idea of Settle's monumental achievements.
137 Westaby 2012: 104.

2
Alternative channels

That morning the whole Colony got up before dawn ... and quickly swallowed cocoa and biscuits, for the business of irrigation is serious and exacting ... boys were working with feverish activity stopping up gaps and preparing new ones in the earth ridges of the terraces, so that when the water came it would inundate first the lettuces and then the potatoes and onions. In the meantime on the terraces below, with the same feverish haste, other boys were transplanting tomatoes and pimientos from the frames and putting in seeds of maize, melons and soya bean. Then at last Pepe, the small black-eyed boy who had been posted as sentinel on the top of the hill, announced the water's coming, and there is was – a yellow, foaming stream rushing through cemented channels and dashing in cataracts over rocks ... the boys soon look well nourished, brown and healthy. On the dark background of the Spanish Civil War the Farm Colony at Crevillente shines out like a lantern on a stormy night.[1]

A tall Englishwoman with short, cropped hair and a voice 'like a rusty saw' watched this busy agricultural activity from a plateau above the fields.[2] Francesca Wilson was responsible for the lives of the fifty Spanish boys living in the converted flour mill high above the Alicante *huerta* stretching towards the Mediterranean

Alternative channels

Sea.[3] The previous day she had bid for, and purchased, four hours of water at 20 pesetas an hour, all the colony budget could afford. The boys had already been displaced twice: once from their homes in Malaga after Franco's troops, aided by Mussolini's Italian soldiers, took the town in early 1937, and again, this year, 1938, from their temporary refuge in Murcia, a close-packed town suddenly home to thousands of refugees where typhoid was endemic. Now the boys were happy, active and learning agricultural skills.

This moment of triumph against the odds, as the water raced through its channels, was recorded by Wilson, who had been volunteering for Quaker Friend relief missions since the First World War, in the Quakers' weekly journal, *The Friend*. The article, 'A Farm Colony in Spain', is a vivid account of the work of a frontline relief worker and not only celebrates a rare moment of optimism in the midst of bloody war, but places Francesca Wilson centre stage in a conflict that, presaging as many feared a greater conflagration, held the world's attention. The article promoted the work of the Friends in Spain, and as such helped raise much-needed funds for relief operations; it also helped promote Wilson's progressive ideas about seeing refugees not just as helpless victims but as people with potential who needed more than just sympathy and blankets. On another level, the article, by placing the power over land and access to water into the hands of the boys, speaks to Republican arguments that the people should have the right to the productivity of the land, denied them through years of Spanish absentee landlordism. The carefully prepared runnels and seedlings, the order and hard work of the boys were evidence that they would be capable of farming the land if it belonged to them. This powerful image echoes the 1937 pro-Republican film *Spanish*

Rebel women between the wars

Earth, directed by Joris Ivens and commissioned by the left-wing US collective Contemporary Historians Inc., which ends with an arresting image of water cascading over the arid earth, directly connecting the needs of the Spanish peasants with that of the land.[4] The film had been widely circulated in late 1937 in union halls and left-wing film groups, raising funds for the Aid Spain movement of which Wilson was a member.[5] It had been reviewed and discussed in the *Manchester Guardian*, a newspaper that Wilson had contributed regularly to since 1921, so it is likely that she was both aware of the film and its themes and had probably seen it too.[6]

Although a Cambridge graduate from a middle-class family, Wilson was not a 'Lady Bountiful'; nor, despite her association with the Quakers, was she a missionary type living purely by ideals of service and self-sacrifice. She expected neither gratitude from refugees, nor sentimentality from relief workers: 'Refugees are often accused of not being grateful. Why should they be. Their misfortune is none of their seeking,' she wrote. Too often, she said, wealthy Victorian philanthropists 'needed the poor' as a sop for their guilty consciences.[7] She 'smoked, swore mildly, and took rum in her tea', she spoke Latin, Greek, French, Spanish, Serbian and Russian, quickly learning the language of every new country she arrived in.[8] In 1938, single and just turned 50, Wilson had escaped to Spain from years of teaching history and geography at the Church of England College for Girls in Edgbaston, Birmingham.[9] The Spanish Civil War finally offered this complex, talented and often frustrated woman the chance to make a difference to the lives of the thousands of refugees the war created.

Sent to Murcia by the Friends' Service Council to communicate the Quakers' refugee work in British newspapers, Wilson

Alternative channels

had been shocked by the conditions of the refugees in the town. They were camped everywhere: in churches, in half-finished apartment blocks, sleeping on flea-infested straw mattresses, living off one meal of potato and rice soup a day.[10] Wilson, along with other Quaker volunteers, had quickly organised feeding stations, providing hot chocolate and biscuits to thousands of children every morning. While Wilson could organise occupations for the girls and adults – sewing, literacy classes and rope sandal-making – the older boys were a problem. 'They hung around the refuges, teasing the girls, or formed themselves into gangs to loot the markets, raid orchards or throw stones at peaceful citizens.' Wilson believed hard physical work and the acquisition of agricultural skills could save them.[11]

With the help of a German engineer and two Spanish teachers, and with funds provided by the Quaker Friends in London and America, Wilson took over the old flour mill at Crevillente, and there established a secure, disciplined colony of boys, just one of many camps and colonies she set up for hundreds of Spanish children displaced within their own country.[12] She called these colonies her 'castles brought down from the sky': real, tangible, lasting help rather than the usual relief work of doling out food, clothes and blankets. Another colony she established on a beach near Alicante provided tented accommodation for a further 60 children. Food was stored in a deep sandy trench and the children's tents were erected in the shade of a ravine hidden by pines and fig trees. These children came mainly from Alicante, as she wrote in another article, 'half paralysed because almost every day there are air raids … The sirens scream and the whole town disappears underground for an hour or two … Every crash they hear may mean their home is in ruins.'[13]

Quaker childhood and Cambridge

Francesca Wilson was born on New Year's Day 1888, the third daughter of a relatively wealthy Quaker family then living in Jesmond, Newcastle. She was an unhappy child and always believed that her character was created from the experiences of her first six years.[14] She wrote: 'I was a bitter disappointment to my mother', who, having already borne two daughters, was desperate for a son. When the longed-for son, Maurice, finally arrived two years later, he was everything the angular, difficult Francesca was not: 'He had large, grey blue eyes, good features, a mass of golden curls and an angelic expression. People used to say he should have been the girl, I the boy.'[15] Her childhood memories were of quarrelling with her sisters, schoolgirl crushes and being at times both a 'prig' and a 'sadist'. Both parents had initially been Quakers, but when Wilson was 12 her mother converted to the Plymouth Brethren and insisted her daughters be baptised into the fellowship. The adolescent Wilson, already doubting her faith, found the ceremony 'extremely embarrassing. It had given me no elation, nor sense of sanctity, only made me feel rather foolish.'[16] Her memories as a teenager were of going out on long, solitary walks in the rain in the hope of finding salvation through the downpour to return a believer: 'But when I got home it was all just the same as before.'[17] She rejected the Bible and instead borrowed 'dirty old books' from the 'dirty Free Library in Elswick Road' swapping religious superstition for Ruskin, Carlyle and Victor Hugo.[18] As a young adult she rejected the Brethren and returned to the Quakers. But even when firmly established as a Quaker volunteer in Spain, she would remain an outsider from a religious point of view. Details of the Friends Service Council's supplies to

Alternative channels

Wilson's projects in Murcia and Benidorm contain the note: 'These are Francesca Wilson's projects, with which we take a fraternal interest.'[19]

Despite being branded the difficult middle child, she was encouraged by her father, a fur trader to whom she was very close, to take the examinations for Cambridge University and went up to Newnham College to read history in 1906.[20] At first Cambridge only underlined Wilson's feelings of being an outsider. Newnham in the early years of the twentieth century was, she remembered, peopled by 'glittering beings, brilliant, witty, some of them beautiful'.[21] Girls such as Ray Costelloe (later Strachey, the writer and suffragist), Katherine 'Ka' Cox (friend

Figure 3 Francesca Wilson, early 1900s

of Rupert Brooke and Virginia Woolf), the classicist Dorothy Lamb (who would later be a pioneering archaeologist) were all her contemporaries. 'I had been lonely at school and at home but I was infinitely lonelier here,' she wrote of her early days at Newnham.[22] Gradually Wilson was brought into the circle of women, which, while to Wilson's eyes seemed glamorous, was also modest and studious. She went on suffragist rallies and her growing knowledge of the world and its injustices sparked a sense of outrage which would later lead her to sympathise strongly with left-wing politics. Although she recorded that she struggled with her history studies, she obtained a solid second class result both in her Part I and in her Tripos examinations in the summer of 1909. No woman obtained a first class that year.[23]

Participation strategy: alternative channels

Despite her commitment, energy and language skills, Francesca Wilson had to enter relief work with the Quakers by stealth, having initially been rejected by the Women's Selection Committee when she first applied to volunteer during the First World War. On 14 August 1914, *The Friend* publicised a call for 1,000 volunteers, initially to help families of servicemen at home, but later to serve abroad.[24] One week later *The Friend* reported that relief organisers already had the names of 1,200 volunteers, 'and further lists are coming to hand by every post'.[25] Volunteers were asked to pay for their own travel expenses, equipment and maintenance, while the Friends organised passports and 'Safe Conduct' passes.[26] From these haphazard beginnings, a vast relief network across France, Serbia, Italy, Russia, Belgium, Holland and North Africa gradually spread,

Alternative channels

with 170 workers, 75 of whom were women (mostly nurses and midwives), operating abroad by 1916, and by 1919 more than 600, nearly 200 of whom were women.[27] A further 60 administrative workers in London were kept busy coordinating funds of £1.5 million, and assessing and deploying volunteers.[28] By October 1914, early coordinators were sending back first-hand accounts of their experiences for Quaker publications, such as a report by the Liberal MP Edmund Harvey who went out on an early reconnoitre: 'We came slowly across the main battlefield of the Marne yesterday ... trenches and graves everywhere, and all littered with tins and scraps like Hampstead Heath after a bank holiday.'[29]

The first teams of relief workers were in France by November 1914, the men involved in reconstructing destroyed villages around Esternay in the Marne Department, and the women working under the direction of Dr Hilda Clark at the maternity hospital at Châlons.[30] The Friends were from the start aware of the value of public support for their work through publicity, and by December 1914 the War Victims Relief Committee had enlisted the help of the *Westminster Gazette* to publicise their work.[31] While the Quakers were more progressive than many religious organisations, women Friends were not recognised as equals until 1896, and even after this date women Friends did not enjoy equality in all areas of Quakerism.[32] The pattern of women's access was similar to other mixed-sex organisations: resistance followed by reluctant acceptance, with a few energetic women occupying positions of status.[33] These women were the 'wives and relations' of prominent Quaker men, adopting a pattern of access to power followed by women in other membership and political organisations such as the Fabians, the Socialist League and the Social Democratic Federation.[34] Early records of First World War relief workers show that women volunteers tended to come from the leading Quaker families: the surnames Fry, Cadbury, Pim and Rowntree predominate.[35]

At the outbreak of war, Wilson, then 26, had just started a job as history teacher at the newly opened County School for Girls, Gravesend. In her memoir she describes how she would take the ferry after work across the Thames and listen to the stories of the bewildered refugees thronging Tilbury Station, 'with their treasures tied up in sheets'. She describes these first experiences of displaced people in covetous, almost venal terms: she 'listened thirstily' to their stories and was accused by officials of trying to 'poach' the refugees; through their tales of burning homes and terrified flight she 'first tasted blood'.[36] Despite her doubts over her faith, the Quakers were a familiar organisation and provided a relief framework that she might join, although her first attempt at volunteering was firmly rebuffed. She applied as a volunteer in November 1914 but was rejected by the administrator, Ruth Fry, who questioned her motivation: was it genuine desire to relieve the suffering of civilians caught up in the war, or a selfish desire for excitement and adventure?[37] It is unclear why Wilson was initially rejected. Letters between Hilda Clark, who ran the Châlons maternity hospital, and the Friends administrators in London suggest that there was no good reason for the rejection, apart perhaps from a suspicion of the assertive young woman, which is surprising considering Clark's long history with the women's movement and her involvement with the International Women's Suffrage Alliance.[38] Wilson clearly had qualifications: although she had no medical experience, she had close family links with the Friends, was a French-speaker and had experience of both teaching and volunteering in England.[39] Hilda Clark thought

Alternative channels

Wilson not '*très serieuse*'. Margery Fry, on the women's committee, had concerns about her 'age and temperament'.[40]

It is worth noting here that Wilson's access was blocked by a group of senior women working within a male-dominated organisation. Doubts about her age were certainly specious: many male volunteers younger than Wilson – including her own younger brother, Maurice – were accepted. This resistance by an older, established group of 'gatekeeper' women in mixed-sex organisations to younger women's aspirations has been noted in other studies of women in hierarchical organisations of this time, notably party political selection committees and women journalists.[41] Women, of course, could also be collaborative and helpful to each other in less hierarchical, single-sex networks and structures, as we have seen. Although later Wilson described the committee's doubts as 'perspicacious', the rejection was a blow.[42]

Quaker records show that Wilson was nearly selected on a number of occasions throughout the first half of 1915, but for some reason, despite the constant urgent calls for more women relief workers, medically trained or not, her application kept being rejected. Margery Fry wrote in a letter to Ruth Fry in July 1915: 'It seems rather to be thought that F. Wilson has had hopes held out – and as she could get half next term off if she comes, please feel free to send her if you think her useful'; however, once again Ruth Fry obstructed her candidature.[43] Wilson instead gained her first overseas relief experience by unofficial means: first accompanying a Belgian refugee whom she had befriended to visit an interned relative on the island of Urk in the Zuyder Zee ('the seas were rough but I was unafraid'), and from there slipping into Holland to join a Friends' mission in Gouda: 'It pleased me to slip into this illicitly and by-pass the

London office, who had detected so efficiently the poverty of my motives.'⁴⁴ Despite this unauthorised entry into the organisation, her work in Gouda was immediately appreciated. Grace Vulliamy, a coordinator in Holland, wrote to Alice Fry in early September, just before Wilson had to leave to return to teaching: 'We want more workers soon. One is urgently needed ... by the 11th when Miss Wilson goes.'⁴⁵

The following year, having proved herself by unofficial means, Wilson was finally successful in her application to volunteer formally, and in August 1916 she went first to Samöens in France and then to Corsica to join the Serbian Relief Fund, where her brother Maurice was also working. It seems that this posting was also obtained by unofficial means. Maurice had put in a good word to Lady Grogan of the Serbian Relief Fund, asking if Francesca could work with him.⁴⁶ From Corsica she sailed to join Maurice in Bizerta in North Africa in early 1918, 'a desolate place as one approaches from the sea ... you only see the barracks and forts, some modern French houses and the bare hills behind, where nothing grows but stubbly grass, a few gnarled olive trees and the ungracious cactus'.⁴⁷ By 1919 she was sending her first vivid despatches to Quaker publications.

This access by unofficial means, finally resulting in acceptance, can be seen in other groups of women who sought participation when barred by conventional or hegemonic obstacles. A significant example comes from the early days of the Women's International League for Peace and Freedom (WILPF), which met in The Hague in 1915 as a group of international women pacifists and suffragists who wanted to influence a speedy resolution to the First World War. The gathering of some 1,136 women from 12 countries resolved to send women's delegations to both neutral and belligerent governments in an effort to

Alternative channels

bring about mediation. The women were received politely by government representatives in 14 countries, conveying information though informal channels between countries otherwise cut off by the state of war. After the delegations had done their visiting, the WILPF released a communique:

> At a time when foreign offices of the great belligerents have been barred to each other, and the public mind of Europe has been fixed on the war offices for leadership, we have gone from capital to capital and conferred with the civil governments ... As a result of this the plan of starting mediation through the agency of a continuous conference of the neutral nations is today being seriously discussed alike in the Cabinets of the belligerent and neutral countries of Europe and in the press of both.[48]

While it cannot be argued that the women's delegations shortened the war in any way, they had opened alternative channels of communication and asserted the competence of women on the international stage, and the WILPF became closely associated with the establishment of the League of Nations. A member of the WILPF, the Dane Henni Forchhammer, was appointed as the woman member on the Permanent Mandates Commission. The WILPF was also successful in pressing for the establishment of a League of Nations commission to investigate the trafficking of women across Europe in the chaos of the aftermath of war.[49]

Salvation in writing

Francesca Wilson was a careful diarist, minutely chronicling her daily life, and recording, virtually verbatim, long conversations she had with other relief workers, diplomats and refugees. These records, combined with her journalism, provide a richly detailed account of the life of a humanitarian activist during this period. More than this, her memoirs reveal a self-confessed adventurer and 'freakish outsider', a brilliant polyglot, and a lonely woman, despite love affairs and the 'family' she created for herself from several adopted refugee children. She described herself as 'on the whole more loving than loved', and her disarming honesty lays bare the complex and contradictory relationship between the relief worker and the victim of war:

> Outsiders think that one has lived a life of sacrifice, that one has 'done good.' How little they understand! The main force driving me, I think, has been first of all, a desire for adventure and new experiences, and later on a longing for an activity that would take me out of myself, out of the all too bookish world I had lived in.[50]

This self-deprecating analysis sheds light on the complicated two-way relationship she had with her work. After graduating she lacked the money or more formal connections with influential networks to engage in politics beyond the fringe. Reluctantly, she accepted the fate of the educated middle-class woman with neither offers of marriage nor independent means: the life of the girls' school teacher, first at Bedales School and then in Gravesend. After four dull years, the First World War brought Wilson, as it brought many women, the chance to break out of her straitjacket.

Salvation for Wilson came from her writing. From a very young age, she wrote stories to escape from an unhappy external world into a make-believe one.[51] When an adult, in the evenings and on her days off from relief work, she would type out her impressions of the refugees, of the strange or unusual locations she found herself in, on reams of flimsy paper, each

Alternative channels

carefully carbon copied and corrected in her spidery handwriting. Sections of much of this 'private' writing, either letters or diary extracts, would end up either in her newspaper articles, her campaigning pamphlets and publications such as *Portraits and Sketches of Serbia* (1920) or in her memoir, *In the Margins of Chaos* (1944). As such the diaries and letters are a reflection that, even in private, she was writing for wider audience than her own or her family's eyes. From her very first writings on relief in 1919 it is clear that she felt a powerful urge to help comfortable British readers understand refugees not as just helpless hordes, but as suffering fellow human beings. She employed multiple media: newspaper and magazine journalism, educational pamphlets, advice booklets, essays, memoirs and even a film script to convey her ideas.[52] Always interested in the means of communication, she later expanded her writing for the *Manchester Guardian* to include articles, for example, on the radio, noting how disembodied words have a greater effect on the audience than images on the screen: 'It is more vivid than if I saw it at a cinema for sounds have a greater power of incantation than sights ... I like to be free from the tyranny of the visual world.'[53] She responded to the various landscapes she was called to – the deserts of North Africa, the icy wastes of Russia – with poetic delight. In the mountains of Montenegro she would sleep rough among the oak and acacia, just to smell the wild thyme and cistus, pine and myrtle above 'the shimmering plain infinitely far below'.[54] She responded, too, to the teeming cityscapes where she and other Friends lodged. She continued her solitary walks into adulthood, roaming the streets at night and reflecting on the nature of solitude and urban living, and always with an eye to communicating her experience to a wider audience.

The Friend and other Quaker publications

Wilson's vivid writing would provide interesting reportage for readers of the Quaker journal, *The Friend*, and would also help generate funds for the hugely expensive relief operations that the Quaker Friends ran throughout Europe from 1914 onwards. Quaker volunteers were encouraged to report their experiences either in *The Friend* or in other Quaker publications, including the *Friends Quarterly Examiner* and, in the immediate post-war period, the journal *Reconstruction*, which chronicled the work of volunteers in Poland, Austria and Serbia. Wilson's first articles were published in 1919 in the *Quarterly Examiner* and *Reconstruction*, and she began writing for *The Friend* in 1934 with an article about a school in Lichtenstein for the children of displaced pacifist and Jewish refugees from Germany.

During the interwar years, *The Friend*, 'A religious, literary and miscellaneous journal', was a weekly periodical, priced at 3d and printed on imperial octavo-sized paper in 24–28 pages. The first number of *The Friend* was published on 15 February 1843, and it is still published today, making it one of the oldest continuously published periodicals in Britain. Its early editors included members of prominent Quaker families such as Joshua Rowntree (1872–75) and Henry Newman (1892–1912). *The Friend* is not an official Quaker publication and editors are appointed by a body of trustees which, during the interwar years, included Arnold Rowntree and William Cadbury. While it maintained a religious editorial every week, through the early twentieth century it increasingly carried a wide range of articles, letters and book reviews on political subjects of interest to Quakers, including prison reform, temperance, the vegetarian movement, pacifism and women's equality. After the First

Alternative channels

World War *The Friend* campaigned for the release of Quaker conscientious objectors, regularly listing the names of men still incarcerated months after the Armistice.

Hubert Peet (editor 1932–49) was a conscientious objector and had spent most of the First World War in Wormwood Scrubs prison. He was the first professional journalist to take charge of *The Friend*, having previously worked for the *Daily Sketch* and the *Daily News*. Under his editorship, circulation of *The Friend* almost doubled from just over 4,000 in the early 1930s to more than 7,000 in the late 1940s.[55] In his inaugural editorial on 1 January 1932, Peet said he wanted *The Friend* to be more than 'a mirror of the Society of Friends … in the city of life we need the troubadour and the artist as well as the watchman, the prophet and the teacher'.[56] He began a process of interviewing returning relief workers from abroad and encouraged them to write for his journal, an editorial process which resulted in *The Friend* becoming, for the first time, self-supporting as its circulation grew.[57] This growing circulation created problems of its own: more organisations wanted to advertise their products to a predominantly middle-class and educated readership, and trustees' communications with Peet show disapproval of advertisements from financial institutions other than temperance building societies, and for 'quack' medications.[58] Peet introduced a policy of encouraging more younger, and more female, correspondents, a policy that slowly paid off. An analysis of non-religious articles in *The Friend* in 1919 and 1939 shows that female-authored articles rose from just under 10 per cent of all named-author articles in the earlier period to just under a quarter in the later period.[59]

From a secular point of view, *The Friend*'s most interesting articles during the interwar years were written by the network of Quaker volunteers who operated from Russia in the east, helping victims of famine, to Spain in the west, where its Civil War work was highly organised. As such, *The Friend*, along with the *Quarterly Examiner* and *Reconstruction*, charted the rise of humanitarian communication across Europe from 1914 onwards. *The Friend*'s reliance on relief workers' journalism to publicise the results of fundraising and volunteer work presents a rich resource of vivid, eyewitness reporting in areas of conflict where journalists were unable to reach. For example, Tessa Rowntree's account in *The Friend* of the German invasion of Czechoslovakia in March 1939, at a time when few British newspapers kept permanent correspondents in Prague, is a valuable description of this early attack by Hitler.[60] She describes seeing swastika flags flying early in the morning of 15 March as she walked through Prague, and seeing 'the German mechanised army moving along the side of the River to the Wenceslas Platz'. On 23 March she took a party of 71 refugees, including 15 children, by herself in a train across Germany to Flushing.[61]

Other Quaker women, including Ruth and Margery Fry, also contributed during these years both to *The Friend* and to mainstream newspapers, notably the *Manchester Guardian* and *News Chronicle*. Similarly, *The Record* (renamed *The World's Children* in 1923), the journal of the Save the Children Fund, offered women activists working for that organisation a platform to describe aid work in Austria, Germany and Poland.[62] These organs, therefore, helped 'normalise' the idea of women's activism and of women's participation in public life beyond the expected role of child welfare and women's interests.[63] These articles, like Wilson's, also normalised the idea of women writing in newspapers outside the realm of the women's page. For example, Margery Fry's series of articles for the *Manchester*

Alternative channels

Guardian on the treatment of prisoners in the Balkans described the 'mediaeval' conditions and discussed the moral implications of extradition treaties.[64] This tradition of women writing about international affairs from a strictly humanitarian point of view can be traced back to the campaigner Emily Hobhouse's reports on the conditions of Boer women and children in concentration camps during the Boer War in 1901. Hobhouse's reports, originally contained in letters for fundraisers and supporters, were published in the *Manchester Guardian*, provoking a shocked response from readers and politicians. Her intensely subjective documentation of the flies, the baking sun and the drenching rain that found its way into overcrowded tents can be seen as a model for much of the style and content of women's international reportage through the interwar years and beyond.[65] While women were unable to get close to powerful figures, they concentrated on the victims of conflict, the 'odds and ends' of war and the results of great men's politicking, as journalist Louise Bryant wrote of her part in documenting the Russian Revolution.[66]

The monthly magazine *Reconstruction* is a very early example of a relief organisation creating its own journal solely from contributions from field workers. It was edited by a committee of relief coordinators from the Quakers' Mission headquarters in the rue de Rivoli in Paris. Its first issue, published on 1 April 1918, called for contributions from relief workers (ignoring the fact that one-third of relief workers were female):

> The editors welcome suggestions, advice, criticism, letters, notes, stories, articles from every man in every equipe. Their chief joy will be a fat mailbag. They count confidently on the support of Englishmen and Americans alike – in France, Italy, Holland, Russia, Serbia – wherever there are Friends at work.[67]

Rebel women between the wars

Reconstruction contains early reportage by Madeline Linford who would later become a groundbreaking women's page editor of the *Manchester Guardian*. Her articles 'Fighting the Typhus Plague in Poland' (February 1920) and 'Life-Saving in Vienna – a Grateful City' (March 1920) offer first-hand accounts of the civilian suffering in post-war Europe, valuable eyewitness reporting of the struggle for survival:

> In summertime I should think that Zawiercie is a very good-looking place in a rugged, untrimmed way. Today – a day of livid cold – it has a wild sort of beauty … In the last two days I have visited a score of families and in no case had any more than one small room to live in; two or three families are quite commonly found living, eating, and sleeping in a hovel not much bigger than an ordinary English scullery and far less well entilated … It is hard to blame these people for the repulsive state of dirt in which the Friends Mission found them.[68]

Despite the call for 'articles from every *man* in every equipe', a large proportion of the articles in *Reconstruction* were written by women: for example 'Châlons Dreams' and 'The Cave Dwellers' by Edith Pye, 'The Expedition to France' by Dr Hilda Clark, 'The Quilts that Really Warm' by Frances Candy Ferbis and 'With the Serbs in Corsica' by Frances Newberry.[69] The monthly journal was thus not only a record of women's participation in war zone relief work (it regularly published lists of names of workers in the field), but was a public platform on which women were able to express their own responses to the suffering they witnessed.

Francesca Wilson's first article, 'The Return of the Exiles with a Serb Transport to Belgrade', was published in both the *Friends Quarterly Examiner* and *Reconstruction* in July 1919, and described the journey across the Mediterranean from North

Alternative channels

Africa that she made in 1919 with 100 returning Serb soldiers. She evokes the men's fear and excitement at returning home, many of them now suffering debilitating and disfiguring injuries, wondering how wives and sweethearts would greet them. While they were all at sea, their small merchant ship was a world of its own, and even though a storm was raging about them, it was a temporary sanctuary between the hospital in Bizerta and an uncertain future back home:

> It was such a homely ship. The gale might be blowing forty knots an hour, the sea might be flashing with magenta lightning and the boat trembling with the shock of thunder, but still one could always hear the Colonel's dog barking, the ship-mate's pigs grunting ... And the ship was so small, that the gales could never quite bear away the friendly odour of soup and the evening's roast. There was nothing lonely in the storm.[70]

This early piece of journalism, like much of her reportage, concentrates on both the author's and her subjects' emotional response to the extraordinary situation they find themselves in, an emotional response often heightened by the powerful forces of nature around the tiny, desperate humans. She and the exiles are in the same liminal space, between land and sea, exile and home, rocked by external and internal storms. Rather than distancing herself from the refugees, Wilson presents herself as one of their number right from the start (as Hobhouse did in her reports): '*Our* transport left Bizerta on January 31 ... *our* boat was small ...' Her sympathy for their plight is also regret for her own situation: we learn from her memoirs that during the voyage she was suffering heartbreak, having quarrelled irreconcilably with her brother Maurice.[71] On arrival late in Ragusa, and not sure where she could stay, Wilson was offered a sofa and a dinner of 'fried pig and tea' by the mother-in-law of one of the soldiers who had accompanied her on the ship, and who learned, on arriving home, that he had lost everything: 'the Austrians hadn't left a stick and worst of all had carried off his books ... when the exile is no longer young and he comes to find his home looted, his little gods all gone and life to begin over again, he needs a brave heart' – words for Wilson as well as the exile and the reader.

Serbia, Austria and Russia

Humanitarian work was during this time still very piecemeal, and for the volunteers it was a dangerous occupation with little in the way of official support. Although more men than women operated through the Red Cross and the Quaker Friends, women were more numerous in the medical professions, such as the Scottish Women's Hospitals and the Women's Emergency Corps.[72] Of the relief work she was part of in Serbia, Wilson wrote: 'There was nothing like it before except in the great ages of Faith when monks and friars poured over Europe, nursing the sick and feeding the hungry.' She was careful to point out, however, that modern relief workers like herself were not concerned with capturing souls for the pleasure of God, but laboured with more altruistic motives.[73]

Humanitarian work would gradually professionalise and organise with the appointment in 1921 of Fridtjof Nansen as the first High Commissioner for Refugees by the League of Nations, and the allocation of funds for relief work in Europe and Russia.[74] But in 1919 in Serbia, volunteers lived either in unhygienic hospitals or in cottages abandoned after the retreat from the advancing Austrian army, whose occupants had either died in exile or had yet to return. In the spring of 1919 Wilson arrived in the village of Gerdalitza (Grdelica, southern Serbia)

Alternative channels

in the Morava Valley, a remote region of wooded hills topped with medieval citadels and monasteries, and wide, fertile agricultural land. She wrote in her diary: 'It is one of the most beautiful parts of Serbia … The glinting river and these hills and the squares of orchard, peaceful as convent courtyards, the fruit trees holding up their slender branches like tapers waiting to be lit.' Within days of arriving she was reminded of the dangers she faced when she attended the funeral of a colleague who had contracted typhus, spread by fleas and body lice, and which was epidemic in Serbia at the time. It was early spring and the peasants came with armfuls of 'anemones and asphodel, bunches of scylla, violets and grape-hyacinths and twigs of cypress'.[75] Gerdalitza, being by a major railway intersection, became a focal point for travellers: exiled Serbs returning home, 'oxcarts full of wounded Bulgars', Greeks, Macedonians and British soldiers kept on duty to help mend roads and bridges. It was a 'funny, fugitive population,' she recorded in her diary, 'everyone bears the stamp of war … and it is a war without gusto, just weary and sordid'.[76] Wilson lived in a tiny cottage, lit 'by the light of a sputtering candle'. She lived off bully beef and tinned food and handed out bales of donated clothing to the 'shockingly ragged' Serbs. Demoralised by the listlessness of officials and frustrated at her limited role, she seized the initiative herself – a familiar pattern – and commandeered a food cart headed for Nis: bags of rice, macaroni, beans and slabs of salt butter. She improvised a canteen to provide a daily meal for the Bulgarians heading in one direction, the Greeks heading in another and the Serbs heading in yet a third. Within a few days, she was providing food for more than 100 men every day out of an enormous copper pot hung over a fire. At last doing what she considered to be useful work, she wrote that she could 'be happy here, almost' in her diary. Much of her Serbian diary is incorporated into her first book, *Portraits and Sketches of Serbia* (1920), written in order to revivify flagging public interest in Serbia after the Armistice.[77]

From Serbia Wilson was sent on to Vienna where again she helped to organise feeding stations and education for orphans. This was where she continued to formulate ideas on education and particularly on the importance of giving traumatised children access to art and music. She visited an experimental art school run by Professor Franz Cizek, and organised a touring exhibition of the children's work to Great Britain in 1920–22.[78] Wilson wrote the pamphlet for the exhibition wherein she expressed very strongly the philosophy that the children of Vienna should not be seen simply as 'poor, half-starved [creating] constant requests of canned milk and cocoa and clothing' but as 'startlingly different', the art education they had been given helping to rebuild their creativity and sense of purpose.[79] Her writing from Vienna also contains an unpublished article, 'Anti-Semitism in Vienna', written in 1920/21, in which she observed that antisemitism played 'a very important part in [Austrians'] social and political life', noting that in the food riots of December 1920, 'a great many small shops and coffee houses were battered in in the Leopoldstadt (the Jewish quarter)'.[80]

From Vienna Wilson journeyed to Buzuluk on the Samara river in southern Russia, where a combination of economic policies and a failed harvest in 1921 had reduced the peasant population to stewing its own boots and leather harness for food: 'They had ground bones for their bread and mixed it with sawdust, barks of trees and acorns – indeed in our district, which was near the forest, people had survived in greater numbers than on the steppe, because acorns were more nourishing

Alternative channels

than camel grass.'[81] The Buzuluk district was one of extremes, with winter temperatures dropping to minus 40 degrees centigrade, and summers soaring to plus 40 degrees. Spring was a fleeting, days-long event; after the snows thawed and the floods subsided, the meadows briefly bloomed with a million flowers before the intense heat left them bleached and dusty. Little wooden villages were far flung and Wilson spent most of her days travelling in horse-drawn sleighs or heavy-duty vans delivering clothes and food.[82] She drank tea brewed from grated pumpkin rind.

This experience marks the point when Wilson began writing for a wider range of larger-circulation publications, including the *Manchester Guardian* and the *Daily News*. Trekking across the vast, empty spaces and suffering alongside the starving Russians helped create for Wilson an unusual persona for a woman: the solitary traveller, the documenter of great events. Wilson's descriptions of the Russian famine represent an important and rare eyewitness account of this disaster, and it is worth noting that here, too, she engaged in a kind of alternative, unofficial form of activity, this time journalistic. Few journalists were granted access to the most devastated areas, and those journalists who did travel to Samara, such as the American Eleanor Franklin Egan, did so under the auspices of aid organisations – in Egan's case the American Relief Administration.[83]

In Russia the early need for adventure that had first spurred Wilson into volunteering gradually transformed into ideas of humanitarian socialism. As well as distributing food, she visited factories and schools and saw how women were paid the same as men, and how girls were given the same educational opportunities as boys. She started writing for Madeline Linford at the *Manchester Guardian*. She had met Linford in Vienna,

Rebel women between the wars

after the *Manchester Guardian* began sponsoring Friends' relief work in post-war Europe, and had sent Linford to report on projects in Poland and Austria. Wilson's article 'The Women of the New Russia', published in the *Manchester Guardian* in May 1923, examined in great detail the Soviet crèche system, through which 'the women are given free time twice a day to feed their infants' and where the schools, attached to the factories, 'are free, paid for by the factory profits'.[84] She suggests that British women, denied help in arranging childcare unless very wealthy, would benefit from a similar state-organised system to help them take their rightful place in the world of work. She discussed Tolstoy and Dostoyevsky with communist officials, and visited orphan colonies where the children were all encouraged to take up musical instruments and so learned to express themselves through art. She saw in Russia a new egalitarian system being firmly, implacably opposed by outside forces. 'I enjoy the classless side of life here very much', she wrote. 'I loathe and despise the snobbishness of England and our artificial class distinctions, which are quite the worst in the world.'[85]

Once, a lone wolf tracked her horse-drawn sledge for miles across the snow. She was afraid and excited at the same time, and for weeks afterwards its 'cruel, thin face' haunted her, a symbol of the Russia of folklore, 'of ikons, samovars, steppes, bearded peasants' that still seemed so present. Wilson's niece, Dr Elizabeth Horder, was her GP during her later years, even though she was thirty years younger than her aunt.

> When I was a girl, I took my family's part, which was to view my bohemian, different aunt with disapproval. We were all pretty straight-laced and Francesca was a socialist, a feminist, cut her hair short, wore extraordinary clothes, did a lot of protest

Alternative channels

marching and drank a lot. When I was older and free from family opinion, I became rather in awe of her. I loved to listen to her stories and she often told me the wolf story, as if it haunted her. She ignored the dangers she faced. She was tough, fit, whipcord thin and strong. She believed in what she was doing, totally.[86]

English schoolteacher

During the late 1920s and early 1930s Wilson spent several years living in Edgbaston, Birmingham, teaching at the Church of England College for Girls but still engaged in work with refugees, bringing several Russian émigré orphans to live with her in a made-up extended family at her large, Victorian home. One of these was the young Micheal Sokolov, who would later marry Shiela Grant Duff (see Chapter 4). Using her educational contacts, she got 'Misha' into King Edward's Grammar School, despite his not speaking any English. He described her as having 'a remarkable gift for helping and collecting young friends'. Another refugee who Wilson helped was Tomas Bartoli, who escaped to England from the Spanish Civil War and lived with four young Basques in her basement. Of her he wrote: 'She was an extremely loveable person. Her qualities included, in very high degrees, intelligence, goodness, generosity, idealism and the will to serve needy people and defend noble causes.'[87] According to her niece, her 'adopted' family was much more important to her than her real one: 'the refugees and émigrés did not judge her'. After Hitler came to power in 1933 she helped bring out several Jewish academics, including the art historian Niklaus Pevsner, who lived in her house in Duchess Road for a while, and she wrote several articles for *The Friend* and the *Birmingham Post* on the impact of Nazism on German Jews. She was in Gottingen in May 1933 and reported for the *Birmingham Post* on the crowds of men waving swastika flags. Women were absent from the rally: 'Hitler wants to revive the good old Germany, in which women stayed at home, rocking cradles and obeying husbands.'[88]

During the school holidays Wilson visited refugee projects across Europe, especially those educating children in innovative ways. The experimental school in Silum, Lichtenstein, for the children of Jewish and pacifist refugees from Germany would be an inspiration to her when she was in Spain later in the decade. The mountain air of the Alps, she wrote in *The Friend*, 'has in it something of the tonic breath of snow-clad heights, and because of its commanding views it is as exhilarating to the mind as to the body'. The children not only received intellectual guidance: 'besides their ordinary lessons they take their share in all the activities of the place, make hay, chop wood, gather vegetables from the garden, help in the kitchens, watch the cows being milked and the butter being made'. She ended this article, as she did many, with: 'Funds are urgently needed.'[89]

Spain

When the Spanish Civil War broke out, the Friends called on Wilson, with her connections with the *Manchester Guardian* and the *Birmingham Post*, to 'do some useful publicity for their work'.[90] It is a measure of the organisation's continued underestimation of Wilson's skills as a relief worker that she was selected initially as a publicist. Throughout the UK, Aid Spain committees were quickly established to organise fundraising, medical care and food ships to go to the aid of Spanish coastal cities besieged by Falangist forces and cut off from their agricultural hinterlands.

Alternative channels

Women nurses, stretcher-bearers, radio operators and administrators joined the International Brigades to go to the aid of the Republic.[91] The British humanitarian effort during the Spanish Civil War was the first instance of a mass civilian response to atrocities committed against non-British civilians on foreign soil.[92] More than 70 British women volunteered for humanitarian work in Spain.[93] Some, such as the writer Jessica Mitford, were committed socialists going to the aid of the Republic. Other volunteers, many of them nurses, simply could not stand by and do nothing after hearing reports of air raids, terrible injuries, homeless children and mass evacuations. Their letters and reports contain evidence of astonishing self-sacrifice: giving so much of their own blood to the patients they were treating that they nearly fainted, working up to 36-hour shifts while under heavy bombardment, treating dying men in a frontline hospital hewn out of a cave near the Ebro.[94]

In early 1937 Francesca Wilson went first to Barcelona, then on to Valencia and Murcia, and then Madrid, and she took special interest in investigating the Spanish educational system under the Republic.[95] In Barcelona she saw the children of the rich and the children of the poor sitting side by side in beautifully designed modern schools, and a society organised with a perfect combination of 'order and freedom'.[96] She believed in the idea of the 'Spanish Renaissance' that had been kindled after the general election of February 1936. 'Perhaps in Spain people live and die for ideas more than in other countries', she wrote. In her article 'The Women of Madrid: Dancing in Food Queues' for the *Manchester Guardian*, she painted a picture of an indomitable populace who responded to Franco's daily bombardments with songs and dance:

This is the difficulty with Madrid. The people are too brave; they will not go. They turn deaf ears to the Government cry 'Evacuate!' It would be cowardice to leave, they say. They will not desert their husbands – they wish to share the tragedy of their city. So the children play in the streets among the debris – once I saw them dancing – '*en Madrid mucha allegria!*'[97]

This method of combining eyewitness reportage with a deeper message – of the beauty of Spain, of the courage of its people in the face of a brutal enemy – appears in much of Wilson's Spanish reporting, even in apparently straightforward accounts of the progress of relief work. Her article 'Relief Work in Murcia', published in *The Friend* in February 1938, begins drily enough with a description of the process of coordinating aid between Valencia and Murcia with the help of the Spanish Ministry of Justice. Then somehow, without even noticing it, the reader is bowling alongside Wilson, 'through groves of date-palms and Moorish-looking villages' and into the 'busy, untidy town with narrow, winding streets … boiling over with refugees … wild, screaming half-starved women and children'.[98] The article appeared alongside an appeal from the Peace Committee to campaign for an armistice in Spain, a calculated placement by editor Hubert Peet to give the Peace Committee appeal maximum impact.

By the spring of 1938 Wilson was finding a safe haven for the unruly boys of Malaga and Murcia. She was now toughened, experienced, knew the sticks she had to wield, and where to wield them, in order to get things done. With her commanding voice she elicited assistance from anyone and everyone who might help with funds, food deliveries and building work. 'She was very good at roping people in, she was completely charming and persuasive.'[99] Colleagues who worked with her spoke

Alternative channels

warmly of her 'charm and sense of humour'.[100] Quaker volunteer Graham Heath, who first met her in early 1940 working for the Polish Relief Fund in Budapest, said of her: 'In a way she seemed to belong to an earlier age – one of those independent-minded single women of the 19th century, who rode side saddle across Arabia or created hospitals from nothing in remotest Indian states.'[101] Back in London, the Friends Service Council coordinated the delivery of thousands of kilograms of milk powder, sugar and cocoa to be distributed among Quaker projects in Murcia. Quaker records show that Wilson regularly flew backwards and forwards between Spain and London, until Air France stopped its flights to Alicante in the autumn of 1938, delivering messages and requests to the highly organised Friends Service Council.[102]

While putting together her memoir, *In the Margins of Chaos*, during the later years of the Second World War, Wilson looked back on her time in Spain as both her happiest and most useful and productive years as a relief worker. In Spain she was not just 'sweeping up the sands with vaster deserts in front', but building lasting hospitals, farms and refuges for the children in her care.[103] She had also learned that while her work was often frustrating, difficult and dangerous, there were moments of peace and calm to be grasped, even in a war zone. She wrote of the beach camp at Alicante:

> Sometimes the camp was very idyllic and I was happier than I had ever been in Spain. There were days when the children seemed the most adorable beings in the world, with their stormy affection, their wild grace, their warm southern charm. Sometimes Alonso taught me the constellations in the quiet night when the camp was asleep and there was no sound but the waves.[104]

Rebel women between the wars

Wilson finally left Spain in January 1939, just before the Republic was defeated. She watched from the deck as, minutes after the British destroyer she was sailing in left Alicante, an Italian squadron flew over and bombed the harbour. Middle-class British members of the diplomatic corps, also being evacuated, pitied her for having had to live with Spaniards, and she wryly realised that not everyone back home had the same sympathy for their plight as she and her fellow relief workers.[105] Before the end of the year Wilson would be called upon by the Friends to organise help for Polish refugees across Eastern Europe, and at one point she played cat and mouse with the advancing German army, fleeing through Hungary. Her aid work continued through the Second World War and beyond, this time with the United Nations Relief and Rehabilitation Administration (UNRRA).

When one assesses the sum of Wilson's work across Europe, it seems astonishing that she so nearly missed her calling and that her requests to volunteer were rejected multiple times. Her ingenuity and willingness to break the rules, to be a 'disruptor', enabled her to participate after more direct routes had been closed to her. While her relationship with Quakerism had always been troubled and at times contested, it was, in the end, the closest she felt to belonging anywhere. Her obituary in *The Friend* records: 'shortly before her death she asserted vehemently that she was a Quaker – if she was anything'.[106] Another obituary, written by her close friend, the literary scholar E. E. Duncan-Jones, described her boundless humanity: 'It seems high-flown to say that Francesca loved more of her fellow-men to more purpose than anybody else one has been lucky enough to know. I do not think it would be untrue.'[107]

Alternative channels

Notes

1 Wilson 1938a: 755–6.
2 Wilson 1995: 27.
3 Figures for the numbers of boys at Crevillente are provided in the Friends Service Council archives, Friends Library (FL), FSC/R/SP/3.
4 For more on *Spanish Earth*, see Archibald 2012: 31–2.
5 Houssart 2016; as well as reporting for *The Friend*, Wilson also sent reports to the Joint Committee for Spanish Relief (Marx Memorial Library archive (MML)).
6 See, for example, '*Spanish Earth*, the Film by Ernest Hemingway and Joris Ivens', *Manchester Guardian*, 9 November 1937, p. 5; 'Films of the Week', *Manchester Guardian*, 14 November 1937, p. 16; 'The Man who Made *Spanish Earth*', *Manchester Guardian*, 18 November 1937, p. 10.
7 Wilson 1945: 7–8.
8 Wilson 1995: 30.
9 Wilson 1944: 171; interview with Francesca Wilson in *The Birmingham Post*, 19 January 1938.
10 Report from Francesca Wilson to the National Joint Committee for Spanish Relief, 10 June 1937, MML.
11 Wilson 1944: 190–3.
12 Friends Service Council archives, FSC/R/SP/3, FL.
13 Wilson 1938b.
14 Wilson 1995: 1.
15 Wilson 1995: 6.
16 Wilson 1995: 13.
17 Wilson 1995: 19.
18 Wilson 1995: 20.
19 Friends Service Council archives, FSC/R/SP/3, FL.
20 Wilson 1947, 'The Author', back cover blurb.
21 Wilson 1995: 95.
22 Wilson 1995: 95.
23 Cambridge Tripos lists, *The Times*, 21 June 1909, p. 3.
24 'Wanted: 1,000 Friends', *The Friend*, 14 August 1914, p. 593.
25 'Society of Friends War Relief Service', letter, *The Friend*, 21 August 1914, p. 626.

26 Fry 1926: xxviii.
27 *Reconstruction*, 2/1, April 1919, p. 19.
28 Fry 1926: xi.
29 FEWVRC/Missions/1/2/6, T. Edmund Harvey correspondence, FL.
30 Fry 1926: 1.
31 Letter from J. A. Spender, editor of the *Westminster Gazette*, to Ruth Fry, 10 December 1914, Missions/1/2/3, FL.
32 'A Centenary Scrapbook', *The Friend*, 12 February 1943, p. 114.
33 For women's involvement in other international organisations, see, for example, McCarthy 2014; Miller 1994.
34 Currell 1974: 11–12.
35 'Friends Missions in the Field', *Reconstruction*, 1/2, May 1918.
36 Wilson 1944: 2.
37 Letter to Hilda Clark from Edith Pye, 4 May 1915, Missions/1/3/2/1, FL.
38 Tusan 2005: 199.
39 Letter to Hilda Clark from Edith Pye, 4 May 1915, Missions/1/3/2/1, FL.
40 Letter from Hilda Clark to Alice Clark, 17 June 1915, Missions 1/3/2/1; letter from Margery Fry to Ruth Fry, 3 July 1915, Missions 1/3/2/2, FL.
41 For women politicians, see Currell 1974; for journalists, see Lonsdale 2018.
42 Wilson 1944: 3.
43 Missions 1/3/2/1 and 1/3/2/2, FL.
44 Wilson 1944: 5.
45 Letter to Ruth Fry from Grace Vulliamy, 6 September 1915, YM/MfS/Missions/9/3/3/2, FL.
46 Wilson 1995: 88
47 Wilson 1943.
48 Bussey and Tims 1980: 23.
49 Bussey and Tims 1980: 37.
50 Wilson 1995: 114.
51 Wilson 1995: 9.
52 For more on Wilson's work on a 'propaganda' film for the Friends in Vienna, see Roberts 2011.
53 Wilson 1937a.
54 Wilson 1944: 100.

Alternative channels

55 White 1993: 659; *Dictionary of Quaker Biography*, Hubert Peet; archives of *The Friend*, Temp MSS 727, FL.
56 'A Message From the Editor', *The Friend*, 72, 1 January 1932, p. 4.
57 White 1952: 35–6.
58 Archives of *The Friend*, Temp MSS 727, FL.
59 Many articles were still anonymous or had only unidentifiable initials after them. Although there were many more female-authored articles in the later period, many of these were book reviews.
60 Tessa Rowntree, 'From Prague to London', *The Friend*, 31 March 1939.
61 Ibid.
62 For example, Beatrice Harraden, 'Tragedy and Hope: A Visit to a Children's Colony in Poland', *The Record*, December 1922, pp. 83–5, and Henrietta Leslie, 'Footprints of Fate: The Present Distress in Germany', *The World's Children*, January 1924, pp. 64–7.
63 For a detailed analysis of women's public roles during the interwar years, see Breitenbach and Wright 2014.
64 Fry 1938.
65 Emily Hobhouse, 'The Concentration Camps: Miss Hobhouse's Report', *Manchester Guardian*, 19 June 1901, p. 10.
66 Chatterjee 2008: 16.
67 *Reconstruction*, 1/1, April 1918, p. 12.
68 Madeleine Linford, 'Fighting the Typhus Plague in Poland', *Reconstruction*, 2/9, December 1919, p. 168.
69 Edith Pye, 'Chalons Dreams', 1/2, May 1918, p. 22; 'The Cave Dwellers', 1/6, September 1918, pp. 85–6; Dr Hilda Clark, 'The Expedition to France', 1/4, July 1918, pp. 50–2; Frances Candy Ferbis, 'The Quilts that Really Warm', 1/6, September 1918, p. 89; Frances Newberry, 'With the Serbs in Corsica' 1/1, February 1919, pp. 172–4.
70 Wilson 1919.
71 Wilson 1995: 89.
72 For more on the Scottish Women's Hospitals, see Storr 2010.
73 Wilson 1944: 268.
74 See, for example, Marrus 1985.
75 'Extracts from my Diary', March 1919, MSS 1006/2, FL.
76 Ibid.
77 Wilson 1920.
78 MS 1006/3/2, FL.

79 Ibid.
80 Ibid.
81 Wilson 1944: 145.
82 Descriptions of the relief workers' day-to-day life in Buzuluk are in letters to Ruth Fry from William Allbright and Ernest Rowntree, relief coordinators for the Friends in Russia, YM/MfS/Missions/7/3/6/1, FL.
83 Hudson 2016: 195.
84 Wilson 1923.
85 Wilson 1944: 157.
86 Interview with Elizabeth June Horder, December 2016.
87 Both Tomas's and Misha's testimonies are in Wilson 1995: 23, 25.
88 Wilson 1933.
89 Wilson 1934.
90 Wilson 1944: 171.
91 See Jackson 2014.
92 Other European countries, notably France, also mobilised a mass humanitarian response to the Spanish Civil War.
93 The figure of 70–80 British women is in Fyrth 1991: 29.
94 From Leah Manning's reports to the Spanish Medical Aid Committee, August 1938, Archives of the Trades Union Congress, 292/946/42/16.
95 Roberts 2006.
96 Wilson 1944: 172.
97 Wilson 1937b.
98 Wilson 1938.
99 Interview with Elizabeth June Horder, December 2016.
100 Wilson 1995: 30.
101 Wilson 1995: 30.
102 Friends Service Council archives, FSC/R/SP/3, FL.
103 Wilson 1944: 267.
104 Wilson 1944: 11.
105 Wilson 1944: 219.
106 'Obituary', *The Friend*, 27 March 1981, p. 375.
107 E. E. Duncan-Jones, 'Francesca Mary Wilson 1888–1981', Newnham College Roll, Newnham College, Cambridge, 1982, pp. 61–3.

3
Parallel platforms and safe havens

Toiling over the glaring surface, I wondered for the first of many times what enthusiasm made one labour so and what was the recompense? Your face streams, your temples pound, your breath is short, you feel that another step and you will lie down on the snow and quickly expire … This was my first close view of a big ice-fall, and it held me spell-bound and somewhat aghast. The waves of ice near to are not like the water's waves. These towers, split and splitting, and leaning forward one behind the other in close-packed ranks over the valley, were all the more terrifying for their beauty of clear white and palest greens and blues against the sky … I had never seen so many tramp-like figures of all nationalities – ragged, dirty and unshaven – as were lolling about the platform, smoking and gossiping, as we trudged up the wooden steps towards them … The reason for Mr Solly's extra special welcome was at once made plain. He had a big pipe and it was unconquerably blocked. What he most needed in life was a hairpin, and what use was woman on the mountains unless she could instantly provide one?[1]

Dorothy Pilley's account of her first experience of climbing in the Alps in the summer of 1920 defiantly places a woman, in breeches, sweating and panting, in a physically dangerous environment amid the 'unshaven' manly mountaineers of the interwar period. It also, unusually, reveals a woman meditating on the beauty and vastness of 'the wild', attempting to understand the urge to propel oneself to the limits of physical strength in order to participate in it. The passage also expresses this woman's sense of being out of place, an intruder, and only of use to supply a hairpin to help unblock a male mountaineer's pipe. This memoir of early post-First World War climbing, published in 1935, is so much more than a technical log of new routes, equipment used and peaks conquered, of which there were dozens published during this period.[2] Interwar interest in mountaineering was part of a new modernity of the outdoors. At one extreme, developments in air travel and technological breakthroughs led to repeated attempts on Himalayan peaks; and at the other, the growth in wages and working-class leisure time led to the mass trespasses on upland moorlands in the late 1930s. The outdoors, however, was very much understood as being an extension of the 'masculine public sphere' and the vast proportion of mountaineering and rambling was undertaken by men.[3] After 1933 mountaineering took on a further masculine dimension as the German National Socialist 'need for heroes' characterised rival British and German Himalayan attempts as a symbolic battle between the two European super-powers.[4] Combining imperialism, racism, aggression, competition and brute strength, and dramatised and emphasised by a new genre of German 'Berg film', this symbolic war was no place for a woman.

Although there is a long tradition of women writing about 'the wild', much is private or overlooked, and the canon tends to foreground the 'lone, enraptured male', as Kathleen Jamie so memorably put it, from Wordsworth to the present.[5] Dorothy Pilley's *Climbing Days* is a radically feminist text: it chronicles the first 'manless' rope ascent of an Alpine peak at a time when women mountaineers who climbed without male guides or leaders were characterised as 'insane' and 'a disgrace' in the leading mountaineering publication of the age, the *Alpine Journal*.[6] For Pilley, writing and mountaineering represented the twin routes of escape from the repressive expectations of a well-to-do family in the early interwar years. Returning from a weekend of climbing in North Wales to the 'gloves and high-heeled shoes, pavements and taxicabs', having the day before lain 'munching a dry sandwich on a rocky ledge, plucking at a patch of lichen', put so much stress on her that 'with a little more strain one would become a case of divided personality'.[7] Her personal achievements were immense: her first ascent, with her husband I. A. Richards, of the north ridge of the Dent Blanche in 1928 is still seen as one of the greatest 'firsts' in Alpine ascents. Equally important, as the editor of the *Pinnacle Club Journal* she helped provide a platform for dozens of hitherto suppressed female voices to write about mud, crampons, ice axes and eating tinned sardines at the top of a mountain.[8] This chapter examines Pilley's method of parallel engagement, of asserting female voices through establishing a separate feminine public sphere in the arena of mountaineering and writing about the wild.

Early years

Dorothea Eleanor Pilley was born on 16 September 1894, the eldest of four children of John James Pilley and Annie Maria (née Young). The family was comfortably off and lived in a large Georgian villa at the top of Camberwell Grove in south London. Her father owned a baby food factory and, an industrial chemist by training, taught science at Alleyn's School in Dulwich.[9] Her mother, described by a family friend as a 'free thinker', was raised among the Plymouth Brethren, but rebelled against the sect to such an extent that she refused to go to church and succeeded in banning her husband from teaching the children the Lord's Prayer.[10] The four children, two girls (Dorothea and Violet, sometimes called Evelyn) and two boys (John and William), born within six years of each other, were imaginative and creative. A 'Family Theatre Programme' dated January 1910 lists the cast of young Pilleys performing a play written by Dorothy, called *The Idea*. The play's setting, a suffragette's cottage, and cast list of suffragettes, politicians and the royal family shows that even at the age of 15, Pilley was interested in politics and the women's movement.[11] Dorothy, of course, played the Queen.

She attended Wentworth Hall School, Mill Hill, in northwest London, where among other more academic subjects the girls were instructed in dance and gardening. A school report dated summer 1908 describes Dorothy as 'A good child' but is damning of her academic achievements. In English, she 'Has done no written work for class. Spelling evidently a great difficulty'; Scripture is simply 'Weak'. In science, although 'No preparation done for class', the teacher noted that she 'shows interest' in nature study. At 16 Pilley went to Queenwood School in Eastbourne, a boarding school on the edge of the South Downs, where she made friends with Winifred Ellerman, who would later become known as the modernist writer and avant-garde film-maker Bryher.[12] Few girls went on to university from the school, and Ellerman's memoir highlights the cold, the regular prayers and an emphasis on good behaviour rather than achievement.[13] In 1912 Pilley sat the Oxford

Parallel platforms and safe havens

Local Examinations and obtained third class Honours in the Associate in Arts, having been examined in English Language and Literature, Drawing, Hygiene, Music and French.[14] She had dreams of careers in horticulture and then Egyptology, but her father refused her permission to study further.[15] Her brothers went to boarding school from the age of 13, and then to university, an unequal investment she always resented. She was, indeed, the classic 'daughter of educated men' of Virginia Woolf's polemic about female inequality based on lack of educational investment in *Three Guineas*.

After war broke out Dorothy, now 20, applied to become an agricultural worker, but her father refused to sign the necessary papers.[16] As Bryher later recalled: 'We helped our mothers in the morning, we went for walks in the afternoon; whenever possible, whatever wishes flowered in us were destroyed.'[17] Pilley also had problems with her sight which meant she suffered from debilitating headaches after two hours of reading, something that had held her back at school.[18] She settled, unhappily, into a life of helping her mother on shopping trips and assisting in the administration of the British Women's Patriotic League, formed in 1908 'to promote patriotic feeling among women of all classes', and which during the First World War instructed women in home defence, first aid and vegetable growing.[19] After the war its aims became more generally focused on promoting women's interests and training women for public life in the wake of the partial suffrage victory. Pilley trained members of the League in public speaking.[20] She was clearly unfulfilled. A diary entry for 8 January 1921 reads:

> I am practically The League; I can do as I like, I meet interesting people; I do not have to work long hours which gives me time for journalism, rest my eyes and earn enough money to

get away to the hills ... I discover most lives are a compromise. Mine certainly is.

The entry for the next day describes a dreary shopping trip with her mother: 'The immense amount of wandering about; the excessive consumption of time, often with so little results ... I am oppressed with a sense of quickly speeding life – of futility.'[21]

Pilley lived only to get away to the mountains, which she discovered on a family holiday to North Wales in 1914. The moment was a revelation: 'It was like waking up from a half sleep with the senses cleared, the self released. It was as if I had never seen anything before to strike me as beautiful ... I was distraught by the feelings that arose.' A habitual recorder of events, conversations, feelings and sights, she then passed hours 'trying to describe, in a notebook, the flowing water, clear, softly lipping over stones with a chase of fleecy foam-mice running out from under them over amber and cat's-eye depths'.[22] The following January she and Winifred Ellerman went on a two-week walking holiday in North Wales where they first experienced rock climbing with a rope up Tryfan. 'Dorothy went up as if she had been used to precipices all her life', recalled Bryher; her friend had 'found her destiny and was in a state of ecstatic happiness'.[23] Pilley simply noted in her diary that she wished 'such a sensation could continue into infinity'.[24]

Pilley was in London on Armistice Day and hearing the news she ran to Buckingham Palace. Her diary of that day evokes a spirited young woman not at all crushed by convention, writing up her ascent of the 80-foot-high Victoria Memorial as a climber would ascending a peak:

Parallel platforms and safe havens

> I saw in a flash the Victoria Memorial waiting to be climbed: white, untouched, a secret ambition of mine to scale its dizzy heights ... Pitches correspondingly tricky; an arm pull, then followed some ordinary scrambling onto a Cherubim's head, from there a delicate traverse had to be made which I found myself accomplishing with my right hand hold on the angel's neck and the left her harp. By this time I was exhilarated as only climbing can make me ... And there, looking across the grey, misty sky, the wind blew gently and the mob gathered til they were so thickly packed that only the vivid colour of the massed hats filled the valley below.[25]

London journalism

Pilley became secretary of the British Women's Patriotic League in 1917, with an income of £200 a year, and began writing for newspapers as a way of promoting the League during the First World War.[26] Her first article, 'Patriotism', was published in the *Lady's Pictorial* on 21 July 1917, and signed 'Diana E. Penrhyn' – her own initials, but anonymised, the surname inspired by her visits to North Wales.[27] The article describes the League's funding of two equipped rooms for disabled soldiers and a day nursery for the children of women doing war work, and asked readers for contributions to funding refugee relief projects. Pilley's early articles were all either for the *Lady's Pictorial*, *Ladies Field* or *The Queen*, for which she wrote up a long series of League lectures on women's war work in France, Italy, Serbia and other countries (for which she was not paid).[28]

Gradually, non-League articles begin to appear in her red, cloth-bound and neatly ruled, dated and indexed cuttings book: 'Dancing: Tips for the Novice' (*Daily Express*, 9 June 1919), 'Ice Axes in Restaurant' (*Daily Mirror*, 5 December 1919), 'London's Thatched Cottage' (*Daily Mirror*, 28 January 1920). Pilley was a

Figure 4 Dorothy Pilley, c. 1926

resourceful journalist, recycling the contents of articles several times, her stock article on women mountaineers and the equipment they need (hobnail boots and brandy flask indispensable) appearing in four different publications over several years. A short piece on the prominent feminist Lady Rhondda being an expert whistler appeared twice ('Lady Rhondda: Siffleuse', *Daily Mirror* April 1920; 'Whistling Peeress', *Sunday Express*, November 1923).[29] A very small piece in the *Daily Graphic* in 1919 comprises a small head and shoulders photograph of Pilley

Parallel platforms and safe havens

wearing a close-fitting bonnet, accompanied by the words: 'Miss D. E. Pilley, the mountaineer, is the first woman to climb the Devil's Kitchen.'[30] The piece reveals a gift for self-publicity; it also reveals a degree of *chutzpah*: Pilley had only been climbing seriously for two years, and never outside the United Kingdom. Appearing on a page of society gossip, where most images of women were of recently engaged débutantes or titled *grandes dames*, the image of a healthy young woman in rugged jacket and climbing hat was both unusual and subversive.

In 1920 she took a regular job on the *Daily* and *Sunday Express*. While she was not a full member of staff, she was obliged to go to the *Express* office several times a week, particularly on Saturdays, to take on assignments.[31] It is unclear why her father, who had refused to allow her to study horticulture or to take on agricultural work during the war, now permitted her to take a bus down Fleet Street and regularly visit a newspaper office. Few women worked as journalists in newsrooms during the interwar period. It could be that Pilley, now 26, and described by a family friend as 'immensely strong-willed', was able to challenge some of her father's edicts.[32] It could be that the injustice of her position *vis-à-vis* her younger siblings encouraged some relaxation of the rules: her younger sister Evelyn was training to be a doctor and her brothers were now at university. Her father also seemed to be withdrawing into himself at this time and perhaps lacked the energy to resist his spirited eldest daughter's persistent rebellion. One diary entry in May 1921 records that her father 'sat all the evening designing a greenhouse ... mixing as he does with so few people ... is it natural this shutting himself up?' Another entry in January 1921 records that her father spent most of a dreary Sunday 'potter[ing] in the garden and admir[ing] his wine collection'.[33]

Rebel women between the wars

By the early 1920s he certainly seemed to have no power to prevent his as yet unmarried daughter from working in Fleet Street as well as travelling to Wales, Switzerland, France and Spain to pursue her passion for climbing. She enjoyed the busyness of a newspaper office: 'got back to the rush of Fleet Street – to write in that heat – among a noisy, moving mob is the most exciting yet nerve-wracking experience'.[34] Although she did begin to use her position to write about the subjects she cared about most – feminism and mountaineering – journalism was, primarily, a means to earn money for her climbing holidays. Although her father supported her financially, he 'wouldn't supply a penny for any mountaineering'.[35]

From 1920 onwards, Pilley began to show a marked interest in writing feminist articles. On 8 March 1920 her article in the *Daily Express*, 'Is Marriage a Necessity – the Modern Girl's Answer', asks:

> Need one simper, faint, be outwardly demure to be feminine? Must one live in a world of ignorance, petted, spoilt, and have only half the intelligent attention of mankind to be possessed of truly feminine charm? This modern girl may smoke cigarettes, but why is that so much less feminine than sniffing smelling salts?

Other subjects included a celebration of the 100th anniversary of the birth of Florence Nightingale: 'Her part was that of a pioneer, and revolutionary at a time when women were relegated to the background and considered fit only for the drudgery of domesticity' (*Daily Express*, 12 May 1920); the expansion of the numbers of women called to jury service ('Twelve Women Good and True', *Daily Express*, 27 March 1920); and an interview with the first qualified woman metallurgist ('I found her a fluffy haired girl with the most charming smile … in neat

Parallel platforms and safe havens

brown overalls ... We are misled by those hardy forerunners of the women's movement who, in the fight sometimes became dishevelled', *Sunday Express*, 25 December 1921).

Pilley was not happy, however. Her diary reveals a young woman seething with resentment at her position, plagued by headaches and forced to watch her younger siblings achieve academic and professional success: 'Argument with father ... women have the most unpleasant time, not men. Violet and I are agreed on the intolerableness of this attitude ... enough to rouse any spirited woman. *Anyway I've had enough of it.*'[36] When her sister qualified as a doctor in January 1922, she wrote in her diary: 'Violet by the by has passed all three divisions and is now called by courtesy Dr Evelyn Pilley.' She then records having to take to her bed with a violent headache and a recurrence of pleurisy from which she intermittently suffered.[37] A particularly heartfelt article appeared in the *Daily Sketch* on 25 February 1923, 'The Age at Which She Chooses Mr Wrong'. The article warns of the dangerous time when a young woman, approaching 30, having rejected several young men 'any one of whom would have made an excellent husband', rushes into a decision 'that means unhappiness for both'. The article examines why educated young women are wary of getting married, and blames the shortage of men and women's unequal status, which leads boys to be brought up to consider girls as less intelligent and capable than they. She also blames marriage bars and other conventions that insisted that a young woman give up her career on marriage: 'At fifteen [today's young woman] shared the liberal education previously only granted to her brothers. At twenty, her mind, alert with a different quality to a man's, was trained for a career.' Small wonder, then that young women are wary of giving up hard-won freedoms, experience and a salary for a life of domestic drudgery and serving a man who considers her his inferior, she wrote.

With this article, Pilley was participating in a familiar contemporary debate, promoted by the more radical suffragists before the First World War, that of spinsterhood as a deliberate political strategy.[38] While the promotion of deliberate 'marriage refusal' faded after 1918, Pilley's views were still widely held by educated young women. Her article reflects her wide interest in and reading of feminist politics and echoes the argument of Christabel Pankhurst in her book *The Great Scourge and How to End it* (1913), that educated, 'spiritually developed' women were condemning themselves to slavery through marriage.[39] Pilley, strikingly beautiful, had been plagued with suitors from about 1918 onwards, and her diary during these years is sprinkled with queasy accounts of awkward interviews and proposals and having to work hard to avoid the topic of 'sex' when alone with a man. In 1925 she wrote a 60-page letter of refusal to her eventual husband, the philosopher and literary critic I. A. Richards. Her closely argued reasons for refusing even 'I. A. R.', to whom she was devoted, were those she had put forward in the *Daily Sketch* article: marriage would mean voluntary subjugation, 'lots of housework and twenty children'. The prospect of this makes her 'go cold and stiff with disdain'. Instead of marrying, she would devote herself to campaigning, through her journalism and organisational skills, for women's equality in Canada.[40] The letter bears striking similarities to the character of Muriel in Winifred Holtby's 1924 novel *The Crowded Street* and shows that this attitude permeated beyond the university-educated members of Holtby's network to a much wider group of young women:

Parallel platforms and safe havens

> I think I've always had in my head somewhere [an] idea of service – not just vague and sentimental, but translated into quite practical things. Maybe I'll do nothing with it, but I do know this, that if I married you I'd have to give up every new thing that has made me a person.[41]

Interwar 'outdoor' periodical print culture, 'insane' lady mountaineers and manly virtue

Life was made bearable by weekend and holiday dashes to Wales, the Lake District, and eventually the Alps and beyond, taking with her a rucksack packed with breeches, rope, ice axe and crampons. While traditional Victorian 'antagonism towards the sporting female' was fading, the 'acceptable' sports for women were tennis, golf, badminton, cycling, ice-skating and swimming, with hockey being the only team sport seen as acceptable for women after the Football Association banned women from playing on its grounds in 1921.[42] Modern studies of women mountaineers suggest that even today the 'rugged' pursuits of rock climbing, mountaineering and wild bivouacking challenge traditional notions of gender, with women mountaineers often working in traditionally masculine fields such as engineering or IT.[43] This gender disruption can be traced back to early mountaineers. In her memoir, the celebrated American climber Miriam O'Brien Underhill, a contemporary of Pilley's, recounts her mother's letter to her grandmother in response to suggestions for a birthday present when she was young: 'One thing's for sure – she doesn't want dolls for her birthday ... buy her a greased pole or a tree to climb or something of that order.'[44]

For a woman in the early twentieth century, mountaineering also required a degree of transvestitism which attracted both opprobrium and hilarity and further blurred gender distinctions. Women walked to the foot of a climb in skirts; these were removed and left in rucksacks or under rocks and the climb itself was carried out in breeches or knickerbockers. The early twentieth-century novelist E. H. Young was a keen mountaineer and wrote of the procedures she and her sister were obliged to undergo when out climbing in Wales:

> a woman in knickerbockers was an object of derision or shame ... the skirt was decently worn for as long as possible, then hidden under a rock or carried in a neat bundle, as circumstances decreed ... just before the [First World] war, people on the road near Ogwen, would walk backwards for quite a long way, in astonishment and mirth at the sight of my sister and me in our corduroy breeches.[45]

Climbing brought rebellious and exhilarating reward, the shedding of the restrictive skirt symbolising the shedding of the rules and regulations governing female behaviour. Women climbers of this period recorded the pleasure and freedom climbing gave them. Both extracts below speak of a kind of magic in bodily liberation and weightlessness. Freya Stark, Pilley's near-contemporary, discovered rock climbing and mountaineering at about the same time as Pilley. In her memoir, *Traveller's Prelude*, she recalls her first climb, in the Val d'Aosta, just before the First World War:

> The happiness was almost frightening ... the feeling was there, the extraordinary sensation of safety, the abyss held in check, the valley with its life of everyday, bridges, tracks, fields and houses, seen from a narrow ledge which made it exciting and remote; this sense of *double life* is, I think, one of the main ingredients of the mountain *sorcery*.[46]

Parallel platforms and safe havens

Another contemporary, the Scottish climber and writer Nan Shepherd, described climbing as 'that joyous release of body ... This bodily lightness, then, in the rarefied air, combines with the liberation of space to give mountain *feyness* ... a malady of which the afflicted will never ask to be cured.'[47]

While there was a rapid growth in outdoor leisure pursuits during the interwar years, culminating in the 1930s 'hiking craze' and the ramblers' mass trespasses, hiking, climbing and mountaineering were predominantly masculine activities.[48] Scholars have contended that the 'social outdoors' is coded as masculine (complicated by the fact that nature, with her abundance, rolling hills and deep valleys, is coded as feminine), and in the early years of the twentieth century was seen as an extension of the masculine public sphere.[49] While young women, in the brief years between leaving school and marrying, did enjoy increased leisure time, and those from the middle and lower middle classes certainly participated in walking and cycling, rambling club structures such as committees and journal editors and contributors were male-dominated.[50] The front covers of the Sheffield Clarion Ramblers handbooks from the 1920s, for example, feature a lone male on top of a cliff, mountain or cairn, glorying in his strength and self-reliance. Although women were invited on some rambles, they were excluded from longer excursions, called Revellers' Rambles. An announcement for one of these in January 1929 reads:

> We go wet or fine, snow or blow, and none but the bravest and fittest must attempt this walk. Those who are unwell, unfit, inexperienced or insufficiently clad should consult their convenience or that of their friends, by staying at home. Ladies on this occasion are requested not to attend. The ramble is not estimated by mileage, but by the amount of stamina you possess.[51]

Rebel women between the wars

The other major northern rambling group, the Manchester Ramblers Federation, was similarly male-dominated. In his study of the Federation's annual handbook during the 1920s and 1930s, Ben Anderson found only one female-authored article in sixteen years of publications and only one female committee member, the club secretary.[52]

The growth in leisure and outdoor activities from the turn of the twentieth century onwards had produced a richly diverse 'outdoor' periodical and print culture. The quasi-scholarly *Alpine Journal* and the *Climbers' Club Journal* had been founded in 1863 and 1897 respectively; others, such as the *Journal of the Fell and Rock Climbing Club* and the *Rucksack Journal*, began in the Edwardian era. These older journals were joined in the postwar period by publications ranging from the eight-page *Country Standard* 'For Peace and Socialism in the Countryside' (price 1d), an agricultural paper aimed at farm labourers and staffed by Left Book Club members, to the *Deeside Field* (3s 6d), a beautifully produced magazine on heavy paper, usually 80–90 pages long, 'issued under the auspices of the Deeside Field Club' and privileging artistic and literary responses to the landscape, particularly the Cairngorms.[53] So numerous were outdoor journals and magazines that in 1920 the leading climber and climbing writer Geoffrey Winthrop-Young predicted a crisis in the genre. The crisis, he argued would be caused by there being not enough contributors to fill the sheer quantity of journals, and the 'immense increase in the cost of production' of so many journals competing for the attention of a small and overlapping readership.[54] The periodicals all provided opportunities for climbers, walkers, geologists, poets and amateur naturalists to voice, in words and images, their experiences in the outdoors, from basic route-finding and climbing technique, to chronicling triumphant ascents, to more personal evocations of the beauty of the mountains and their flora and fauna.

Over all these publications towered the *Alpine Journal*, the twice-yearly 300-page publication of the Alpine Club, in a sober dark green cover, priced 10 shillings and 6 pence, which recorded new ascents and published lengthy essays on mountaineering history.[55] It had a regular 'Alpine Accidents' section which often ran to several pages. The Alpine Club had always been both a mountaineering and literary society: in the tradition of the Victorian gentlemen's club a candidate for membership, as well as being male, needed to submit 'a list of his literary contributions' as well as successful ascents to the committee.[56] The journal had grown out of the Alpine Club's tradition of having members read out a summary of their adventures and excursions at twice-yearly meetings. Embedded in English nineteenth-century imperialist and colonial tradition, the journal developed an aggressive and militaristic written style in which peaks were 'laid siege' to and 'defeated', virgin territory was 'attacked' and 'conquered' in 'great campaigns' and, it seemed, Englishmen were the first to go or discover everywhere: 'Englishmen had the field more or less to themselves ... Cecil Slingsby did single-handed for Norway what Packe and Count Henry Russell had done for the Pyrenees.'[57] The journal referred to the Alps as the club's 'playground', denoting domination, pleasure and ownership.[58]

Women's voices were initially absent from the journal, as might be expected; gradually, as editors canvassed for contributions beyond the membership, articles by women began to appear in the interwar period.[59] Dorothy Pilley's name first appeared in the November 1921 issue, in a short note in the 'New Expeditions' section of her ascent, with I. A. Richards, of the Pointe Sud des Bouquetins (4,000 metres).[60] One of her first articles on the Alps appeared in the May 1923 issue, detailing her summer 1922 ascent of the Jungfrau, as well as other climbs she accomplished, along with her friend Dorothy Thompson and Richards, without a guide. Pilley led one climb up the Rothorn, something that caused 'surprise' and 'amusement' among other climbers on the mountain that day.[61] Her written style in the article is noticeably different from either the matter-of-fact technical articles on the use of ice axes or the relative strengths of different ropes, or the triumphalist genre of attack and victory. There is a lyrical, philosophical quality to her writing, and always nature is respected, admired and trod upon only with her consent:

> To go up by a route unknown to the party, to come down over slopes never seen before into valleys where the rocks, the trees, the houses, the very flowers are different, seems to us the way to wring the best joys from mountaineering … The Trift glacier itself, as the crystal clearness of the sunrise crept down upon it was a thing *almost too exquisite to walk upon.*[62]

Other women climbers, including Dorothy's friend Lilian Bray, and Miriam O'Brien, another pioneer of 'manless climbing', also contributed articles to the journal during the interwar years.[63] It appears the then editor of the *Alpine Journal*, E. L. Strutt, actively sought permission to reproduce two of O'Brien's articles on the Bernese Oberland in 1931 and 1932, which had first been published in the *American Alpine Journal*.[64]

Women's contributions were not without challenge. When Sheila Macdonald's account of her ascent of Mount Kilimanjaro (the first female ascent to the summit) was published in the *Alpine Journal*, there followed several pages of claim and counter-claim, by men challenging, and then defending, her assertion that 'no woman has ever succeeded in getting there before'.[65] A short article, 'Lady Mountaineers', on Miriam O'Brien's first traverse of the famously difficult Aiguille de Grepon 'without guides' in the May 1929 issue is footnoted by the editor with a smirking reference to Victorian mountaineer A. L. Mummery's 'worn-out jibe' that all peaks were doomed, eventually, to go from 'inaccessible' to 'an easy day for a lady'.[66] This news item was followed by an anonymous article, 'Foolish Mountaineering', describing reports of women climbers attempting the Vajolet Towers, a series of difficult peaks in the Dolomites, as an 'insane performance' and a 'disgrace'.[67] This undermining and challenging of the truthfulness of women's accounts of their travels has been noted elsewhere.[68] Criticism of 'Lady Mountaineers' did not prevent O'Brien, who was rapidly becoming a climbing superstar, from stating her preference for 'manless' climbing in subsequent articles. Her long description of climbing in the Mont Blanc massif in the November 1931 edition begins: 'Sometimes with guides, sometimes guideless and sometimes – best of all – manless.'[69]

The *Alpine Journal*'s attitude to women climbers contrasts with the praise of the 'manly virtue' and 'heroic effort' of male mountaineers when they undertook climbs sometimes so dangerous as to be fatal. The November 1924 issue of the journal, for example, was dedicated to celebrating the life, and death, of George Mallory and Andrew Irvine, Britain's 'glorious sons' who had died in an attempt on Mount Everest in the summer of 1924. Rather than being described as 'foolish' or 'insane', the men are 'brave, high-minded and energetic', their deaths a 'tragic mystery'.[70]

Initially Pilley had strongly negative views of the Alpine Club. A diary entry in the summer of 1921, just her second

Alpine season, reports seeing, in a hotel lobby in Zermatt, 'A.C. dotards with green ties who sit at a table and talk to no one. What a fatuous set of mandarins.' The entry suggests that although still an Alpine novice, she saw the 'A.C.' as an ancient guardian of an elitist and outdated system that she and other women were fighting against. Her attitude would soften, however, and on her death she left two beautifully wrought, short, slender ice axes to the club, one engraved 'D. E. P. 1919' and the other 'D. Richards 1933'.[71]

Despite the antagonism and sometimes deliberate exclusion, the interwar outdoor periodical press did provide an important platform for women who wanted to write about both the sporting opportunities and the aesthetic beauty of the outdoors. During the period of 'high imperialism' (1850–1930), women's travel writing, as well as having different perspectives and interests than men's, was often private, contained in diaries and letters, rather than published in books and periodicals.[72] Encouraged by women's greater visibility in public life during the First World War, women in increasing numbers presented their responses to exotic and unusual environments on more public platforms. Sheila Macdonald's account, for example, of her ascent of Kilimanjaro (initially recorded in a letter sent to her parents, which they then presented for publication) contains, as well as the technicalities of the climb, masses of detail on the flora, fauna and geology of the region:

> Above the cloud belt into the sun again through a district of sweet-smelling shrubs, protea, giant heather and gladioli ... We saw plenty of eland standing as high as cattle ... The inside of the crater is amazing. Imagine a huge bowl of ice with hanging glaciers all round its inside walls and two great lakes of greeny-blue ice at the bottom, huge crevasses and *séracs* around its rim.[73]

Parallel platforms and safe havens

Perhaps the most startlingly original example of women's nature writing in interwar periodicals is Nan Shepherd's essay 'The Colours of Deeside', published in the 1938 issue of the *Deeside Field*. The lengthy essay is more like a prose poem and takes the reader through every colour and every element:

> Blue. For the most part our blues are cool – slate-blue, steel-blue, ink-blue, ice-blue, milk-blue. The hot mauves of rainy land in the west are absent. Here, rain in the offing, the land grows navy-blue. Corries take on the depth of gentian, shadowed with hyacinth and violet. But the most characteristic blue of Deeside space and distance is one that I find hard to name. It is azure thinned out till all its vivid intensity is gone, but not the purity of its colour: beaten to a transparency of itself, but still itself … Grasses, both stalk and flower have heat. Their ripeness is a pinky russet …[74]

Dorothy Pilley published a prose poem in the 1920 issue of the *Journal of the Fell and Rock Climbing Club*, 'Rain in the Mountains'. The piece expresses the frustration of the office girl, watching the rain fall in the city, turning the dust to mud and ruining shoes and feathers and flowers in hats, and imagining what that same rain is like in the mountains. She contrasts the originally natural articles, the suede of the shoes, the flowers and feathers, wrenched from their natural environments and rendered artificial in items of fashion, with the sodden moss, bracken and rocks of the hills:

> Rain falls in the mountains. The wind comes with the rain. Both rush up the valleys, whirl across the fell side, circle in a mad vortex, and mount triumphant to the summit ridges. Imperishable is the joy of this rain. To surprise it, in solitude over the great spaces of the mountains, is to grasp immortality.[75]

The Fell and Rock Climbing Club ('Fell and Rock'), founded in 1906, was mixed-sex, but the committee and the contributors to the journal were predominantly male. Pilley made an immediate impression when she joined in the autumn of 1919, making a 'neat little' speech to the 107 assembled members at the annual dinner and committee meeting.[76] By the time the 1921 issue of the journal was published, she was listed as one of the three female committee members (out of 23) and was honorary secretary and treasurer of the London section, writing up accounts of dinners and walks held by Fell and Rock members 'who had the misfortune to live in the South'.[77]

In the same issue another article, 'The Pinnacle Club', written by Mrs Pat Kelly, laid out the formation of an important new women-only climbing club. The article explained that while women climbers had always appreciated the kindness of men prepared to take a woman on an expedition, it really was time that women now forged their own way:

> As in other walks of life, women wanted to find their own feet; it was very splendid for some women always to be able to borrow crutches in the shape of a man's help, and a man's rope, but it is even better to find we have feet of our own.[78]

Parallel platforms, safe havens: interwar women's leadership, the Pinnacle Club and journal

The inaugural meeting of the Pinnacle Club was held at the Pen-y-Gwryd hotel in Snowdonia on 28 March 1921, immediately attracting 41 members, a figure that would rise to 80 by 1935.[79] An article in the *Manchester Guardian*, published shortly after the meeting, recognised the importance of the club, and expressed the hope that it would shortly produce a journal that would enable women climbers, and people in general, to 'assess the proper place of women's climbing, *as a distinct thing*'.[80] As has

Parallel platforms and safe havens

been noted, while women did contribute to existing outdoors and travel media, their contributions were minority items in a predominantly masculine and often disapproving sphere. To compete equally for space and voice when many of the most important clubs were either men-only or male-dominated, and with all the leading journal editors male, would have been a long and difficult struggle. A women-only club, with its own public platform in the tradition of suffrage newspapers, would enable women's voices to be heard clearly, undiluted and without snide comments from male editors, in effect bypassing masculine power structures.[81] The club and journal would help normalise climbing as something that all women could do, not just a few extraordinary women, often characterised as deviant or insane in the traditional climbing press.

Organising separately during this crucial transitional time as women negotiated various routes out of the domestic sphere has been seen to have worked for other groups of women, helping develop confidence and ensuring that, in the absence of men, women would assume positions of leadership.[82] This method of beginning activism and organising within a homogeneous group to either challenge or thrive parallel to entrenched power has been observed in other contexts, and has been described as a 'safe havens' strategy, particularly in cases where ethnic minorities or diaspora populations attempt to assert their will to political participation within an established political structure.[83] Segregation and separatism were arguments put forward by anti-suffrage campaigners before 1918: if women wanted to participate in public life, they should form clubs and parliaments of their own, it was argued.[84] Feminists after 1918 and particularly after 1928 were, however, divided as to whether separate organisations, which had certainly helped women learn leadership and debating skills during the pre-suffrage years, should continue after the vote was won, or whether this would now put them at a disadvantage. In a newspaper debate in 1932, Nancy Astor argued that 'separate women's organisations must go on existing in order to hasten the time when separate women's organisations need not exist'.[85] Margaret Wintringham, former MP for Louth, argued the opposite: remaining in separate organisations would undermine women's claims to be equal citizens. 'Woman serves in Parliament not as a woman but as a capable public servant. Woman possesses the parliamentary vote not because she is a woman but because she is a citizen, having interests equal to those of men in the welfare of the state.'[86] Pilley's friend and fellow climber Lilian Bray expressed this unease over segregation in a letter in the early years of the Pinnacle Club: 'I think sex distinction in climbing ought to be given up ... What we want is to have some standing as Alpine climbers.'[87] The Pinnacle Club founders were not, however, wholly separatist in their intentions. Both Pat Kelly and Dorothy Pilley emphasised that the Pinnacle Club did not want to antagonise men's climbing, but rather to give women the chance to feel what it was like to be a leader in a specific activity, which could then be translated to other walks of life, through the increased confidence it gave them.[88]

Training women for leadership, and for more generally taking their place in public life in the immediate post-suffrage years, was a focus for women keen not to lose momentum following the attainment of the vote.[89] Studies have shown that women were more likely to emerge as leaders during the early years of the twentieth century if they had come up through women-only or women-dominated organisations, such as women's unions, suffrage societies or the nursing and

Parallel platforms and safe havens

teaching profession.[90] Clubs such as the Women's Citizens Associations in Britain, and women's dressmaker unions in Australia, encouraged activities such as debating, voice training, singing and excursions to develop expertise and confidence.[91] Women's potential to play a greater role in public life was a subject that Pilley wrote about regularly in the press and about which she felt keenly, given her role as voice trainer for women hoping to make public speeches.[92] Her diary entries recording the voice-training sessions refer to her pupils' lack of self-confidence but also their desire to overcome this obstacle ('a room of nervous women bent on making speeches which they are sure are awful').[93] Pilley, a founding member of the Pinnacle Club, describes the essence of the club's ethos in *Climbing Days*, emphasising this transferable skill, as we would call it today. The club was formed with 'a rooted sense that training in the fullest *responsibilities of leadership in all its aspects* is one of the most valuable things that climbing has to offer, and that women could hardly get such training unless they climbed by themselves'.[94]

There was, of course, the Ladies' Alpine Club, established as a 'child' of the Alpine Club, with Mrs Aubrey Le Blond as president, in December 1907. The club produced its own annual report of women's climbing activities, but this was little more than a list of peaks ascended with no narrative contributions. Papers in the Alpine Club archives show that Pilley tried to persuade the Ladies' Alpine Club that it should produce a proper journal. Her requests were met with regular refusals from the club officers, citing lack of need, until in June 1923 she forced a members' vote on this issue. Of the 17 members who voted, six were in favour of a regular journal, two were 'maybe' and nine voted 'no'. A letter to Pilley from Lilian Bray, urging her to contribute to a nascent Pinnacle Club journal, complained that the Ladies' Alpine Club could never provide an appropriate platform as it only existed as subordinate to the men's club:

> I am not keen on the Ladies Alpine at present, I don't think it can ever be made a success after all this time, we could never so alter it, there would always be perpetual and very powerful opposition from the old members, and unless it was very completely changed it will never have any real standing in the climbing world.[95]

This characteristic, of a female club often controlled by an older generation of women and having internalised the patriarchal structures of the dominant 'brother' men's club, has been noted in other interwar networks. Women's clubs formed as offshoots or adjuncts in this way tended to be conservative and possessed an uncritical, 'don't rock the boat' mentality.[96] The disappointing vote and Bray's letter appear to have been the catalysts for Pilley to turn her attention to a Pinnacle Club publication. The novelist E. H. Young had initially been tasked with the editorship, but she wasn't enthusiastic and for three years no journal appeared.[97] With Pilley's energy, the first issue, co-edited with Lilian Bray, appeared within months.

Its front cover was a bold and deliberate contrast to that of the Ladies' Alpine Club annual report. On the latter, a lone female in breeches and hobnail boots stands, leaning on an ice axe, in a triumphant pose mimicking that common image of men's journals, atop a rugged peak. On the cover of the *Pinnacle Club Journal*, by contrast, a lone woman, rope around her shoulders, sits, pausing for breath by a mountain tarn, further and higher peaks to climb surrounding her. It is a meditative pose and she seems overwhelmed by how far she still has to go. The rope, of course, is a subversive image. She is alone and thus

Parallel platforms and safe havens

Figure 5 Ladies' Alpine Club annual report cover

intends to climb 'manless'.[98] That first issue contained a tribute to founding president Pat Kelly, who had died in an accident on Tryfan in 1922, and E. H. Young's previously quoted reminiscences of climbing before the First World War. It also carried articles by several other women including Pilley's friend Dorothy Thompson ('On Snowdon Summit in a Gale') and Eleanor Winthrop-Young ('Rain and Storm in Norway'), and, by Pilley herself, an extraordinary account of a journey across

CONTENTS.

		Page
Club Proceedings	*The President*	1
As it was in the Beginning	*B. Eden Smith*	3
Heat and Cold on the Cuillin Ridge	*Lilian Bray*	7
The Crowberry Ridge by Abraham's Direct Route	*Ella Mann*	16
A Bird's Eye View of Scottish Climbing	*Mabel I. Jeffrey*	20
L'Année de Misère, 1928	*E. Wells*	28
Ten Days at La Grave	*Dorothy E. Thompson*	36
On Trying to Climb in Iceland	*E. M. Hall*	47
Hills versus Mountain Peaks	*Sylva Norman*	58
Reviews		63
Climbing Notes		68

Copies may be obtained from Mrs. H. Summersgill, 61 Moorside Road, Heaton Moor, Stockport.

Published by the Pinnacle Club. Price 3/6

Figure 6 *Pinnacle Club Journal* cover

Parallel platforms and safe havens

the Pyrenees from Spain into France in a raging blizzard. The article, 'Into Spain and Back Again', is partially reproduced in a chapter of *Climbing Days* and was her first major attempt to capture the fierce beauty of the mountains and their elements, and to examine the human urge to explore that characterises so much of the longer book. It is interesting to note that even though Richards had also climbed with them on the expedition of March 1923, in the account published in the *Journal* the '*deux jeunes demoiselles*' are the only protagonists, along with their ancient Pyrenean guide, Bernard Salles, 'infinitely old and worn out … his hands gnarled and corded with great veins', part of the mountain itself. There is, then, a deliberate attempt to avoid the over-used trope of the 'bold adventuring hero' of male travel texts.[99] The three participants form an ever-changing trio, sometimes one ahead, sometimes another, taking turns when the leader becomes exhausted, cooperating not competing. The article has fabular elements, placing two young women, fit, healthy and brave, in a perilous situation, toiling over an almost mythically threatening landscape; when they are at the limit of their endurance the travellers come upon a miraculously placed hut, where they rest around a blazing fire. The wordless, ancient guide, the mountain's spirit, acts as a magic charm, leading the heroines through the storm:

> Two-thousand-foot-high cataracts of snow dust. There was little to see now as we took the upward way to the Boucharon except coloured rocks rising in to a yellow opaqueness out of which snow flakes steadily silted downwards, the darkness of the roaring gulfs below and the laden, uneasy forest trees … Every few moments the blast which roared endlessly overhead would drop upon us, and the slope would dissolve into a race of white, writhing smoke that seemed to eat one's skin …[100]

Rebel women between the wars

Contributions to the *Pinnacle Club Journal* between the wars challenge assumptions that during this period women's writing about travel and the outdoors was either of poor quality or not concerned with more philosophical ideas on the nature of exploration and travel.[101] While not all the writing could be described as 'literary' in quality, certainly Dorothy Pilley's intentions in the Pyrenees article, and in others, go far beyond the matter-of-fact travelogue and leave the domestic far behind. The sheer range of contributions and subject matter, from easy walks in the hills to serious climbing, also served to encourage readers not to consider mountaineering as only the preserve of extraordinarily talented or unusual women. Pilley would continue to edit the *Pinnacle Club Journal* for twenty years. The circumstances of the journal's genesis and editorship show that although it was first and foremost a climbing magazine, Pilley and Bray saw it as part of a larger enterprise in post-suffrage print culture to help women achieve and make something of their lives.

Leaping crevasses in the dark

In 1925, Pilley left England for an extended trip to North America. Family friend Richard Luckett describes this journey as 'an attempt to leave both her family and [I. A. Richards] behind'.[102] A letter to Richards suggests that she wanted this emigration to be permanent, and that she would be supporting herself initially by journalism.[103] When she arrived in the United States in the early autumn of 1925, she was treated like a celebrity by the local newspaper, the *Nelson Daily News*: 'English Girl of Alpine Fame is in Nelson; climbs peaks and edits the Pinnacle Club Journal.'[104] Her cuttings books contain

Parallel platforms and safe havens

articles published in various American and Canadian newspapers, including the *Daily Colonist* (British Columbia), the *Sunday Province* (Vancouver) and the *Bellingham Herald*. Several articles show her genius for recycling content, with her stock 'mountaineering for women' article appearing again, as well as her 'Rain in the Mountains' piece. After her rejection of Richards's proposal, he travelled to North America to persuade her otherwise, and together at the end of August 1926 they scaled Mount Baker (10,781 feet) from the north-east side, Pilley becoming the first woman to do so.[105] This joint achievement convinced Pilley that 'I. A. R.' would not try to dominate her or hold her back, and they married in Honolulu in December 1926. Despite her fears, she found in Richards a meeting of minds: 'You were the first original thinker I had met and in your conversation I discovered even as barely more than a schoolgirl the "something more in life" which I had ever so vaguely suspected – a country of the mind.'[106] Richard Luckett described the marriage as an 'exceptionally happy one'.[107] In July 1928 they made the first ascent of the north ridge of the Dent Blanche in the Alps, described as 'still one of the great mountaineering achievements of the century', which brought the 'lady mountaineer' fame across Europe.[108]

Pilley was first approached by Alan Harris of publishers George Bell and Sons on 11 December 1928 regarding the possibility of her writing a book on mountaineering. The letter suggests that while the publishers wanted to make the most out of Pilley's being a woman ('there is still something striking and original in such a book being written by a woman at all'), they wondered if it might be a joint project between Pilley and Richards.[109] Richards, by now a respected critic and philosopher, was already in discussions with the publishers about a possible volume on criticism, and it is not clear whether they felt that this was a project that Pilley could not pull off by herself, or whether, for commercial reasons, it would be helpful if Richards was involved as co-author. Harris wrote again in March 1929: 'It is of course an important fact that you are a woman climber but I don't think too much attention should be drawn to the woman business in the book.' He once again asked ('we should awfully like it') if Richards could share authorship.[110] Pilley sent Harris a synopsis on 19 May 1929, together with her 'Into Spain and Back Again' article that would eventually form part of chapter 10 of the book. She commented, 'I haven't been able to persuade my husband to join me yet', adding that she hoped to have a manuscript finished by the autumn of 1930. However, the book took another five years to write. By then they had moved to China, Richards having taken a chair at Peking (Beijing) University, and travels and illness contributed to the delay. When it was finally published, only the name 'Dorothy Pilley', devoid even of the suffix 'Richards' that she sometimes now used, appeared on the cover.

On publication *Climbing Days* received highly favourable reviews in the *Manchester Guardian*, *Times Literary Supplement*, *Liverpool Post* and *Time and Tide*, and the *Observer* put it on its recommended summer reading list for that year.[111] The review in the *Journal of the Fell and Rock Club* described Pilley's narrative as 'intensely alive and the sense of adventure always present, sometimes so poignantly ... that one holds one's breath as one reads.'[112] In the end, there was a fair amount of 'the woman business' in it and it is now seen as something of a classic in mountaineering circles. It is interesting to note that Pilley, who saw herself as having to fight for every scrap of freedom and

Parallel platforms and safe havens

agency she had in her life, also appears to have had to fight to assert sole authorship of her book.

Subsequent uncollected accounts of her climbs throughout China, Japan and Canada are equally compelling, and space only allows for brief fragments of these in the Appendix. In 1959 she broke her hip in a car accident, which finally put an end to serious climbing at the age of 65. While she was in hospital Richards wrote a poem for her, 'Hope', and although it seems against the spirit of this volume to end this chapter with someone else's voice, this poem, recalling a night that they accidentally spent on a treacherously crevassed glacier before they married, sums up the indomitable spirit that radiated from her, but crucially, also, shows how her words could inspire others: 'Recall the Epicoun: / Night welling up so soon, / Near sank us in soft snow ... / "Leaping crevasses in the dark, / That's how to live!", you said / No room in that to hedge. / A razor's edge of a remark.'

Notes

1 Pilley 1965: 108–9, 112.
2 The twice-yearly *Alpine Journal*, the leading publication discussing British and international mountaineering, reviewed around twenty new volumes on climbing and mountains in each issue during the 1920s and 1930s. These included poetic and artistic responses to mountains, as well as technical 'how-tos' and guides. There were attempts on Mount Everest in 1921, 1922, 1924 (Mallory's ill-fated expedition), 1933, 1935, 1936 and 1938. See Hobusch 2009: 624.
3 See Tebbutt 2006.
4 See Hobusch 2009.
5 For an analysis of the predominantly 'private' nature of women's travel writing, see Mills 1993: 40–2; Jamie 2008. Jamie's article in the *London Review of Books* is a review of Robert Macfarlane's *Wild Places* (2007).

Rebel women between the wars

6 'Foolish Mountaineering', *Alpine Journal*, 41/238, May 1929, p. 423.
7 Pilley 1965: 36.
8 The headline is slightly misleading as Pilley climbed the north ridge with her then husband, the English literary critic I. A. Richards, in the company of two Swiss guides, Joseph and Antoine Georges.
9 Luckett 1990: xlii.
10 Richards 2016: 135; Luckett 1990: xiv.
11 Theatre card for 'The Idea' in 'Ephemera', I. A. Richards collection, Magdalene College, Cambridge (RCM).
12 Ellerman was the daughter of a wealthy shipping owner; rebelling against her traditional upbringing, she became the lifelong companion of the poet H.D. and used her money to fund the literary magazine *Life and Letters Today*, and the journal *Close Up*, which launched the concept of film as an art form. In 1948 she adopted the name Bryher, after one of the Scilly Isles.
13 Bryher 1963.
14 School report and examination result in 'Ephemera', RCM.
15 Pilley makes reference to trying to pluck up courage to broach the subject of studying horticulture in her diary on 13 September 1912; the reference to wanting to study Egyptology is made in *Climbing Days* (1965: 2) – the attempt at which she writes mysteriously as requiring, afterwards, 'a two-months rest'.
16 Bryher 1963: 185.
17 Bryher 1963: 123, 150.
18 She makes reference to these reading-induced headaches in her diaries. In a 1925 letter to her future husband I. A. Richards, she wrote: 'My eyes which I hoped were stronger are in no ways fit … I rarely do more than an hour or two of close work at a stretch … my school girl headaches have returned' (1 December 1925, RCM).
19 'Letter to the Editor', *Spectator*, 5 April 1913, p. 19.
20 There are various diary references to this, for example 18 January 1921, 3 March 1921.
21 Dorothy Pilley's diary, 9 January 1921, RCM.
22 Pilley 1965: 2.
23 Bryher 1963: 172.
24 Dorothy Pilley's diary, 25 January 1915, RCM.
25 Dorothy Pilley's diary, 11 November 1918, RCM.

26 Her salary for her work for the League is mentioned in a letter to Richards on 1 December 1925; it may have been slightly lower when she first started work for the League, RCM.
27 Dorothy Pilley newspaper cuttings, RCM, not catalogued.
28 Newspaper cuttings; a diary entry for 8 October 1918: 'Spend last night and this evening writing up lectures for the *Queen* and *Ladies Field*. Shall not get paid for any probably but the advertisement may be worth while and the League gains into the bargain' (RCM).
29 Both pieces are undated but appear under the relevant newspaper name and column in the cuttings book.
30 The Devil's Kitchen is the name for a steep rocky cleft on Glyder Fawr in Snowdonia. The clipping appears in the 1919 section of her cuttings book but there is no date. In *Climbing Days*, the event is recorded as being at Whitsuntide 1918.
31 Her diaries for 1920 and 1921 contain several references to going to the *Daily Express* offices and taking assignments from a man named Bishop.
32 Luckett 1990: xiv.
33 Dorothy Pilley's diary, 16 January 1921, 31 May 1931, RCM.
34 Dorothy Pilley's diary, 21 January 1921, RCM.
35 Dorothy Pilley's diary, 3 March 1922, RCM.
36 Dorothy Pilley's diary, 10 July 1921, RCM (italicised section underlined).
37 Dorothy Pilley's diary, 22 and 23 January 1922, RCM.
38 For more on politicised spinsterhood, see Oram 1992.
39 Pilley's annual diaries list books read for that year. They reflect a wide interest in mountaineering literature, classics and contemporary literature and politics. They also list lectures attended and show that she attended Fabian lectures before the war and Six Point Group lectures after the war.
40 'Sixty Page Letter', Pilley to Richards, 1 December 1925, Box 29, RCM.
41 Holtby 1981: 270.
42 There was also among working-class women a very vigorous participation in team rounders. Langhamer 2000: 4, 82.
43 See, for example, Dilley and Scraton 2010.
44 Underhill 1956: 13.
45 Emily Hilda Daniell (E. H. Young), 'Reminiscences', *Pinnacle Club Journal*, 4, 1929–31. E. H. Young challenged conventional notions

of gender and propriety in a number of ways, including living in a *ménage à trois* for many years. While best known as a 'domestic middlebrow' writer, her writing was also inspired by the outdoors. Her unsettling short story 'The Stream', first published in *Good Housekeeping* in 1932, concerns the deaths of two men in the trackless wilderness of North Wales.

46 Stark 1950: 135.
47 Shepherd 2011: 7–8.
48 For more on interwar leisure, see, for example, Anderson 2011; Lowerson 1980; Matless 1990.
49 See Tebbutt 2006; Schaffer 1989; Cosgrove 1984. Rebecca Solnit writes engagingly on this subject in her book *Wanderlust* (2014).
50 Langhamer 2000: 77. Langhamer points out that rambling, though 'free' in itself, was prohibitively expensive for the poorest women as they could not afford the train fares and footwear required.
51 Reprinted from the 1929 Sheffield Clarion Ramblers Handbook, in Sykes and Sykes 2001: 47.
52 Anderson 2011.
53 Reference to the staffing of the *Country Standard* appears in an article 'The Left Book Club and the Countryside', *Left News*, June 1938, p. 855. *Left News* regularly promoted rambling and outdoor activities among its members.
54 G. Winthrop-Young, 'To the Members of the Mountaineering, Climbing and Rambling Clubs of Great Britain', *Journal of the Fell and Rock Climbing Club*, 5/2, 1920, p. 209.
55 The journal had been quarterly until the First World War.
56 Mumm 1921: 4.
57 Mumm 1921: 12–13. This 'vicarious imperialism' in nineteenth-century mountaineering attitudes has been noted by other scholars, including Peter Hansen (2013) and Clare Roche (2013), although Roche challenges Hansen's assertions that women were rare in Victorian mountaineering.
58 Collie 1923: 1.
59 A survey of the journal during the years 1904–14 shows not a single woman-authored piece, although in the 1904 volume there is a review of Mrs Aubrey Le Blond's book *Adventures on the Roof of the World* (1904). The February 1908 number notes the establishment of the Ladies Alpine Club with Mrs Aubrey Le Blond as president. It is described as a 'child' of the Alpine club 'of unique character

Parallel platforms and safe havens

and formidable dimensions ... many of whose members have every qualification for our own Club, except that of sex' (pp. 10–11).
60 'New Expeditions', *Alpine Journal*, 34/223, November 1921, p. 476.
61 Pilley 1923: 162.
62 Pilley 1923: 165.
63 For example, Lilian Bray, 'The Kaisergerbirge', *Alpine Journal*, 37/231, November 1925, pp. 279–97, a lengthy (18-page) article on climbing in the Austrian Alps; Miriam O'Brien, 'In the Mont Blanc Massif and the Oberland', *Alpine Journal*, 43/243, November 1931, pp. 231–7, another long article, with photographs taken by the author.
64 'Editor's Note', *Alpine Journal*, 43/243, November 1931, p. 231.
65 Macdonald 1928: 77.
66 'Lady Mountaineers', *Alpine Journal*, 41/238, May 1929, p. 422.
67 'Foolish Mountaineering', *Alpine Journal*, 41/238, May 1929, p. 423.
68 See Mills 1993: 13. In *Climbing Days*, Pilley notes the *Alpine Journal*'s 'incredulity and stern disapproval' of women's ascents, 'announcing the first woman's lead of the Grepon with a hesitating "it is reported"' (1965: 130).
69 O'Brien 1931: 231.
70 'In Memory of the Men Killed on Mt. Everest', *Alpine Journal*, 36/229, November 1924, pp. 273–7. This fetishisation of the heroic male mountaineer was satirised in W. H. Auden and Christopher Isherwood's play *The Ascent of F6* (1937), in which a party of young men are sent to their deaths climbing a notoriously difficult peak in the defence of British colonial interests.
71 These are kept in the basement at the club's Charlotte Road headquarters, Old Street, London.
72 The major exception to this is the work of Gertrude Lowthian Bell, who began publishing travel guides from the turn of the twentieth century, for example *The Desert and the Sown* (1907) and, with William Ramsay, *The Thousand and One Churches* (1909).
73 Macdonald 1928: 78–81.
74 Shepherd 1938: 8–9.
75 Pilley 1920: 172. The piece was originally published in the *Daily Express*, 28 May 1920.
76 'Our Club in 1920', *Journal of the Fell and Rock Climbing Club*, 5/2, 1920, pp. 184–7.
77 Pilley 1921: 331.

78　Kelly 1921.
79　'Rock-Climbing for Women', letter in the *Manchester Guardian* by Pat Kelly and Eleanor Winthrop-Young, 2 April 1921, p. 12; in *Climbing Days*, Pilley notes that in 1935 the club had 80 members (1965: 84).
80　'Rock-Climbing for Women', anonymous leading article in the *Manchester Guardian*, 2 April, p. 8 (emphasis added).
81　For example, *The Vote* (1910–33), *International Woman Suffrage News* (1913–45) and *The Common Cause* (later *The Woman's Leader and The Common Cause*, 1909–33). See also 'Introduction' above, and Tusan 2005.
82　See, for example, Hannam and Hunt 2002: 90–1; Ward 2019: 43.
83　Kaya 2004: 234.
84　See, for example, Harrison 1986.
85　Contributions to 'Should Women Organise Apart from Men?', *Christian Science Monitor*, 15 October 1932, p. 16.
86　Ibid.
87　Lilian Bray to Pilley, 23 November 1923, Alpine Club archives.
88　See Kelly 1921, and the unsigned article on Kelly in the first issue of the *Pinnacle Club Journal*, assumed to have been written by Pilley.
89　See, for example, Ray Strachey's chapter on the aftermath of suffrage in her book *The Cause* (1978: 367–85); see also Gottlieb and Toye (eds) 2013.
90　See, for example, Jackson and Tyler 2014; Theobald 2000. The Australian activist and poet Lesbia Harford, who campaigned for the rights of women machinists during the First World War, wrote her poem 'Fatherless' on this subject. The poem is not only about the loss of her own father, but the metaphorical lack of repressive male father figures in her working life, which enabled her to form her own ideas and speak her own mind: 'For since no male / Has ruled me, or has fed / I think my own thoughts / In my woman's head'; quoted in Frances 2013: 12. See also Pat Thane's (2001) work on the National Union of Societies for Equal Citizenship (NUSEC).
91　See, for example, Frances 2013: 21; Thane 2013: 58.
92　See, for example, her article 'Orators in the Making', *Daily Express*, 18 March 1921: 'The demand for women as speakers on social, economic and political questions is steadily increasing. It is even said that certain persuasive female orators have won by-elections for their party. Many women however, when asked to assist their party retort: "I'll help, but I'm no speaker." As if a speaker were born, not made!'

Parallel platforms and safe havens

93 Dorothy Pilley's diary, 3 March 1921, RCM.
94 Pilley 1965: 84 (emphasis added).
95 Dorothy Pilley papers, Alpine Club; letter from Lilian Bray to Pilley, 13 November 1923.
96 See, for example, Lonsdale 2018. The Ladies' Alpine Club in effect disappeared in 1975, when the Alpine Club became mixed sex and the two clubs merged.
97 The struggles to get Young to produce the journal are conveyed in Lilian Bray's letter to Pilley, 13 November 1923. Dorothy Pilley papers, Alpine Club.
98 This image, whose creator is not known, remained the cover image of the journal until the 1963–64 issue (Clennett 2009: 9).
99 Mills 1993: 22.
100 Pilley 1924: 43–6.
101 See Mills 1993 and Fussell 1980 for two opposing views on this.
102 Luckett 1990: xv.
103 Letter from Pilley to Richards, 1 December 1925, RCM.
104 *Nelson Daily News*, 30 September 1925.
105 *Bellingham Herald*, 8 and 10 September 1926.
106 Letter from Pilley to Richards, 8 December 1925, RCM.
107 Luckett 1990: xliv.
108 Williams 1973: 107.
109 Letter from Alan Harris to Pilley, 11 December 1928, archives of George Bell and Sons, Archive of British Printing and Publishing, University of Reading (ABPP).
110 Letter from Alan Harris to Pilley, 27 March 1929, archives of George Bell and Sons, ABPP.
111 'What to Pack', *Observer*, 11 August 1935.
112 Display advertisement, *Observer*, 5 May 1935, p. 4.

4
Risk-takers

The million swastikas which hang on the walls in the Saar give the impression that a plague of spiders has descended, and already they are weaving the web which will bind the Saar to Germany. Every town and village is decked in flags and streamers, and at night mighty swastikas stand out against the sky. Bare walls and empty buildings alone testify that for more than 46,000 people the popular slogan 'Die Saar ist frei' has no meaning ... The position of the minority is pitiful. They have no work, no country and no money. They have no confidence in a police which is already the agent of a Government for whom they are traitors ... The Nazis can tell their enemies by their eyes. Panic can be seen in all the gestures and bearing of working class women who tell how they have been threatened, how they have been mocked at and spat upon ... Others ... tell how their doors have been broken open in the middle of the night, their drawers turned out, and everything turned upside down while members of the Ordnungsdienst searched for arms.[1]

This important account of the mistreatment of anti-Nazi activists in the Saar region just days after the plebiscite of 13 January 1935 appeared in the *Observer* newspaper on 20 January. The article meticulously details the house-to-house searches, the

Risk-takers

protestors being taken to German prisons and concentration camps. It describes police prejudice and an international peace-keeping force – to which Britain had supplied 1,500 soldiers – incapable of protecting the anti-Nazi minority.[2] In a series of articles, which appeared throughout January and early February 1935, the writer warned both of the brutality of the Nazis when in the ascendant, and of the complicity of the German people in supporting this brutality. The journalist was Shiela Grant Duff, a 21-year-old Englishwoman, operating freelance, just months out of the sheltered cloisters of Oxford University. Grant Duff had arrived in Saarbrucken, its streets 'clogged and cluttered with snow' and its Christmas decorations still hanging across the main streets, at New Year.[3] Within a fortnight these 'streamers of lights' and 'garlands of evergreen' would be replaced with the swastika 'spiders'.[4] Within a fortnight, too, of arriving in the disputed zone, she would succeed in getting her newspaper temporarily banned from Germany because of the anti-German tone of her Saar reports.[5]

The Saar plebiscite was at the time considered of only minor interest to British newspapers (which is why a young woman just out of university and on her first reporting assignment was there representing the *Observer* newspaper). Most British newspapers used Reuters or their Berlin or Paris correspondents to cover the run-up to the vote, only sending in a 'Special' for a few days either side of the plebiscite, which is now seen as a pivotal moment in Hitler's journey to war. As part of the Treaty of Versailles, the 730-square-mile coal-rich territory abutting France and Luxembourg had been governed by the League of Nations for a fifteen-year period, with France benefiting from the coal mines. The plebiscite, deemed free and fair by a team of international observers, was overwhelmingly in favour of a return to German rule. The result boosted Hitler's confidence, laid bare France's inability to contain German expansion and, according to historian Christopher Hill, revealed that, among the German people, 'nationalism was a stronger attraction than barbarism was repellent, and, therefore, that dreams of German public opinion being sufficiently revolted by Nazi terror-tactics to move against the Hitler regime were pure delusion'.[6] Grant Duff's reports exposed Hitler's willingness to sanction violence and intimidation in a vote that was always going to be won comfortably by his supporters.

Figure 7 Shiela Grant Duff, 1939

Risk-takers

Shiela Grant Duff had finished three years studying Modern Greats (PPE) at Oxford that summer, and while at university she had enjoyed the company of a group of well-connected and politically active young men including the political philosopher Isaiah Berlin, the aristocratic German Adam von Trott, the novelist and academic Goronwy Rees, and the economist Douglas Jay. Both Rees and Jay walked effortlessly into jobs at the *Manchester Guardian* and *The Times* respectively. Grant Duff, desiring to be a journalist to work towards 'preventing the outbreak of a major war', expected to be able to do the same.[7] However, following an interview at *The Times*, she received a sharp rebuff from editor Geoffrey Dawson: 'The conditions of work in this office are such as to make it awkward to accept women as foreign sub-editors, which we regard as an essential part of the training of young foreign correspondents', he wrote to her.[8] While in his letter he accepted that women could, and did, make good journalists, he created such obstacles as to prevent their being able to work in the *Times*'s office. He advised her, if she was going to the continent, to send the paper some 'fashion notes' instead. So she took off, alone, ironically exposing herself to far greater risk than any 'awkwardness' in the *Times*'s sub-editors' room. Indeed, if Graham Greene's and Claud Cockburn's memories of the sub-editors' room at *The Times* during the interwar years are reliable, the greatest risks amounted to being asked to translate texts from Greek into Mandarin as the hot coals softly thudded into the fireplace grate.[9]

Having a private income of £3 a week and no father to prevent her, in October 1934 Grant Duff went to Paris and took a room, decorated with 'a reassuring pattern of large Tudor roses', beneath the eaves of the Hotel Britannia, rue d'Amsterdam, in the 9th arrondissement.[10] Her romantic imagination was charmed by the idea of living in Paris alone. She wrote to her friend Adam von Trott:

> I like the street of public bars in which I live, and I like the grand restaurants where the walls are made of glass and have a sky and sea and trees painted on them with love-birds and canaries flying through the lighted fountains – oh it's a gay and beautiful place.[11]

Her one connection in Paris, through her friend Goronwy Rees, was to Edgar Ansel Mowrer, the highly regarded Paris correspondent (and former Berlin correspondent before he was expelled by Hitler in 1933) of the *Chicago Daily News*.[12] Grant Duff met Mowrer for a drink in the Jardins de Luxembourg on her second day in Paris and afterwards recorded in her diary how acutely aware she was of the significance of the day, addressing herself as 'you' as an encouragement.[13] Under Mowrer's fond yet also gruff and at times harsh tutelage, she began to learn the rudiments of journalism. His letters to her, tracking her journeys around central Europe during the 1930s, are a mixture of avuncular concern, saloon-bar coarseness and sexist assumptions about women foreign correspondents ('You ought to behave in a more feminine way … you ought to keep your mouth shut more and listen better').[14]

It was on Mowrer's recommendation that Grant Duff gained the job of reporting on the Saar plebiscite for the understaffed *Observer* newspaper. The letters of authorisation from 22 Tudor Street, signed by editor J. L. Garvin, are carefully preserved in her personal papers, as are communications with the distinguished diplomatic correspondents she mixed with in Saarbrucken, including Vernon Bartlett of the *News Chronicle*

Risk-takers

and Frederick Voigt of the *Manchester Guardian*. Staying on in Saarbrucken long after the other correspondents had left for the next big story, she observed the brutality of the victorious Germans, something that most newspapers missed. The general line taken by the British mainstream press was that the plebiscite had passed off peacefully and that the vote, by satisfying Hitler, 'has brought new hope of a European Settlement', as the *Sunday Times* reported the following week – the very day Shiela Grant Duff was describing the brutal treatment of anti-Nazis.[15] In mid-February, she reported, this time for the *Manchester Guardian*, on the withdrawal of British peacekeeping troops and how soldiers from the first battalion of the Essex Regiment sang 'Tipperary' and 'Pack up Your Troubles' as they marched through the Saar, songs reminiscent of the Great War implicitly warning of the war to come. She pointed out that while the British troops were ordered to embark at small provincial stations, to minimise the potential for cheering crowds, the Italian troops, also heading home, were accorded a Guard of Honour and a military band to see them off.[16]

'Not reckless, but fearless, certainly, and very brave and determined'

For a young woman from an upper-middle-class background to go, unaccompanied, to Paris in 1934, to stay alone in a low-quality hotel frequented by prostitutes, and then to travel to Saarbrucken, with all its potential for violence, was brave, risky even, but not uncharacteristic. Shiela Grant Duff had already travelled through Germany and Austria alone earlier that summer, trying to understand for herself the political changes taking place:

Rebel women between the wars

> I want to know the history of Europe in the last 20 years – or at least since the War – why such peaks of idealism, hope and bravery are followed by such pits of despair, anarchy and oppression. I want to … contribute something to prevent war and bring about better peace conditions in Europe – especially in Austria and Germany.[17]

She would, for the next few years, take enormous risks, socially, politically and physically, to achieve political engagement in the fight against fascism. A diary entry written when she was just 19, towards the end of her first year at Oxford, acknowledges that she would do anything dangerous if the ends justified it.[18] Her daughter, Penelope Newsome, describes her mother as 'not reckless, but fearless, certainly, and very brave and determined'.[19] This willingness to put herself in harm's way to achieve political participation deviates from the correct gendered behaviour regarding courage. Studies of the representation of female courage suggest that its correct manifestation is either endurance of pain (childbirth, domestic abuse) or defence (of children, of honour). Masculine manifestations of courage include active resourcefulness, verbal repartee and physical aggression involving risk.[20] Women activists of the early twentieth century demonstrated a new kind of female courage that went beyond the correct behaviours. This can be seen in the direct activism of the suffragettes in picture slashing, brick throwing and arson attacks, as well as their enduring sexual harassment at demonstrations, prison and force feeding.[21]

The evolving nature of female courage has often been overlooked in histories of post-suffrage activism, but as we shall see throughout this chapter – and book – hundreds of women were at this time redefining the limits of female action and courage. Part of the work done here will be to theorise the attributes

Risk-takers

and dispositions required for a woman to 'bravely [precipitate] herself out of a pink miasma of sloth and stagnation' to engage with the world, as one woman expressed it during an earlier phase of women's political and social evolution, that of the 'New' or 'Advanced' woman of the 1890s.[22] The generation of young women who grew up having witnessed, or if too young learning, that their father or brother had participated in the First World War may well have been a factor. Shiela Grant Duff's daughter, Penelope Newsome, puts her mother's courage down to the fact that her father's bravery was a constant narrative through her childhood.[23] Her father had been killed early in the First World War, her two uncles in 1917 and 1918, and having no paternal figure to exercise control over her, she enjoyed more freedom than most young women of her class. She would use those freedoms to the limit: travelling to some of the most dangerous parts of 1930s Europe, including Civil War Spain and contested Czechoslovakia, occasionally blurring the lines between newspaper correspondent and activist. Always putting her passionate causes ahead of regard for her reputation and career, she supplied information to communists in France and to Spanish government agents during the Civil War, made links with the anti-Hitler 'Black Front', resigned from the *Observer* over disagreement with the editor's support for appeasement and turned down a job offer at the Royal Institute of International Affairs (Chatham House) over the British approach to the Munich Agreement.

Despite Edgar Mowrer's advice to her in the Saar – 'Don't get entangled in anything political there of any sort. Observe, advise but keep out' – she ignored him.[24] While in the Saar, as well as reporting events for the British public, Grant Duff admitted in her memoir that she used her position as a British journalist 'quite shamelessly to ease the escape of anti-Nazis ... Most of those who came forward for my help were German communists; many of them I now suspect ... were Comintern agents.'[25] On one occasion she had to dispose of a pistol, hidden in her underwear drawer, given to her by an anti-Nazi activist; she threw it into the Saar river.[26] This mirrors Tessa Rowntree's hiding of a Jewish refugee's pistol under a pile of sanitary towels, before disposing of it in the Vltava river after the Germans invaded Prague in March 1939.

Childhood and family background

Shiela Grant Duff was born the youngest of four children on 11 May 1913. The family was wealthy, connected and influential in the fields of politics, science and banking. Her paternal grandfather was Sir Mountstuart Elphinstone Grant Duff, a Liberal MP and governor of Madras, and her maternal grandfather Sir John Lubbock, the first Lord Avebury, was an eminent Victorian scientist and friend of Charles Darwin. But she took most delight in listing her maternal grandmother's maiden surnames: 'Lane Fox Pitt Rivers', the daughter of the famous Victorian anthropologist. Adrian Grant Duff, her father, was fatally wounded on 14 September 1914, and she and her siblings lived with their mother in a smart Edwardian townhouse at 16 Mulberry Walk, Chelsea. They spent most holidays at High Elms in Farnborough, Kent, the family seat of the Lubbocks: a 260-acre estate and a 27-bedroomed mansion which burned to the ground in 1967:

> High Elms had everything a child could want – swings, dogs, stables, a farm, woods, ponds, a walled kitchen garden, rabbits. There were flat-bottomed boats we could row out to islands in

Risk-takers

the ponds, a red cart we could drag round the woods ... For us it was all joy, but we were aware of the sorrow.[27]

Her father's absence, and the cause of it – war – lived with her throughout her childhood: 'We were aware that our grandmother hated the Germans with all her heart. My mother was wiser and more compassionate. She taught us to hate war.'[28] In a letter to her friend Goronwy Rees written while she was at Oxford, she confessed that the thing she wanted most in the world was a father.[29] Grant Duff's mother, after her father's death, 'was determined that her daughters should have the same education and the same opportunities as her son', and Shiela, who displayed precocity in every area, was sent to St Paul's Girls School. Her two older sisters, Jean and Diana, were born six and five years before her. Being the baby of the family, her mother 'always clung close to [me]'. Her sisters 'thought I was spoilt', their feelings confirmed when she was given emerald green ribbons to wear in her beautiful red hair when they, with plain brown hair, had to wear black ribbons.[30]

She won a place to study PPE at Lady Margaret Hall, Oxford, one of the first women to do so. She went up in the autumn of 1931, and through her friendship with Peggy Garnett she met Douglas Jay and Goronwy Rees, three years her senior, the summer before she went up, which was also the summer she 'came out' as a débutante. A dance card for an Oxford ball held on Wednesday 24 June 1931 shows that she reserved the first, eleventh and last dances for Rees, who had just finished his finals. The two would shortly begin a relationship which would shape her political development as events in Germany began to overshadow her studies. At Oxford she joined the Labour Club and the communist October Club, and in the summer of 1932, during extended travels around Europe, she went to Russia with Rees and her brother Neill, visiting Leningrad and Moscow and touring a number of Soviet technical institutes. She became friends with the young political theorist Isaiah Berlin, with whom she travelled through Eastern Europe in 1933, and who took over the care of her two dogs after Lady Margaret Hall objected to her having them in her rooms.[31] She read left-wing literature, much of it at Rees's recommendation, as indicated by a letter from Rees dated 16 April 1933, shortly after Hitler became Chancellor of Germany:

> I wish you had finished your essay. I am very glad you are not a society girl and do not have what my communist book calls 'The traditional parasitism of the female' ... the communist book *The Condition of the Working Class* is very good and you must read it ... Internationalism is the only possible way of avoiding war.[32]

Her final year at Oxford was marked by persistent impulses to leave as European politics intruded ever more urgently. Diary entries from the rise of Hitler in 1933 track the Nazis' progress anxiously. While she would later come to reject communism, particularly after 1945, her undergraduate self saw international socialism as the only way to eliminate war. A diary entry dated 4 October 1933 predicts another European war within five years and that communism was the only way to prevent it. After the hunger marchers passed through Oxford on 19 February 1934, an event that coincided with the shelling of workers' flats by fascists in Vienna, she nearly left Oxford: 'It seemed preposterous to be living a useless life in this ivory tower when such things could happen.'[33] The principal of Lady Margaret Hall, Lynda Grier, wrote to advise her that it would be better, at this stage of her undergraduate career, to finish her course. She did, and gained a good second class degree.[34] After a summer travelling through Germany she decided to become a foreign correspondent.[35]

Women and interwar foreign correspondence

Asking the editor of *The Times* for a job as a foreign correspondent was, in 1934, an astonishingly bold act, as there were no women foreign correspondents on the staff. Foreign affairs were widely assumed to be of interest only to men and there was a distrust of women's political judgement.[36] Even *Time and Tide*, the feminist weekly review largely directed and edited by women, kept women's names off its weekly notes and leaders, which editor Lady Rhondda saw as 'the soul of the paper', for fear of reducing its authority in this area.[37] Winifred Holtby, who wrote widely on international affairs for the paper and was one of its directors, struggled both for bylines and acceptance from male contributors on these pages.[38] Elite women did edit small-circulation niche journals with an international outlook: Violet Milner, Lord Alfred Milner's widow, commented on imperial politics when she became editor of the *National Review* in 1929, taking over from her brother; Lady Houston was a 'diehard' Conservative commentator in her *Saturday Review*; on the other side of the political spectrum, the prominent feminist internationalist Helena Swanwick edited the pacifist journal *Foreign Affairs*.[39] It must be stressed, however, that writing about and commenting on international affairs is not the same as reporting from the field. The restriction of commentary and reporting on foreign affairs to elite women matched the outlook of the British Foreign Office and diplomatic service, which was in the interwar years a 'significant bastion of male upper-class power and privilege', with women, apart from diplomatic wives and aristocratic society hostesses, 'almost wholly excluded'.[40] The complex set of diplomatic and political manoeuvrings that led, ultimately, to the Second World War are thus seen as predominantly male-authored in anglophone journalism, narrated by men such as Norman Ebbutt and George Steer of *The Times*, and the Americans Ed Murrow and Ernest Hemingway, despite women's organisations increasingly commenting on events from the sidelines as the 1930s wore on (see Chapter 7 for women's internationalism in the 1930s).

While the occasional woman had previously reported for mainstream newspapers from foreign parts, they were either well-connected peeresses, or extraordinary, or both. The acclaimed nineteenth-century journalist Harriet Martineau's *Letters from Ireland*, published in 1852 in weekly articles in the *Daily News*, are considered to be the first example of female foreign correspondence, although these articles were anonymous and written as from a masculine viewpoint.[41] Lady Florence Dixie, who reported on the Zulu Wars for the *Morning Post*, Flora Shaw (later Lady Lugard), *The Times*'s colonial editor in the 1890s, and Lady Sarah Wilson, who reported from the siege of Mafeking for the *Daily Mail*, enjoyed aristocratic, diplomatic and military connections at the highest levels.[42] Lina Duff Cooper, later Mrs Aubrey Waterfield, reported on Italy and the rise of Mussolini for the *Observer* newspaper from 1921 to 1935 from her castle in the Apennines, facilitated through her friendship with *Observer* editor J. L. Garvin.[43] During the interwar years high-profile women writers such as Vera Brittain and Winifred Holtby commented on international affairs, often from personal overseas experience – Holtby wrote extensively on Africa, much of her opinion coloured by a lecture tour for the League of Nations Union in 1926, where she met the prominent South African statesman Jan Smuts; Brittain wrote of her experiences in France as a VAD (volunteer nurse), after the publication of her war memoir *Testament of Youth* in 1933 and particularly as another war loomed.[44] The Labour MP Ellen Wilkinson travelled to Germany as a journalist in 1933 after losing her seat in 1931, and wrote of the 'orgy of cruelty' that she observed in *Time and Tide*.[45] Other women wrote humanitarian pieces for publications such as the Quaker *Friend*, but these focused on the victims of conflict, not the powerful belligerents.

Women's voices, then, were not entirely absent from commentary on international affairs. What they did not have, however, was the status and security of a staff position, and none of them were in the small and close-knit group of diplomatic correspondents who shaped public understanding of the rise of Hitler and the slow collapse of the League of Nations. Women who wanted to report for mainstream newspapers on diplomatic affairs were embattled outsiders. Shiela Grant Duff, her fellow Czechoslovakia expert Elizabeth Wiskemann and the French diplomatic correspondent Genevieve Tabouis were accomplished, intelligent and outspoken journalists, but their outsider status, while resulting in some of the most interesting interwar commentary on fascism and the rise of Hitler, meant that their roles were very precarious. Tabouis was forced to leave both *Le Petit Marseillais* and *La Petite Gironde* because of her support for Republican Spain during the Spanish Civil War, although she did continue her weekly column in the *Sunday Referee* throughout the late 1930s. Wiskemann, a freelance writer who reported on international affairs for the *New Statesman*, *The Scotsman* and *Time and Tide*, was arrested by the Gestapo in Berlin on 11 July 1936. She was taken to their headquarters on Prinz Albrechtstrasse and questioned about an article she had written for the *New Statesman*, 'A Land Fit for Heroes', published on 13 July 1935. The article begins: 'The general line in England today is, it seems, that Germany is settling down quite nicely ... Nothing could be more disastrously deceptive than this impression ... the maltreatment of the Jews is being carried out to hitherto unknown lengths.' She was ordered to leave Germany and did so the next day, travelling back to England via the Hook of Holland; she did not return until 1945.[46] She did, however, continue to report on the threat of Hitler right up until 1939, travelling extensively to Austria, Czechoslovakia and Yugoslavia, her path sometimes crossing with that of Shiela Grant Duff.

Coverage in the mainstream press of the major events in Europe, the rise of Hitler, the League of Nations and the disarmament conferences in Geneva was dominated by a powerful all-male group of diplomatic correspondents. Most took direction from the Foreign Office News Department run by Rex Leeper, under the leadership of Permanent Under-Secretary Robert Vansittart: Frederick Voigt of the *Manchester Guardian*, Victor Gordon Lennox of the *Daily Telegraph*, Norman Ewer of the *Daily Herald*, Vernon Bartlett of the *News Chronicle*, Harold Cardozo of the *Daily Mail* and Victor Poliakoff of the *Evening Standard* (who later moved to *The Times*).[47] Geoffrey Dawson and J. L. Garvin, editors of *The Times* and *Observer* respectively, and Lords Rothermere and Beaverbrook, proprietors of the *Daily Mail* and *Daily Express*, took personal interest in diplomatic coverage and had close personal relationships with members of the government. Women were excluded from these networks of power, many forged at public school and later through London clubs. The uncritical acceptance by the British press, especially *The Times*, *Daily Mail* and *Daily Express*, of Chamberlain's policy of appeasement has been commented on by scholars of this period.[48] Individual correspondents, however, often had very different views from their editors. Norman Ebbutt of *The Times* and Pembroke Stephens of the *Daily Express* were expelled from Nazi Germany in August 1937 and May 1934 respectively.[49] Frederick Voigt was the target of an SS assassination attempt at the end of 1933. Despite correspondents' personal concerns over appeasement, their reliance on Rex Leeper for information meant that when Vansittart and Leeper were sidelined by Chamberlain during the run-up to the Munich crisis in the summer of 1938, their sources of information virtually dried up and they were left helplessly reliant on Chamberlain's direction.[50]

Shiela Grant Duff and Elizabeth Wiskemann, however, having carefully constructed a network of independent information sources, wrote articles, pamphlets and then books on Czechoslovakia throughout 1937 and 1938, which were marked by their knowledge and authority. More women began reporting from Spain during the Spanish Civil War, especially Americans, but as will be seen it was often by accident and in unusual circumstances.

Spain

In February 1937 Grant Duff travelled alone to Spain via North Africa. Her mission, mysteriously given to her by Edgar Mowrer, was to obtain evidence of the Spanish rebels' brutality since taking Malaga, and also to obtain evidence of Italian involvement in Spain to prove that Italy was breaking the international Non-Intervention Agreement.[51] A further aim of the trip was to try to find the writer (and secret Kremlin agent) Arthur Koestler, who had been captured in Malaga and had subsequently disappeared. The mission, organised by Mowrer and Otto Katz, a Czech Comintern agent, and with the Spanish government paying her expenses, was both bizarre and risky.[52] It is not clear why Mowrer enticed Grant Duff into this venture, or indeed why Mowrer, who although openly critical of European fascism was equally critical of Soviet communism, should liaise so directly with a known agent of the Kremlin.[53] Mowrer's instructions were hardly designed to preserve the safety of a young, unaccompanied English woman: 'You wear your prettiest dress and stand by the side of the road with a bunch of flowers, and an Italian officer will give you a lift.'[54] Grant Duff was aware of the dangers, half-joking in a letter to Adam von Trott just before her departure: 'I think Mowrer is to be trusted and it is not a wild goose chase nor means I will be raped by Moors nor shot for treason.' She did, however, make a point of not telling her mother of the trip.[55]

She was originally to fly to North Africa from Bordeaux, cross into Gibraltar from Tangier, and then take a bus to Malaga. The final journey varied significantly from the original plan: she went by train to Barcelona and then on to Alicante, flying from Alicante to Oran, and then making her way to Tangier, spending four nights on trains and buses crossing North Africa.[56] The stop-overs in Barcelona and Alicante, still in Spanish government hands, are significant and suggest that she was taking messages to, or from, Spanish government agents. She returned by the same route. On her return she submitted a lengthy and highly detailed report of all she had observed to someone she only referred to as 'our friend' in a letter to Mowrer.[57] In her two published accounts of the trip – in her memoir *The Parting of Ways* and in 'A Very Brief Visit', a chapter in a collection of Spanish Civil War memoirs published in 1976 – she focuses on one minor episode when she attempted to meet the American Consul, who Mowrer had assured her was 'pro government'.[58] Although she makes light of this episode – after climbing over a wall into the Consul's garden at night, she discovered that he had pragmatically switched sides and was entertaining several of Franco's officers to dinner – it was a moment of danger. In neither published version of the trip do the stop-overs in Barcelona and Alicante appear. Throughout the journey she collected evidence of troop and ship movements, information which, if her notes had been found by Italians or Franco-supporting Spanish, could have been disastrous. In the report of her journey, preserved in her private papers, she records two French destroyers in the port of Tangier and that all the Italian sailors in the port vanished after 9 p.m. for fear of encounters with French seamen. The report also describes how Spanish rebel agents and Italians were fomenting discontent among the native population and against French Morocco. It also notes that the Spanish rebels' office in Tangier had pictures of Franco and Mussolini on the walls and notices exhorting people to denounce suspected spies. The report describes how agents of Franco travelled secretly by boat across the Straits of Gibraltar to give evidence against prisoners held in Malaga.[59]

A receipt in her archives shows that she stayed at the Caleta Palace Hotel on the seafront in Malaga on the night of Friday 19 February 1937, and deposited 175 pesetas in the hotel safe. She had arrived in Malaga ten days after it had been taken by the Falangist forces and the town was full of mourners: 'Every woman seemed to be draped in black, every man – but men were few – seemed to wear a black armband. Their hair was black, their eyes were black, their faces grey and pinched.'[60]

Rebel women between the wars

She attended a court hearing and watched 26 people, six of whom were women, three under 20 years old, tried for pro-government acts, found guilty and sentenced to death, with executions at 3 a.m. She was invited to observe these by a group of Franco's officers, but declined. At the harbour she reported the presence of two rebel destroyers and one Italian and one Greek destroyer, and a Moroccan troopship disembarking mules. As for evidence of fortifications, she described a sentry lying asleep on sandbags. There were four rifles lying beside him and a machine gun pointing out to sea.

Grant Duff wrote to Mowrer on her return, with a cryptic reference to Valencia, but Mowrer replied sharply: 'You ought to learn to keep your mouth shut more and listen a little better and work systematically. Have no illusions about the warmth of the Castilian Plateau.'[61] This warning suggests that Mowrer wanted to close down any recorded discussion of the trip. Reading the details of the report, it is astonishing to note quite how much danger Grant Duff had put herself in. She was, essentially, spying, either for the Spanish government or for the Kremlin, or both, deep inside Franco-held territory. That she accepted the mission in the face of such danger reveals either extraordinary courage or intense desperation to prove herself, to be involved.

The Spanish Civil War was a time when women's voices on international affairs, via the widespread network of Aid Spain committees, public fundraising, anti-fascist and pacifist groups, began to be raised beyond the fairly narrow (by class) confines of the Women's International League for Peace and Freedom and the International Alliance of Women for Suffrage and Equal Citizenship (IAWSEC; see Chapter 7 on these two organisations).[62] Women started to report from Spain for newspapers and magazines, although most were marginal and precariously employed. Even Martha Gellhorn, who became famous for her literary reportage, only had a freelance arrangement with the American *Colliers Weekly*.[63]

Perhaps the most romantic character was the Welsh-born Florence Roberts, who with her father, Captain William Roberts of the Welsh-registered merchant ship *Seven Seas Spray*, broke through Franco's naval blockade of the Basque coast several times between April and July 1937 with a cargo of olive oil, honey, beans, peas, salt, almonds and barrels of cognac to deliver to the starving Basques besieged by land and sea.[64] She sympathised with the Republican cause and, after having spent two months as a prisoner in the Spanish port of Santona in autumn 1937, said she 'would do it all again'.[65] The blockade of the Basque coast began in early 1937 after Franco failed to take Madrid, and by April the populace was reduced to eating donkeys and dogs. On the night of 19 April the *Seven Seas Spray* left St Jean de Luz on the French coast. After ten hours' uneventful sailing the ship's arrival in Bilbao was feted by the Basque authorities. English newspapers celebrated the 'pretty, 20-years-old' captain's daughter sporting a jaunty sailor's cap.[66] The *News Chronicle*, no doubt appreciating the appeal to readers of having a real-life English heroine reporting for them, hired her to write about her experiences with Bilbao's starving women and children. She reported, in her first despatch for the *News Chronicle*:

> I have seen children and even women run after lorries leaving one ship with loads of salt and snatch a handful of it. Hordes of children gather round the food shops from early morning till dusk pleading for food. What they prize most are pieces of white bread … despite their hardships they would rather starve than surrender.

And, in a deliberate dig at the British prime minister, Stanley Baldwin, she added: 'If only those in authority in Britain could see these starving, homeless women and children – the sight of whom brings a lump into my throat, there would not long be a shortage of food in Bilbao.'[67] Later one of the first correspondents to report from the bombing of Guernica, she wrote: 'Amid the ruins mothers are still seeking children and children their parents. No cattle remain. They were machine-gunned in the fields as were their fleeing owners. Two unexploded bombs bearing German marks of identification help to place the responsibility for this inhuman massacre.'[68]

Instead of calling her a 'special correspondent', however, the *News Chronicle* gave Roberts the gendered byline 'Foodship Girl' or the diminutive 'Fifi' Roberts. This was the fate of many female newspaper correspondents, and implies that editors assumed that readers' interest would be roused more by their status as female curiosities than by the words they wrote. Virginia Cowles, who reported on the Spanish Civil War first for Hearst newspapers and then the *Sunday Times*, was bylined 'American Girl' and 'NY Society Girl' as she reported on fighting in the trenches around Madrid.[69] The newspapers would often introduce her as 'Virginia Cowles, daughter of Dr Edward Spencer Cowles and New York Social Registerite, who made her debut in Boston Society in 1928–9' and as a 'young, dark, glamorous American', not only defining her by her gender, but by class, looks and parentage. These gendered bylines are reminiscent of Edith Shackleton's description as 'a woman correspondent' as she made history by being the first female newspaper correspondent to report on parliamentary proceedings for the *Evening Standard* in 1923.

Risk-takers

Roberts's youthful bravery caught the imagination of the left-wing poet Edgell Rickword, who wrote about the 'brave lass' in his famous poem 'To the wife of any non-interventionist statesman', published in the *Left Review* in March 1938. The poem contrasts the pampered politician's wife in her 'boudoir's pleasant shade' with the 'Victims of Franco's sham blockade' and 'Potato Jones and his brave lass' who through their courage had 'proved this husband knave or ass'.[70] Literary scholars have criticised the misogyny of the poem in holding the powerless wife responsible for her husband's political cowardice. They all overlook, however, the heroine of the poem, romantically played by Florence Roberts, the young woman who scorned danger to help the 'thousands left to Franco's hate'.

Another 'accidental' war reporter was Elizabeth Wilkinson, a member of the British Communist Party and the British Women's Committee Against War and Fascism, a communist-sponsored organisation. She was in Bilbao to gather evidence on the effects of the blockade at the time of the bombing of Guernica, and cabled an article to the *Daily Worker*. Her report, headlined 'Wounded People Roasted in Hospital', made the front page and is an outraged, lucid account of the bombing:

> Where Guernica, ancient capital of the Basque country, stood on Monday there is today a ruin, wrapped in smoke, illuminated by the flames of still burning buildings. Where men, women and children went quietly about their business two days ago there are now only silent figures twisted in the agony of death or burned beyond recognition.[71]

Thus the young daughter of a merchant seaman and a communist activist were able to address an audience of millions on an atrocity that came to define the Spanish Civil War.[72] Their strange, hybrid position as humanitarian activist and accidental news correspondent enabled them to express outrage and point the finger of blame at the Germans, while other correspondents, writing for more mainstream newspapers, either had their reports suppressed or toned down.[73]

The American poet Muriel Rukeyser had perhaps the most serendipitous of accidental reporting experiences. Sent to cover the People's Olympiad in Barcelona in July 1936 for the English literary journal *Life and Letters Today*, her train from Port Bou on the French border was caught up in the first hours of the Spanish Civil War, when military garrisons throughout Spanish Morocco and mainland Spain rebelled against the government.[74] The article on the People's Olympiad became instead an eyewitness account of the opening days of the war. Her experience on the train, which was held up at the town of Moncada by a spontaneous general strike was, for Rukeyser as for many writers of the left during this decade, the moment when 'I began to say what I believed.'[75] Of wider importance was her framing of these early days of the conflict not simply as the outbreak of a civil war, but the beginning of a revolution, foreshadowing George Orwell's later observations in his more famous *Homage to Catalonia* (1938). Rukeyser, only 22 at the time, had already made a name for herself as a poet of the left, but the events of July 1936 strengthened her convictions and she spent the rest of the duration of the war publicising and raising money for the government cause.

The article she wrote for *Life and Letters Today* was thus an unlikely scoop by an unlikely correspondent in an unlikely publication. As yet uncollected, the article, across eight pages of the literary journal, is a hybrid of documentary, poetry, scrapbooking from other media and creative non-fiction, and is an

Risk-takers

extraordinary piece of modernist reportage. It is worth quoting at length:

> As the train began to wake up, Cerbere was reached, the last town in France, and the old water, the Mediterranean. Very quickly, the terraces became mountains, covered with cactus and olive, the Pyrenees produced their little pale villages, stone masonry and plaster and stucco became prominent as we crossed the Spanish border.
> *Torchlight Procession through the City of Barcelona. Finish of the International Relay courses. Program. People's Olympiad First Day.*
> ... A wildfire of rumours goes through the train from that moment on. The Catalonians, who have been fighting, leave the train, buy bread and sausages and wine, and begin lunch on the benches; the foreigners begin to meet each other after two hours of waiting. Word goes through, the news of a general strike. This, a slogan at the end of a pamphlet, the last words of a poem.
> *Moncada is a little town between Geronna and Barcelona, on the inland route. There is nothing in it that will need detain the tourist, who will do well to proceed to the capital immediately. Guidebook of N. Spain.*
> ... The tourists begin to make themselves at home. The handsome young English couple, on their way to Mallorca, have it in for the man at Cook's, who should have told them there was to be a revolution.[76]

Her observations on the spontaneous collectivisation of the town, its brutal treatment of the Catholic priest and his church and the confiscation of all vehicles in the town by the workers' committee show that she was politically astute, seeing that these were no mere reactions to military aggression, nor a defence of the status quo, but revolutionary acts.

Rukeyser's experience proved artistically productive, and as well as writing a long poem, 'Mediterranean', about her journey out of Spain, she wrote a novel, *Savage Coast*, which, rejected by her publisher, remained forgotten until recently discovered misfiled in her archive in the US Library of Congress.[77] Analysis of the text of the novel, written after the article for *Life and Letters Today*, shows how she borrowed phrases and ideas from her journalism for inclusion in *Savage Coast*. The Mediterranean, for example, is, in both the novel and the article, the 'old water', emphasising Spain's location at the heart of early Western civilisation, its history and permanence now under threat from military-backed fascism and warfare. An ephemeral piece of journalism published in a quarterly periodical thus became the basis for a lengthy and lasting work of prose fiction. Words, initially recorded rapidly to be discarded rapidly, cross the journalism–fiction boundary, transforming into a more permanent genre through the catalyst of seismic political events of which she had accidentally become a part. The novel's powerful opening image – 'The train went flashing down France toward Spain, a stroke of glass and fine metal in the night' – conveys the transformative power of the journey into Spain for Rukeyser.[78] Her experience in Spain can thus be seen as the fount of multiple texts in multiple media: journalism, poetry and prose fiction, all of them excavating and giving voice to a key moment in her development as a writer.

The Spanish Civil War is now seen as an 'important moment in women's visibility in public political life'.[79] These examples serve to deepen our understanding of the commitment, artistic, humanitarian and political, shown by women in wartime and the risks they took in order to enable their engagement. They also show how the process of reporting and recording legitimated female presence in a war zone. Despite the 'NY Society Girl' byline, Virginia Cowles's reportage from Civil War Spain received critical acclaim, and after the Second World War she was awarded an OBE for her war reporting. Shiela Grant Duff's trip to Spain marked a moment of acceptance by Edgar Mowrer, that she was not just a society girl on the lookout for adventure, but a serious activist, as he acknowledged in a letter: 'I was proud of the way you overcame your scruples and did the Spanish job … You stepped up three degrees.'[80]

Czechoslovakia

After Hitler entered the Rhineland in March 1936, Grant Duff asked Hugh Massingham, foreign editor of the *Observer*, to appoint her to represent the newspaper again. His response – 'I think we've got a correspondent in Prague. Oh no I think he died' – reveals how low down Czechoslovakia was on the list of foreign interests in 1936.[81] On arrival, Grant Duff found that she was the only resident British foreign correspondent, as well as the only woman journalist among the foreign press corps.[82] She lived in the centre of Prague old town, underneath the eaves of a red-roofed house at number 1 Bartolomejska, and was, her daughter Penelope Newsome wrote in her obituary, 'lonelier in the company of cynical and uncaring British diplomats than when alone'.[83] Both first minister Sir Joseph Addison and his deputy Robert Hadow were convinced appeasers. Addison thought Czechoslovakia 'a bizarre mongrel state' and socialised only with Bohemian Germans, and offered her little help or encouragement.[84] Not only was Grant Duff refused help by the British Legation, but she aroused suspicion in the Czech police, who thought she was a German spy, and in the foreign press corps, which denied her membership of their club, declaring her not a '*Journaliste de Profession*'.[85] In a letter to the *Daily Telegraph*'s diplomatic correspondent, Victor Gordon Lennox, she said that the Legation was intensely suspicious of her and offered her no help, and she knew not where to start.[86] These multiple difficulties stemmed to no little extent from her being the only woman in a man's world of diplomacy and foreign correspondence. Male correspondents sexualised and fantasised about her. Edgar Mowrer wrote to warn her that rumours were flying around diplomatic correspondent circles that she had been sleeping with 'a Nazi boy from Germany', and that she ought to behave in a more feminine way, 'which doesn't necessarily include promiscuity'.[87]

Frozen out of political and professional circles, Grant Duff also struggled to get anything published in the *Observer*, which took an increasingly pro-appeasement line and rejected many of her submissions.[88] The only article of any major interest that she published with the *Observer* during those months was one about the author and German exile Thomas Mann becoming a Czech citizen.[89] She was, however, assiduous and conscientious, travelling widely through the countries of the 'Little Entente' (Czechoslovakia, Romania and Yugoslavia), making several trips to Berlin, and compiling a wide-ranging card index of everyone she met, often making crisp notes on whether or not they would be helpful, such as Dr Frantisek Bayer from Bratislava, whom she described as small and beady-eyed, and who didn't look very intelligent. She dismissed Dr Frantisek Kubka of the Czech Press Department at the Ministry of Foreign Affairs as a complete fool altogether.[90] She was never a detached observer. She met Otto Strasser, leader of the anti-Hitler 'Black Front' group, several times in the autumn of 1936 and they corresponded regularly.[91] She corresponded too with the prominent Labour anti-appeasement campaigner Hugh Dalton, passing him any information she thought he might find useful.[92] She also began

Risk-takers

writing to Winston Churchill and, through a family connection on her mother's side, was able to meet him on 13 July 1937. In a diary extract she described how he appeared to her, with a sprightly, intelligent ugliness. She agreed with Churchill's assessment that the only way to contain Germany was a network of European alliances so tight and strong that internal pressure would build until some kind of political civil war would erupt, resulting in the destruction of Hitler and his circle.[93]

Her despair at the *Observer*'s appeasement line reached breaking point, and on 24 May 1937 she wrote a three-page resignation letter to the editor J. L. Garvin, disagreeing with his stance over Czechoslovakia point by point. She described her resignation as 'an immense liberation' although she also admitted to fearing what she would do next.[94] To discard, deliberately, her tenuous connection with the foreign press corps might be seen as another reckless act, but she was now placing her articles in other publications, including the *Manchester Guardian*, *Spectator*, *London Mercury* and *Political Quarterly*.[95] These articles show that she was beginning to find a voice, distinguished in three ways: command of detail, a controlled sense of outrage at events and a literary style using simile and metaphor:

> Any schoolchild in Eastern Europe could write today the communique that will be issued tomorrow. It will reaffirm the indissolubility of the Little Entente; the unity of purpose and endeavour which animates its governments, the lasting affection of the people for each other and the honour which Yugoslavia feels in the presence of Dr Benes. But what is the real position?[96]

> To Western eyes, the events in Romania appeared nothing more nor less than the suicide of parliamentary democracy. According to Romanian statistics more than four million people voted for

the virtual abrogation of the democratic regime and willingly accepted the rule of a royal dictatorship.⁹⁷

Strange though it may seem, Czechoslovakia is not alarmed ... She is isolated in middle Europe, a democratic island with martial dictatorships or their satellites bearing down on her from all sides. Her allies are far away.⁹⁸

'Meddling in foreign affairs'

Her authorship of a pamphlet, *German and Czech: A Threat to European Peace*, published by the New Fabian Research Group in November 1937, confirmed Grant Duff as an expert on Czechoslovakia and attracted the attention of Allen Lane at Penguin. From then on her *Spectator* articles were bylined rather than anonymous, although they used the gender-neutral 'S. Grant Duff'. She saw with a clarity that evaded many that the fall of Czechoslovakia would inevitably lead to a British war with Germany. Writing in the *Spectator* in March 1938 after the Austrian Anschluss, she made much of the Czechoslovak military defences. This had a twofold intention: warning Germany of the dire consequences of any invasion of Czechoslovakia, and warning the Allies of the consequences of these arms falling into German hands: 'With Czechoslovakia will go down the last resistance to German aggression in central Europe. What will happen when Germany can spare all her troops for the Western Front, all her bombers for Paris and London?'⁹⁹ She became a regular correspondent with Churchill, and his article on the folly of a German invasion of Czechoslovakia, published in the *Daily Telegraph* on 23 June 1938, was heavily influenced by her knowledge of Czech military preparations: 'A well-conceived system of forts and concrete pill-boxes,

Risk-takers

a judicious improvement of natural obstacles, the thorough mining of roads and bridges should, if backed by a stubborn army, bring any rapid thrust to a standstill.'[100]

For the next two years, Grant Duff's travelling, writing and campaigning against appeasement became increasingly frantic and active. In the autumn of 1938 she campaigned in two of the so-called 'Munich by-elections' for anti-Chamberlain candidates, making political speeches, though 'I am speaking badly, and I feel too empty to go on', as she confessed during the Duchess of Atholl's campaign to be re-elected as an Independent.[101] Once more, her activism challenged gender stereotypes: not only was anti-appeasement hawkishness seen as unbecoming in a woman, but political commentators generally agreed that Chamberlain's policy was widely supported by women, who were 'for peace at any, or Mr Chamberlain's price', and that Chamberlain's policy was partly shaped by the fact of women's enfranchisement.[102] Grant Duff crisscrossed Europe, attending diplomatic functions in Romania, Yugoslavia and Czechoslovakia. Watching in Romania as the parliament voted itself into a royal dictatorship, she bitterly wrote: 'It will be fun to tell my grandchildren how I assisted, in one country after another, at the suicide of democracy. I shall tell them how pleased and self-congratulatory everybody was at having lost their freedom.'[103]

Allen Lane commissioned her to write a book for his 'Penguin Specials' series. The series of distinctive books with orange and black covers at 6d each included a reprint of Edgar Mowrer's *Germany Puts the Clock Back* (1933) and Genevieve Tabouis's *Blackmail or War* (1938). The series was conceived as list of 'topical importance published within as short time as possible from the receipt of the manuscript'. While intensely factual and dealing with the history of the Czech and Slovak peoples, the origins of the Sudeten Germans and the complex political machinations between the countries of Eastern Europe since Hitler gained power, the book's central organising theme was a warning to the world of how important it was that Hitler should not get hold of the country. *Europe and the Czechs*, published under the name 'S. Grant Duff', was rushed out on 30 September 1938, the day after the Munich Agreement, and within six months had sold nearly 190,000 copies, for which Grant Duff was paid £1 per 1,000 copies. She had been in Paris the day before and returned on the boat train to Victoria Station to see her book in print for the first time, next to the newspapers with their banner headlines about Munich, an irony not lost on her: 'Against a background of a Europe all in black, its cover showed the blood-red outline of a Czechoslovakia that no longer existed. It was my first sight of this now useless book.'[104]

Europe and the Czechs brought a further book commission, this time from Macmillan, and an offer of work in the Czech section of Chatham House 'in the event of war'.[105] The letter also enquired whether she might be able to support herself, as the Institute was short of money. The letter, received the day after Munich, provoked a furious response. She was ashamed of her government she told the director of studies, Arnold Toynbee, over Munich, and she could not possibly work for an organisation so closely linked to the British foreign policy.[106] She spent the months between Munich and the invasion of Czechoslovakia writing for newspapers and gathering information about German preparations for invasion and British complicity over the fate of the doomed country. This included, in a memo dated 5 March 1939, the information that German students at the University of Prague had received orders to learn Czech and to prepare to become administrators, and that the British Embassy in Prague had been informed, at least a week before the invasion, of Germany's intentions.[107] Now fully revealed in newspaper bylines as 'Miss Shiela Grant Duff', her forthright articles attracted attention and opprobrium from readers. One reader of the *Cheshire Observer*, objecting to an article she wrote for the *News Chronicle*, accused her of hawkishness and of wanting young men to be killed in another war: 'We all realise the tragedy of Czechoslovakia without having the deplorable fact of its extinction rammed down our throats as if we were responsible.' The letter, filled with disapproval of a woman having such views, urges 'Miss Grant Duff' to study her history books and stop meddling in foreign affairs.[108] After the German invasion of Czechoslovakia she continued to write vivid pieces of reportage from Prague, detailing how the Czechs whistled in derision at the German invaders, as well as more analytical articles pointing out the illogicality of the British position: 'British unpreparedness will never explain the necessity to hand over to a potential enemy, forty motorised Czech divisions, the biggest armament works in Central Europe and a tidy air force'; she predicted, correctly, that Czech armaments would shortly be used against Britain and its allies.[109] After war broke out Grant Duff was appointed Czech editor of the BBC's new European Service, where she met her future husband, the former *Telegraph* journalist Noel Newsome, who was head of the service.

* * *

Shiela Grant Duff's strong and spirited personality enabled her to participate in a field of work where women were not just scarce, but actively excluded and marginalised. Over the years 1934 to 1939 we see her emerge from a precarious and anonymous freelance contributor, to the gender non-specific 'S. Grant Duff', to the full 'Miss Shiela Grant Duff', and then to recognition as one of the foremost experts on Czechoslovakia as war broke out. Her brave and passionate disposition enabled her, through sheer force of personality as well as plenty of youthful energy, to excel in the masculine world of foreign correspondence, although, as we have seen, her name was linked to sexual scandal by the diplomatic press corps. Her writing echoes the humanitarian precedents of Emily Hobhouse and Francesca Wilson: passionately outraged accounts of human suffering are privileged over interviews with powerful men. This was partly because she was distrusted by the Czech authorities, and refused help by the strongly pro-appeasement British Legation officials in Prague. Also, as an embattled outsider herself, she identified with those on the receiving end of abuses of power. She never forgot that the only reason she was refused a job on *The Times* was because her gender would make it 'awkward'. This idea of 'feminine' and 'masculine' treatments of international news – reinforced by the newspapers' gendering of women's dispatches from Spain – represents both an opportunity and a problem for women journalists, who even today feel stereotyped into the kind of news they report.[110]

Unlike many of the other women in this volume who benefited from mutually nurturing friendships with other women, or from formal and informal networks of women, Grant Duff journeyed and worked alone. She was not a member of English PEN, nor the Society of Women Journalists, nor of any other organisation of women writers or campaigners. Having been barred from working for *The Times*, she nevertheless forced herself into the public sphere, taking on assignments that others would not, and although clearly dejected by efforts to exclude her, she battled to maintain and build on her precarious position. Her principles almost got the better of her: even having gained a precarious foothold, she was not afraid of rejecting patronage if its issuers' opinions appalled her, as in her resignation from the *Observer* and her initial rejection of a post at Chatham House. She, as well as other women such as Elizabeth Wiskemann and Martha Gellhorn, began the slow process towards the acceptance of women as foreign news correspondents. In October 1938, on her return from Prague, deeply distressed at the fate of a country that had come to represent her coming of age as a respected writer and commentator on international affairs, Churchill told her, 'You have fought well', a statement that could accurately describe her entire life since leaving university.[111]

Notes

1. Grant Duff 1935b: 15.
2. Grant Duff 1935b.
3. Letter from Shiela Grant Duff to Adam von Trott, Saarbrucken, 13 January 1935 (von Klemperer (ed.) 1988: 65).
4. Descriptions of Saarbrucken before the plebiscite in Grant Duff's article 'The Saar at the Polls', *Observer*, 13 January 1935, p. 15.
5. Letter from Grant Duff to von Trott, Saarbrucken, 13 January 1935 (von Klemperer (ed.) 1988: 67).
6. Hill 1974: 142.
7. Grant Duff 1982: 66.
8. Letter from Geoffrey Dawson to Grant Duff, 30 October 1934, MS Grant Duff 2, file 5, Bodleian Library, Oxford (Bodl.).
9. Claud Cockburn: 'In the Foreign editorial room a sub-editor was translating a passage of Plato's *Phaedo* into Chinese, for a bet' (1957: 123); Graham Greene: 'I remember, with pleasure … the

slow-burning fire in the sub-editors' room, the gentle thud of coals as they dropped, one by one, in the old black grate' (1972: 125).
10 Grant Duff 1982: 67.
11 Letter from Grant Duff to von Trott, Paris, 13 November 1934 (von Klemperer (ed.) 1988: 56).
12 Mowrer 1970: 226.
13 Diary entry, 28 October 1934, MS Grant Duff 71, file 2, Bodl.
14 Edgar Mowrer to Grant Duff, 5 April 1937, MS Grant Duff 2, file 1, Bodl.
15 'No Election This Year', *Sunday Times*, 20 January 1935, p. 17.
16 'Saar Gives British Troops a Warm Send Off', *Manchester Guardian*, 19 February 1935, p. 12.
17 Letter from Grant Duff to von Trott, Salzburg, 25 August 1934 (von Klemperer (ed.) 1988: 43–4).
18 Diary entry, 8 June 1932, MS Grant Duff 71, file 2, Bodl.
19 Interview with Penelope Newsome, 16 February 2018.
20 See, for example, Simpson 1991.
21 See, for example, Lawrence 2001; Wheelwright 1992.
22 Dr Arabella Kenealy, *Idler*, IX, 1894, 'Advanced Woman Number', p. 209.
23 Interview with Penelope Newsome, 16 February 2018.
24 Letter from Mowrer to Grant Duff, 23 January 1935, MS Grant Duff 2, file 1, Bodl.
25 Grant Duff 1982: 84.
26 Grant Duff 1982: 85.
27 Grant Duff 1982: 21.
28 Grant Duff 1982: 21.
29 Letter from Grant Duff to Goronwy Rees, 12 April 1932, MS Grant Duff 45, file 3, Bodl.
30 Grant Duff 1982: 22.
31 Grant Duff 1982: 37.
32 Letter from Rees to Grant Duff, 16 April 1933, MS Grant Duff 45, file 5, Bodl.
33 Grant Duff 1982: 54.
34 Email from Lady Margaret Hall archivist, 22 January 2018.
35 Grant Duff 1982: 66.
36 Gottlieb 2013: 159.
37 Clay 2018: 142.
38 Clay 2018: 143.

Risk-takers

39 Riedi 2013: 944–5; Gottlieb 2015: 55.
40 Gottlieb and Stibbe 2017: 176.
41 Duspati 2017.
42 For a lively overview of these extraordinary and unusual women journalists, see Sebba 2010.
43 Waterfield 1961.
44 Holtby wrote on international affairs for the *Nation and Athenaeum* and *Time and Tide*; Brittain wrote for the *Manchester Guardian*, the *New Clarion*, *Modern Woman* and *Peace News*.
45 Ellen Wilkinson, 'Thinking with Blood', *Time and Tide*, 1 April 1933, pp. 381–4.
46 Elizabeth Wiskemann recounts this incident in her memoir *The Europe I Saw* (1968: 56–60).
47 For a detailed study of the role of British newspapers during the 1930s, see Cockett 1988.
48 See particularly Cockett 1988; Gannon 1971.
49 On 25 May 1934 Stephens had written a particularly caustic attack on the Nazis' treatment of German Jews in the *Daily Express*: 'German Jews are facing their darkest days – Denied a Living – Savings Gone – Friends Dare not Greet them – their children play at home'. This led to his expulsion, but did not have the desired effect of shutting him up: 'My Expulsion by the Nazis – Article about Jews that angered Hitler – *Daily Express* to prove its truth', *Daily Express*, 2 June 1934, p. 1. Stephens had been arrested on 31 May and made his way back to England via Amsterdam.
50 See Cockett 1988: 64–9.
51 The French had proposed a non-intervention agreement, which would prohibit the provision of arms and military support to either side in the Spanish Civil War, in August 1936. This was eventually signed by 27 countries including Britain, Germany, Italy, USSR and Portugal. It was flouted on both sides, with the Soviets helping the Spanish government and the Germans and Italians helping Franco. Of the Great Powers, Britain maintained most neutrality. See Little 1988.
52 Letters between Grant Duff and Mowrer about this trip, letters between Grant Duff and Koestler's wife, and Grant Duff's report, prepared for a Spanish government agent, are in the Sokolov Grant papers (MS Grant Duff 3, file 1, Bodl.); Grant Duff 1976.
53 Mowrer writes about Katz in his memoir *Triumph and Turmoil*: 'Otto Katz, a Czech some thought an agent of the Kremlin. Good looking,

sharp of mind ... I ran into Otto in the strangest of places, Paris, Mexico City and the like ...' (1970: 171).
54 Grant Duff 1976. This account plays down the importance of this visit, and makes no reference to the detailed report she prepared for the Spanish government afterwards.
55 Letter from Grant Duff to von Trott, February 1937 (von Klemperer (ed.) 1988: 210–11).
56 There is a map of her final route in her papers, MS Grant Duff 3, file 1, Bodl.
57 Letter from Grant Duff to Mowrer, 'End Feb 37', MS Grant Duff 2, file 1, Bodl.
58 Grant Duff 1976.
59 Spanish itinerary and report in MS Grant Duff 3, file 1, Bodl.
60 Grant Duff 1976: 84.
61 Letter from Mowrer to Grant Duff, 5 April 1937, MS Grant Duff 2, file 1, Bodl.
62 See Fyrth 1991.
63 Dell'Orto 2004.
64 *Western Mail*, 21 April 1937, p. 10.
65 *Daily Mail*, 3 November 1937, p. 15.
66 *Daily Mail*, 21 April 1937, p. 13.
67 *News Chronicle*, 27 April 1937.
68 Florence Roberts's reports from Guernica appeared in the *News Chronicle* on 29 and 30 April 1937, pp. 1 and 2, respectively.
69 Articles published in Hearst Sunday Syndicate newspapers, collected by Cowles in her scrapbook, Imperial War Museum, Docs. 20478/20.
70 *Left Review*, March 1938, pp. 834–6. Like many at the time, Rickword confused Captain Roberts with the more famous, but actually less successful, blockade runner, Potato Jones.
71 *Daily Worker*, 28 April 1937, p. 1.
72 The circulation of the *News Chronicle* at the time was 1.6 million.
73 For a thorough overview of reporting on Guernica, see Rankin 2004.
74 The People's Olympiad was to be held in Barcelona on 22–26 July, as a response to Hitler's Berlin Olympics. Six thousand athletes from 22 nations were to attend but the games were cancelled because of the Civil War. Many athletes stayed and joined the first International Brigade. The People's Olympiad should not be confused with the International Workers' Olympiads, held between

Risk-takers

1925 and 1937 and organised by the Socialist Workers' Sports' International.
75 Quoted in Kennedy-Epstein 2013: ix.
76 Rukeyser 1936.
77 Kennedy-Epstein 2013: x.
78 Rukeyser 2013: 7.
79 Kennedy-Epstein 2013: xiii.
80 Letter from Mowrer to Grant Duff, 5 April 1937, MS Grant Duff 2, file 1, Bodl.
81 Grant Duff 1982: 116.
82 Grant Duff 1982: 126. Elizabeth Wiskemann and Virginia Cowles visited extensively during this time, but cannot be described as 'resident' as Grant Duff was.
83 Newsome 2005: 81.
84 Neville 1999: 259.
85 Letters to Mowrer, dated 5 February and 13 April 1937, MS Grant Duff 2, file 1, Bodl.; Grant Duff 1982: 152.
86 Letter from Grant Duff to Gordon Lennox, 7 August 1936, MS Grant Duff 2, file 4, Bodl.
87 Letter from Mowrer to Grant Duff, 5 April 1937, MS Grant Duff 2, file 1, Bodl.
88 Grant Duff 1982: 152.
89 'Thomas Mann in Exile', *Observer*, 24 January 1937.
90 MS Grant Duff 1, Bodl.
91 MS Grant Duff 3, file 4, Bodl.
92 Letter from Grant Duff to Hugh Dalton, 19 June 1937, MS Grant Duff 2, file 4, Bodl.
93 MS Grant Duff 3, file 4, Bodl.
94 Letter from Grant Duff to von Trott, 30 May 1937 (von Klemperer (ed.) 1988: 239).
95 For example, 'Czech Attitude to Germany More Favourable?', *Manchester Guardian*, 17 June 1937; 'Rumania', *Political Quarterly*, April–June 1938; 'Rivalries in South-East Europe', *Spectator*, 2 April 1937; and 'The Czech Nation', *London Mercury*, November 1938.
96 'Rivalries in South-East Europe', *Spectator*, 2 April 1937, p. 618.
97 'Rumania', *Political Quarterly*, April–June 1938, pp. 238–53.
98 'Czechoslovakia's Confidence', *Spectator*, 5 February 1937.
99 'Czechoslovakia after the Anschluss', *Spectator*, 25 March 1938.

100 Winston Churchill, 'Factors which Sway Europe's Fate over Czechoslovakia', *Daily Telegraph*, 23 June 1938.
101 Letter from Grant Duff to von Trott, 20 December 1938 (von Klemperer (ed.) 1988: 345); Grant Duff also supported fellow foreign correspondent Vernon Bartlett in his successful by-election contest at Bridgewater on 17 November 1938.
102 'Mass-Observation', *The Pioneer*, 4 February 1939. For more on the impact of gender on the Munich by-elections, see Gottlieb 2013.
103 Letter from Grant Duff to von Trott, 28 February 1938 (von Klemperer (ed.) 1988: 297).
104 Grant Duff 1982: 188.
105 Macmillan commissioned Grant Duff to write *A German Protectorate: The Czechs Under Nazi Rule* (1942). Letter from Arnold Toynbee to Grant Duff, 30 September 1938, MS Grant Duff Box D2, Bodl.
106 MS Grant Duff Box D2, Bodl. A staff list of Chatham House dated 23 November 1939 lists Shiela Grant Duff, showing that she did, after all, decide to serve her country after war broke out.
107 MS Grant Duff Box 5, Bodl.
108 'Fighting for Czechoslovakia', *Cheshire Observer*, 25 March 1939.
109 Grant Duff 1939a; 1939b.
110 Franks 2013: 23.
111 Newsome 2005.

5

Parental influence and family networks

Downstairs in the smoking-room members had fallen into their first afternoon sleep. The deep armchairs held them tenderly. The cigars grew ashy white in their unconscious fingers and the pages crept about with a trained, inaudible tread. It was afternoon in the Devonshire Club. Was it possible that a desecrating female foot should have trod those hallowed carpets while they slept? I am glad to say the members did not wake as I looked at them (a little guiltily) and they only stirred in their sleep. They did not know that in the dining room above, between twenty and thirty of their fellow members were consenting to sit down to a princely luncheon – to sole, lamb, asparagus and Stilton – with one of the Unhallowed Ones. A woman in the Club! ... 'You may say,' said the member on my right at luncheon, nursing his cigar and warming his brandy in a generous palm, 'Or you may think, dear lady, that we are going to pieces by allowing ladies into the Club.' 'But I remember,' protested one of the members in a frail voice, 'I distinctly remember ladies in the club before. No, my dear madam you are not the first, we had ladies here at the Coronation, though of course, we only allowed them on the balconies.'[1]

In April 1933, Margaret Lane became the first woman (apart from servants) to set foot inside the Devonshire Club. Situated behind a classical stone facade in St James, the heart of

Rebel women between the wars

London's smart clubland, the Devonshire was the quintessential gentleman's club, with panelled walls and deep leather armchairs from which politicians and aristocrats discussed the great affairs of state in the absence of women. During the club's previous sixty-year history, there had been five separate proposals to allow women in, and all had been defeated by large majorities.[2] Only a fire in 1930, which destroyed part of the club, and declining membership due to the club's close ties to the equally declining Liberal Party, forced members finally to allow women guests into a new ladies' dining room, painted a pale pistachio green, on the first floor. Lane, then the *Daily Mail*'s 'star' descriptive writer, was invited in to sample the new facilities.[3] If the gentlemen of the club were hoping for a gushing, wide-eyed paean to its tradition and grandeur, they were to be disappointed. Instead, Lane, who had been a member of the Labour Party since university, composed a devastating satire in her characteristic, delicately humorous but nevertheless well-aimed prose.[4] The members, supposedly representatives of Britain's economic and political elite and guardians of national identity and masculine power, are depicted as babies sleeping in their cradling chairs, and possessing a baseless sense of superiority, revealing themselves as pompous, discourteous and irrelevant.[5] The mischievous 'first afternoon sleep' implies that these great men spend half their days semi-comatose. Her language also suggests her own delighted transgression: 'hallowed/unhallowed', 'desecrating female foot' and 'invades' combine to create an image of trespass into sacred enemy territory. This notion, in the context of the stuffy old Devonshire, would certainly have pleased her, a lifelong feminist who used her position to campaign on a wide range of women's rights, despite the *Mail*'s conservative politics.

Parental influence and family networks

Material from Margaret Lane's childhood and youth helps explain, in part, the personality of this bold and self-assured young woman who successfully invaded the masculine world of news reporting and became the highest paid woman on Fleet Street when she signed a contract with the *Daily Mail* in 1932.[6] In 1931, at the age of 24, she travelled incognito to the town of Evarts in Kentucky, a lawless place at the heart of the mining riots, checked into a hotel under an assumed name, 'Mrs Campbell', and, with the help of a tiny camera, filed news agency reports while other journalists were being run out at gun point (indeed, two journalists had been murdered).[7] She also travelled to Chicago to cover the Al Capone trial, the only woman journalist to do so, and flew to Germany in a two-seater plane with a drunken pilot in 1933, after the notorious Nazi 'mass marriages' in Berlin, to interview Magda Goebbels, who darkly warned her that the 'era of strong men' had arrived.[8]

This chapter not only examines Lane's participation strategy, which in this case is the established one of parental/familial influence and access through her newspaperman father, but also seeks a possible source of her fearlessness and unusual self-assurance. These dispositions enabled her, once her easy introduction was obtained, to convert that access into a successful career in journalism and then in literature, winning with her first novel a prestigious literary prize previously won by Virginia Woolf and E. M. Forster. A notable theme of her actions, from a young child onwards, is *knowing transgression*: she was very much aware that what she was doing was not 'normal' or 'correct' for a middle-class girl or woman of her time, but she did it anyway, and took pleasure in doing so. In addition, for someone repeatedly described by those who met her as utterly charming and polite, she possessed a dauntless determination.

Figure 8 Margaret Lane, c. 1930s

This propelled her not only to pursue Al Capone for a snatched, scooped interview amid the press maelstrom of his trial, but also to approach the notoriously prickly Beatrix Potter who, even as an elderly lady in 1939, left her publisher terrified, and who sent Lane the 'rudest letter I have ever received in my life'.[9]

Journalists are, of course, the embodiment of transgression. With their press pass they can gain entry into the homes of the highest and lowest, adventuring, as Rudyard Kipling put it, 'in the fourth dimension'; and through the power of the press they

Parental influence and family networks

can make the private public.[10] Indeed Margaret Lane acknowledged this in an article about her experiences in America for the *Daily Express*:

> Myself, armed with an American press pass, I have fetched judges off the bench, sheriffs from their offices and policemen from their stations, and chiselled my way into prisons, morgues, the fastnesses of Chicago's 'Scotland Yard' and a thousand places where I had no earthly business.[11]

Perhaps one of her boldest and most transgressive moves was in breaching the gulf between journalism and literature, a gulf established and deepened during the 1920s and 1930s by the highbrow literary elite actively demarcating and defending the boundaries of high culture against mass reading, the middlebrow and the feminine.

A precocious, transgressive, imaginative child

Margaret Winifred Lane was born on 23 June 1907 in Manchester, where her father, Harry George Lane, was a sub-editor and drama critic for Edward Hulton's popular newspaper the *Sunday Chronicle*.[12] Harry Lane was a 'modest, self-made man' who moved his family into the middle class through a combination of talent, hard work and the opportunities provided by a rapidly expanding news industry.[13] In 1909 Lane was appointed to a new Hulton title, the heavily illustrated *Daily Sketch*. The paper was launched in Manchester but quickly moved to London to compete head-on with Alfred Harmsworth's *Daily Mirror*.[14] The family moved south along with Hulton's ambitions, their fates as entwined with the business interests of the newspaper barons as those of Edith Shackleton and Alison Settle. In an interview Lane gave to the *Yorkshire Post* in 1936, she said she 'learned to walk in the newsrooms of Fleet Street'.[15] The quote not only underlines that she was familiar with the busyness, noise and smoke of newspaper offices from youth, but that her proud father, with whom she had an exceptionally close relationship, would bring her to work and show her off. This familiarity with Fleet Street is displayed in her first piece of published prose, written in October 1922 when she was 15, for the *S.S.C. Magazine*, the journal of her secondary school, Saint Stephen's College in Folkestone in Kent:

> The newsboys are yelling in Fleet Street, and the traffic is at its height. It is four o'clock of an autumn afternoon, and the evening papers have just been issued. The motor vans from the different offices are loading up with stacks of newspapers, their ink still wet from the press ... and beautiful London river lies like a chain of diamonds flung across the City.[16]

The article, titled 'The Hub', is a celebration of the capital city, particularly its noise, its crowds and the busyness of the roads, the shops and the river. Fleet Street is the beating heart of this hub, linking London to the rest of the world with its transmission of news through the voices of the newsboys, the engines of the motor vans and the barges on the sparkling river. The young girl finds nothing to be afraid of and instead sees beauty in the crowded tea shops, rich with the 'fragrance of toasted muffins', the flocks of pigeons, the lights of the barges and roaring traffic.

She was an only and sometimes lonely child; one of her sharpest memories of her childhood was watching alone at the banister and listening to 'the sound of musical evenings going on downstairs ... my first introduction to an enormous nameless melancholy which I still find it impossible to define'.[17]

Parental influence and family networks

The house was 'full of books', so she read widely and avidly, saving up her pocket money to build her own collection of Robert Louis Stevenson novels in special children's editions, at two shillings each.[18] This love of stories and of storytelling can be seen in Lane's very young childhood. She was sent to stay in Luton several times between 1915 and 1918 when Zeppelin raids threatened London. A fellow evacuee who wrote to her in the 1960s remembered her as unusually calm and self-assured for an eight-year-old sent away from home. Margaret would give the much older girl tips on what colour clothes suited her most, and would entertain the other evacuees with poems and stories: 'I often think of the funny things you used to say ... You used to sit up in bed with a pad and pencil writing til it was time to get up.'[19]

She attended a day school until she was 12, just a short walk from home in Gordon Square, Bloomsbury, and would walk to and from home alone, letting herself in with a latchkey attached to a ribbon around her neck.[20] She described herself as a good child, though possessing an 'undisciplined imagination'.[21] This was fed by her mother who had an extraordinary habit of playing terrifying pranks on her daughter. These tricks included hiding in the cellar, growling like a 'Jabberwock', and dressing 'in shrouded white with dishevelled hair carrying a greenish flame', having lain in wait for her daughter's return from school, then advancing 'eagerly but hauntingly, like Lady Macbeth sleep walking, rather impeded by her draperies'.[22] (One must, regrettably, put aside here meditation upon the state of mind of a mother who had apparently spent the afternoon preparing so thoroughly to scare her young daughter.) After this, Lane wrote, she never again believed in or feared ghosts. Her scepticism and rationalism became 'impregnable'.[23]

Rebel women between the wars

Shortly after this episode, she stumbled at school across a copy of a popular horror book for boys, *The Wolf Men* by Frank Powell (1906), and was intrigued by the cover depicting an Edwardian adventurer wrestling with a horrific creature, an air of calm detachment on his face even as he and the monster plummet down a sheer cliff face. She was immediately fascinated by the descriptive images: 'It is a twilight world lit only by the phosphorescence of the fungus forest. Giant squids and loathsome forms inhabit its waters ... The underworld is inhabited by creatures straight from the subconscious.'[24] She asked her parents for the book for Christmas and became fascinated by it, reading it over and again. Her fascination with the story puzzled her:

> These are the very creatures that have always lurked on dark landings and on the tops of wardrobes, known to every child long before he opens the page of *The Wolf Men* or comes on their modern counterpart in the horror-strip ... What does seem rather a puzzle, one which perhaps only an analyst can solve, is how once, as a normal and reasonably well-behaved little girl, I responded with such satisfaction to the descriptions aimed at the fantasies and primitive instincts of little boys.[25]

Indeed, she confessed that it was the discovery that the book was meant only for boys that was the most fascinating and tempting thing about it. What, she wrote later, gave her most satisfaction was that the world she was reading about was the world of men: not a single female character, good or evil, inhabited it: 'There are not only no women in it, there is not even a breath of a suggestion that more than one sex exists, either on this planet or inside it.' Her 'voluptuous terror' which gave her such pleasure was, then, partly based on knowing that she was straying into a world forbidden to most little girls, seeing

Parental influence and family networks

things she shouldn't. It also endowed her with a fearlessness that would enable her to face down doubts when embarking on dangerous journalistic missions: 'the primitive instinct of flight which was so stimulated and fed, leaving me for life a skilled and resourceful evader'. For that, she wrote, she had her parents, 'who were neither Freudian nor squeamish', to thank, for giving her the book and not removing it from her even after it clearly provoked such a strange tension in their daughter.[26]

As with so many of the women in this study, the preparedness to stray from 'correct' gender roles is an essential prerequisite for success in achieving one's goal of participation in public life. In the case of Margaret Lane one can see that this 'deviance' – in this case from the ideal of the sweet little girl who yearns only for domesticity – can be deliberately pursued from a relatively young age.[27]

Secondary school and Oxford

In 1919 Lane's father was made editor of the *Daily Sketch* and, now comfortably off, he sent her to a smart, yet modest boarding school for young ladies. St Stephen's College in Folkestone, no longer in existence, was founded by nuns in the nineteenth century for deserving daughters of the poor, gradually transforming to cater for the rising aspirations of middle-class parents for their daughters.[28] The year-groups were small, about 16–18 in a year during the 1920s, and 'Peggy' Lane was involved in most school societies and clubs. In her first year she was a regular contributor of poems to the school magazine, graduating to longer pieces of prose and literary essays, and she was its editor in her senior year. She was honorary secretary of the Debating Club, and in 1924 was part of the school's *annus mirabilis* when nearly all the sixth form won places at university. Lane outperformed everyone: in July

> the whole school went home for the long summer holidays bursting with gratitude to Peggy Lane and Joan Briggs who by their brilliant successes in the University Entrance Examination had won them all an extra five days' holiday. Peggy ... had just been awarded the Top Scholarship at St Hugh's College, Oxford, over nearly 500 other competitors.[29]

At Oxford she joined the University Labour Club and at the end of her first year wrote a musical comedy on the theme of the national strike that had taken place in May. She was also vice-president of the Oxford English Club, started up several college publications, and was given a 'job ... rather fun', as she wrote back to her school, on the *Oxford Magazine*, the university literary journal that published the early poetry of many interwar authors including W. H. Auden and C. S. Lewis.[30] What these upbeat letters back to her school don't reveal is her dismay at coming face to face with the class prejudice that was rife at Oxford during the late 1920s. This was the era of Harold Acton, Brian Howard and the 'dandy-aesthetes', mostly Eton-educated, self-consciously affected and snobbish young men who would progress to dominating English cultural life for the next thirty years, and who ran the *Oxford Magazine*.[31] It would not take long for Lane, clever and capable but of lower-class origins and the daughter of a popular newspaper editor, to discover how easy it is to be frozen out with a look or a careless word.

To get a hint of Margaret Lane's own experience, we can look to the fictional Oxford portrayed in her first novel, *Faith, Hope and No Charity* (1935). The novel's protagonist, Charlotte Lambert, the daughter of a painter and decorator who has

Parental influence and family networks

moved into classless 'bohemia' through her beauty and talent as a dancer, is courted by Tom Ackroyd, a member of the landed gentry who takes her to lunch in Oxford. Despite Charlotte not interacting with the students beyond exchanged looks, it is as if they can immediately see she is not 'one of them':

> Three very young men were standing at the head of the stairs with wet umbrellas. They stared coldly at Charlotte, making no move to let her pass until Tom elbowed them. 'I shall see to it I don't come here again,' said one of the young men with almost morbid distinctness, as Tom and Charlotte passed them ... It was not, she decided on examination, so much their appearance one disliked as their air ... It was their air that marked them, as distinctly as if they had been wearing a badge. It was an air of such profound self-confidence that Charlotte, who knew the value of such things, at once envied it. Because we are here, said the confident air, and at this particular moment everything we say and do is of more interest than anything else in the world. People outside our sphere do not know.[32]

The passage shows not only the rudeness of these privileged young men but the protagonist's instinctive, visceral feeling of being an outsider, without a single word passing across the great social gulf that divides them. The novel reveals Lane's dislike of upper-class snobbery, a dislike that would inform much of her work, both journalistic and literary, throughout her life (even though, ironically, on her second marriage she would become a countess, albeit her similarly rebellious husband, Jack Hastings, 15th Earl of Huntingdon, known as 'The Red Earl', was a member of Clement Attlee's post-war government; see Appendix).[33] She did, however, persevere on the *Oxford Magazine*, writing short theatrical reviews and two longer essays, one on the Parliamentary Bill which would finally give women the vote on equal terms with men, and another, very witty account of the poet Edith Sitwell's visit and lecture at the university ('Miss Sitwell spoke on "Sitwellism", a subject on which, it would seem, she is an authority').[34]

Family networks, dynasties and male equivalence

Lane graduated with a second class degree in English Language and Literature in 1928 and went to work in Fleet Street, despite her aspirations to become an author. In 1979 she told an interviewer that

> Journalism wasn't what she had hoped to do, she wanted to write books, and had gone to university with this in mind, rather than just a general education. But living had to be earned, and as you can't live on the proceeds of books not yet written, journalism it had to be.[35]

Her father, now a well-connected editor-in-chief of Northcliffe Newspapers, could well have supported her, but they both preferred that she worked for herself: 'He was a self-made man, had worked for everything he achieved and he wanted, above all, for her to make something of herself, an enlightened view for a father in the 1920s.'[36] Harry Lane helped her get a job on the popular *Daily Express*, then owned by Lord Beaverbrook and edited by the American journalist Ralph Blumenfeld.[37] Despite his obsessive rivalry with the *Daily Mail*, Beaverbrook was a loyal and helpful newspaperman, open to giving chances to the children of fellow journalists and editors.[38] She began work as a general reporter in 1929, on a basic reporter's wage of £9 9s a month.[39] A contemporary commentator wrote of her easy access: 'When she came down from St Hugh's College, Oxford at twenty-one and joined a daily

Parental influence and family networks

paper as a reporter, there were plenty of Fleet Street people to sniff "influence" and prophesy a gloomy downfall for her. She is, you see, the daughter of a well-known journalist.'[40] She had few options. During the first half of the twentieth century the National Union of Journalists deliberately restricted the number of girls permitted to be taken on as apprentices by regional newspapers, the traditional route into Fleet Street for news reporters.[41] Although, as we have seen, women were able to establish – albeit precarious – freelance careers especially in the realm of features and the women's pages, becoming a news reporter was still extremely difficult.

Family networks were, then, a shortcut for women into the profession and had been used by several other prominent women journalists. These include Emilie Peacocke, first a news reporter then women's page editor of the *Daily Express* and the *Daily Telegraph* (née Marshall, she was daughter of John Marshall, editor of the *Northern Echo*); Rachel Beer, who married into a newspaper-owning dynasty and who eventually became editor of the *Sunday Times* and *Observer* newspapers in the late nineteenth century; and *Guardian* 'doyenne' Mary Stott, who began her newspaper career on her father Robert Waddington's paper, the *Leicester Mail*, in 1926.[42] A survey of early American women war correspondents shows that before the First World War virtually all women who wrote for US newspapers did so while accompanying husbands, fathers or brothers who were either members of the military or war correspondents themselves.[43] This phenomenon can, of course, also be observed among sons and brothers of powerful media barons, the most obvious being the Northcliffe/Rothermere and Beaverbrook/Aitken and, latterly, Murdoch dynasties. Indeed, family networks have always been pervasive in many professions and trades and in all classes, from the professional intellectual elite 'tribes' of Stracheys, Bell/Stephen/Duckworths, Nicolsons and Macaulays to the unnamed father-to-son passing down of jobs and union cards.[44] Women's early participation in the professions through family connections or influence has been observed in other areas, particularly politics and academia.[45] The archaeologist Dorothy Garrod, who would become the first woman professor at Cambridge in 1936, was born into an academic scientific family and was specifically encouraged by her father, then a professor of medicine at Oxford, to take her diploma at Oxford after all three of her brothers died in the First World War.[46] Wilhelmina Gordon became, in 1909, the first woman lecturer at Queen's University in Kingston Ontario, even though her father, the principal who appointed her, had asserted his opposition to women lecturers.[47] This privileged access is, however, a double-edged sword. Certainly a powerful father or husband in a profession can smooth the way, but studies have also shown that women thus favoured must then be 'better' and harder working than the best men in their organisation in order to win respect and quell 'resentful mutterings'.[48]

Male equivalence, where a daughter or wife takes over the role of a father or husband, is another form of familial influence from which women benefited, the most famous example being Nancy Astor, the first woman to take her seat in the House of Commons.[49] Two of the first three women Liberal MPs, Hilda Runciman and Margaret Wintringham, also benefited from male equivalence.[50] Male equivalence can extend from the real to the symbolic family network, and has worked as an access method for women assistants of prominent men who successfully filled their shoes during their absence or after

Parental influence and family networks

their retirement. Examples of non-familial male equivalence (although this could be seen as a symbolic father/daughter or husband/wife relationship) are the microbiologist Harriette Chick, who discovered the link between poor nutrition and rickets, and the entomologist Evelyn Cheesman, whose interwar solo insect-collecting expeditions to the Pacific islands yielded tens of thousands of specimens for the Natural History Museum.[51] Both women, obstructed in their early attempts to make careers for themselves in science, gained lowly assistant roles at the Lister Institute and London Zoo respectively, and filled their male superiors' positions during the First World War. Once established, during the interwar years they went on to become enormously successful, both making important scientific breakthroughs.

Lane described herself as 'by nature a thorough and painstaking person', and her work ethic impressed Ralph Blumenfeld, who promised to send her to New York as a member of the *Daily Express* staff.[52] This posting, however, failed to materialise, so she resigned from the paper, and, 'armed with a book of cuttings and letters of introduction', in October 1931 she used her final month's wages to buy her fare and went to the US as a freelance, selling stories to the *Express* as well as to Randolph Hearst's wire agency, the International News Service.[53] A contemporary commentator wrote romantically of her:

> At the beginning of the thirties, as a young Oxford graduate and the daughter of an editor and publisher, she was one of the brightest things in Fleet Street. When she crossed the Atlantic as a freelance the Americans were dazzled to find that anyone could be both so beautiful and so brilliant. She brought off some notable coups, including an interview with Al Capone and his henchmen in their lair.[54]

Her reports from the US included an account of the hypocrisy of prohibition, which, she claimed, led to enormous pressures on young people to drink 'synthetic gin' heavily in speakeasys as a matter of pride. 'During my first week here,' she wrote, 'I poured more liquor out of windows and under tables than I could see at home in six months.'[55] When the Capone trial opened in Chicago on 6 October 1931, Lane was there to describe to readers Capone's 'natty black suit, a soft white collar and shirt and a black and yellow striped tie' and the 'sparkling gold chain that stretched straight across his expansive chest'.[56] Now billed as a 'special correspondent', she entertained readers of the *Daily Express* with her witty observations of 'Scarface':

> I have sat behind 'Scarface' Al Capone in court every day this week … I am quite familiar now with six of his suits, two overcoats, the careful selection of pearly white hats, and the neat way in which his blue-shaven neck rolls over his collar.[57]

She charted the drama of his downfall from glossy-haired rogue to bewildered defendant, reporting as the jury retired to deliberate:

> He whistled bravely when the jury left to consider their verdict – for all the world like a small boy summoning up courage. But when he was summoned to the court room to hear the result he appeared panting, wiping the perspiration from his forehead. He threw his green overcoat and green hat on the table, mopped his brow, and swung round, facing the jury.[58]

Two days after the guilty verdict, Lane managed to snatch an interview with Capone as his lawyers returned to court to ask for bail until a motion for a stay of judgement was heard. She asked him whether he expected to go to prison soon: '"Don't hold your breath on it," the swarthy gang chief snapped', she

Parental influence and family networks

reported. '"Scarface" Al Capone bared his teeth today: "It's a raw deal and you can bet your life I'm not giving up the battle until the higher court has had the say-so."'[59] Precariously freelance, Lane was now providing the *Express* with front page copy. Like Shiela Grant Duff, in order to participate in the public sphere she had to choose precarity and an outsider status.

After she joined the *Daily Mail* (the announcement of her appointment in the trade paper *The Newspaper World* commented 'Not only is she the prettiest girl in the Street but she can write', as if it were somehow astounding that a woman could combine the two traits), Lane became the butt of ribald gossip in the newsroom. Her daughter Selina Hastings said her mother rarely got angry, but 'At one point she absolutely lost it with all the sexual innuendo. She stood on a desk in the middle of the office to proclaim that the rumours she was having affairs with two men on the paper were untrue.'[60] These incidents illustrate the 'price' women had to pay in order to access the masculine world of news and politics: like Shiela Grant Duff, Lane was both idealised and sexualised in the almost entirely male environment of the *Daily Mail* newsroom, and had to go to extreme lengths to protect her reputation and professionalism.[61] It is interesting to note that the other newspaper journalists in this study, Alison Settle and Edith Shackleton, did not report this harassment. It could be that Grant Duff and Lane, both news reporters rather than feature or women's page writers, presented more of a threat to the masculine power structure. Studies have shown that women are more likely to suffer sexual harassment in the workplace where they are perceived to be making inroads into traditionally masculine areas.[62]

Despite this harassment, which could be seen as a form of professional intimidation, Lane used her position to campaign for a wide range of women's rights and interests, including equality for unmarried women's pensions and equal pay for women at the BBC. She also tirelessly, if wearily, inveighed against the persistent prejudice shown towards 'University Women': 'That bogy of the corrupting effect of university life on female manners and morals is a very old one. It is hoary and feeble with age,' she wrote in her third article in as many years on the subject.[63]

The 'lady novelist' and the Prix Femina-Vie Heureuse

In 1933 Margaret Lane went to live in Spread-Eagle Yard, just off Whitechapel High Street, lodging with the artist and lithographer Pearl Binder, who was then a student at the Central School of Art and Crafts.[64] After her reporting shifts for the *Daily Mail*, in the evenings, wrapped in a tartan dressing gown, she sat in a Victorian armchair she had bought at Caledonian Market in Bermondsey and wrote her first novel, which she dedicated to Binder.[65] It is a measure of the importance this period had in her life that in 1979, some forty-five years later, this battered old armchair still had 'pride of place' in her sitting room.[66] The gulf between journalism and literature was, by the early 1930s, growing rapidly. While writers of earlier generations, from Charles Dickens and George Eliot to Arnold Bennett and Rudyard Kipling, had moved between newspapers and literature with ease, defensive action by the so-called 'highbrow' writers of the interwar period was making that transition harder.[67] Any author or literary figure aspiring to signal 'intellectual seriousness' would publicly denigrate newspapers, and anyone associated with mass-market newspapers *de facto* debarred themselves from being called literary.[68] Lane, a

Parental influence and family networks

student of English literature at Oxford and, through her work on the *Oxford Magazine*, familiar with the prejudices of highbrow literary class and culture, was well aware of the gulf, and of the risks she was taking. Her sex, of course, doubled these risks. While, as saw in Chapter 1, there was a thriving and artistically rich parallel 'middlebrow' culture, Lane knew that with one slip she could become 'that figure of fun, the Lady Novelist', widely lampooned in contemporary popular culture as quietly desperate and peddling 'sentimental and curiously invertebrate "middle" articles' to newspaper and magazine fiction editors.[69] In addition, her reporting for the *Daily Mail* involved attending literary functions where she experienced at first hand the physical distance between journalists and authors that so eloquently expressed the metaphysical gulf between the two different groups of cultural producers. As she described it in a speech to the Society of Authors in 1937:

> Always in the past, at these gatherings [I have] been accommodated *with my kind* at some small table well into one of the corners of the room, where it was difficult to see the guests and almost impossible to hear the speeches and have been expected nevertheless to reproduce their pearls of eloquence by 11 o'clock the same night for the benefit of the late edition of a morning newspaper. This extraordinary reversal of all that I am used to has produced an almost *dreamlike, upside-down state of mind, rather like Alice Through the Looking Glass*.[70]

The telling phrase 'with my kind' emphasises the contemporary view that journalists and authors were two very distinct species. Lane's bold and deliberate crossing the species barrier, as it were, turned contemporary cultural convention on its head, but, as with all her transgressions, she clearly enjoyed the process.

Rebel women between the wars

Faith, Hope and No Charity, despite being a successful first novel and despite winning a prestigious literary prize, has disappeared without trace, suffering the fate of so many accomplished 'middlebrow' novels.[71] While much work has been done recently to redress the imbalance of the once 'almost exclusively male' literary history of the 1930s, the extraordinarily rich and ebullient flowering of women's interwar writing has still to be fully excavated.[72] This section explores some of the themes of Lane's novel and examines the circumstances of its prize winning. The Prix Femina committee's deliberations on the novel, and the other novels up for the prize that year, offer telling insights into the English literary culture and networks of the time. The novel emerged from the very East End streets it fictionalised, Lane undergoing an 'immersive' experience pursued by other journalist-novelists including Charles Dickens and George Orwell.

We know something of the atmosphere of the now vanished Spread-Eagle Yard, described by East End contemporary Thomas Burke in his book *The Real East End*:

> It is in one of the old yards that Pearl Binder has made her home, and she has chosen well. She enjoys a rural atmosphere in the centre of the town. Her cottage windows face directly onto a barn filled with hay wains and fragrant with hay, and a stable, complete with clock and weather vane ... one realises here how small London is, how close it still is to the farms and fields of Essex and Cambridgeshire.[73]

Binder and Lane, both engaged in creative projects, shared the tiny cottage tucked into the side of the yard, next door to Bill and Emmie, the ostler and his wife. Both women found artistic inspiration in the location; Binder included Bill and Emmie in her illustrated book *Odd Jobs*, also published in 1935:

Parental influence and family networks

> The sweet smell of hay in the lofts, and the peaceful cooing of the pigeons in the yard seemed so remote from the cosmopolitan roaring of the city just outside the gate, that Emmie imagined herself in the country. In the cool of the evening, Bill would take his stumpy pipe and sit outside the yard, in the doorway of the big gate, watching the swirling life of the city go by and resting his aching feet after his day's work.[74]

In Lane's novel the ostler and his wife are Bill and Rose Viner: hard-working, struggling, buffeted by the chill winds of technological change that mean that dray horses are no longer needed and the yard changes hands swiftly between increasingly hard-nosed and unreliable clients. Through all this, Rose and Bill maintain a quiet dignity and gentle humour, a strength of the novel noted by reviewers, who compared it to Arnold Bennett.[75] Its detailed observation of the social ills in London's East End, just miles from the opulence, furs and modernity of the West End, reminds us, as historian Juliet Gardiner wrote in her history of the decade, that in the 1930s there were several Englands, or Britains, coexisting, each separate from the other.[76] Depression-era England is highlighted in the desperate dockers waiting for work and the luxurious Christmas packages they are unloading:

> Certainly there was always a crowd of men, breathing frostily and stamping on the muddy cobbles by half-past seven in the morning whenever a ship was known to be coming in. The casuals would be there too, wary and anxious on the fringe of the crowd, afraid to shove in with the registered men and afraid of missing a chance ... The warehouses smelled strongly of tangerines, and were stacked full of thin-looking, beautifully stamped crates of fancy goods from Japan, tinsel and Christmas decorations from the Baltic ports, frozen turkeys from Poland.[77]

Rebel women between the wars

This is an environment that eventually kills young Arthur Williams, the Viners' son-in-law, aggravating the tuberculosis he acquired in a previous job in the Welsh coalmines, and Lane implies that this is no accidental death but murder by an unequal social and economic system.

Superimposed upon this background of economic hardship run the lives of two (and towards the end of the novel, three) young women. Each represents a different class: Ada Viner, the ostler's daughter, represents the lower classes; Charlotte Lambert, the struggling artisan class; and Margery Ackroyd, the landed bourgeoisie. All three are trapped, living lives mapped out for them by the vastly overpowering economic, gender and social strictures of the time. Where Ada, a widow at 19, is passive, patient and dutiful, Charlotte sets out to marry a besotted young man from the landed middle class in a doomed attempt to alter her destiny. Margery, the most actively rebellious of the three, boards a train to London to escape a future of subjugated tedium in a damp country house. Charlotte, prepared to trade her beauty for security in what she sees as a 'fair exchange', fails most spectacularly, but none of the women ends up in a happy ever after.[78] At the end of the novel, Charlotte questions her attempts to escape her fate, wondering 'how life would have shaped itself if she had never struggled to twist it to her own pattern, had lived it out acquiescently, taking things as they came'.[79]

In the bleak final scene, on a freezing December evening each woman contemplates her entrapment; but the scene also points to a way in which the three might help each other defy society and their destiny through their own collaborative efforts:

> The three sat together for a little while in silence, finding a quiet comfort in the still room and the fire, the hot tea and fiery brandy they sipped so cautiously, and in each other. The coals

Parental influence and family networks

settled and blazed behind the bars of the grate; the gas in its white globe purred hoarsely.[80]

The image of the fire echoes a previous fireside image conjured in Charlotte's head as she imagined a comfortable life with Tom Ackroyd before her 'cheap defeat':[81]

> Everything in the world that had embittered and defeated her, Tom would shut out forever. It would be like coming in from the chill of a winter afternoon, coming in to the warmth and welcome of firelight, and shutting the door behind one.[82]

Although it is not located in a country house but in the nonetheless sheltering old pierhead house in Wapping, the fireside image provides the reader with a small shard of hope that, rather than struggling hopelessly and individually, together these three women might eventually lead fulfilling and free lives. More importantly, this is neither Ada's nor Margery's restrictive parental/marital home; it is a liminal urban space, and a home for characters on the edge of society: unmarried women and homosexual male dancers, surrounded on three sides by water. While it is firmly located in London's East End, it is also 'otherland', an extraordinary island of bohemia sandwiched between the working-class tenements and the industrial docks, and as such represents escape of a kind.

The novel, dealing with feminine disappointment and domesticity, is recognisably part of the interwar feminine middlebrow genre.[83] Yet its interesting structure and movement – each woman takes a different journey, Ada on foot, Charlotte in a car and Margery in a train, to reach the pierhead – and its examination of the 'new public woman' gives it a modernity that was recognised by the Prix Femina committee.[84] There are ongoing efforts by some literature scholars to question the distinctions between 'modernist' literature and the rest of the rich, vibrant narrative output of the early twentieth century.[85] These distinctions were, of course, successfully created by the modernists themselves and unquestioningly accepted by the academy, consigning to oblivion and the dusty shelves of second-hand bookshops so many interwar novels, the famously termed 'slaughterhouse of literature'.[86] *Faith, Hope and No Charity* would certainly be a useful exhibit in the case for reassessing overlooked commonalities between different narrative methods of this time.

An interwar literary prize committee deliberates

The Prix Femina-Vie Heureuse committee for novels published in 1935–36 shortlisted nine other books for consideration, pretty much all of them by writers now much better known and studied than Margaret Lane: *The Weather in the Streets* by Rosamond Lehmann, *A Gun for Sale* by Graham Greene, *Keep the Aspidistra Flying* by George Orwell, *Bird Alone* by Sean O'Faolain, *The Last Landfall* by Desmond Malone, *Summer Will Show* by Sylvia Townsend Warner, *The House of Women* by H. E. Bates, *The African Witch* by Joyce Cary and *Novel on Yellow Paper* by Stevie Smith. This was a strong line-up, and it is worth examining the committee's deliberations that finished with Margaret Lane's novel winning the 1,000 franc (£40) prize. The Prix Femina-Vie Heureuse prize was established in France by the publishers Hachette with two popular women's magazines in 1904, to encourage new authors and to be decided by a group of literary women. After the Armistice, as part of a general post-war effort to improve international relations across the continent, the prize was offered to other

Parental influence and family networks

European countries, and the inaugural English committee meeting was held at Bedford College, London, on 20 June 1919, chaired by the literary critic Professor Caroline Spurgeon.[87] Other founding members included Naomi Royde-Smith and the writers Rebecca West, Evelyn Sharp, Winifred Stephens, Ethel Clifford (Ethel Fisher Dilke) and Violet Hunt (Violet Hunt Hueffer). At its first meeting the committee stated that the establishment of the English version of the prize sprang from 'the movement that was taking place all over the world, and which was one of the results, one of the greatest and most miraculous results of the War, a drawing together of the intelligent and intellectual members of the community in every civilised nation'.[88]

As well as awarding the annual prize, the committee's main role was to foster strong ties between the literary women of England and France. The committee thus deliberately located itself in the post-war literary and cultural internationalism that would also include English PEN, and was grounded in the belief that nations with strong cultural ties and understanding would find it harder to go to war with each other. The English committee's criteria were that the winning novel should be a 'strong and imaginative' work, that the author should show promise for the future, and that there should be something in the novel that would reveal the 'true character and spirit' of Englishness to French readers. Two books were chosen from each year's British shortlist and sent to the French committee to decide which would be the ultimate winner of the British prize. The committee awarded its first prize in 1920 and its last in 1939, and as such it perfectly mapped and critiqued the literary history of the interwar years, awarding prizes to E. M. Forster, Virginia Woolf, Rose Macaulay, Cicely Hamilton, Radclyffe

Rebel women between the wars

Hall and Robert Graves among others, with an almost fifty-fifty gender balance among the prize winners.

The committee for the 1935–36 prize met in November and December 1935, and in April, October and December 1936. The chair was shared between the novelists Kate O'Brien and Margaret Kennedy, incoming and outgoing presidents respectively. Other members for this year included the artist Laura Anning Bell, the novelists Sylvia Lynd, Amabel Strachey and Netta Syrett, and the poet Ethel Clifford. Lehmann's novel was dismissed for being by an already well-established writer, although many on the committee agreed that it was one of the better ones in the selection. Similarly Cary's *The African Witch* was disqualified for not being a sufficiently 'English' topic. Other books were dismissed for their lack of literary merit. The committee agreed that Bates's *The House of Women* was 'not a patch' on his short stories. Ethel Clifford dismissed it as 'com[ing] into the category of dreary farm books', the agricultural middlebrow being a popular sub-genre during the interwar period.

One of the most outspoken contributors was the 70-year-old late Victorian popular author Netta Syrett. Her comments (most of which went unchallenged) illustrate how committees of this kind can be swayed by just one or two domineering characters. She described *Novel on Yellow Paper*, perhaps the most accomplished submission from a literary point of view, as 'a journal kept by a lunatic'. The novel's proposer, the novelist Margaret Kennedy, did not put up a fight, saying: 'I wouldn't mind it coming off. It is full of promise but not a Prize book. We should keep an eye on this author.' That *Novel on Yellow Paper*'s literary merit was obliquely recognised, but that it was not considered a 'Prize book', helps define what the committee

Parental influence and family networks

was looking for in its selections, favouring accessibility and straightforward narrative over playful innovation.

Syrett also dismissed Greene's and Orwell's novels. She said of Greene's *Gun for Sale*: 'I do think the details are so improbable. Especially the idea that they would choose an agent with a hair lip.' She was supported by Kennedy, who added: 'It is a bogus book. Intensely insincere.' Only Sylvia Lynd stuck up for Greene, telling the committee she thought him the most talented author on the list that year. The committee all agreed that Greene's *Stamboul Train*, considered for a prize five years previously, was a much better book. Syrett reserved her most caustic comments for Orwell's *Keep the Aspidistra Flying*, saying that 'It would take a genius to make a work of art out of this material and lacking this the book seems to me compounded of dirt, squalor and loose thinking.'[89] Lynd, although acknowledging Orwell's writing talent, said: 'As with all his other books he displays a most unpleasant personality.' Clifford agreed that although she found the novel and its protagonist 'tiresome', there was no doubting Orwell's distinction as a writer. Perhaps the committee had identified Orwell's own dislike of his second novel, which he refused to have reprinted in his own lifetime; perhaps the theme of a struggling literary life was too close for comfort. The novel was, however, allowed to go through to the final round of voting. Throughout the discussions, Margaret Lane's novel, though described as 'distinguished' and having been a pleasure to read, never raised much comment or opprobrium.

Personal animosity seems to have played its part in the committee's deliberations. Unable to attend one meeting, writer and committee member Amabel Strachey (the wife of the architect Clough Williams-Ellis) wrote in to suggest W. H. Auden and Christopher Isherwood's play *The Dog Beneath the Skin*, a bizarre choice both for being a play rather than a novel, and jointly authored. The critic and former suffragist E. M. Goodman acidly pointed out that 'Books suggested by Mrs Williams-Ellis never have done anything.'

In the final round of voting, the first-placed novel was Desmond Malone's fictionalised First World War memoir *The Last Landfall*, described by Kennedy as 'the best book on the list. It is beautifully written and the most moving and it stays in one's mind.' *Faith, Hope and No Charity* came second and went through to the final judging in France, where it was awarded the prize. *A Gun for Sale* and *Keep the Aspidistra Flying* came last.

From journalist to writer

Faith, Hope and No Charity marked a turning point in Lane's career. Not only did it win the Prix Femina prize, but it gained her the representation of literary agent Laurence Pollinger of Pearn, Pollinger and Higham, who secured a three-book deal with her publisher Heinemann. The £300 advance for her second novel, *At Last the Island* (1938), and £750 for each of the next two novels allowed her to leave her job at the *Daily Mail* in 1938 and take up literature full time.[90] She had already embarked on what would be her first biography, of the journalist-turned-thriller-writer Edgar Wallace, and the narrative she constructed for his life, that of mass-produced craftsmanship preventing careful artistry, acted like a cautionary tale on her. She had no desire for Wallace's 'facile rapidity', which, she judged, destroyed his style:

> Years of newspaper work, in which speedy delivery had been essential and the quick death of everything he wrote inevitable, had ingrained in him the habit of writing crisply, superficially,

Parental influence and family networks

and for the moment ... one is tempted to think that, differently circumstanced, he might have developed into a serious artist.[91]

In addition, while journalism had brought her experience and interest and had launched her career, she always preferred book writing, as she wrote later:

> I need a book to give my life impetus. Everyone needs the illusion of creative effort ... You only have to lift the lid of your subconscious and it's all there: all the evil you depict in your bad characters must be inside you somewhere. Your upbringing has made you repress it, but I know the seeds of my evil characters are within me. So every novel is a form of self-exploration.[92]

Edgar Wallace: The Biography of a Phenomenon (1938) brought her more success. The bookshop Foyles made it their book of the month for December 1939, ordering 120,000 copies, for which Lane received 1½d per copy.[93] Lane combined meticulous research with compelling storytelling and the book, like its subject, was an instant best-seller. She evoked sympathy for her subject, his struggles and setbacks, even though the reader is left with the unavoidable impression that Lane disapproved of Wallace's recklessness and the slapdash approach to his work that earned him two libel writs and several sackings. She certainly sympathised, perhaps because she recognised it in herself, with his determination to make something of his life:

> Dick [Wallace] would take up his Collins Large Type Pronouncing Dictionary and go up to the top of Zig Zag Hill behind the town, where he could stare out across the bright waters of the bay and learn new words for the adornment of his poetry ... He was determined to improve himself and Collins' Pocket Dictionary was the best means to his hand; he went through it page by page, enjoying the words and the sense of power they gave him.[94]

Rebel women between the wars

Her next biography, of Beatrix Potter, would prove more challenging, particularly with regard to access to her subject, who she first approached in 1939, 'when I was very sharply sent about my business'.[95] Undaunted, Lane approached Frederick Warne, Potter's publisher, who told her that 'nobody must ever be allowed to write her a letter'. Lane did so anyway, describing the rebuff as 'a challenge to ingenuity', and was rewarded with 'the rudest letter' mentioned at the beginning of this chapter. Only after Potter's death in 1943 was Lane able to obtain enough material through her widower, who received Lane with a 'trembling blend of terror and courtesy', her research resulting in one of Lane's most admired books, *The Tale of Beatrix Potter* (1946).

* * *

In this chapter we have seen how family networks benefit aspirants in two distinct ways: first, a familiarity with Fleet Street from childhood meant that, although a woman and still certainly an outsider, Margaret Lane also felt comfortable in and indeed excited by the energy and busyness of a newsroom. That her father was one of these suited men behind a great desk must surely have removed some of the terror and feelings of being an impostor. Secondly, her father was able to use his influence to help her find her first position. When she joined the *Daily Mail* and the Northcliffe papers, where her father was now a senior editor, her surname would have been familiar to many of her colleagues in Fleet Street, and while she suffered from sexual harassment in the newsroom, her robust way of dealing with it again might have stemmed from her knowledge that a powerful father belonged to the same organisation as she. She

Parental influence and family networks

also worked ferociously hard, and her daughter Selina Hastings remembers her mother, who did not have 'a room of her own', writing for hours and hours at her little desk in the corner of the family drawing room.

While a willingness to transgress certainly played a role in Lane's ability to capitalise on her fortunate fatherly connection, she still maintained, through her famous charm, politesse and neat and feminine presentation, many of the 'correct' gendered qualities expected of a woman in the interwar years.[96] In the next chapter we will see a further example of deliberate transgression, though in this case one that departed greatly from correct gendered behaviour.

Notes

1 Margaret Lane, 'A Woman Invades the Devonshire Club', *Daily Mail*, 28 April 1933, p. 10.
2 'The Devonshire Club: Provision for Lady Guests', *The Times*, 4 October 1932, p. 17.
3 'Miss Margaret Lane Joins the *Daily Mail*', *Daily Mail*, 21 November 1932, p. 11.
4 Margaret Lane, 'St Hugh's Coll', *SSC Magazine*, July 1926, pp. 14–15, Margaret Lane Papers, St Hugh's College, Oxford (ML.SH).
5 Evans 2019: 131–3 gives a good account of late Victorian and early twentieth-century men's clubs.
6 *The Newspaper World*, 19 November 1932, p. 15.
7 An account of Margaret Lane's activities in Evarts is in Ross 1936: 213; there are multiple sources for the events in Evarts during May 1931.
8 The drunken pilot incident is recounted by Selina Hastings (interviewed 6 June 2018). The interview with Magda Goebbels, 'Nazi Creed for Women: Marriage First but Beauty is a Duty', was published in the *Daily Mail*, 3 July 1933, pp. 11–12.
9 Lane 1966: 207.
10 Kipling 2008: 30.

11 Margaret Lane, 'Gentlemen of the Press: Meet an English Sob Sister', *Daily Express*, 15 March 1932, p. 3.
12 Bibliographical note, *The Newspaper World*, 18 November 1932, p. 15.
13 Interview with Margaret Lane's daughter, Selina Hastings.
14 Cox and Mowatt 2014: 52.
15 'Journalist and Author', *Yorkshire Post*, 31 January 1936.
16 Peggy [Margaret] Lane, 'The Hub', *SSC Magazine*, October 1922, pp. 10–11.
17 Lane 1965: 506.
18 Franklin 1979: 55.
19 Letter from A. M. Watling to Margaret Lane, 30 October 1966 and 13 November 1966, MLSH.
20 Lane 1966: 221.
21 Lane 1966: 221.
22 Margaret Lane, 'A Mother Who Played at Ghosts', *Evening Standard*, 1 March 1965, p. 10.
23 Ibid.
24 Lane 1966: 227.
25 Lane 1966: 227.
26 Lane 1966: 227.
27 This 'deviance' has been shown in other studies, for example in Melville Currell's study of women MPs, *Political Woman* (1974).
28 Balston 1994: 3–7.
29 Balston 1994: 127.
30 Lane, 'St Hugh's Coll', *SSC Magazine*, July 1926, pp. 14–15.
31 See Green 1976, and, as a corrective, Stannard 1978: 85–90.
32 Lane 1935: 185–6.
33 In her archive at St Hugh's there is a marvellous comic poem mocking aristocratic pretension and inspired by a clearly uncomfortable visit to Eske Castle in Donegal. The poem is undated but probably relates to the time she eloped to Ireland with Viscount Hastings, during the early years of the Second World War:

> 'Eske Castle, County Donegal' (Now a Select Hotel):
> Gothic structure
> bold cement
> Uphold the pretentious battlement …
> Above in large and cheerless cases

Parental influence and family networks

>   Salmon display despondent faces ...
>   (The radiator on the stair
>   Is not for drying underwear ...
>   The lady and the desk laments
>   The social gaffes of residents ...
>   Also when conversation fails
>   Edward the Seventh as Prince of Wales
>   And calms the gentlewomen's fears
>   With faded photographs of peers ...
>   How many stags have met their doom
>   To ornament the dining room ...
>   Beneath their calm disdainful faces
>   Abashed we meekly take our places ...
>   Behold this deep and spacious bath
>   The boring evening's aftermath,
>   Its marble sides, its taps of brass
>   Which only tepid water pass ...
>   O surely grandeur counts for much,
>   Though everything's too cold to touch?

   For more on the 'Red Earl', see Hastings 2014.
34 Lane 1927a; 1927b.
35 Franklin 1979: 54.
36 Interview with Selina Hastings.
37 Brooks 1998: 51. Lane and Blumenfeld were old friends, having worked together on various Fleet Street papers for the previous twenty years (Griffiths 2006: 38–41).
38 Beaverbrook's private papers contain several memos to his editors about what his newspapers missed in comparison to the *Daily Mail*; see, for example, letter to Ralph Blumenfeld, 8 August 1929, asking him to give Tom Clarke, the son of author and agricultural expert Sir Ernest Clarke, an interview for a possible job, BBK/H/62.
39 Beaverbrook Papers, staff salary information, BBK/H/19.
40 Review of *Edgar Wallace* (no date; 1938) in Add.MS8900, PFVH.
41 Gopsill and Neale 2007: 36–40, 75–6.
42 Emilie Peacocke began her career on the *Northern Echo* but became women's page editor of the *Daily Telegraph* and wrote a seminal handbook, *Journalism for Women* (1936); for details of Rachel Beer, see

Koren and Negev 2011; Mary Stott, who became celebrated editor of the *Guardian* women's page, wrote entertainingly of her early years in journalism in her memoir *Before I Go* (1985).
43 Edy 2017: 21.
44 See, for example, Laband and Lentz 1992; in many working-class trades, including mining, dockers and printers, jobs were often passed down from father to son.
45 For politics, see Melville Currell's analysis of the first women MPs in Britain (1974), and for academia, see Pickles 2001, who analysed how the first women academics in Australia, Canada and New Zealand obtained their positions.
46 There is an article on Garrod's discovery of Neanderthal skull fragments in Gibraltar in *The Oxford Magazine*, 17 June 1926, p. 569; biographical details from Bar-Yosef and Callender 2004.
47 Pickles 2001: 275.
48 Pickles 2001: 275.
49 Nancy Astor stood for Parliament after her husband Waldorf was elevated to the peerage and was MP from 1919 to 1945. For a discussion of 'male equivalence' and the 'politicised family' in early women MPs, see Currell 1974: esp. 164–72.
50 Currell 1974: 58.
51 For details on Harriette Chick's career, see Carpenter 2008; for Evelyn Cheesman, see her memoir, *Things Worth While* (1958); see also Laracy 2013, and 'Woman Collects 42,000 Insects', *News Chronicle*, 16 June 1934.
52 Margaret Lane, from the text of a speech given to Society of Authors, 9 November 1937, MLSH.
53 Franklin 1979: 55; 'Writing Best Sellers', press cutting (no title or date; 1939), PFVH; 'Notes and News', *The Newspaper World*, 7 November 1931, p. 15.
54 Robert Pitman, 'New Books' (no date), MLSH.
55 Margaret Lane, 'America is so Proud of Synthetic Gin Parties', *Daily Express*, 3 October 1931, p. 3.
56 Margaret Lane, 'Capone Faces his Judge', *Daily Express*, 7 October 1931, p. 3.
57 Margaret Lane, 'Capone's Polite Trial', *Daily Express*, 15 October 1931, p. 3.
58 Margaret Lane, 'Puzzle of Capone Guilty Verdict', *Daily Express*, 19 October 1931, pp. 1–2.

Parental influence and family networks

59 Margaret Lane, 'Can Scarface Escape Going to Prison?', *Daily Express*, 20 October 1931, p. 2.
60 Interview with Margaret Lane's daughter, Selina Hastings.
61 There is a deep and wide literature on sexual harassment in the workplace, particularly in sectors where women are under-represented or perceived to be making inroads in traditionally masculine territory. See, among others, MacKinnon 1979; Fitzgerald 2017.
62 See, for example, Fiske and Glick 1995.
63 See, for example, 'Spinsters Must Have Pensions, Declares Margaret Lane', *Daily Mail*, 18 February 1938, p. 12; 'BBC Television Girls "Thrilled with Our Job", but "Hush Hush" about Salaries', *Daily Mail*, 14 May 1936, p. 11; 'Manners and Morals of University Women', *Daily Mail*, 3 February 1937, p. 10.
64 Margaret Lane, 'Dedicatory', in *Faith, Hope and No Charity* (1935: n.p.); details of Pearl Binder's time at Whitechapel thanks to her daughter, Josephine Gladstone. Binder's archives are held with the MSS Lord Elwyn-Jones, Flintshire Record Office.
65 Franklin 1979: 56.
66 Franklin 1979: 56.
67 For discussions of Victorian writers' negotiations between literature and journalism see for example McDonald 1997; Liddle 2009; Rubery 2009. For a detailed account of how individual writers and journalists negotiated the widening gulf between literature and journalism between 1900 and 1939, see Lonsdale 2016: chs 1–4.
68 See Collier 2006.
69 Margaret Lane, from the text of a speech given to Society of Authors, 9 November 1937, MLSH; the 'sentimental' quote is from Stephen McKenna's novel *Sonia* (1917), satirising literary and political life during the First World War.
70 Lane Margaret, Society of Authors speech, 1937, MLSH.
71 Virginia Woolf won the Prix Femina with *To the Lighthouse* in 1928, E. M. Forster with *A Passage to India* in 1925.
72 Light 1991: 6.
73 Burke 1932: 23.
74 Binder 1935: 19–20.
75 See, for example, 'A Remarkable First Novel', *Gloucestershire Echo*, 8 October 1935: 'The detail has something of the Arnold Bennett quality … One is tempted to say of *Faith Hope and No Charity* that it is a great novel.'

76 Gardiner 2010: xiii.
77 Lane 1935: 225–6.
78 Lane 1935: 188.
79 Lane 1935: 169.
80 Lane 1935: 357.
81 Lane 1935: 339.
82 Lane 1935: 182.
83 For a discussion of 'feminine disappointment' in the interwar domestic middlebrow novel, see Hinds 2009.
84 For a discussion of the 'new public woman' in literature, see Evans 2019.
85 See, for example, Snyder 2008; Evans 2019.
86 Virginia Woolf's famous essay 'Mr Bennett and Mrs Brown' (1924) is often seen as the starting point for these distinctions, although the essay itself puts the date of the start of these changes 'on or about' December 1910. For the 'slaughterhouse of literature', see Moretti 2000.
87 Ad 8900, PFVH.
88 Ibid.
89 Ibid.
90 Contractual details from Penguin Random House archives, with particular thanks to Kirby Smith, senior archive assistant.
91 Lane 1939: 281.
92 Margaret Lane, 'Margaret Lane', *Illustrated London News*, 18 January 1969, p. 21.
93 Penguin Random House archives.
94 Lane 1939: 76–7.
95 Lane 1966: 206.
96 Many newspaper descriptions of her attending public functions after 1935 describe, approvingly, her 'slim figure', 'chestnut hair with its quaint curled fringe' and feminine attire.

6
Rejecting the feminine

I have discovered, through bitter experience, that a would-be engineer must have a wide knowledge beyond the art of slide rules, micrometers and permutations, etc. It is just as essential to her career to know how to soothe turbulent landladies, to know the ways and habits of a 'penny in the slot' gas machine, to know the art of keeping clean without the aid of hot water, and on half days and holidays she must be able to conform to the amusements of the neighbourhood in adopting a wild enthusiasm for watching Rugby matches ... Even after the novelty of a totally unique existence has worn off, when the fascination of wearing trouser overalls is forgotten because familiarity has bred contempt, when the first delight in actually helping in engineering construction has become a matter of fact, when everything looks rather hard and unappetising, all the same, you know you would hate to give it up ... there is something strangely fascinating in the hum of the machinery: it is a soothing sound, perhaps it is melodious after all. Even an engine has a stately way of being picturesque and the smell of hot oil – an old bête noire soon becomes as familiar as the varied odours of the many fish and chip shops you pass on your way to your lodgings. Funny life – but it grips![1]

Rebel women between the wars

Claudia Parsons, the author of this article, published in 1921 in the *Woman Engineer*, was 19 years old and one of just three women among 200 men to enrol in the first post-war diploma-level engineering course at Loughborough Technical College in the autumn of 1919.[2] Women, and men classed as medically unfit, had been taken on training courses and as apprentices to enable them to work in munitions factories during the First World War, giving many young working-class women skills and opportunities they had never dreamed of. After the Armistice, however, most factories and technical colleges, under pressure from unions, and also giving priority to soldiers returning to complete interrupted studies and apprenticeships, ceased training women. Loughborough, which had trained nearly 1,400 women in milling, gauge making and welding between 1915 and 1918, was the one further education college where a woman serious about a career in engineering could study for a diploma leading to a BSc course in engineering after the Armistice.[3] The Women's Engineering Society was founded in 1919 to protect the right to work of all women employed in the engineering trades during the war, who were being routinely dismissed to make way for returning male engineers under the government's Restoration of Pre-War Practices Act.

The society's magazine, the *Woman Engineer*, was one of several professional women's magazines to be launched in response to this pressure on women to 'return to home and duty' during the early 1920s.[4] The magazine was edited by the society's secretary, Caroline Haslett, an engineer who had worked at the Cochran Boiler Company in Dumfries and Galloway during the war and who, with Lady Rhondda, was one of the first executive members of the influential feminist Six Point Group.[5] The *Woman Engineer*'s launch issue, published

Rejecting the feminine

in December 1919, declared the pressing need for the magazine to encourage and stimulate women interested in engineering and as an instrument to help towards 'removing the prejudices and artificial restrictions which now prevent women from taking up engineering as a trade or profession'.[6] Quoting Olive Schreiner's foundational book *Woman and Labour* (1911), which demanded equality of opportunity for women, the first issue's editorial described the position of women engineers as 'hopeless'. Despite this gloomy opening editorial, the magazine contained useful articles on engineering jobs still open to women, and reports by women engineers about their work. On the whole, however, the content was forbiddingly dry, dominated by lengthy technical pieces, line drawings of machinery and a series 'Views of Distinguished Engineers' authored by men.

Claudia Parsons' personal article was an attempt by the young engineering student to cheer the *Woman Engineer* up.

> It is a bit serious. I fear some day some kindred spirit to mine will come along aspiring to be an engineer and looking within these pages will tremble from head to foot and say, 'This is no profession for me. Behold these people are all bright and brilliant, absolute cheek for me to take it up.'[7]

Parsons' article unusually tried to express what it *felt* like to be a woman in a wholly male-dominated industry: wearing gunmetal grey 'trouser overalls', living in boarding houses run by suspicious landladies, with the only weekend entertainment geared towards male workers. The article captures the loneliness of being an outsider, but also the quiet pride and fascination in leading this 'totally unique existence' and the pleasure of following one's dream. It must have been a revelation to young women engineers to see themselves thus represented on the printed page.

Representations of munitions girls during the First World War had been aimed at helping the nation accept the idea of women doing traditional men's jobs, and at inspiring and encouraging women to 'do their bit'. The most famous image is the painting *The Munition Girls* by Stanhope Forbes (1918), presenting weary yet surprisingly clean young women illuminated by brightly burning furnaces at the Kilnhurst Steelworks in Rotherham. The image is idealised: not a drop of sweat or smear of grease can be seen either on the women's brows or overalls, and there is an unreal sense of calm and order to the scene. Prior to this, the *Daily Mail* had carried an article in 1917, authored by an anonymous factory welfare supervisor, that celebrated munitions workers in all their sweaty, smelly reality, a surprisingly poetic and highly unusual image for a popular newspaper to present:

> It was at the end of the night shift in a munitions factory. Through the open door of the workshop I could see the meagre grey light of a winter's morning, and the rain falling like threads of steel – the cold raw wind driving in cut like a knife across the vitiated air, tainted with the smell of stale food, sweat and fumes from the braziers we had breathed all night … the smell of fruit, the smell of cough lozenges, the musty smell of damp clothes steaming in the warmth of the gas overhead, cheap scent and cigarette smoke … an icy draught playing around our swollen feet …[8]

Parsons' article, published some four years later, was an attempt to marry this realism with encouragement to women floundering before the obstacles they faced, 'the *man-made* constraint' as Parsons described it.[9] While during the war women's

Rejecting the feminine

Figure 9 Stanhope Forbes, *The Munition Girls* (1918)

labour in traditionally male workplaces had been accepted because it was needed, as Parsons was writing her article most women engaged during the war in traditionally male employment had been dismissed. The image of the plucky women ambulance drivers, bus conductors and aeronautical engineers as celebrated in the popular press during the war had been replaced by calls for women to return either to middle-class domesticity or domestic service from those same newspapers.[10]

Throughout her life, Parsons would endeavour to explain to women the pleasures, as she saw them, of engineering, particularly automobile engineering. Hard-won skills obtained in Loughborough's workshops would bring her not only employment through the 1920s and 1930s as a chauffeur but also the

Rebel women between the wars

freedom to travel, which brought her adventures across interwar Europe and, in 1937–38, the opportunity to circumnavigate the world, much of the time alone, by car, boat and train.

Parsons' determination to acquire engineering skills, drive a motor car and travel alone broke multiple social rules. She did not merely push at the boundaries of acceptable feminine behaviour, she rejected them altogether. The realm of engineering was an almost exclusively masculine one and the car, since its development in the late nineteenth century, had been identified with technical and itinerant masculinity: this new and powerfully liberating technology associated with speed, adventure and dominion over time and space had from the start been a wholly male fiefdom, with women, if ever they did enter a car, firmly in the passengers' seats.[11] This bias against women drivers – the butt of countless jokes down the decades – lasted well into the twentieth century, with only 13 per cent of women holding a driving licence as late as the 1960s (compared to 56 per cent of men). When the first female driving-test examiners began work in the late 1930s, an enormous controversy emerged, whipped up by the magazine *Autocar* and leading to questions in the House of Commons, over whether women should be allowed to examine men.[12]

Women traveller-explorers were, if anything, more suspect than women drivers. From Odysseus, Aeneas and Gilgamesh, the myth of the heroic male traveller covering vast distances away from home as a means of gaining immortality has associated mobility with masculinity; the myths were then embedded in waves of explorers from Marco Polo to Roald Amundsen, Captain Cook to David Livingstone, conquering and often enslaving virgin territory. Conversely, itinerant women, from street walkers to Little Red Riding Hood, have been associated

Rejecting the feminine

with immoral behaviour and the risk of abduction and rape.[13] While the Victorian and Edwardian periods were characterised by the emergence of the woman explorer-adventurer, she was always wealthy, often aristocratic and usually travelling in groups with male companions; even when claiming in fêted memoirs to have travelled alone, she was escorted by unacknowledged armies of native bearers, mechanics and servants. Parsons spent long periods of her travels actually alone, but as we will see, she would be the focus of men's persistent attempts to 'correct' her behaviour, whether by anonymously buying her a berth in first class to put her out of sight of multiple third-class eyes, offering her alternative, private transport, or buying her garments to cover herself with. Parsons deliberately rejected marriage, knowing that in the 1920s and 1930s it would mean restraint, and believing that most husbands 'thought women's whole purpose in life was to work for men'.[14]

As we have seen, during the interwar years women were making steady, incremental progress in moving into public life, even if that progress came about through socially transgressive actions, subterfuge or 'unwomanly' courage (Margaret Lane, Francesca Wilson, and Shiela Grant Duff, respectively). However, there was also a sense that certain codes of behaviour, such as the way they dressed and the public selves they presented – humanitarian, writer, teacher, magazine editor – still respected accepted feminine identities. This cautious approach has been observed in other interwar studies of women taking their place in the public sphere for the first time, with women political activists who joined parties after 1918, for example, taking on the role of fundraising organiser, envelope filler and tea and cake maker for committee meetings rather than more public roles.[15] But if women were ever to press forward on all fronts, some would have to go where no woman had gone before and establish a foothold in territory only ever previously occupied by men. This chapter presents Claudia Parsons, who spent many years tearing up the gender rule book in her pursuit of a life as an engineer, motorist and adventurer, and in so doing it also examines attitudes towards, and representations of, the woman traveller.

'I must not watch the puddings coming in'

Claudia Parsons was born in the hot-season hill station of Simla (now Shimla) in northern India, in August 1900, in a modest bungalow with 'thick walls and deep verandahs', cooled by the 'rhythmic swish of the punkah'.[16] Her father was a major in the Indian army, and her mother was from a family that had spent generations in the service of the East India Company: the were a typical Anglo-Indian family, not hugely wealthy but certainly rich enough to have native servants, one of whom, the ayah, fed Claudia's older sister Betty with opium in an attempt to make her sleep.[17] Three-year-old Betty became so ill that their mother took her and Claudia, who was only two, back home to England, where the girls were looked after by a grandmother and aunt in Guildford; their mother returned to India to be with their father. Betty and Claudia's childhood then took on the pattern of that of many so-called 'Raj orphans', perhaps most famously epitomised in Rudyard Kipling's lonely and neglected early days: separated from parents with only the random and unreliable eyes of distant relatives upon them.[18] This sense of abandonment in the Parsons girls was reinforced after the birth of a third daughter, Avis, who stayed in India with her parents.

Rejecting the feminine

Aunt Muriel, who was in her late twenties when the two little girls were deposited with her, was prone to towering rages, black moods, shouting and cruelty. In her memoir Parsons attempted to be as loyal as possible: 'Her aim was to turn us out obedient, tidy, truthful ... one covered up injury or hurt ... when she was in a good mood we did in fact enjoy our aunt's company.'[19] However, much of her childhood was unhappy. The girls were educated at home by a 'conscientious' governess and were made repeatedly to write lines by Aunt Muriel when 'naughty'. Parsons kept these exercise books well into her nineties, recording in her memoir the pages of lines she had to copy out: 'I must not slam the door or I am punished' and 'I must not watch the puddings coming in', this latter denoting the emphasis on self-denial and repression in the Guildford house.[20]

The young Claudia began to show an interest and expertise in rudimentary craft and engineering skills: she asked for and was given a small carpentry set when she was seven, and erected a 'water garden' by connecting piping from the lavatory cistern to a flower bed, held together with plasticine; when she was nine she began riding a cousin's bicycle, revelling in the freedom it brought her, venturing out of the front garden and on to the street – which brought her severe punishment when caught – learning how to mend punctures and replace chains. At the age of 14, as the First World War broke out, Parsons was sent to boarding school in Hertfordshire; in her memoir she records that while she was good at mathematics, and while she had always loved composition, she struggled with literature and history. She was pronouncedly left-handed but was forced to write right-handed, which, she believed, left her a poor speller and rather clumsy. In the summer of her eighteenth birthday she missed matriculation, the equivalent of A levels, due to a double attack of tonsillitis and a severe bout of the skin infection erysipelas on her head.[21] The option of going to university was thus closed to her. Still fascinated by machinery, however, she attended evening classes on auto-cycle engines at Guildford Technical School, convincing her now widowed mother, who had returned from India with Avis, to allow her to go to Loughborough to study on the new engineering diploma. The wider family was scandalised at the thought of Claudia attending a mostly male college and her mother admitted that she would never have been allowed to attend had her father been alive.[22] In addition, now aged 21, Parsons received £16 a quarter from her father's pension, enough to keep her at Loughborough.[23]

Absent fathers

The crucial role that the absence or death of a father played in endowing a woman with the energy to achieve exit velocity from the domestic sphere has been noted earlier in this book: both Edith Shackleton's and Alison Settle's fathers had abandoned them while they were children; Shiela Grant Duff's and Claudia Parsons' fathers died while they were young; and we will see later that Una Marson also lost her father as a child. Leah Manning lived apart from her father from childhood; the Australian author Kylie Tennant deliberately abandoned her own family at the age of 18 to escape patriarchal oppression. By contrast, Francesca Wilson, Stella Martin and Margaret Lane had unusually supportive and indulgent fathers – Lane's was particularly keen she should earn a living, Martin's father was plagued by lifelong financial worries and Naomi

Rejecting the feminine

Royde-Smith's father, having been ruined in business, had no option but to allow his talented daughter to leave the family home to find employment.[24] Only one woman in this study, Dorothy Pilley, had a father who can be considered to have been the traditional Victorian patriarch, successful in keeping his daughter under-educated and at home. As we have seen from Pilley's diaries, this repression of a spirited young woman wrought severe emotional and physical harm and may well have played a part in propelling her, almost beyond human endurance, to scale unclimbed peaks.

While only a decade or two earlier the loss of a father might well have meant disaster for a young woman, the social and economic context of the 1920s and 1930s meant that many were able to take up employment and educational opportunities that would not have been open to them even twenty years earlier. Another major result of losing a father was that mothers often had to step in and become the head of the family, taking decisions on money and education (as in the case of Parsons) that might well have been different to those of their husbands. Mothers and grandmothers would then become strong role models of independent womanhood for the younger women, often transforming, out of necessity, from a passive creatures confined to the domestic sphere to financially active agents. After Shiela Grant Duff's father died, for example, her maternal grandmother, a strong-willed and outspoken woman, took a much more active role in her grandchildren's lives. For Alison Settle, widowed with two young children, the experience of having been abandoned by her own father and seeing her mother coping on her own gave her the resolve and inner strength to take on the editorship of *Vogue* as a means of protecting her children's economic security.

Rebel women between the wars

This kind of 'critical life experience' was common to many activist women of the early twentieth century. In her study of women in leadership roles in Australian unions before the Second World War, for example, Frances Raelene finds an unusually high number of women in the upper echelons of the notoriously macho Australian unions who had lost a father.[25] Raelene quotes machinist Lesbia Keogh, better known as the poet Lesbia Harford, who became a union executive on the Victorian Wages Board during the interwar years. Harford's father deserted his family when she was 12, and in a poem she attributed her courage and ability to think independently to that potentially disastrous moment:

> For since no male
> Has ruled me, or has fed
> I think my own thoughts
> In my woman's head.[26]

While the emotional impact of losing a parent might well have had a disabling effect, it might have been that for some women there was also, within that loss, an impetus to resist reliance on a male breadwinner, to reject submission to gendered divisions of labour and to learn to take responsibility for the direction of one's life at a younger age. In the case of Parsons, we can see that she embraced all these options.

Writing and engineering at Loughborough

Soon after beginning her studies, Parsons began contributing both to the *Woman Engineer* and *The Limit*, the Loughborough College magazine. Writing, as we have seen for all the women in this book, offered a means of escape and expression. Claudia

Rejecting the feminine

and her older sister Betty from an early age had sought escape from their aunt's dark moods in the world of the imagination, telling each other stories. At the age of nine Claudia began producing her own magazine, *The Jester* (with a readership of two), as well as writing a steady stream of stories and plays. Betty would later become a published novelist: 'Writing was almost a disease in the Parsons family.'[27] Indeed, writing for public platforms would not only give Claudia Parsons a voice but the financial means for travel: the £156 royalty payment received in 1936 for her novel *Brighter Bondage* funded the start of her journey round the world; writing articles and short stories for publications including *The Bystander*, *Japan Times* and *Calcutta Times*, with spasmodic cheques arriving at *postes restantes* across the globe, would allow her to continue travelling.[28]

Parsons threw herself into the life of the college even though she was in a tiny and much-observed minority – the arrival of women in autumn 1919 was announced in the college magazine with the headline: 'New Students not all Men!' The article went on to apply conditions to women's participation: 'the male sex will have no cause to complain' as long as the women showed 'the same purposeful energy' as those who trained for munitions work during the war.[29] Parsons' college activities show her to have been an active joiner-upper, willing to try her hand at almost anything. She established the Midlands branch of the Women's Engineering Society at the college, was elected to the social committee of the College Union, joined the newly formed Stage Society as secretary and took part in debates for the Literary and Debating Society. She won a large majority opposing the motion 'That Women should not Smoke'. She also joined the college Burlesques Society, dancing the lead

Figure 10 Claudia Parsons, c. 1920s

role in a production called *The Enchantress*, and helped set up a local branch of the Workers' Educational Association at the college.[30] Her contributions to *The Limit* reveal her as a humorous and skilful writer, unafraid to criticise the college authorities and even *The Limit*'s own editorial board, made of up of college masters.[31]

Parsons achieved a pass diploma in the summer of 1922, and signed her name on the Roll of Graduates in 1923.[32] As an interesting side-note, and possibly evidence of prejudice

Rejecting the feminine

against women students, Parsons and her friend Dorothea Travers, the only other woman studying for the automobile engineering exam in May 1921, were suspected of cheating and an investigation was undertaken by the qualifying body, the Institution of Automobile Engineers. Notes from the Institution exam committee record that 'In the case of the papers of Miss D Travers and Miss C Parsons, both of Loughborough, the examiners found that in one question the wording of the answer was practically identical.'[33] Parsons was suspected of having copied Travers's paper and, combined with her low marks, she failed the exam; Travers passed. No other records relating to this incident exist and Parsons went on to achieve her diploma in her final year. There is, however, a short story by Parsons published in the April 1922 issue of *The Limit* which could be an oblique reference. In the story, 'History of a Guileless Student, or, Tossed on the World', the unnamed narrator, an engineering student, has committed some ill-defined crime. She is sent to see 'the Great Man – (Hons. B.Sc., London)' in his office: 'I fought my way past the amanuensis, Dictaphone, theodolite and protoplasm. There sat the Great Man. With water-cooled slide rule in hand and table of Havasine and Covers beside him, he made a few rapid calculations.'[34] The narrator is doomed to be expelled, 'never again to take laminas of triangles and find their moments of inertia, never again to eat chocolate biscuits in the Canteen'. She is offered a last-minute reprieve, however, by the Student Representative Committee, and eventually, after submitting to a series of gruelling panels chaired by increasingly elite judges, the last being the King, she is readmitted. Whatever its relevance to her failing her exam, this and other contributions show that while Parsons enjoyed the social side of Loughborough and the company of other students, she cared little for the college authorities and what she clearly saw as a fusty, hierarchical structure.

Despite the diploma, finding a job in a traditional engineering workshop proved impossible.[35] 'I had brandished my Loughborough diploma round local garages, hoping to be taken on as assistant, to find them suffering a surfeit of applicants', she recorded in her memoir.[36] This 'surfeit of applicants' in 1925 may well have been the result of qualified men returning to civilian work or, more plausibly, a way of rejecting her application from an industry that was vigorously resisting female encroachment. Car ownership, although still at low levels, was growing exponentially throughout the 1920s and automobile mechanics and other related services were rapidly expanding.[37] During the war, a handful of mostly upper-class women had distinguished themselves driving ambulances in France, and a few women-run garages and chauffeur services catering for the wealthy and leisured flourished, most notably the Honourable Gabrielle Borthwick's Ladies' Automobile Workshops in Piccadilly.[38] In the immediate post-war years, women motorists were briefly glamorous and fashionable; in 1918 *The Woman's Motor Manual*, featuring on the cover a cheerful, uniformed young woman driving a pair of moustachioed generals, promised plentiful work for the woman 'chauffeuse' as long as she possessed a 'fairly muscular physique' capable of 'cranking up, washing a car and fitting tyres'.[39] The clean-lined uniforms and practical gabardine and leather driving coats advertised for lady motorists also caught the spirit of the age.[40] A concerted pushback, however, from drivers' organisations, engineering unions and motoring media soon saw women mechanics and drivers associated strongly with immorality, deviance and lesbianism.[41] Despite this, women chauffeurs and chauffeur-companions were in demand from wealthy widows and younger unmarried women wishing to avoid the innuendo and ribald jokes associated with male chauffeurs.[42]

The *Woman Engineer* and interwar women's professional magazines

Through all these obstacles, the *Woman Engineer* was stolidly and reliably published once a quarter, informing a growing readership of the slow and hard-won gains made by fellow members and other women engineers. The magazine's character and fortunes were closely tied to the Women's Engineering Society, and early committee meeting notes show that it stumbled and nearly fell several times during the 1920s and 1930s as the society's funds teetered precariously.[43] The founding members were wives of senior engineers and the society survived on donations from the richest of these. Society membership rose from the inaugural group of 20, which met in March 1919, to 337 in January 1922.[44] A note of the magazine sub-committee held in March 1921 puts the circulation of the magazine at 1,000 copies, of which half were paid for and half distributed freely to libraries and workplaces. The magazine rarely paid for itself and nearly closed on a number of occasions; at one point, a merger with the feminist magazine the *Woman's Leader* was proposed, in order to sustain it; however, this was rejected on the grounds that the two magazines' aims differed too widely. The *Woman Engineer* did survive, unlike many interwar women's feminist and professional magazines, and is still published today.

The first issue, published in December 1919, was eight pages long and priced at 3d, with a simple two-column layout and only one photographic image. The price rose to 4d in its third, ten-page issue. By its sixth issue it was 20 pages long, priced at 6d and included advertisements, book reviews, a letters page and several regular features such as 'Notes and News' and 'Members' Activities', two upbeat columns on women's achievements in education, technical expertise and motoring and aviation. These columns reported, for example, 'To one of our members, Miss W. L. Hackett, belongs the distinction of winning the Bowen Scholarship for Electrical Engineering at Birmingham University, and of being the first girl to achieve this success' and 'Miss Amy Johnson, a twenty-two year old member of the London Aeroplane Club, is the first woman to gain an Air Ministry ground engineer's license.'[45] The entire September 1925 issue was dedicated to reproducing papers from the first International Conference of Women in Science, Industry and Commerce, held at the British Empire Exhibition at Wembley in July 1925.

Depressingly, the magazine also reported on the many cases brought by manufacturing unions, particularly the Amalgamated Society of Engineers, against firms that continued to employ women after the passing of the Restoration of Pre-War Practices Act. It kept readers informed about other legislation and regulations affecting women's employment prospects, particularly the International Labour Organisation's (ILO) Night Work Convention, passed at the first ILO Conference in Washington in 1919, which effectively banned all women from working night shifts in factories from 10 p.m. to 5 a.m. Ostensibly devised to protect women, it was in fact part of a major pushback from the almost entirely male ILO to restrict women's work opportunities after the war.[46] Sweden refused to ratify the Convention, under pressure from feminist organisations, but the UK did, although from 1931 the British

Rejecting the feminine

government tried to introduce amendments to the Convention exempting women in managerial 'technical and advisory posts' from the ban.

The magazine did not, however, publish much of the more personal and anguished correspondence from dismissed former 'munitions girls' received by the society, over which there was much hand-wringing during committee meetings. One such letter came from a young member who, having been dismissed from her factory job, was then suspended from the Labour Exchange in Manchester and had her 25 shillings a week unemployment benefit withdrawn for refusing to take a position as 'third housemaid'. This was the usual alternative position offered to many of these young working-class women who, having experienced the camaraderie and relative status of a munitions job, quailed at the thought of long, lonely hours in domestic service.[47]

Notwithstanding its silence in this area, the *Woman Engineer* was a strongly feminist magazine at a time when the women's movement, somewhat splintered and directionless after the achievement of 1918, was stumbling in its response to concerted efforts once more to circumscribe women's activities after the war.[48] Among advertisements for grinding, lathe and glass manufacturers, the magazine carried notices for other interwar magazines including *Time and Tide*, the *Woman's Leader*, the *Woman Journalist* and the *Vote*. Many of these advertisements were reciprocal, and thus the magazine consciously presented itself as part of a network of interwar feminist journals in dialogue with each other.[49] It also operated as a network organiser for widely flung and often embattled society members, promoting lectures and social events at the society's Club Room at 46 Dover Street, offering visiting members 'the excellent selection of papers and magazines' and 'the most excellent tea that is obtainable by an extremely cosy gas fire'.[50]

As well as lectures and teas, the society arranged visits to factories for members as part of a wider associational culture. These visits were often enthusiastically written up for the *Woman Engineer* by Claudia Parsons, whose vivid writing style captured the wonder of modern manufacturing. Her description of visiting the new Ford works at Dagenham in March 1933 combines wide-eyed awe with professional satisfaction at being one of the first to see the huge factory on the edge of the Thames:

> That imposing frontage sparkles like a jewel at night and at all times presents a picture of energy and even of beauty. For there are now broad acres of solid earth where formerly existed marsh and refuse, and twenty-eight of these acres are covered with Ford workshops. The long, even lines of roofing advance towards the river and culminate in a tall building, a veritable palace, sitting so comfortably and majestically on the river bank.[51]

After describing the process that converted iron ore into motor cars – one came off the production line every 30 seconds – Parsons was able to refer to her own recent journeys across Europe, marvelling that the car she had driven across '8,000 miles of the worst European roads. Sometimes there was no road' had been produced so quickly. This opportunity, via her profession's public platform, to promote her technical achievements and present herself as an active participant in public life was something that many professional women's magazines offered at this time. While popular newspapers certainly celebrated women's achievements, from swimming the Channel to becoming barristers, reports were always couched in gendered terms and somewhat sensationalised: women pilots, for example, were described as 'air-girls' or, as was often the

Rejecting the feminine

case, 'beautiful flying débutantes'. In the crowded arena of flying, in addition, newspapers tried to whip up 'cat-fight' rivalries where none existed, as, for example, the *Daily Express* did with reference to Amy Johnson and Peggy Salaman.[52] Women were also increasingly sexualised in the popular press, whereas professional journals allowed women to speak without being packaged in the trappings of popular journalism.[53] It is worth noting that while 'frivolous' popular papers puffed these 'superwomen', women's papers took a far more sober approach and often expressed despair at the promotion of these 'dangerously spectacular' icons, which forced less talented and extrovert women into 'a forbidding and seemingly priggish austerity'.[54]

Alternative and more realistic accounts of women's professional lives, from the humdrum to the exhilarating, but always on their own terms, can be found in a wide range of interwar professional titles, from the *Woman Journalist* (for example, social justice reporting from the Paris slums, and the only woman journalist on the *Egyptian Mail* in Cairo) to the *Woman Teacher* (on improving the life-chances of 'backward' children in deprived areas and educational tours of Soviet Russia).[55] The *Nursing Mirror and Midwives' Journal*, though founded earlier (1888), also reported on women's engagement with the public sphere, including nurses' presence in field hospitals during the Spanish Civil War. From January 1937 onwards the *Journal* carried articles on subjects such as the use of canned blood for transfusions on the Madrid Front and the delivery of chilled food and supplies to hospitals in Barcelona.[56] The magazine carried a regular section, 'Incident in a Nurse's Life', to which nurses could contribute articles about their unusual or dangerous experiences, from reminiscences of the First World War to being offered a gift of a lamb by a grateful farmer who had received treatment on an isolated farmstead.

Indeed, reading a sample of these magazines, one wonders why the popular press made such a fuss about any woman doing anything at all. It is clear that, even if not all were circumnavigating the globe or winning motor races at the Brooklands circuit, women in their thousands – middle-class women, at any rate – were quietly and persistently active and making progress in most walks of life, and the reality presented a very different picture from the sensationalised 'othering' of the popular press. Certainly, the perfectly serious feature published in the popular *Bystander* in June 1935, 'What Women Do all Day', which had attending a tea party as the most arduous activity, presented a wholly distorted picture.[57]

Writing, motoring and freedom

When in 1926, after four years of being a governess, then a ladies' companion and occasional driver, Parsons placed her details with London employment agencies, 'applications came pouring in'.[58] For the next ten years she earned her living as a chauffeur, driving wealthy women – and one monk – around Britain and Europe, the high point being a five-month road trip across Eastern Europe and the Balkans in 1931 with American heiress Dolly Rodewald. After years of dull sequestration in the English and Swedish countryside as governess and companion, this adventure with a carefree young woman who defied all accepted mores brought Parsons an exhilarating taste of freedom. It was, literally, a 'journey without maps' (from Paris to Thessaloniki, where the maps finally turned up at a *poste restante*) in a four-door A-model Ford saloon. In it the pair criss-crossed

Rejecting the feminine

forests, snow-covered mountains, wide baking plains and trackless bogs: 'Balkan roads were either a series of hard ribs or a glut of potholes or plain bog. Bridges, if wooden, had rotting or missing struts, so one drove through the rivers.' Apart from endless puncture repairs, a broken windscreen wiper in a blizzard ('the one of us not driving had to hang out keeping the screen clear') and a broken gravity feed, 'The only casualty was the bar across the front of the Ford, coupling the two front wings, on which the headlamps were mounted. It fractured but we spliced it with the bough of a tree.'[59]

Young middle-class women's education in the late nineteenth and early twentieth centuries focused on preparation for marriage and motherhood, and cultivating a certain feminine helplessness, especially when outside the home, so discovering resilience, resourcefulness and self-reliance was an exhilarating experience for Parsons.[60] Memoirs and diaries written by women during this time reveal the frustration, boredom and desperation of these cloistered lives. The film-maker Bryher recalled her late teens and early twenties as a time of mind-numbing tedium:

> Almost everything outside the home was forbidden ground ... I was not allowed to go to public lectures or accept invitations to lunch in restaurants ... I was reproved, aged twenty, for writing a business letter to a publisher to inquire about the fate of a manuscript ... we sat sedately on chairs ... I must never 'show off' ... I was supposed to put on a hat and gloves if I went to the post box at the corner.[61]

When she was old enough to understand that the reason for this repression was to protect her only apparently valuable asset, her virginity, she was shocked and angry. A clearer example of this attitude can be seen in the memoir of Kylie

Tennant (Chapter 8). After she ran away from home at the age of 18 to escape her repressive father, the first thing he did when he found her was to send her to a doctor to examine whether she was still *virgo intacta*.[62] Hence for Parsons, each time she cranked up a jack to change a tyre or lay sprawled under the chassis inspecting the car's mud-caked underside was a moment of triumph, even though passing motorists flung the derogatory '*chaufette!*' at her. As a female motorist she was regularly stopped by police and asked for her licence; many times they advised her to abandon the car and retreat home by train, but no setback or disparagement overcame her.[63] Encouraging self-reliance is now a major development goal for organisations that seek to encourage the participation of repressed or subjugated populations. In recognition of the importance of instilling self-reliance in women as a tool in the search for global gender equality, the United Nations High Commission for Refugees has recently made the encouragement of this quality part of its protection policies.[64] It is interesting to note that a hundred years ago a woman such as Parsons, intent on breaking out of the domestic sphere, instinctively understood self-reliance as a major tool in her armoury.

As a chauffeur, Parsons was, however, always in a subordinate position to her wealthy employers. Motoring memoirs of early twentieth-century adventurers reveal that they saw their domestic entourage, often including chauffeur, navigator/mechanic and maid, as 'non-persons', barely meriting inclusion in their tales of derring-do. Despite her cheery disposition, Parsons resented many of her employers. In a letter sent to her publisher Harold Raymond, of Chatto and Windus, shortly after the publication of her novel *Brighter Bondage*, she described one set of clients, 'the old lady and the monk', as

Rejecting the feminine

'hang[ing] over me like vultures'.[65] In another letter in response to criticism by Chatto's readers of an early version of her travel memoir *Vagabondage* (1941) as being too insipid, Parsons ruefully agreed, admitting that she had felt under obligation to paint a falsely rosy picture in the section of the book describing her crossing America in a car as chauffeur to two wealthy clients:

> If I had been free to describe three people who only found how unsuitable they were to travel together across the States after they had bound themselves to each other with possession of one car ... then *Vagabondage* would have started out a far more entertaining book and you would not have complained of a want of venom.[66]

Parsons' experience, both her grim and lonely employment as a lady's companion and the more entertaining, yet nevertheless problematic adventures as a chauffeur, inspired her to write a semi-autobiographical novel, *Brighter Bondage*, about a young widow fallen on hard times and surviving as a companion and 'chauffeuse'. The dedication at the front of the novel, 'in retrospection of the years of bondage, which began in 1925', implies that under the gentle humour there is a more serious intent. The novel, though as light as whipped air, discusses the condition of the lady's companion, kept in semi-slavery and at the whim of a bullying employer who expects the 'chauffeuse-gardener-companion to help also in the house, do a little mending, play bridge and read aloud to invalid [employer]'.[67] Published in May 1935, *Brighter Bondage* was well received and reviewed widely and quickly went into two further editions. Chatto and Windus also sold the translation rights in Norway, Sweden and Denmark, where it was published as the slightly less cheerful *I Dag ar det Varst* (The days are the worst). Readers were delighted with the unlucky yet constantly optimistic young widow Antonia March, who took misadventure, snubs and financial ruin in her stride. Sean O'Faolain, the poet and literary critic, wrote of it in the *Spectator*:

> It is hard to believe that Miss Claudia Parsons has not written before now or that her book is a first novel. In effect it is much more like the merry diary of a young woman who has actually been paid companion to all those odd, sometimes unpleasant, but mostly pleasant people whose adventures she shares from time to time.[68]

It is apparent from letters between Parsons and her editor at Chatto that from this moment on she saw herself as a writer above all else, and whenever she could she spent her time bashing out stories on an old typewriter at her home in Wonnersh, which she shared with her mother and her sister Betty. Chatto, too, seemed delighted with their new find and Harold Raymond wrote several letters to her inquiring about her next project, and every Christmas sent her gifts. After *Brighter Bondage*, she struggled fruitlessly for over a year trying to write a novel based on Romanian folktales that she had heard on her travels. Although satisfying her craving to write, the most important outcome of *Brighter Bondage* was the £156 it brought her in royalties, which paid for a third-class boat ticket to New York, part-ownership of a car, and enough petrol to take her and her passengers who also invested in the car across the United States. She planned then to sell the car in Vancouver, take a job for a few months and then get a cargo boat home. She actually ended up circumnavigating the globe, including driving a 1925 Studebaker from Calcutta to Calais on a journey that took fourteen months. It becomes clear reading her letters to Harold Raymond that she was not at all sure the trip was a good idea, but he convinced her:

Rejecting the feminine

> Though I dare not give you advice ... I would pawn my last pair of shoes but one and go that America trip ... If I were what is called 'a young writer of promise' I should try to beg, borrow or steal sufficient to get me across to New York, buy me a second-hand Ford and keep me in the States for about six months ... If as a result I could not interest readers in what I had seen and above all what I had heard, I should chuck writing. I well picture how delightfully you would handle all the dialogue.[69]

Raymond's encouragement and generosity clearly played a role in transforming Parsons' view of herself from chauffeur/engineer to writer, looking for 'copy' in her day job. While little had materially changed for Parsons, apart from the fact that she was now a published author, the confidence that this new persona of 'writer' gave her enabled her to pitch ideas and articles as well as short stories to a variety of magazines and newspapers, and to assert her right to participate at least at the edges of the public sphere. Whereas her previous contributions had been confined to her student newspaper and her professional magazine, she was now asked, through her agent Curtis Brown, to contribute short stories to the popular *Bystander* magazine. She also planned right from the start to sell articles from her American trip and enquired of her agent and publishers whether they would represent her in this endeavour.[70]

Suspicions aroused by the solitary mobile woman

For the journey across the United States, Parsons had two female companions, but as she stepped on to the SS *Hikawa Maru* at Vancouver in September 1937, she became that most suspicious character: the solitary mobile woman. While women had been explorers and adventurers in the Victorian and Edwardian era as colonial exploration, rail and road travel opened up new travel routes, they rarely travelled alone. Famous women travellers such as Freya Stark and Stella Court Treatt were accompanied by native servants and male companions, their native servants often getting them out of terrible scrapes.[71] Mary Hall was another 'explorer', whose account of her travels, *A Woman's Trek from the Cape to Cairo* (1907), became an Edwardian publishing sensation, and purported to show how a white Englishwoman could conquer trackless Africa 'quite alone'.[72] Early on in the book, however, and somewhat ingenuously, Hall reveals that when not travelling in trains, she was carried a lot of the way by native pole bearers 'in smart red uniforms', virtually dehumanised into machines by her description: 'two boys at either end of the pole act as bearers … and entwine their arms around one another in such a manner that it is difficult to say where one boy begins and where the other ends'.[73] Similarly, Harriet White Fisher's early motoring book, *A Woman's World Tour in a Motor* (1911), apparently makes play of the lone woman adventurer, but then reveals that in her four-seater with her were 'Mr Harold Fisher Brooks, who acted as my chauffeur; Albert, an English servant who can cook a good dinner or write a business letter; and Maria, my Italian maid, typical of her country: always bright, cheerful and sunny.' It would be enlightening to read Maria's account of the same journey. Even Margaret Belcher's *Cape to Cowley via Cairo* (1932), supposed to be a more down-to-earth account of how the ordinary woman could now aspire to make this legendary journey, glosses over the fact that she and her companion Ellen Budgell also brought their cook, given the impersonal name 'J. M. O. Day' or 'official tin opener', with them.[74]

Rejecting the feminine

The truly solitary mobile woman was a focus of suspicion and carried with her a whiff of scandal: her vulnerability and thus suspected sexual availability and untrustworthiness suggested that she was either destitute, a prostitute, or a spy. Working-class women had always been forced, through financial necessity, to leave the protecting confines of home to seek employment. The middle-class woman who chose to leave the protection of her father's home and expose herself to prying eyes was seen as perverse, but also a symbol of social change and modernity, and thus, for the forces of reaction, someone to fear.[75] Often she was suspected of espionage, the underlying assumption being that a solitary mobile female must perforce be at best duplicitous, at worst a traitor to her country.[76] The German journalist and traveller Rosie Grafenberg, for example, who travelled to French West Africa in the late 1920s, was suspected by French Intelligence of being a Russian agent, a communist agitator and a German spy, and agents followed her, taking copious notes.[77] Kylie Tennant aroused intense suspicion through her journalistic trips alone across Depression-era Australia to gather material for her novels, which exposed the hardship of the slums and the farm workers. Briefly a member of the Australian Communist Party, she was spied on by the fledgling Secret Intelligence Service, which kept a file on her from 1935 onwards, opening letters and collecting press cuttings on her.[78]

Parsons was also suspected of being a spy as she crossed Japan alone, and at one point she was arrested.[79] At every step of her journey she was the focus of attempts to circumscribe or control her travels, from the booking office clerk in Victoria, Canada, who tried to avoid selling her a third-class ticket because she was a 'solitary woman', to the anonymous man in Siam (modern-day Thailand) who bought her a first-class train ticket because he could not bear to see a lone woman in second class: 'He saw me as a victim when really I was nothing of the sort, or perhaps he saw me as somebody lowering the standards of the white races.'[80] Here she was not only a threat to standards set by class, but also those of race. Her journey was characterised by continual resistance on her part to being curtailed by the keepers of these standards, be they clerks, chief petty officers, the military or other travellers: 'Wars and finance might, and did, deter me from getting to some of the places I wanted to visit. But "because of what people might think" was not likely to put me off.'[81]

As we have seen, her first attempt to write up her travels was met with disappointment by her editor and rejection by Chatto's readers because she felt inhibited when writing passages that involved other people. Only when she was completely on her own and 'not bothered to be polite' did her writing really sing.[82] The final, published version of *Vagabondage* was reduced in size by a quarter and was spikily outspoken, particularly towards the travellers and officials she met who objected to her travelling alone.[83] In one exasperated aside, recording a train journey across Malaysia and Cambodia when a series of priests, officials and boys 'walked one after another along the line to look at me in my compartment as at something in a cage', she expostulates: 'this is not an impossible expedition for a woman travelling alone, it is only impossible for a woman to travel alone'.[84]

The book records the hard-won triumph of a woman of meagre means following a long-cherished dream of seeing the world on her own terms. Unfortunately there is not space here to record more than a single extended passage from the final

Rejecting the feminine

edition of *Vagabondage*, written in the evenings after 'ten hours of the day as a turner on a central lathe', after Parsons had returned to the factory floor and munitions work during the first twelve months of the Second World War.[85] But here is a flavour of how, alone, she responded to the landscape and the flora and fauna she passed through:

> Towards evening, strange birds flew out of the jungle. Herons rose lazily from the water but the tick birds refused to be agitated by our passing … for a long time I lay in bed with the blind drawn up, looking at the jungle and the moonlight. And, as it always does, the train sang to me … Its rhythm seemed here to be beating out, measure for measure, this continuous silhouette of trees and creepers, the future becoming the present and the present at once falling away into the past. A grand lesson this strange, revolving scenery, in living for the now. Though what business had I to call it strange? Was I not myself who was the stranger? The jungle and its creatures belonged here, but this train, this lighted phantom stealing through the forest with its all-seeing eye, its great head-lamp on the engine, was the real and only eccentricity.[86]

This passage reveals Parsons as a sensitive and thoughtful traveller, and in a mould very different to conventional imperial globe-trotters. Although she acknowledges that the railway line she is travelling on is British-built (and she admires the 'engineering of the embankment only slightly above water-level'), she conveys awareness of the illegitimacy of its occupation of the landscape and that the true and legitimate occupants, the trees and jungle creatures, were there before, and will be there long after, her uninvited trespass. In this sense she brings an almost Conradian view to her travel memoir, the sinister 'phantom' train a symbol of the antagonism between imperialism and colonial territory, 'the intrusion of machines into jungles … a world in which progress drinks nectar from the skulls of the slain'.[87] The image, too, of the lone traveller in a small lighted space, isolated from nature and subject to compressions and distortions of time, reveals a poetic response, all the more impressive since it was conjured after ten hours' work as a lathe-turner.

It may be that her second attempt at having *Vagabondage* published, this time after the outbreak of the Second World War, brought with it a more thoughtful consideration of her and Britain's place in the world, and that events on her journey, such as her decision to drive back through North Africa rather than Eastern Europe because of the Anschluss, had been thrown into sharp relief by the outbreak of war. It may also be that she actually wrote better when doing other things, as she confessed in a letter to her publisher, now that she was not writing full time, but squeezing it in after a long day at the munitions works: 'I find I always write magnificently when I am supposed to be doing something else.'[88] *Vagabondage*, published in August 1941, ran to two editions, as much as was allowed during wartime paper rationing. The book was rejected by publishers in the United States as they were uncomfortable with a story about an unmarried woman who either travelled alone, or in the company of a man, as she did on the final leg of her journey by car from Calcutta to Calais.[89]

One magazine that carried an account of Parsons' travels, the *Studebaker Journal*, inserted the words 'old man' into her description of her companion, the anthropologist Kilton Stewart, who was actually a vigorous 36 years old, to make her account more palatable to conservative readers.[90] Thus her then still unusual method of adventuring continued to be circumscribed and

Rejecting the feminine

edited. The Women's Engineering Society had no such qualms and invited her to give a public lecture on her adventures at its Annual General Meeting on 29 November 1938, where 'many beautiful slides were illustrated by Miss Parsons' entrancing descriptions'.[91] Here we have an example of how an organisation and publication aimed at men (the *Studebaker Journal*) saw fit to criticise and censor Parsons' habit of departing from correct gendered behaviour, whereas a woman's organisation, established for the purpose of furthering women's equality, celebrated and promoted her.

In choosing her path, Parsons, as we have seen, suffered multiple setbacks, from being accused of cheating at Loughborough, to struggling to find employment once qualified, to being the subject of attempts to control and censor her wherever she travelled. To have survived all this, she was clearly endowed with deep reserves of self-belief and an inner confidence, something which many women of her era lacked. For less self-assured women, other methods of engagement were necessary, the most powerful being organised networks, which will be discussed in the next chapter.

Notes

1 Parsons 1921a: 66.
2 The college magazine, *The Limit*, records new enrolments in the Engineering Department in October 1919 as 203, with three of those being women: Claudia Parsons, Dorothea Travers and a Miss B. Lees. 'New Christmas Term', *The Limit*, 2/1, October 1919, p. 25. One further woman, Verena Holmes, enrolled in 1920.
3 'Editorial', *The Woman Engineer*, 1/1, December 1919, p. 2. By 1930, a further 13 technical colleges across the country offered training courses for women engineers (Women's Engineering Society 1930). Vanishingly few women studied engineering at university at this time.

Rebel women between the wars

Nina Baker (2009) records six women graduating from all Scottish universities with a BSc in Engineering between 1919 and 1939, although several more did during the 1940s. Another reason why so few women were offered places to study engineering at university was because for several years after the war, universities reserved places to men returning from war service, who had interrupted their studies after 1914. A letter to the Women's Engineering Society from Imperial College, then the leading institution for engineering degrees, dated March 1919, makes this point. NAEST 92/4/1/10, archives of the Institution of Engineering and Technology, London (IET).

4 Professional women's magazines launched during this period include the *Woman Teacher* (1919), the *Woman Journalist* (relaunched in January 1923, having closed down in 1920) and *Opportunity* (for women civil servants, 1921).

5 Thompson 1989: 1; DiCenzo and Eustance 2018: 321. Haslett was friends with Lady Rhondda, and from the start the *Woman Engineer* had close links with Lady Rhondda's *Time and Tide*, advertising regularly in its pages. The two journals, though radically different in readership and aesthetics (the *Woman Engineer* was forbiddingly dull in its early issues), shared a similar outlook on women's place in the modern world. For more on the close links between *Time and Tide* and the *Woman Engineer*, see Clay 2018: 22.

6 'Editorial', *Woman Engineer*, 1/1, December 1919, p. 1; the cover price rose to 6d to pay for more pages from March 1921.

7 Parsons 1921a: 66.

8 'The Real Life of the Girl Worker', *Daily Mail*, 1 January 1917, p. 4.

9 Parsons 1995: vii.

10 For a study of the changing image of women workers in the popular press between 1914 and 1919, see Lonsdale 2015; Beddoe 1989. Although in recent years scholars have challenged much of Beddoe's work in this area – and this study is another contribution to this – it is nevertheless true to say that the pressure on women from, for example, articles in the popular press to return to the domestic sphere was very great indeed. See also Chapman 2020: x.

11 See, for example, O'Connell 1998: esp. 43–76; Smith 2001: esp. 167–201.

12 O'Connell 1998: 59.

13 For more on this, see Leed 1991.

14 Parsons 1995: 226.
15 Stephanie Ward's study (2019) of working-class Labour women activists reaches this conclusion.
16 Parsons 1995: 6.
17 Parsons 1995: 7.
18 Allen 2007: 64–91 is particularly good on Kipling's terribly painful days in Southsea; see Kipling's own short story, 'Baa Baa Black Sheep' (1888).
19 Parsons 1995: 10–11.
20 Parsons 1995: 14.
21 Parsons 1995: 32.
22 Parsons's father had died of a heart attack when she was 12; Parsons 1995: 38.
23 Parsons 1995: 36.
24 Benton 2015: 56.
25 Frances 2013.
26 Harford 1941.
27 Harford 1941: 36; Betty Parsons' *The Dove Pursues*, published under the pseudonym G. M. T. Parsons, was published by Constable and Co. in 1933.
28 Parsons 1941: 1.
29 *The Limit*, 2/1, October 1919, p. 27.
30 Various entries in *The Limit* magazine 1919–22.
31 See, for example, 'To *The Limit*', July 1921, p. 127, and her poem 'A Third Year Lament', July 1922, p. 115.
32 Loughborough University Archives, LC/AD6/5.
33 IAE/1/1/7, archives of the Institution of Mechanical Engineers, London.
34 Parsons 1922: 75.
35 From the age of 21, Parsons received an army pension through her father's service of just over £5 a month, which was not enough to allow her to buy a car or travel.
36 Parsons 1995: 65.
37 In the twenty years between 1919 and 1939 car ownership in Britain grew from just over 100,000 to two million (O'Connell 1998: 17).
38 Clarsen 2008: 30–45.
39 De Havilland 1918: 5.
40 The *Woman's Motor Manual* features an advertisement for a Burberry 'Weatherproof Motor Dress', featuring an austere-looking woman

wearing a peaked chauffeur's cap sporting a shin-length coat with lapels and vast pockets (De Havilland 1918: ii).
41 Clarsen 2008: 30–45.
42 Smith 2001: 172–3.
43 NAEST 92/1.1.1, 2 and 3, IET.
44 Emergency meeting, 13 January 1922, NAEST 92/1.1.2, IET.
45 *Woman Engineer*, 3/1, December 1929, p. 4, and 3/2, March 1930, p. 24, respectively.
46 For more on this, and rampant sexism in the ILO, see Natchcova and Scoheni 2013: 52–4.
47 WES meeting, 15 May 1919, NAEST 92/1.1.1, IET.
48 See, for example, Bingham 2004b; Innes 2004; Pedersen 2020.
49 This is similar marketing activity to other professional women's magazines, such as *Opportunity* (for women civil servants) and the *Woman Teacher* (Glew 2018: 366–7).
50 'Correspondence', *Woman Engineer*, 1/6, March 1921, p. 68.
51 Parsons 1933: 215.
52 'Miss Salaman Flight Controversy', *Daily Express*, 3 November 1931, p. 1; Peggy Salaman flew from London to Cape Town, South Africa, in six days in November 1931. In fact, like most women explorers of this time, she was not alone, travelling with her navigator Gordon Store.
53 On the sexualisation of women in the popular press during this time, see Bingham 2004a: 248.
54 'Pioneer Women and the Press', *The Lady*, 12 May 1932, p. 744.
55 *Woman Journalist*, April 1933, p. 2, and September 1924, p. 20; *Woman Teacher*, January 1937, p. 118, and February 1937, p. 193; for more on the *Woman Journalist* and *Woman Teacher*, see Lonsdale 2018 and Goodman 2018, respectively.
56 For example, 'Blood Transfusion in Spain', *Nursing Mirror and Midwives' Journal*, 23 January 1937, p. 323; 'Cargo for Spain', *Nursing Mirror and Midwives' Journal*, 6 February 1937, p. 360.
57 *The Bystander*, June 1935, p. 121.
58 Parsons 1995: 67.
59 Parsons 1995: 83–4.
60 See, for example, Mullaney and Hilbert 2018: 73–8.
61 Bryher 1963: 149–50.
62 Tennant 2012: 69.
63 Parsons 1995: 80–5.

Rejecting the feminine

64 Maynard and Suter 2009: 127–49.
65 Letter from Parsons to Harold Raymond, 5 February 1937, CW 73/12, ABPP.
66 Letter from Parsons to Harold Raymond, 5 April 1940, CW 88/11, ABPP.
67 Parsons 1935: 16–17.
68 'Fiction', *Spectator*, 14 June 1935, p. 1036.
69 Letter from Harold Raymond to Parsons, 6 February 1937, CW 73/12, ABPP.
70 Letter from Harold Raymond to Parsons, 3 May 1937, CW 73/12, ABPP.
71 For an account of Stella Court Treatt's 'Cape to Cairo' journey, see Wolf 1991.
72 Hall 1907: v.
73 Hall 1907: 24.
74 Belcher 1932: 3.
75 For an excellent discussion of the genealogy of the 'new public woman', see Evans 2019: esp. 22–7.
76 Women aviators, who perforce travelled alone, were often thought to be spies; other lone women travellers were often not issued with papers or permits and were followed by secret service agents. See, for example, Boittin 2014.
77 Boittin 2014.
78 National Archives of Australia, A6119/283.
79 Parsons 1941: 117.
80 Parsons 1941: 72, 134.
81 Parsons 1941: 162.
82 Letter from Parsons to Harold Raymond, 21 January 1941, CW 91/17, ABPP.
83 Ibid.
84 Parsons 1941: 130, 159.
85 Letter from Parsons to Harold Raymond, 21 January 1941, CW 91/17, ABPP.
86 Parsons 1941: 133.
87 Jonah Raskin, quoted in Giddings 1991: 1.
88 Letter from Parsons to Harold Raymond, 15 April 1940, CW 88/11, ABPP.
89 Letter from Parsons to Harold Raymond, 24 November 1941, CW 91/17, ABPP.

90 Ibid.; her companion was the controversial pioneer psychoanalyst Kilton Stewart, author of *Pygmies and Dream Giants* – but that's another story.
91 Account of Parsons's travels published in the *Woman Engineer*: '"Baker", the Anthropologist and Claudia Parsons', June 1939, pp. 292–5.

7
Formal networks

Without any clear idea of where I wanted to go, I drove my car out of its garage on the first Saturday in the month and headed for the Great West Road – out of a dripping, mackintoshed and umbrellaed London, away from an office envious of my foresight and discontented with its wet half-day, into a country flaming with orange and red, madder and bronze; a country of warm scented airs and soft blue skies shot with ragged gleams of gold; a country plenteous with cider and cheese, honey and clotted cream […] Somebody had turned on the wireless. Suddenly I was startled into thrilled attention. What was the announcer saying? 'In Madrid yesterday steps were taken to confine the troops to barracks for forty-eight hours. Fighting has taken place in the suburb of Tetuan. There is no further news from the Asturias where armed miners have seized, and are successfully holding, the Government centre, Oviedo.' The artificial peace of the quiet room was shattered. Something tremendous had been flung into it across the ether. I stayed in Cornwall for several days, walking, motoring, but thinking most of the time of Spain. The newspapers contained little or nothing to show which way the struggle was going. Like most other English Socialists I waited in sickening suspense to know what the issue would be. Reverberations of suffering, pain, death, from the mountains of Asturia seemed to fill my ears, even as I walked by quiet grey seas, or drove in the dim twilight through the narrow, twisted Cornish lanes. I did not dream that in less than three months I would be finding the answers to all these questions for myself.[1]

So opens the former MP Leah Manning's evocative account of her visit to Spain in December 1934, shortly after the country had been rocked by a series of disorganised and short-lived workers' uprisings against the right-wing government. A particularly sustained rebellion by the miners of Asturias in northern Spain had been brutally suppressed by troops led by General Franco and some 40,000 trade unionists had been imprisoned. Manning formed part of a Committee of Inquiry invited by the Spanish Workers' Alliance to hear evidence of torture and violence by the Spanish military.[2] She visited activists in jail and spoke to their leaders, uncovering evidence of shocking cruelty meted out to political prisoners. 'As we turned to go,' she wrote, 'the tears pricked my eyes and my throat choked. I was free to walk out again into the bright sunlight, the clean sweet air. Behind me four thousand men were jailed for believing what I believed.'[3] Her visit was published the following year by Victor Gollancz, under the title *What I Saw in Spain*, a piece of book-length reportage describing the quasi-anarchic state of Spanish politics just before the country tipped into bloody Civil War. It was something of a scoop: a more high-profile English deputation, led by the prominent former MP Ellen Wilkinson and the Labour peer Lord Listowel, had been ignominiously turned away at the border. Manning and her group, which included Professor Lascelles Abercrombie, travelled incognito as tourists until they reached their socialist guides.[4] At the end of the book, she warned, all too presciently, of the 'ten thousand rifles [that] lay oiled and buried' in

Formal networks

the coal and steel towns of the Valgrandi river valley against the day that tensions in Spain would finally break the country apart.[5]

Recognised as an important piece of writing at the time, garnering praise from Clement Attlee and the author Naomi Mitchison among others, the book called for a united international front against the rise of fascism across Europe.[6] When war did eventually break out, Manning would play a major role in coordinating the delivery of medical supplies to International Brigade units and in organising the evacuation of 4,000 Basque children to England in May 1937. This latter was an astonishing feat under strong prevailing headwinds: Stanley Baldwin's government was at best lukewarm and at worst hostile to the idea of committing to an action that would compromise Britain's neutrality, and that would also stoke a growing anti-immigrant populist right led by Oswald Mosley's fascists.

Manning had been a political and trade union activist since before the First World War. A committed and progressive teacher, she served as president of the National Union of Teachers in 1929/30, when in her fight to raise the school leaving age to 15 she was dubbed a 'Savonarola in Petticoats', and she briefly held the parliamentary seat of East Islington in 1931.[7] From her days at Homerton Teacher Training College (1906–08) onwards, Manning was involved with a wide range of informal and formal organisations and networks associated with the women's movement, teaching, pacifism and left-wing politics. These included the Fabian Society, the Young Liberals' League, the Socialist League, the Independent Labour Party (ILP), the Cambridge branch of the Trades and Labour Council, the National Union of Teachers and before that the National Federation of Class Teachers, the National

Association of Labour Teachers (for which she was founding chair), the National Council of Women, the County Insurance Committee, the Tuberculosis Sub-committee and the National Federation of Women Workers; she ran the first family planning clinic in Cambridge; she served on the Cambridge Borough Juvenile Employment Committee and was secretary of the Borough Teachers' Association; during the First World War she sat on the Borough Food Control Committee; after the war she joined the Fellowship of Reconciliation; in 1920 she became one of the first three women Justices of the Peace to serve in Cambridge; during the General Strike of 1926 she sat on the trades unions' General Strike Committee; during the 1930s she joined the Left Book Club and became, with John Strachey, joint secretary of the Co-ordinating Committee Against War and Fascism and in 1936 honorary secretary of the Spanish Medical Aid Committee.[8] Suspected by the leading Labour politician Herbert Morrison of being a communist, enquiries were made of the then Communist Party secretary Harry Pollitt, who replied cryptically: 'We much admire Leah, but this is a disciplined movement.'[9]

Manning believed strongly in the power of organisation as a way of underpinning activism and confronting entrenched power, and although she supported women's enfranchisement, like many on the left she saw the struggle to get women enough to live on as a more pressing issue.[10] Entering the teaching profession in the early years of the twentieth century, she joined the most populous profession for women: the 1911 Census shows that three-quarters of all teachers were women (183,298 in total), a ratio that had not changed since the beginning of the century.[11] This preponderance of women had long since 'normalised' their presence at all levels of several teaching unions

Formal networks

and associations, and when Manning became NUT president in 1930 three women had already held this post ahead of her. She was, however, the first married woman president as most borough education authorities operated a marriage bar at least until the First World War, and many until the mid-1930s.[12] The densely woven and often interconnecting network of organisations that she joined, many of them statutory or quasi-governmental, served to facilitate her access to the public sphere and, eventually, to propel her into the House of Commons on one of the NUT's parliamentary tickets. If one measures public sphere success purely in political terms, then, of all the women discussed in this book, Leah Manning achieved the most. Although her first spell as an MP was short-lived, lasting just eight months between a by-election and the disastrous (for Labour) general election of 1931, it endowed her with status as a public figure and a network of powerful contacts that would enable her activism throughout the rest of the 1930s.[13]

This chapter also examines the author and activist Una Marson, who, arriving from Jamaica as an already published poet, journalist and editor in London in 1932, expected to find a welcoming intellectual culture. Instead she encountered an excluding and bewildering racism operating administratively as the colour bar, but which informally permeated social, political and literary London, where writers and socialites watched 'exotic' black dancers and musicians performing in racy West End clubs, and where even progressive organisations and intellectuals were prone to patronising and pro-imperial attitudes.[14] In Peckham, where Marson first lodged on arrival in 1932, her 'otherness' was brought into sharp focus by a 'pygmy woman' freak show operating in a nearby draper's shop, where the public paid threepence to look at a black African.[15] Marson faced the double obstacles of gender and race in 1930s Britain, where the 1919 Aliens Restriction Order and its subsequent amendments had embedded racism into state structures, and where a black face drew suspicion and even ridicule, prompting her to write the poem 'Nigger' shortly after her arrival:

> They called me 'Nigger',
> Those little white urchins
> They laughed and shouted
> As I passed along the street
> They flung it at me:
> Nigger![16]

The poem, published in the journal *The Keys* in 1933, bursts with bewilderment and anger. Even the 'little white urchins' – the lowest in white society – point and laugh, making a spectacle of her colour. There is a violence, both in the urchins' words (they 'flung' the insult at her) and in Marson's response: she imagines herself 'choking the words in their mouths'. Another verse describes the British upper-class appetite for 'Nigger Minstrels' as a 'cause for merriment', criticising the fashion in London for 'singing Negroes [which] caused white men to laugh'.

The poem is not just a personal cry of hurt: it is also an expression of bitter disappointment at the English response to her presence in the 'mother country', problematising the colour of her skin in obvious and exclusionary ways. In Jamaica, Marson had favoured a cross-colonial model for political activism that would promote harmony between black and white, a 'world-wide commonwealth [in which we] are members of one another'.[17] The racism that she encountered in London – she was turned down for secretarial jobs and from accommodation in boarding houses on account of her colour – shattered this optimistic vision. From now on she would see England as the

Formal networks

country of her 'enemy', as it looked on her as 'a member of a servile and dull race'.[18]

This poem would be just one of many creative expressions produced during Marson's time in London, revealing a growing race consciousness and dissent against colonial power even as she lived and worked in the heart of the imperial metropolis. However, she quickly joined the burgeoning networks of anti-racist and colonial activists beginning to organise and operate in London in the 1930s, including the West African Students' Union, the International African Friends of Abyssinia and, most importantly, the League of Coloured Peoples (LCP), of whose magazine, *The Keys*, Marson was an early editor and thus influential in shaping the LCP's public image. She also joined the British Commonwealth League, established to try to encourage understanding between black and white citizens of the Empire, while still accepting British colonial hegemony. She was also involved in women's organisations, including the International Alliance for Women's Suffrage and Equal Citizenship and the Women's International League for Peace and Freedom, which, as we will see, formed a dense, supportive and multi-noded network for interwar feminists. In recognition of the work of feminist networks, Marson wrote the poem 'To the I. A. W. S. E. C.', in which she praised 'Women of England who in freedom's name / Work with courageous women of all lands' and recognised the 'bitter struggles' women have fought, both 'in public life and in the quiet home'.[19]

Marson's relationship to these predominantly white women's groups was not, however, straightforward, as we will see, and she came up against obstacles to her participation in unexpected and painful ways. Social networks have been shown both to enable and constrain the performance of a particular entity within them, depending on their structure, size and agency, and part of the work of this chapter will be to understand the limitations of social networks, particularly where the goal of an individual clashes with the goal of the network as a whole.[20]

Leah Manning: nonconformist childhood to radical teacher

Elizabeth Leah Perrett was born in Droitwich, Worcestershire, on 14 April 1886, the third of twelve children, of whom only six survived into adulthood.[21] Her paternal grandfather had been a baker, then grocer and confectioner, and on her mother's side there were assorted silk weavers and timber traders, several of whom had emigrated to Canada: artisans and craftspeople of the aspirational lower middle class. The young Leah Perrett's mother and father also emigrated to Canada while she was still a child, the result of a family row, and she moved to London to be brought up by her maternal grandfather and his new, much younger wife. In her memoir, she claims not to have been concerned about this arrangement, although she also acknowledged the potential for psychological damage: 'This might seem a catastrophe in the life of a child. However ... I loved the idea of being the petted, youngest member of a family of grownups, rather than the eldest daughter of a rumbustious brood whose intake was one per annum.'[22] This arrangement may have proved crucial in Leah's development on two grounds. It removed her from her father's control, which, as we have already seen, was a significant factor in increasing a young woman's likelihood of breaking free from traditional gender expectations. It also brought her under the influence of her grandfather, a

Formal networks

radical Methodist minister. There were pictures of Gladstone in every room in the house, and the young Leah was permitted to sit in during the heated political discussions that went on 'in the cosy back parlour between tea and supper':

> The rights and wrongs of Charles Bradlaugh; the vicious sentence on Oscar Wilde; the queer ideas of Mrs Besant; Mormon missionaries and the white slave traffic; General Booth and Mrs Josephine Butler; Dr Campbell and the immanence of God; above all the iniquity of the Boer War.[23]

While underlining the caveat that the women in this book do not constitute a representative sample, it should be noted that of the thirteen principal characters, a significant number, seven, were born into (or in this case raised in) families with strong nonconformist traditions. The others are Naomi Royde-Smith (Presbyterian/Methodist), Francesca Wilson (Quaker), Dorothy Pilley (Plymouth Brethren), Una Marson (Baptist), Kylie Tennant (Presbyterian/Christian Science) and Stella Martin (Methodist). It does not seem unreasonable to assume that in nonconformist groups that rejected established orthodoxies and tolerated and even promoted women as lay preachers well before the established Church, you might also find more progressive attitudes to women generally, and women's education in particular.[24] Stella Martin, for example, recalled in her memoir of her father that her mother organised Methodist women's meetings on a large scale. Some of the earliest women social reformers and nonconformists such as Elizabeth Fry (Quaker) and Catherine Booth (Salvation Army) had 'created for themselves [a space] to occupy outside the domestic sphere'.[25]

Of course, belonging to a well-organised network which defined itself by public service and charitable work was also very important. It could also be that an openness to complex philosophical or controversial ideas might have instilled in nonconformist women a more enquiring and adventurous mind that would help them navigate their way out of the domestic sphere. Constance Maynard, who founded Westfield College in 1882 as a Christian college for young women, noted that among students attending her Divinity lectures, which questioned the biblical origins for the idea of separate spheres for women, 'Quakers and Independents will listen' but students from the established Church would not.[26] In her important study of the women's movement, *The Cause* (1928), Ray Strachey also noted the preponderance of women from nonconformist backgrounds among those who had managed to escape the domestic sphere:

> If you were a Buxton, a Gurney, a Fry, a Wedgwood, a Bright, a Fox, a Barclay or a Darwin it was not such a very great misfortune to be born a woman ... you would be allowed and expected to be educated and intelligent, and you would be considered an equal in family life.[27]

While education was certainly valued in her grandfather's house, university was never an obvious option for the young Leah, and after matriculation she assisted at a London school and then undertook teacher training at Homerton College in Cambridge, her fees paid for by a small bequest from her grandfather, who had since died. Like Margaret Lane at school and university, and Claudia Parsons at Loughborough, Leah threw herself into student life, became chair of the college debating society and the drama club, and of the college's branch of the student Christian Union while also founding the college Socialist League. She joined the University Musical Society (she always loved choral singing) and was a member of the Cambridge Teachers' Dramatic Society, playing Maria in Shakespeare's *Twelfth Night*.[28] Through a teaching contact in London, she was invited by Cambridge undergraduate Hugh Dalton to join the University Fabian Society, and so the fledgling network of politics and influence that would help her so much began to form. Records from her time at Homerton suggest that while she did not shine academically (she came halfway up the results table in her final examinations), she achieved the highest, alpha, grade

Figure 11 Leah Manning, c. 1920s

for her teaching placement, despite her tutors' criticism of her lack of 'refinement' and her 'ungainly ways'.[29]

In July 1914 she married Will Manning, an assistant at the University Observatory, and although, as was the custom, she handed in her notice just before her marriage, she was called back in almost immediately after the outbreak of war. Will Manning is barely mentioned in his wife's memoir, and reading between the lines it seems that they did not spend much time together. Political friends often said they had never met him.[30] Their marriage was hit very early on by the loss of a baby daughter, and it is possible that they could not overcome this tragedy. During the war she taught all day and then went to work as a VAD in the evenings. In 1915, possibly through exhaustion, she went into early labour and her baby daughter died three weeks later: 'I couldn't grieve. All my tears were shed.'[31] She had no more children of her own.

Networks

After qualifying, Manning began her teaching career at a former Ragged School for 'pauper' children in New Street, Cambridge, where even in a relatively affluent city, poverty and neglect were rife, and it was a challenge to inspire any of the 70 children in her class to take lessons:

> Poor mites! Under-fed, over-worked, lacking sleep, I often wished for a bit of real naughtiness; but they didn't have enough spirit … our children were out on the streets late at night selling and delivering papers, up early in the morning on a milk, paper or baker's round, and at school all day. In the winter, blue, chilblained fingers, running noses and toes sticking out of ruined shoes were the hall-mark of their poverty.[32]

Formal networks

After a child in her class died of starvation, Manning organised a public meeting, inviting the local newspapers, and spoke out over the local education authority's refusal to provide the children of New Street with free milk, then a discretionary benefit. She was ordered to attend a disciplinary hearing before the education committee and was defended by her union, and by members of the local branch of the National Council of Women (NCW), which included Clara Rackham, secretary of the National Union of Women's Suffrage Societies, and Mrs Florence Keynes. Some members of the Council, who also sat on the education committee, had been impressed already by Manning's institution of an evening play centre at New Street, which helped keep children off the street.[33] She was cleared of any wrongdoing, without having to apologise or retract. Her networks were already working for her.

Networks have always helped women challenge the masculine 'dominative mode' through an alternative 'interactive mode' that foregrounds collaboration and the sharing of resources, including knowledge and capital.[34] Recent work has shown how networks of women helped build communities in the arena of the arts and culture during the interwar years, with wealthier women such as Bryher, Nancy Cunard and Lady Rhondda funding or initiating networks of literary magazines for which artistically and intellectually gifted but less economically powerful women could write.[35] Studies of women's political activism have tended to focus on political parties, or a single organisation, such as the suffragist Women's Social and Political Union; this approach tends not to reveal the whole picture and does not show how organisations, often with overlapping memberships, shaped and influenced each other.

Rebel women between the wars

In addition, by examining the group and not the woman (apart from well-studied figureheads, such as Emmeline Pankhurst or Nancy Astor), we are in danger of missing some of the more subtle and nuanced ways in which multiple membership of organisations helped women. Activist women such as Manning tended to belong to a whole interconnected and overlapping raft of organisations, supporting a range of causes such as women's rights, suffrage, pacifism, temperance, educational rights and social justice. The Women's International League for Peace and Freedom, for example, formed in 1915, was founded by women who already belonged to a range of organisations and networks right across the globe. These included multiple national branches of the International Suffrage Alliance including those from India and China, the Women's Peace Party of America, the International Federation of University Women, the International Council of Women of the Darker Races, the Women's Social and Political Union, the Danish Council of Women, the Italian Workers' Party, the Association of Hungarian Women Clerks, and numerous other smaller groups representing women workers, educationists, pacifists and suffragists.[36] In 1930 the WILPF joined with seven other international women's organisations to form the Liaison Committee of Women's International Organisations, to press for the World Disarmament Conference. These organisations were the International Council of Women, the International Alliance of Women for Suffrage and Equal Citizenship, the World's Young Women's Christian Association, the International Federation of University Women, the World's Women's Christian Temperance Union, the International Council of Nurses and the World Union of Women for International Concord.[37] The WILPF also provided a platform for Una Marson, who spoke

Formal networks

on inequality between black people and whites in Jamaica at the 'Africa: Peace and Freedom' conference held in London in 1934.

Similarly, the International Council of Women (ICW, formed in 1888) and its hundreds of branch organisations comprised women from pre-existing temperance, missionary, anti-trafficking and penal reform organisations, as well as suffrage organisations.[38] By 1913 its membership was six million women across 23 countries, mostly from Europe and North America, but also Turkey, India, Argentina and Persia (present-day Iran).[39] If we examine just one dynamic node in this network, the Danish suffragist and educator Henni Forchammer, we see she was a founder member of the WILPF and a vice-president of the ICW, as well as president of the Danish NCW. She was appointed technical adviser to the Danish government delegation to the League of Nations and spoke at the League's first plenary session, held in 1920, on the subject of the international traffic in women and children. She succeeded in persuading the Assembly to establish a commission to investigate the trafficking of women and children between Armenia, Turkey and the Near East. She was also the only woman appointed to the League of Nations' Permanent Mandates Commission. Her membership of both these large, active and diverse women's organisations helped propel her to a major role on the international stage: 'This was the first time a woman addressed a Plenary Meeting of the League Assembly and her intervention was greeted with marked applause.'[40]

Recent work on the role of networks in enabling individual women's participation and activism before they gained full equal rights as citizens has now begun to show just how valuable these networks were to women, even as politics and political activism were still very much a man's game.[41] Multiple networks particularly helped women in the Labour Party, who lacked the powerful elite contacts, education and economic capital of Conservative or Liberal women politicians. Labour women activists, for example, who successfully stood as councillors in Manchester in the interwar period were members of multiple groups including various unions, the Coal Control Board, the ILP and Women's Co-operative Guild.[42] One of the first women Labour MPs, Margaret Bondfield, started her working life at the age of 12 and was apprenticed as a shop assistant aged 14; she joined the Shop Assistants' Union and from there was invited to join the socialist Social Democratic Federation. At 24 she became assistant secretary of the Amalgamated Union of Shop Assistants, Warehousemen and Clerks.[43] A general rule of thumb seems to be that the more organisations a woman belonged to, the more likely it was that she would attain some kind of position of public influence.

This is, of course, not just about the combined influence of networks but about the individual woman. If, like Manning, a woman chose to join multiple political, professional and social organisations she was clearly focused on gaining the benefits of collaboration, support, information sharing and policy influence that these offered, and was probably a good communicator too.[44] The nature and size of these organisations also affected what kind of influence they could exert, both outwardly on society and politics, and inwardly on the individual member. While it was Manning's membership of the broad-based Labour Party and NUT that helped propel her into Parliament, it was her membership of the Cambridge branch of the National Council of Women, numbering only a few dozen members, that enabled her to keep her job at the New Street school. The Cambridge

Formal networks

NCW and Manning were working, at the group and individual level, very much towards the same goal, that of women's increased opportunities and equality, an important factor in predicting the success of an individual within a network.

In the case of Una Marson, the League of Coloured Peoples, which was to be transformative in terms of her participatory trajectory, had a membership of less than 300 in 1933/34 and clearly lacked the numbers to exert much external influence. However, in becoming the League's secretary, Marson practised leadership, administrative and communicative roles that all provided valuable training and experience. This can be measured against women who enjoyed another kind of network altogether, such as the Conservative and Unionist MP Nancy Astor, the first woman to take her seat in the House of Commons in December 1919. She famously did not support suffrage organisations, yet she enjoyed enormous wealth and the network that counted most for her was her marriage to Waldorf Astor and the powerful and wealthy clique that they moved in.[45] Although after becoming an MP Astor formed the Consultative Committee of Women's Organisations, it was boycotted by the Labour Party and its federation of women's organisations from the start, and the National Union of Societies for Equal Citizenship (NUSEC) withdrew over disagreements about Astor's views on protective labour legislation.[46] Astor also lobbied hard for women to be allowed in the diplomatic service, and was famously charming and brave, withstanding severe heckling when she stood up to speak as, initially, the only woman MP in the House of Commons.[47]

Astor needed only a single, powerful network. Manning was in the mould of Labour and union women, who not only overcame gender obstacles by joining organisations but also benefited from their combined power to get an outspoken and unusually progressive and experimental teacher out of trouble. She in turn helped to strengthen other groups. Her recognition of the value of mutually supportive networks threads through all her public speeches, most noticeably in her election address of October 1931 and her maiden speech in the House of Commons. At her election address, quoting Saint Paul, she described the nations of the world as

> roped together like Alpine climbers. If one falls over the precipice, the others have to stand the strain. Great Britain cannot thrive if its neighbours are poor any more than a tradesman can be prosperous if the community in which he plies his business is plunged into poverty. Applied to international relations, the saying of St Paul, 'Ye are members of one another' is truer than ever.[48]

In her maiden speech, which she timed to coincide with the debate on international arbitration on disarmament, she acknowledged that 'my voice is enlarged and enhanced by the feeling and aspiration of thousands of women outside the House'.[49]

Bilbao and the evacuation of the Basque children

After leaving the New Street school, in 1920 Manning had become head of an experimental 'open air' school for tubercular and 'MD' ('mentally defective') children in Vinery Road, and then from 1927 in Ascham Road, Cambridge, in a purpose-built building with large south-facing windows, an open 'rest shed' and expansive grounds.[50] Her experience convinced her that every child should be given a chance, and when she became an MP she continued to campaign for the right of

Formal networks

every child to an education: 'You can take a child who appears to be entirely antisocial, and by careful, patient methods of education, you can give that child a place in society ... we must not allow such children to sink because he or she is uneducated.'[51]

As an MP Manning also continued her campaign to raise the school leaving age to 15 and for a national maternity service at a time when, for every 250 babies born, one mother died in childbirth.[52] Although she lost her only child, she spent the rest of her life campaigning for the rights of other people's children; and so, when in 1937 she was approached by the Basque government's delegation to London asking her to help evacuate children from Bilbao, she naturally agreed immediately to help.[53]

In April 1937 Bilbao was at imminent risk of falling to General Mola's besieging troops, who were daily advancing closer over the mountain passes, aided by German and Italian bombers. The populace had been reduced to eating cats and dogs, buoyed by the occasional British merchant ship that had successfully outfoxed the naval blockade (as we saw in Florence Roberts's story in Chapter 4). However, Baldwin's government had yet to approve the evacuation: the Home Office had expressed doubts over the country's ability to absorb so many children, and the question of the cost to the public purse was also raised.[54] The British Ambassador to Spain, Sir Henry Chilton, cruelly dismissed the evacuation plan as removing 'useless mouths' that would have the effect of prolonging the siege, thus irritating Franco and his belligerent ally Germany at a time when British rearmament had only just begun.[55] The navy complained that ships undertaking humanitarian service in Spain – any refugee ship would need naval protection – would be unfairly prevented from attending the Coronation Naval Review, due to take place at Spithead on 20 May to celebrate the coronation of George VI.[56] In addition, Sir Samuel Hoare, First Lord of the Admiralty, was pro-Franco and wanted to avoid any possible clashes with the Spanish rebel navy.[57]

Thus a barricade of hugely powerful men was aligned against Manning when she arrived in Bilbao on 24 April in a small plane from St Jean de Luz. She drove straight to the British Consulate to ask for help in persuading the British government to approve the evacuation. Ralph Stevenson, a 'pleasant and courteous gentleman', was, however, a Foreign Office conservative who would do nothing without following protocol.[58] Indeed, his preference was for the Basque government and leading families to be evacuated, while women and children were sent to refugee camps inside Spain.[59] After Guernica, just a few miles up the coast, was bombed on 26 April, resulting in the deaths of nearly 1,700 civilians, British public opinion began to move towards supporting the idea of bringing the Basque children to England. Manning visited the town the night after the raid with the *News Chronicle* journalist Philip Jordan, and promised that the children of Bilbao would not suffer a similar fate. She broadcast criticism of the British government nightly from Bilbao, cabling off telegrams to all her political contacts, the Archbishop of Canterbury and the Catholic Archbishop of Westminster. One cable that she sent to her friend, the MP for Jarrow Ellen Wilkinson, on 3 May was designed to provoke both pity for the children and national shame at Britain's inertia. She sent it knowing it would end up in the public domain, as it did: in the House of Commons Wilkinson waved the telegram at Foreign Secretary Anthony Eden, and then made its contents available to any newspaper that wanted it. Manning's words appeared on the front page of the *Leeds Mercury* the next day:

Formal networks

> Arrangements proceeding rapidly for the evacuation of 2,300 children to France, who will be provided for by the French trade unions. More than 20,000 other children ready. Deep anxiety felt in Bilbao as to what arrangements will be made for caring for children. Would also like to send young mothers. Constant air raids on city. Repetition of Guernica feared any day.[60]

However, still Baldwin prevaricated, placing conditions on the ages of the children to be evacuated, meaning that siblings from the same family would be separated: 'The Basques had no sympathy from the Home Office or Foreign Office ... both regarded the whole thing as a nuisance and myself an officious busy-body.'[61] However, Manning had an ally in the Spanish Pro-Consul, Angel Ojanguren, and on 17 May, while Stevenson was absent, Ojanguren sent a cable to London at Manning's request to say that plans for the children's departure were so well advanced that any changes would mean a delay of up to ten days, which might be too late.[62] In her memoir, Manning claims she and Ojanguren had in effect 'conned' the Foreign Office into finally approving the evacuation to Britain with this telegram.[63] This may not be entirely true, but she certainly had public opinion on her side, and the large amounts of money now raised by the Aid Spain Committee for the children's upkeep meant that Whitehall's objections over cost were neutralised. On 21 May the yacht *Habana*, with a capacity of 800, began loading the young passengers, with the help of two British doctors, Audrey Russell and Richard Ellis, and nurse Aileen Moore.

Moore's subsequent article, published in the *Nursing Mirror and Midwives' Journal*, provides a dramatic eyewitness account of the days before and during the evacuation, beginning with her first-time experience of flying:

Rebel women between the wars

> The little monoplane was perched, glittering, in a field of clover and daisies against a background of blue, snow-covered Pyrenean peaks. Her weight was 25 kilos ... Up, up, up, so high that the rolling Atlantic seemed only a corrugated gleaming blue surface, broken by deep patches of shadow ... with fighting units to my left beyond the long yellow fringe of sand and the purple piled ranges. Far, far down, miniature destroyers rode on the white specked blue sheet of sea.[64]

Waiting for final embarkation orders, she records eating rice, beans and cat and donkey steak, and dodging German air raids as she escorted distraught children away from their weeping mothers.[65] Before the *Habana* was fully loaded, the nationalist air raids on the port had become so intense that the ship left without all of the children on board. They were later embarked on a smaller yacht and caught up with the main convoy at Bordeaux.[66] Apart from severe bouts of seasickness ('for two dreadful days and nights Richard, Audrey and I slipped and slithered from one pool of vomit and diarrhoea to another'), they arrived safely in Southampton on 23 May.[67] Two weeks later, Bilbao fell. Leah Manning had literally snatched nearly 4,000 boys and girls out from underneath Franco's nose.

Once they arrived and had been put in temporary tents outside Southampton, Manning did not give up fighting to find them homes and schools. In a foreword to a pamphlet for an exhibition of drawings by Spanish children from Madrid, Valencia and Malaga, she wrote: 'To have become, by a miracle, the "accidental" mother of 4,000 children, gives me a mother's right to speak on their behalf.'[68] The children, as adults, and either returned to Spain or settled in Britain, remembered her fondly. One woman, Esta Nickson, who had been on the

Formal networks

Habana, wrote in 1991: 'I remember her very well, we all loved her, she always had a smile and a cuddle for all of us.'[69]

How instrumental was Manning in the evacuation? One historian is convinced that she made all the difference: 'Without her flaming zeal, her emotional outbursts, her real organising abilities, her broadcasts and her telegrams to all and sundry, the obstacles erected in London to the reception of the Basque children might not have been overcome.'[70] It was a Basque women's group, Emakume ('Free Women'), which in the early years of this century began agitating for a memorial to Manning in Bilbao, and on 13 November 2002 the Plaza de Mrs Leah Manning, a quiet, leafy square, appropriately situated in the schools district of Bilbao, was opened.[71] Twenty-five years after her death, her women's networks were still working for her.

Una Marson: the League of Coloured Peoples

Una Marson, poet, playwright, journalist and activist, has been described as 'the most significant black British feminist of the interwar years', although her activism and literary output reached far beyond the boundaries of gender politics.[72] One of her many outstanding features was her modernity: she crossed the Atlantic three times during the 1930s, making the 'reverse colonial voyage' at least a decade before the main period of Caribbean emigration; she was one of the first women poets to write down the local dialect, as used by Jamaican women, in her poetry; and in 1938 she became the first black woman to work for the BBC through its newest technology of mass communication: television.[73] Her experience of and response to English racism foreshadows that experienced by the later wave of Caribbean immigration after the Second World War, which first drew sociologists' attention to the 'new' problem of race relations.[74] Her response in turning a critical eye on the system that turned her into a form of spectacle is another sign of Marson's modernity, and prefigures the work of later Caribbean writers, such as the Trinidadian Sam Selvon's *The Lonely Londoners* (1956).

Marson has recently been the subject of much recovery work, having been virtually ignored for the first thirty years after her death in 1965.[75] Studies have concentrated on her literary output, particularly her plays and poetry, and her work for the BBC during the Second World War.[76] There is much still to recover, and this chapter examines her work as editor of *The Keys*, the quarterly magazine of the League of Coloured Peoples, as well as some of her other English journalism and activism. In collating contributions to *The Keys*, and in particular writing '*The Keys* Disclose' sections, Marson helped to draw together the threads of a disparate network of black and white members of the League right across the world in the early years of its formation, setting its character as an organisation not only interested in the politics of race, but also in arts, culture and anthropology. She also helped foster a wider associational culture, reporting on the activities of League members to try to create a united and cohesive unit within an organisation that suffered from internal rivalries and factionalism almost from the start.[77] As editor of *The Keys* Marson gave a platform to female voices, both poetic and journalistic. It will be seen that the number of female names recorded in the journal under her editorship was about double the quantity recorded in issues edited by men, and thus, consciously or unconsciously, she was instrumental in including women in the newly establishing black public sphere in interwar London. In 1938 she would be invited

Formal networks

Figure 12 Una Marson at the BBC, 1941

to speak as a witness to the West India Royal Commission alongside the KCMGs and CMGs of the Colonial Office. She founded the Jamaican branch of Save the Children and also would become the first black woman radio producer employed by the BBC, producing wartime cultural programmes with George Orwell and T. S. Eliot.[78]

Una Maud Victoria Marson was born in the village of Santa Cruz on 6 February 1905, the youngest of nine children of the Revd Solomon Isaac and Ada Marson. Her father is described as a 'stern Baptist parson' and Una, being a 'wayward' child, often fought against the restrictions imposed by custom, tradition and religion.[79] The family lived in a house that was large, light and airy by rural Jamaican standards, and Marson won a scholarship to attend the academic Hampton High School for Girls in Malvern. There, 'more than half the staff was English' and, she later wrote, 'I was taught nothing about my own island.'[80] When Marson was born, Jamaica's slaves had only been free for eighty years and her mother and father, she said, 'never spoke of the past, maybe because it was so sad'.[81] So, though she responded poetically to the island's natural beauty, the 'cool sea breezes', lush vegetation, the 'silent hills where the cadences of Nature's voice tempt one to answering song', she was aware of a strange vacuum, a history and voice of a whole people waiting to be recovered and written down.[82]

Marson's father died while she was still at school, and she went to work in Kingston, sharing a house with her sister, Etty. After a few clerical positions, Marson found a job as assistant editor on the *Jamaica Critic* in January 1926, where she 'began to learn how journalism worked', learning the skills of writing, editing, proofreading and publishing.[83] Through the *Critic*, Marson made links with poets and writers in Kingston and became an active member of the Jamaica Poetry League where she was encouraged to start writing her own verse. Frustrated by the *Critic*'s traditional view of women, she left two years later to edit her own monthly magazine, *The Cosmopolitan*.[84] The full title of the magazine, funded by a businessman of Marson's acquaintance, was *The Cosmopolitan: A Monthly Magazine for the Business Youth of Jamaica and the Official Organ of the Stenographers Association*, and it contained an eclectic mix of fashion and housekeeping tips, feminist politics and a page dedicated to

Formal networks

'Short Poems by Local Poets' where Marson published some of her own poetry.[85] However, *The Cosmopolitan* struggled to find a viable readership among the small population of the educated middle classes in Kingston, and in spring 1931, even after a jaunty relaunch, it closed indefinitely.

Marson, always struggling for money, returned to secretarial work and writing in her spare time. She published two volumes of poetry, mostly romantic in nature, and staged a play meditating on the status of women, *At What a Price*, to wide acclaim at the Ward Theatre, Kingston. The proceeds from *At What a Price* were enough for Marson to go travelling as a way of raising her public image as a writer and to satisfy her curiosity about what lay beyond the island. It was a choice between the United States and the United Kingdom, and she chose the latter due to her 'passionate longing for the land of Shakespeare, Milton, Tennyson, Keats, Shelley, Byron and Wordsworth'.[86] In addition, Britain and France, and London and Paris in particular, were, in the interwar years, 'critical contact zones for African diasporic formation, intellectual production and political organisation' and thus London represented for Marson a more fruitful arena in which to develop her literary talent.[87]

The two-week crossing of the Atlantic, in the summer of 1932 on the SS *Jamaica Settler*, transformed Marson from acclaimed poet and playwright into an undesirable alien, an unexpected and unwanted metamorphosis. Marson ended up, as many West Indian travellers did, at 164 Queen's Road, Peckham, 'often a first place of call for many who came to Britain': medical students, graduates seeking employment and political activists as well as 'those who encountered obstacles in their path, and difficulties arising from their colour, which thwarted the achievement of their objective'.[88] The large, rambling Victorian villa was the home of Dr Harold Moody, another Jamaican who had made the crossing thirty years before Marson. Moody had qualified as a doctor at King's College Hospital, winning several academic medals and awards, but, prevented by the colour bar from getting a job in a London hospital, he set up his own private practice in Peckham.[89] The visitors' book at 164 Queen's Road 'read like a who's who of black historical figures': the actor Paul Robeson; the socialist intellectual C. L. R. James; Jomo Kenyatta, who would become the founding president of the Republic of Kenya; the Trinidadian cricketer Learie Constantine; and the barrister Stella Thomas, who would later become the first female magistrate in West Africa.[90]

Marson became unpaid secretary to the new group founded by Moody in 1931, the League of Coloured Peoples (LCP), and in so doing went straight to the heart of a network of activists, helping to organise conferences, social events and Moody's series of lectures on race relations around the country. The LCP, which had a black leadership but included during its first ten years a large proportion of white members, was a moderate organisation with the central aim of 'stating the cause of our brothers and sisters within the British Empire' while also acknowledging the 'struggles of peoples of colour throughout the world'.[91] It was a middle-class organisation, with Moody hosting tennis parties and garden parties, and members' children being taken to the country for picnics in the manner of the English upper and middle classes. Importantly, one of the LCP's key objectives was to 'co-operate and affiliate with organisations sympathetic to Coloured People'. In other words, it was a collaborative organisation, and it was through the broad collection of African activists and British progressives and feminists who sympathised with the League's objectives that Marson

Formal networks

began to make vital connections in the arenas of feminism, pan-Africanism, international development and child poverty.[92] For Moody, the LCP was primarily 'to serve a Christian purpose, not a political one', and this is possibly why various London and African activist groups were often impatient both with the LCP and Moody, who endured harsh criticism from various quarters and threatened to resign his presidency on several occasions.[93] *The Keys* also reported resentment from Indian members of the LCP who complained about under-representation on the officers' committee at 'stormy' annual general meetings.[94]

Editorship of *The Keys*

The LCP's journal, first published in July 1933, was named *The Keys* in allusion to the ebony and ivory keys on a piano creating harmony together, from the much-quoted phrase coined by the Gold Coast educational philosopher James Aggrey.[95] But its first editorial stressed the other meaning of 'keys' as a means of opening doors previously locked:

> We are knocking at the door and will not be denied. *The Keys* will, we trust, be an open sesame to better racial understanding and goodwill. The name is symbolic for what the League is striving for: the opening of doors and avenues now closed to Coloured people.[96]

Marson's two-year editorship of *The Keys* was always contested, as evidenced in her various appellations of 'editor', 'acting editor' and 'associate editor' through the issues she was involved in. Although Harold Moody was a loyal supporter, other members of the LCP's executive committee chafed at the direction of both the magazine and the organisation. Some wanted it to take a less conciliatory, less accommodationist and more radical approach to race politics. Others wanted to move it away from its overwhelming emphasis on West Indian and African politics and membership to include people from China and India. Still others wanted the LCP to embrace communism, seeing the ideology as the only means of ultimately freeing black people.[97] It could also have been, as would be repeated in her 'peculiarly embattled' period as producer for BBC radio during the Second World War, that some people simply objected to a woman (and in the case of the BBC, a black woman) occupying such a prominent position in an overwhelmingly male-dominated organisation.[98]

The editor of the first issue of *The Keys* is named as David Tucker, a Bermudan lawyer who would eventually become an MP and newspaper editor on that island.[99] In the second issue, October 1933, Marson is named as 'acting editor' and a short note explains: 'We regret to inform our readers that Mr David Tucker, our able Editor, left London for his home in Bermuda shortly after he produced the first issue. His departure was sudden and we are very sorry to lose such a splendid worker.'[100] In the third issue, January 1934, Tucker is once again named editor and Marson as 'associate editor', even though Tucker had still not returned, and indeed would not return from Bermuda during the next two years. This pairing of titles, Marson as associate editor to an absent editor Tucker, who by this time was in any case the editor of the Bermuda weekly paper *The Recorder*, is maintained throughout the next four issues.[101] Only in the last issue that Marson was involved in, January–March 1935, is she finally named as editor. Marson's biographer and other scholars agree that she was wholly, or mostly, responsible for the first two years of *The*

Formal networks

Keys. Analysis of various sections of the paper shows editorial cohesion across different issues, such as the '*The Keys* Disclose' section, throughout these first two years, a section that disappeared with the end of Marson's editorship.

The 20-page quarterly journal cost 6d, and came in a pale blue cover carrying, initially, a photograph of palm trees bending over a deserted tropical beach, captioned 'By palm-fringed shores'. Analysis of the editorial content shows that in the first issue, edited by David Tucker, male names outnumber female names by a ratio of 6:1 (in total 36 different male names and 6 different female ones). In the next seven issues, for which Marson was responsible, that ratio falls to the region of 3:1 (for example, Vol. 1/2: 45 male names, 16 female names; Vol. 1/3: 63 male names, 23 female names; Vol. 1/4: 32 male names, 12 female names; Vol. 2/3: 55 male names, 17 female names). In the first and subsequent issues after her resignation, the ratio returns to a range of 6 male names to every female one (Vol. 2/4: 108 male names, 20 female names).[102] This unconscious bias of male editors against commissioning or even mentioning women has long been observed in media studies and partly explains women's continued 'symbolic annihilation' from the public sphere even after they obtained equal rights as citizens.[103] This is still an area of contention, with campaigns such as 'Women on Air' and 'Women Also Know Stuff' monitoring this bias and offering female experts to journalists and editors as commentators.[104] Under Marson's editorship circulation reached 2,000 copies per issue, sold in London and throughout the world.[105] Marson's editorship of *The Keys*, then, intensified women's presence in what was the most important interwar British black activist publication, and thus did more than anything else in asserting women's rights to be part of the developing black public sphere.[106] Marson was also a gifted publicist, with her own name appearing several times in each of the issues she edited, reaching a peak of nine times in the January 1934 issue with coverage of the performance and reception in London of her play *At What a Price* and reports of her attending various social functions.[107] She also published her photographic portrait, again in a journal where images had almost entirely male subjects.[108]

As well as doubling the ratio of women's names in the magazine, Marson also commissioned and reported their work. In the October 1933 issue Marson published a poem by Sylvia Lowe, another Jamaican woman residing at the Moodys' home, who served on the LCP executive committee. Lowe's poem, 'Disillusionment: After Seeing the Trooping of the Colour', is similar in theme to Marson's 'Nigger' of the previous issue, although less angry. It contrasts the love and loyalty felt by black citizens towards king and country and the 'bitter insults' encountered when they arrive in 'the land that lies/ Far in our dreams, dreams which alas are dead'.[109] In the January 1934 issue, Marson published a long report by social investigator Nancie Sharpe into the living conditions among the estimated 3,000 'coloured' seamen in Cardiff, of whom 'more than 2,000 ... are Negroes'.[110] One-tenth of these men had fathered families who were living in Tiger Bay, 'the dock area, which is ... on a long narrow peninsula very much cut off from the rest of the city'. The report notes that the West Indian seamen tended to marry women of a lower social class than themselves, and that 'he afterwards finds [her] to have lower standards of cleanliness, general attainments and ambitions for the children than he has'. In the April–June 1934 issue, Marson included a report of a lecture given to the LCP by the

Formal networks

historian Margery Perham on 'Indirect Rule' in small African countries.[111]

Marson used the '*The Keys* Disclose' section to increase the presence of women in the magazine. The section contained short newsy snippets, both serious and entertaining, concerning black people around the world, for example: 'In USA from January to June 1st there were two lynchings, from June to August 31st there have been 13'; 'Mr George Headley, famous West Indian batsman has sailed from Jamaica to take up his appointment with a Lancashire cricket club here in England.'[112] Marson made sure to include news and names of women in this section, for example: 'Miss Edna Elliott of Sierra Leone, is the first African lady of West Coast to obtain B. A. of Harvard University ... Miss Anna Philips of Liberia, M. A. of Columbia University USA is doing 2 years post-graduate work in Geneva'; 'Mrs D. E. Armstrong of British Guiana has sent two fine pictures for our headquarters'; 'Miss Nancy Harris in her report on London and Cardiff seamen stated that Negroes in England are intellectually and morally starved.'[113] Read as a whole, '*The Keys* Disclose' section asserted the journal as the central node in a comprehensive and densely woven, pan-Africanist global network of information gathering and dissemination, helping to unite a dispersed and often subjugated population with optimistic stories of achievement, as well as publicising white outrages. One item, on a report on the 'vigour and independence' and, crucially, the ability to reproduce of Australian Aboriginal people 'not in contact with whites' is of particular note.[114] Not only does it show that Marson was interested in pushing the scope of *The Keys* beyond a middle-class and Western-centric focus, but that she was also prepared to contradict white Australian 'doomed race' narratives that were being used at the time to justify ill-treatment and seizure of Aboriginal lands. This theme will be pursued in the next chapter, which examines the Australian writer and activist Kylie Tennant and her Depression-era novels.

As her last act as editor, for the spring 1935 issue, Marson introduced a books section and commissioned a review of the black American novelist Zora Neale Hurston's first novel, *Jonah's Gourd Vine* (1934). Marson commissioned the review from the Harlem Renaissance writer Eric Walrond, who had moved to England in the early 1930s and whom Marson met over tea with their mutual friend, the writer Winifred Holtby. Walrond praised *Jonah's Gourd Vine* for its use of 'Negro dialect ... which is disturbingly eloquent of the break with the English literary tradition that is so characteristic of the work of the young writers of the American Negro renaissance'.[115] The new review page, which also included a review of a collection of short stories, *The Ways of White Folk* by Langston Hughes, added a rich intellectual and literary dimension to the magazine, and leads to speculation as to the kind of direction and scope *The Keys* would have taken had Marson remained editor.

Beyond *The Keys*

Marson's resignation as editor coincided with her departure from Queen's Road to take her own flat at 29 Brunswick Square, Camberwell.[116] This was a time when Marson's interests were moving beyond the LCP. She had already spoken at a British Commonwealth League conference in 1933, and in June 1934 she spoke on 'bars to careers' (reporting her speech in *The Keys*), sharing a platform with Jomo Kenyatta; there she met Winifred Holtby, forming a friendship that would last until

Formal networks

Holtby's death a year later.[117] Here we see another group of networks opening for Marson, albeit of mostly white progressives with whom Marson would feel increasingly impatient, particularly after the Italian invasion of Abyssinia.[118] Holtby was a member of the League of Coloured Peoples and also the London Group on African Affairs, the Joint Council to Promote Understanding Between White and Coloured Peoples in Great Britain, and the Council for Promoting Equality of Civil Rights Between White and Coloured Peoples. Holtby herself founded the Friends of Africa, established to raise funds for the Scottish trade unionist William Ballinger, who was trying to organise the Industrial and Commercial Workers' Union, a trade union for black South Africans.[119] Marson also spoke at the WILPF's London conference on 'Africa: Peace and Freedom' on 20 November 1934, alongside Ballinger. The WILPF had begun debating anti-imperialism at its 1924 international congress, with the demand that 'subject nations must be freed'; however, this demand was also framed by the British branch of the WILPF's assertion that 'The European "invasion" of Africa has already brought many benefits to her people – Christianity, Western education, engineering achievements, modern medicine and surgery.'[120] Marson clearly found the conference exhilarating. She dedicated a page of the subsequent issue of *The Keys* to covering it, and wrote a poem, 'Education', inspired by Ballinger's speech, which highlighted the difference in spending on white and black schoolchildren in South Africa (£25 per head and £2 3s 7d per head respectively), a corrective to the WILPF's assertion of the 'benefits' that the European 'invasion' had actually brought to Africa.[121] Her own speech, on 'Social and Political Equality' in Jamaica, urged caution on those who saw Jamaica as a model of colonial progress. It was true, she said, that five heads of government departments were black, and that 'Nearly the entire professional class is black or coloured – magistrates, a judge of the supreme court, many of the finest barristers and doctors are men of colour.'[122] However, it was certainly not 'the Paradise it is painted to be'. The only reason Jamaica was held up as a model of how colonies could order their own affairs was because in comparison with Africa, Jamaica appeared to be doing so well.[123] This view would harden over the next few years, with Marson's submission to the Moyne Commission asserting, 'We are handicapped for our colour in Jamaica and in London.'[124]

In April 1935, shortly after renouncing the *Keys* editorship, Marson travelled to Istanbul to deliver a speech at the IAWSEC's annual congress on the effect of the colour bar on African students at English universities, 'bringing tears to the eyes of her audience'; however, this sympathy, which she increasingly saw as irrelevant and patronising, was not enough.[125] The extent of her feelings about being patronised by white progressives can be seen in her poem 'Little Brown Girl', published shortly after her temporary return to Jamaica in 1936. The poem reveals the gulf of understanding between the white spectator and the 'Little brown girl' who is rendered mute by the narrator's barrage of questions:

> Little brown girl
> Why do you wander alone
> About the streets
> Of the great city
> Of London?
> ...
> Little brown girl
> Why did you leave

Formal networks

> Your little sunlit land
> Where we sometimes go
> To rest and get brown
> So we may look healthy?
> ...
> I heard you speak
> To the Bobbie,
> You speak good English
> Little brown girl,
> How is it you speak
> English as though it belonged
> To you?[126]

The woman immediately 'others' the girl by emphasising the difference between the strange 'brown' of the poet and the aspirational 'brown' of the suntanned Westerners who see her island as their pleasure playground. The woman cannot understand why the 'little brown girl' is more interested in looking at the books, newspapers and cinema listings than the coats and clothes in the shop windows. The girl's interest is in the cultural production of London rather than in trivialities, as she seeks to understand the metropolis that creates a spectacle of her. Her inarticulacy in the face of apparently well-meaning and friendly questioning must be read in conjunction with Marson's publicly stated views on the colour bar, which she described at the British Commonwealth League conference in 1934. Here she used an early opportunity to speak in public to emphasise the silencing effects of racism:

> In America they tell you, frankly where you are not wanted by means of big signs, and they don't try to hide their feelings. But in England, though the people will never say what they feel about us, you come up against incidents which *hurt so much that you cannot talk about them.*[127]

Rebel women between the wars

Marson's poetry became a vehicle for her activism and a means of expressing the gulf that existed between her and even progressive white feminists. Her activism, as the writer and activist Alice Walker would later say, became her 'muse', inspiring her to produce some of her best literary work.[128] In 'Little Brown Girl' the narrator's surprise that, on overhearing her speak to a 'Bobbie' she can actually speak English 'as though it belonged / To you', indicates that despite the apparent friendliness she is both patronising and affronted by the girl's use of the imperial language. The question locates the point of conflict at that juncture where speaking, writing, oppression and language meet, and foreshadows French feminist Hélène Cixous's commentary of fifty years later that 'Woman must put herself into the text – as into the world and into history.'[129] The poem thus speaks volumes for the years that Marson endured in London of being the 'token black woman' at various progressive events, and the ultimate betrayal that, in the end, even apparently forward-looking feminists put Empire and the interests of the West above racial equality. This was exemplified in IAWSEC president Margery Corbett Ashby's response to Marson's impressive performance at the Istanbul congress – Ashby immediately joined the LCP and became a generous donor, but at the same time asserted women's duty to work for a better Empire rather than to dismantle it.[130] Marson's experience here is similar to that of the African American activist Mary Church Terrell, an early member of the WILPF, who spoke at the Zurich Women's Peace Congress in 1919, the only woman of colour among hundreds of delegates.[131] Despite Terrell's campaigning and speaking abilities, her two-year period as a board member of the US branch of the WILPF was contested and embattled, the

Formal networks

politics of race that had so infected US suffragism still infecting interwar feminist activism. Despite the WILPF's work in challenging racism across the world and US politics, 'it struggled when it came to identifying and abolishing racism within its own organisation'.[132]

We can see here both the strengths and the limitations of networks, in the interests they serve and the direction as dictated by leading members. Ultimately the WILPF, IAWSEC and the National Council of Women were organisations for white, middle-class, educated women, and thus were limited in the kind of change they wanted and agitated for. Both the WILPF and IAWSEC did extraordinarily good work in asserting women's rights and in seeking pathways to peace during the interwar years, as well as providing a platform for women to speak publicly on world affairs and to forge supportive links across the world. The WILPF, particularly, in its individual branches and also as a whole campaigned against the evils of imperialism. However, both organisations failed to challenge what Marson saw as one of the biggest obstacles to equality and peace: attitudes to race and Empire within its membership. As we will see in the next chapter, the Australian branch of the WILPF likewise failed to challenge the White Australia Policy in any meaningful way. The WILPF and IAWSEC were, in turn, circumscribed and limited by other, more powerful organisations, such as the League of Nations. While WILPF members were very much involved in the League of Nations, one of their earliest policy demands, that women should be entrusted v ith negotiating the 1919 peace treaty, having identified the nr prevent the isolation of Germany, 'was completely ign We will never know what direction history would h had the WILPF's demand been accepted.

Rebel women between the wars

During the Second World War Marson began to suffer from severe bouts of depression, partly caused by the enormous stress placed on her by widespread resistance to her role as the producer of the *Calling the West Indies* programme at the BBC.[134] Marson had begun working at the BBC as a freelance in 1938, encouraged and promoted by individual producers, especially Cecil Madden at the Empire Service, and was given a job on the BBC staff in 1941.[135] The black, journalistic and feminist networks that Marson was part of, although nurturing to some degree, were ultimately unable to resist the more powerful interests of the Colonial Office and the West India Committee, which took an active interest in the *Calling the West Indies* programme. The committee represented white West Indian interests, and, according to one internal BBC memo, 'the resultant envy, constantly chewed over, developed a hard core of people who, not only criticised Miss Marson, but were prepared to go to the length of doing something about it'; an anti-Marson group was 'out to get Miss Marson and anyone who protected her out of the BBC at all costs'.[136] The West India Committee had direct and personal connections with politicians and civil servants at both the Ministry of Information and the Colonial Office, circulating their interests directly to the heart of government. Some networks are, ultimately, better connected and have more agency than others.

* * *

Both Manning and Marson recognised the value of forming and belonging to networks of people sharing similar ideas and motivations, as ways of overcoming obstacles to their participation in public life. Both women achieved phenomenally more

Formal networks

than might have been expected, of a woman school teacher and a black woman poet and journalist, through their collaborative approach to networks, and this method has been recognised, and employed, by minority groups throughout history. Like Manning, Marson overcame almost insuperable odds partly through her recognition of the power of networks and organisations within which she found a protective, if ultimately limiting space to hone and promote her talent. She performed not only as cultural producer in her own right, but as a collaborator, cultural facilitator for other writers and disseminator of information, all vital roles in building and strengthening the status of marginalised groups and organisations. Her ultimate withdrawal from IAWSEC, and disillusionment with it, stemmed from an irreconcilable clash between her own goals as a black activist and those of the organisation.

Notes

1 Manning 1935: 11–13.
2 Interview with Leah Manning, published in the *Labour Monthly*, February 1935, pp. 95–8; Manning went on behalf of the World Committee for Anti-Fascist Activities.
3 Manning 1935: 59.
4 'Fascist Influence in Spain', *Manchester Guardian*, 19 January 1935, p. 8; *Daily Herald*, 27 June 1935 (from Gollancz press cuttings, MSS.318/7/Qu/5/3, Warwick Modern Records).
5 Manning 1935: 166.
6 *What I Saw in Spain* was widely reviewed, and was in several 'book of the week' or day columns (Gollancz reviews, MSS.318/7/Qu/5/3, Warwick Modern Records). The review in the *Manchester Guardian*, while quibbling with some of her conclusions, agreed that her 'evidence does strongly suggest that there has been shocking cruelty to the imprisoned revolutionaries, and it is high time that the Government put an end to it' (3 July 1935, p. 5); the *Daily Herald*

called it an 'indispensable well documented' record of 'the medieval horrors' taking place in Spain (27 June 1935).

7 'Savonarola in Petticoats', *The Schoolmaster*, 20 November 1930.

8 Manning 1970; see also 'Active Lady Liberals', *Cambridge Independent Press*, 1 July 1910; 'Cambridge Teachers' Salaries', *Cambridge Daily News*, 20 June 1917; 'Ladies on the Bench', *Cambridge Press and News*, 27 August 1920; 'Cambs. Insurance Committee', *Cambridge Independent Press*, 18 July 1913; 'Letters to the Editor', *Cambridge Daily News*, 7 May 1918.

9 Bill and Newens 1991: 42.

10 See Nan Sloane's compelling account of the conflict on the left between suffragism and women workers' pay and conditions (2018: esp. 3–12); in addition, from the beginning of the interwar period there was active hostility (leading to local proscribing) from the Labour Party towards the feminist but non party-political Women Citizen Associations, to prevent a watering down of the Labour message (Hunt 2009: 213–14).

11 1911 Census report, www.visionofbritain.org.uk/census/EW1911 GEN/5 (accessed 7 June 2019).

12 The previous three women presidents of the NUT were Miss I. Cleghorn, MA (1911), Miss E. R. Conway CBE (1918) and Miss J. F. Wood MA (1920) (NUT Annual Report, 1929, Warwick Modern Records).

13 She became an MP again in the 1945 Labour landslide and served in Attlee's government.

14 For attitudes towards black performers among London's intelligentsia, see Bush 1999: 211–14. See also Evans 2019: 165–7.

15 Bush 1999: 215.

16 Marson 1933.

17 Marson's journalism in the magazine that she founded and edited in Jamaica, the *Cosmopolitan*, shows a desire for 'cross-empire migrations between colony and metropole and across colonies' (Emery 2007: 120). An editorial in December 1929 points to Ghanaian educator James Emman Aggrey, who favoured cooperation between peoples, as a role model. Another article that Marson commissioned from the Revd Leslie J. White envisioned a potential world unity where 'these gifts [of all nations] are to be pooled for the benefit of all'. 'On being a Cosmopolitan', *Cosmopolitan*, 1/6, October 1928.

18 Una Marson, 'Editorial', *The Keys*, 2/3, January–March 1935, p. 45.

Formal networks

19 Marson 1937: 80.
20 Westaby 2012: 9.
21 Biographical details from Manning 1970 and Bill and Newens 1991.
22 Manning 1970: 12.
23 Manning 1970: 20; Charles Bradlaugh was a prominent Victorian atheist and Liberal MP; Oscar Wilde had been imprisoned in Reading Gaol for gross indecency; Annie Besant was a women's rights campaigner, socialist and supporter of both Irish and Indian home rule; Josephine Butler was a social reformer and feminist; William Booth founded the Salvation Army, another nonconformist church focused on social justice. Perrett's grandfather supported the Boers in the Boer War, a radical Liberal position and very unpopular in the atmosphere of jingoism and patriotism whipped up during events such as the siege of Mafeking.
24 While, as we saw in Chapter 2, Quaker women did not enjoy complete equality with men, debate about whether women might speak at public meetings had been common among Quakers since the seventeenth century. John Wesley had also encouraged women preachers within the Methodist movement since the 1760s, although after his death the Methodist Conference in 1803 declared that women should not be allowed to preach. There are, however, numerous instances of women travelling preachers throughout Methodist history. Similarly the Salvation Army was progressive on the issue of women's equality. See Johnson 2004; Morgan (ed.) 2002; Englander and O'Day (eds) 1995.
25 O'Day 1995: 357.
26 Johnson 2004: 259.
27 Strachey 1978: 44.
28 Unpublished MS for a planned biography of Manning by Betty Vernon, Essex County Records Office (ECRO), Acc A13957, Box 1, LM 3b: 295.
29 School Practice Reports, 31 May 1907 and 14 December 1907, Homerton College Cambridge.
30 Acc A13957, Box 1, LM 3b p. 298, ECRO.
31 Manning 1970: 54.
32 Manning 1970: 44; the Ragged School Union was founded in 1844 after benevolent patrons of a range of 'schools for the destitute', 'fragment schools' and 'Sabbath schools' banded together under one umbrella organisation. By 1860 some 170 schools across the

country were providing education for about 50,000 children, either on Sundays, after their work in factories or during the day. Most teachers were voluntary, although a few were paid by local education boards; however, these schools were often avoided by ambitious teachers and the pay was often lower than in ordinary schools. New Street School was built as a Ragged School in 1854 but was taken over by Homerton College as a training school in 1901, when an infants department was built; in 1911, when Perrett was teaching there, there were 370 children enrolled. Grigg 2002; Anon., 'The Origin of Ragged Schools', *Ragged School Union Magazine*, November 1860, pp. 241–5; 'The City of Cambridge: Schools', in *A History of the County of Cambridge and the Isle of Ely: Volume 3, the City and University of Cambridge*, ed. J. P. C. Roach (London, 1959), pp. 141–5, British History Online, www.british-history.ac.uk/vch/cambs/vol3/pp141-145 (accessed 21 June 2019).

33 Manning 1970: 45; Acc A13957, Box 1, LM 3b p. 294, ECRO.
34 See Williams 1997: 181, in conversation with Edward Said.
35 See Camboni 2004: 10–24; for more on Bryher, who helped fund *Life and Letters Today* and *Close Up*, see Chapter 3.
36 Bussey and Tims 1980.
37 Davies 2007: 91.
38 International Council of Women 1966: 11–15.
39 International Council of Women 1966: 39.
40 International Council of Women 1966: 47–8; Bussey and Tims 1980: 37.
41 See, for example, Marjorie Theobald's work on how Australian interwar women teachers bolstered their precarious presence in an aggressively masculine arena by joining multiple groups such as the Lyceum Club, Women Graduates Association and the National Council of Women (2000: 66). See also Beaumont 2013 on the policy work of more conservative women's organisations such as the Mothers' Union and the Women's Institutes.
42 Hunt 2009: 217.
43 Sloane 2018: 34–6.
44 Being sociable and a good communicator is one of the prerequisites for political participation (Milbrath 1960).
45 See also Fort 2013.
46 Jones 2000: 132.

Formal networks

47 For Astor's work on arguing for women diplomats, see McCarthy 2014: esp. 115–17.
48 'Election Address of Leah Manning', pamphlet, 27 October 1931, Acc A13957, Box 1, LM 160, ECRO.
49 *The Vote*, 13 March 1931, p. 1.
50 Acc A13957, Box 1, LM 3b p. 300, ECRO; the building is now listed, cited by Historic England as the most intact of the early twentieth-century open-air schools in England, https://britishlistedbuildings.co.uk/101331961-roger-ascham-school-gymnasium-and-attached-classroom-cambridge#.XSG1MOhKiUk (accessed 6 July 2019).
51 Hansard Series 5, Vol. 255, cols 837–842, 16 July 1931.
52 Hansard Series 5, Vol. 255, cols 2393–2401, 29 July 1931.
53 Manning was secretary of the Spanish Medical Aid Committee and thus part of the National Joint Committee for Spanish Relief which coordinated the Basque children's evacuation.
54 Cable 1979: 117.
55 Cable 1993: 340.
56 Cable 1993: 341.
57 Alpert 1984: 433.
58 Manning 1970: 124.
59 Cable 1979: 108.
60 '4000 Children from Bilbao', *Leeds Mercury*, 4 May 1937, p. 1.
61 Manning 1970: 127.
62 Cable 1979: 124.
63 Manning 1970: 130.
64 Moore 1937: 192.
65 Moore 1937: 194.
66 National Joint Committee for Spanish Relief, Bulletin no. 7, 10 June 1937, MML archives.
67 Manning 1970: 131.
68 Acc A13957, Box 1, LM 156, ECRO.
69 Esta Nickson, letter to Ron Bill, 12 September 1991, Acc A13957, Box 1, LM142, ECRO.
70 Cable 1979: 125.
71 Flier, Acc A13957, Box 1, LM125a, ECRO.
72 Anna Snaith (2014: 155) describes her thus, having weighed her against the 'only [two other] black female activists of any prominence in the 1930s' living in Britain (Bush 1999: 219), Amy Ashwood

Garvey and Eslanda Goode Robeson, the wives, respectively, of Marcus Garvey and Paul Robeson.
73 Tomlinson 2017: 30; Jarrett-Macauley 1998: 144–6; Procter 2015: 7. She also, more famously, worked in radio during the Second World War.
74 See Banton 1955.
75 The most important of these recovery works, upon which most others are founded, is Delia Jarrett-Macauley's widely respected biography, *The Life of Una Marson* (1998). Rhonda Cobham and Merle Collins acknowledge Marson's influence as 'foremother' of a new generation of black women writers in Britain (1987: 3).
76 See, particularly, Snaith 2014; Donnell 2011a, 2011b; Covi 2004; Rosenberg 2001; Evans 2019; and Procter 2015.
77 For more on the 'many violent disagreements' between the LCP's executive members, see Vaughan 1950.
78 West India Royal Commission Report ('The Moyne Report'), (Cmd. 6607), Appendix A, p. 457.
79 Jarrett-Macauley 1998: vii.
80 Marson 1939: 166.
81 Marson 1939: 166.
82 Marson 1930: v.
83 Jarrett-Macauley 1998: 26.
84 Jarrett-Macauley 1998: 26–8.
85 Donnell 2011b: 22.
86 Jarrett-Macauley 1998: 45.
87 Matera 2015: 4.
88 Vaughan 1950: 47; Macdonald 1976: 7.
89 Macdonald 1976: 6.
90 Bourne 2008: 10.
91 Macdonald 1976: 7.
92 *The Keys*, July 1933, inside front cover.
93 Killingray 1999: 11; see, for example, *The Keys*, 2/3, January–March 1935, 'President's Message', p. 46, and 'Attack on LCP', p. 58.
94 'Third Annual General Meeting', *The Keys*, 1/4, April–June 1934, p. 70.
95 Macdonald 1976: 5.
96 'Editorial', *The Keys*, 1/1, July 1933, p. 2.
97 Vaughan 1950: 64.
98 Procter 2015: 6.

Formal networks

99 *The Keys*, 1/1, July 1933, inside front cover.
100 *The Keys*, 1/2, October 1933, p. 21.
101 'Students Return Home', *The Keys*, 2/3, January–March 1935, p. 54.
102 This analysis was conducted by verifying and counting every different name except for the list of officers in the inside front page; where names were repeated in an issue only one was counted. Where women were mentioned only in their function as wives to their husbands, such as names of guests at social events where the woman was only there as adjunct to a celebrated husband, their name was not counted. It must be noted that issue 2/4, edited by George Brown, did included four female bylines as well as five male ones.
103 The phrase 'symbolic annihilation' was originally coined by George Gerbner in 1972 and has since become a widely used expression to describe how media representation (or non-representation) of women succeeds in effacing them from the public sphere (Gallagher 2014: 23).
104 Howell and Singer 2017.
105 'Third Annual General Meeting', *The Keys*, 1/4, April–June 1934, p. 70.
106 In his introduction to the republication of the entire run of *The Keys* in 1976, Roderick Macdonald writes: '*The Keys* may fairly lay claim to pre-eminence among those publications edited and published by blacks resident in London during the 1930s' (1976: 5).
107 The performance of *At What a Price* at London's Scala theatre, with a black writer and director and a black cast, has been described as a significant moment in the black visual culture of Britain, appearing a full two years before C. L. R. James's *Toussaint Louverture*, although it passed virtually unremarked and under-reviewed at the time (Emery 2007: 124).
108 *The Keys*, 1/3, January 1934, p. 49.
109 Lowe 1933: 28.
110 Sharpe 1934: 44.
111 'Lecture on Indirect Rule in Africa', *The Keys*, 1/4, April–June 1934, p. 67.
112 *The Keys*, 2/3, January–March 1935, p. 62; *The Keys*, 1/4, April–June 1934, p. 71.
113 *The Keys*, 2/3, January–March 1935, p. 62; *The Keys*, 1/3, January 1934, p. 58; *The Keys*, 1/2, October 1933, p. 31.
114 *The Keys*, 1/2, October 1933, p. 32.

115 'Book Reviews', *The Keys*, 2/3, January–March 1935, p. 61.
116 Jarrett-Macauley 1998: 80.
117 'The Colour Bar in England', *The Keys*, 2/1, July–September 1934, p. 17. Vera Brittain records in her biography of Holtby, *Testament of Friendship*, that one afternoon she went to visit her friend at her home in Glebe Place, Chelsea, where 'an incongruous quartette gathered in her study for tea: Eric Walrond, a negro poet from New York; Una Masen [*sic*], a Jamaican dramatist who was writing *The Autobiography of a Brown Girl* for Victor Gollancz; Winifred's cousin, Daisy Pickering; and the vivacious cosmopolitan writer Madame Odette Keun … It was interesting. Discussed the colour question, miscegenation, birth control and race prejudice inside out' (1987: 380). Marson's *Autobiography* was never finished and no one has been able to find the manuscript.
118 Matera 2015: 126–8.
119 Regan 2012: 103–34.
120 Stockman 2017: 230; Women's International League 1934: 2.
121 Marson 1935.
122 Marson 1934: 18.
123 Marson 1934: 18.
124 Matera 2015: 137.
125 Schreiber and Matheison 1955: 48–9.
126 Marson 1937.
127 Marson's speech at the British Commonwealth League, reported in the *News Chronicle*, 15 June 1934 (emphasis added).
128 Walker 1997: xiii.
129 Cixous 1981: 45.
130 Matera 2015: 127.
131 Plastas 2011: 22.
132 Plastas 2011: 20.
133 Stockman 2017: 228.
134 For a detailed account of Marson's difficulties at the BBC, see Procter 2015.
135 Procter 2015: 7.
136 African Services Director to Assistant Controller (Overseas Services), 11 March 1942, quoted in Procter 2015: 17.

8
Explosive engagement

There was something about Plug Alley that made it unique. People maintained that those mean stone houses, narrow and verminous and dark, had been built by convicts, and if so, some of the convict tradition had soaked into them. Of course, they were not the same as they were, say in 1850. Reluctantly old Mr Bross had moved with the times and had put in gas rings with penny-in-the-slot meters. There were even taps in the back yards … The yards were paved with brick and all the drainage and rubbish ran cheerfully down a grating in the middle. This usually stank to Heaven and gave rise to the belief that the drainage also dated from the convict days. Besides the tubs, copper, woodpile, dustbins, lavatory and washing, the yard was the only place for the children beside the street. They preferred the street. All the houses had at least two rooms, some three. Of course there were no baths but anyone who wanted a bath, could always rig a screen round the copper in the back yard. The bathing and sanitary facilities gave rise to the kind of crude jokes that Plug Alley most enjoyed. The inhabitants would sit on their front doorsteps in the evening and crack shameless and ribald jokes about their neighbours. Plug Alley had no secrets.[1]

Rebel women between the wars

Kylie Tennant's second novel, *Foveaux*, published in 1939 but written in 1937, is an Australian *Road to Wigan Pier*: a forensic examination of the poverty, desolation, inequality and insanitary living conditions of Depression-era Sydney's sizeable underclass.[2] Tennant's intention was to reproduce with photographic accuracy the stinking drains, the rickety furniture, the broken windows, the dashed hopes and the ever-present threat of violence. There is an earthy physicality in the evidence: the foul detritus, the water running from taps to open sewer, the imagined bodies of the tenants bathing in their back yards, observed by their snarking and curious neighbours. Even the street's name suggests that it is at the very bottom of a giant receptacle used for collecting filth and through which all waste passes. While sparing no detail of the realities of life in the slum tenements of the fictional Sydney suburb (easily recognised as Surry Hills, near the city's main railway terminus and close to where Foveaux Street still runs), Tennant enlivens the story with her characteristic dry humour and compassionate irony that lifts the reportage: 'There were *even* taps in the back yards', she writes, as if this was some kind of miraculous luxury. In so doing she gives the colourful array of characters – the battlers, the aspirants, the ne'er-do-wells and the gritty campaigners – a sympathetic humanity. Beneath the humour, however, there was a serious intent: she didn't want just to report but to ask 'what makes a slum, what economic forces deprive people of decent living conditions?'[3]

The Great Depression hit Australia and New Zealand much harder than many other Western countries as wheat and wool prices, on which both economies relied enormously for export, fell steeply. Rural unemployment rose to 30 per cent in some parts of New South Wales, causing an influx of

Explosive engagement

desperate, out-of-work farm workers and their families into the cities. Travelling 'bagmen' and 'swagmen', now part of Australian national myth, took to the roads in vast numbers. 'Never before in Australian and New Zealand history had there been such a huge social trauma ... The Depression dominated the consciousness of the Australian and New Zealand nations from the close of the 1920s to the close of the 1930s.'[4] As a national psychic event, writers and artists responded to the lasting effects of deprivation and social breakdown, producing a rich body of 'Depression fiction'. Among the many novels, short stories and poems inspired by the Depression, Tennant is, however, unique in that her contributions were contemporaneous with events, and her insistence on living the lives of her subjects brings a raw, immediate realism to her narratives.[5]

Similar to Orwell's approach in *Down and Out in Paris and London* (1933), Tennant lived for several months on mattresses seething with lice and bedbugs, taking transitory jobs as a barmaid and social worker. In other novels she would repeat this 'Gonzo' style of immersive reportage, getting herself arrested and imprisoned, impersonating prostitutes, and living with the itinerant agricultural workers who traversed the vast spaces of outback Australia searching for work.[6] Tennant was just 25 when she wrote *Foveaux*, and 22 when she wrote her first novel, *Tiburon* (1935), about the bagmen and squatters scratching out a precarious living in rural New South Wales. In many ways *Tiburon* is an even bolder work than *Foveaux*, and a precocious first novel, which examines the brutally impoverished lives of the 'relief' workers and their families, paid a bare unemployment benefit only if they were prepared to accept ferociously hard and low-paid work from local farmers. The novel also, unusually for the period, critiques the treatment of Aborigines and mixed-race families in an overtly racist society that was officially pursuing the White Australia Policy, which was tacitly accepted even by progressive, liberal organisations.[7]

Tennant, who joined but was swiftly expelled from the Australian Communist Party in 1935, pursued her activism and independence with a single-minded rigour throughout her life.[8] She campaigned on a wide range of progressive causes, from Aboriginal rights to nuclear testing, peace and women's rights, and in so doing attracted the attention of the Australian Secret Service, which compiled a 30-page dossier on her, intercepting personal letters and recording her activities, including meetings with journalists.[9] The daughter of an authoritarian and repressive businessman, Tennant's method of engagement was the most extreme of all the women discussed in this book. She had to force her exit/access at considerable personal risk, first by running away from home while still a teenager and then, having been 'recaptured', by walking, alone, across 600 miles of New South Wales to underline to her father her desire for freedom from his influence. Tennant found self-expression through escape and punishing journeying: she would walk until her feet were bloody and blistered and would spend many nights alone and vulnerable, hiding from drunken travellers in bushes.[10]

This chapter will examine Tennant's powerful determination and willingness to outrage any form of repressive authority, from parents to police to political leaders, to achieve her goal of writer-activist, what I call 'explosive engagement', detonating a force so powerful that it jolted her out of the orbit planned for her. She accepted the risks of her method, recording in her memoir:

Explosive engagement

> When later people told me I would be raped and murdered if I persisted in going on lonely tramps by myself, I thought, 'Why, dammit, I've been raped already.' But I didn't tell anyone because they might be sorry for me and my main object in life was not to be in a position where anyone could be sorry for me.[11]

She would rather face the dangers of the open road than be trapped inside her father's house.

This chapter also examines Tennant's position as a colonial writer, one very much in opposition to that more famous antipodean, New Zealander Katherine Mansfield's European modernism. Tennant disparaged modernist narrative technique as simply inadequate to perform what she considered the writer's primary goal of holding a mirror up to society. Whereas Mansfield, who travelled to Britain while still a schoolgirl, embedded herself in the tight networks of literary London, becoming 'star' reviewer of the *Athenaeum* journal and promoted by her writer husband John Middleton Murry, Tennant chose to stay in Australia and work for social change from within.[12] As a result, her work is virtually unknown outside Australia, and she is not particularly well known or studied within Australia either, partly due to literary Australia's embrace of modernism after the Second World War, when the novelist Patrick White emerged as the leading practitioner in modern Australian letters. Tennant's courage, her clear-eyed awareness of the divisive forces at work in society and the sheer brilliance of her writing, much of which is underestimated, merit her inclusion in this volume.

'I dropped my suitcase over the front verandah and jumped after it. It was my eighteenth birthday': Kylie Tennant and explosive rebellion[13]

Kathleen 'Kylie' Tennant was born on 12 March 1912 in Manly, a pretty Pacific-facing Sydney suburb on the north shore of the harbour, a half-hour ferry journey from the central Circular Quay. A younger sister, Dorothy 'Doffie', was born two years later. From the moment she picked up a pen Tennant was markedly left-handed, a trait, she recorded later, which at the time 'sets a child a little apart from other children'.[14] She would later describe herself as an anxious child, the anxiety stemming from an inescapable sense of loss: that she had forgotten her life before her birth and that 'I was exiled into life.' It was this sense of being an outsider, an exile, which, she said later, would produce such an extraordinary sense of affinity with society's other outcasts.

Her parents were unhappily married and the family home echoed to the sound of angry exchanges. Several times her mother decamped, with her daughters, to her parents' home, also in Manly. In her elliptical memoir, *The Missing Heir*, Tennant traces a link between her authoritarian father's domineering ways, his love of pomp and ceremony, and the suppressed but ever-present threat of violence that turned her into a natural born rebel:

> When I was a child I detested the Tennant family. The Parent's pompous references to his cousin Margot, who had married Prime Minister Asquith, his side glances at Lord Glenconner and so forth sickened me. I became a terrible little anti-snob and decided to join the Communist Party when I grew up ... I remember being taken to see lines of khaki-clad soldiers

Explosive engagement

marched down Macquarie Street to the troopships [during the First World War]. Some kind of road repairs were going on and we stood on the edge of a ditch of yellow clay as though it were an open grave ... I hated the procession – I hate all processions because they are a false showing, changing individual worth to a fused, blind clamouring of power.[15]

This moment of revelation struck Tennant at a precociously young age – born in 1912, she could only have been six, and maybe younger, when she experienced these feelings of revolt, associating the soldiers with death in the image of the open grave. Tennant's testimony contributes to our understanding of the personal dimension to activists' commitment and political awakening. Some of our case studies here, such as Dorothy Pilley and Claudia Parsons, took action because of personal injustices and desires: to be treated the same as one's brothers, or to be able to fulfil one's dream. For Tennant it was the hubris of power and the tragedy of the unknown victims of war that provoked the young rebel. Tennant instinctively responded to issues that she believed required action, with very little thought or planning: 'Unfortunately my interest is attracted to something that needs immediate action. I have this terrible habit of doing things without thinking. I am a pacifist, an internationalist, a multi-racialist. If anyone tried to do anything unjust, I would attack them.'[16] Like so many other women in this study, while still at school Tennant began to produce a family 'newspaper', her sister, mother and grandparents all demanding copies of her mixture of family notices and poems, so that her 'hand ached from writing out copies'. Her first poems were published in the *Farmer and Grazier* magazine when she was just 11.[17]

Tennant's father Thomas, described as 'The Parent' in her memoir, underlining her desire to distance herself from his patriarchal control, was the son of a doctor from a middle-class settler family. Unlike her famous fellow antipodean of a generation earlier, Katherine Mansfield, Tennant was not sent to a London finishing school (the family was not as wealthy, nor as prominent as Mansfield's). She did, however, attend the private Brighton College in Manly, where she excelled at public speaking and English literature.[18] She described herself as being a 'complete social misfit' at school, mostly because she was bookish and poor at sports. 'The only thing I could do was swim underwater so far that everyone thought I had drowned but you don't win prizes for that.'[19] While she was brilliant at literature, she came bottom of her class at maths: 'I was enchanted by the figures which, I thought, had personalities ... I was so busy considering their characters and adventures that I never learned arithmetic.' This lack of numeracy did not prevent her from achieving the highest marks in what her school described as a 'vintage' year. However, 'The Parent', who always worried about money and who wanted for his daughter only the life of a middle-class Australian woman – a little job, then marriage and children – refused to pay her university fees.[20]

Tennant left school at 16 and began work as a secretary at the newly established Australian Broadcasting Corporation in Sydney, then ran away from home to Melbourne, where she sold magazines at a station kiosk until her father found her and brought her back home to Manly. She had been sexually assaulted by a neighbour as a very young child, and in her typically wry style, she records in her memoir the irony of her father's insistence, after he found her on the streets of Melbourne, that she should be checked by a doctor to see if she was still a virgin.[21]

Explosive engagement

Tennant did then attend the University of Sydney for a term, the fees paid for by her uncle, but still needing to earn money to support herself, she dropped out, unable to combine the demands of a job and of studying. She was there long enough to be introduced to the works of the nineteenth-century 'bush balladeer', Henry Lawson, in a series of lectures given by the leading Australian literary critic Henry Mackenzie (H. M.) Green.[22] She worked freelance for a few newspapers: 'I thought I might become a journalist to present facts of corruption and misuse of power.' However, Australian newspapers were an even harder place for a woman wanting to be a serious journalist than English ones, and she was 'relegated to the Woman's Page reporting balls and that was not my idea of journalism'. She then started experimenting with writing fiction as a way of conveying her politics:

> So I thought, 'I will write novels and I will make them as accurate as I possibly can and I will make people listen to the truth in the form of fiction' ... I cloaked it in a kind of story. I said exactly what I wanted to say about the conditions people were living in. I had notebooks full of all kinds of observations.[23]

Tennant's commitment to telling the truth of what she saw pushed her to the limits of her endurance. Several times, either walking the roads of New South Wales, or living in slum tenements, often incognito, sometimes even disguised as a young man, she became so ill that her doctor advised her to stop what she was doing.[24] This willingness to suffer malnutrition, exhaustion and multiple insect bites and stings, and to efface her personality, has led some critics to speculate about her mental health: 'Copy is one thing, but this is evidence of a human being driven to extreme measures. Was it a form of psychological release to escape to another life because she could not bear to dwell on her own?'²⁵

Tennant engaged in direct action wherever she went. She married Charles Lewis Rodd, a radical teacher, in 1932, when she was only 20, and later remarked, drily, that she was in the habit of escaping one form of control only to embrace another. Rodd, however, encouraged her writing, something her father only did after he belatedly realised his daughter's prodigious talent. She lived with Rodd in the New South Wales

Figure 13 Kylie Tennant, c. 1930, 'Buchner Portrait'

Explosive engagement

outback towns of Coonabarabran and then Canowindra, where she organised soup kitchens and free legal aid for the local rural unemployed. She began a left-wing newspaper, *The Bush Worker*, produced in the hotel bedroom where she and Rodd lived – annoying the landlady with ink stains on the sheets – and irritated the local police who organised the payment of scant dole money, often on an arbitrary basis.[26] She also wrote her first short story, 'Strawberry Jam', published in the Sydney-based literary and political magazine, *The Bulletin*, which was influenced by Henry Lawson's well-loved short story 'The Drover's Wife', and by the tales she heard on the road. Despite being far out in the bush, there was a good postal book service and Tennant ordered, and voraciously consumed, literary and political magazines including *The Bulletin*, and volumes ranging from Harold Laski's *The State in Theory and Practice* (1935) to Mary Webb's *Precious Bane* (1924).[27]

Both she and Rodd were Christian Socialists and, as Europe began its predictable pathway towards war, and Australia's role in providing troops became increasingly inevitable, they became involved in the peace and disarmament campaigns led by Christian, student, socialist and former suffrage groups.[28] Rodd, already honorary secretary of the Teachers' Federation Peace Committee, became founding chairman of the Australian Peace Pledge Union in 1938, with Tennant the union's secretary.[29] While Rodd wrote letters or opinion pieces to the newspapers, Tennant, characteristically, took direct action. On 11 October 1939 she made the front page of the *Sydney Daily Telegraph* when she and two other women forced their way into the Anglican Synod meeting at St Andrew's Cathedral in Sydney to distribute leaflets to the clergy of Australia, urging them to support calls for an international peace conference.

'We are militant pacifists', she said as she forced embarrassed clergy to take her leaflets. The newspaper reported that while a few recipients read them, most hurriedly stuffed them into their pockets, unread, unable to refuse Tennant's forceful admonishments.

Thousands of miles away from Britain, Tennant's writing is a distant but chiming echo of the deeply politicised literary culture that dominated Britain in the 1930s, with writers from Virginia Woolf and Storm Jameson to W. H. Auden and Christopher Isherwood engaging in the 'well-chronicled shift to the left'.[30] As Tennant put it: 'I grew up a political person because there was no way of being anything else if you were born to live between two wars.'[31]

Tiburon: workers' and Aborigines' rights and the Australian national literary tradition

What began, in 1932, as a 600-mile journey on foot through the Blue Mountains of Australia to escape her father's reach transformed into a literary journey in the manner of two of Tennant's contemporaries, George Orwell and J. B. Priestley, who travelled the length of Depression-era England to expose social injustice.[32] On her route, Tennant met the unemployed who were then walking across rural Australia in great numbers, searching for work. This was 1932, the worst year of the Australian Depression, when for a while unemployment reached a quarter of the adult male workforce, more than in the US.[33] Tennant slept by the side of the road and on outback verandahs with her fellow 'tramps', attended unemployment meetings in rural town halls and helped out in soup kitchens, aware that her experiences would make valuable material

Explosive engagement

for a book: 'I was perfectly happy peeling vegetables in the soup kitchen and sleeping on the verandah of a nice married couple … I was filling my notebooks.'[34] When Tennant arrived at Coonabarabran, the small outback town where her soon-to-be-husband Lewis Rodd was working as a teacher, the contrast between the desperation of the itinerant families and the smug comfort of the settled middle classes who sparingly doled out charity with their fingers metaphorically holding their noses inspired Tennant to political revolt:

> The revulsion against middle class living was that there were so many facades, so many false fronts and these made me impatient. When you're on the breadline you haven't got time to put on any frills.[35]
>
> I'm born under the Chinese sign of the water rat; it can do anything. As a little water rat, I scampered around everywhere, I proceeded to horrify the locals as usual. I made friends with the Aboriginals at the camping ground. I made friends with all the travellers who came through. I was doing all the sorts of things people thought were shocking in a schoolmaster's wife.[36]

Her first novel, *Tiburon*, features as its central hub a large, disreputable family, the Whites, who provoke fear and disgust in equal measure in the settled community with their drinking, fighting, fornicating and irresponsible poverty. They live on the slopes of Warning Hill on the outskirts of town in a makeshift 'peasey hut', several children to a bed. Each member of the family shadows and affects different inhabitants of the town, from Brian Scorby, the flinty young police constable, to Jessica Daunt, the new schoolmistress sent to educate the barefoot children of the travellers' camp, to Jeffery Harper, the shopkeeper. The Whites are, in effect, the guilty conscience of Tiburon's settled class who one by one fail the town's needy through their inadequate response to the economic ills that have visited them. At the end of the novel the White family is completely broken up and scattered, into prison, to find work in Sydney, on to the endless road, the girls into forced or pragmatic marriages and the youngest under the care of other, equally straitened but nevertheless sheltering, poverty-line families.

Tennant's novel self-consciously locates itself within the Australian national literary tradition, acknowledging as her influences Henry Lawson and the lyric poet Shaw Neilson. Neilson is directly quoted in an early scene between Jessica Daunt and Paul White, a young cowhand and bibliophile, and member of the infamous White family. Paul and Jessica take long, night-time walks together to discuss poetry under the tall black pines at the top of Warning Hill. Soon after they meet, Jessica lends Paul a volume of Neilson's poetry and together they quote Neilson's 'Lament for Early Buttercups', about the passing of the seasons and bad timing:

> The lambs are white and lavender, the frost is with the moon,
> The mushrooms go to God and say they cannot die so soon
> Oh! They would see the love-works of the birds sent up to sing.
> And I – I mourn for buttercups that stay not till the spring.[37]

The poet initially celebrates the signs of early spring, the 'white and lavender' new lambs dappled under the light of an Australian moon, and the buttercups, whose golden colour lights up the endless prairie waking from winter, but which die before the season reaches its glorious peak in December: 'Oh, had their gold delayed until the last moon of the year, / When maids bedeck themselves … / They *would have* loved with a warm love.' Giving of themselves too soon, they miss the rapture of midsummer, a whole world of regret and longing

Explosive engagement

conveyed in the past conditional 'would have'. The poem predicts, well before Paul and Jessica realise it, that their relationship, unable to span the vast class difference between them, is doomed. Tennant crushes the reader's romantic desire to see the pair live happily ever after. 'Who are you kidding?', she seems to say; 'This can never happen in real life.'

As well as locating *Tiburon* within the Australian nationalist tradition, the reference to the poem is an early hint at the reversal of reader expectations that is to come. Instead of the pretty, young, middle-class schoolteacher extracted from 'civilisation' to give culture to the young tearaways of Warning Hill, it is Paul, the young 'clodhopper of a boy [who] should find a kin in the sweetest lyrist Australia ever produced', with whom the reader eventually finds sympathy.[38] Daunt cannot wait to get out of Tiburon and back to the intellectual milieu of Sydney. Her initial impression of the town, 'What a ghastly hole', does not change over the course of the school year, and even though she makes efforts to paint the classroom, she believes the children are irredeemable and requests a transfer during the annual school inspection.[39]

Although the more famous Australian writer Lawson is not directly quoted in *Tiburon*, his presence is acknowledged and critiqued through the text. The Whites' home, built from bark, mud bricks and galvanised iron, is central to the story, and it is where every major family drama is played out. It is the same makeshift hut in which Lawson's bush dramas also played out a generation earlier. Here is the opening description of Lawson's most famous short story, 'The Drover's Wife' (1892), about the quiet, heroic courage of the women of the bush, left to defend their children and property while their husbands went to find work: 'The two-roomed house is built of round timber, slabs, and stringy bark and floored with split slabs. A big bark kitchen standing at one end is larger than the house itself, verandah included.' This is remarkably similar to the Whites' 'mud hut with two rooms roofed with galvanised iron', and considered 'something of a masterpiece by the residents of Warning Hill'.[40] Unlike the drover's wife, however, who keeps her hut neat and clean, the Whites are unable to assert order over the chaos of their lives: the White house is in a state of perpetual mess. While the drover's wife gives her all in defending her children from the dangers of the bush, personified by the large black snake that terrorises them, in *Tiburon* the patriarch Dave White is a feckless drunkard whose stoical wife has died of pneumonia, and the thirteen children are left to fend for themselves. Tennant is telling her Depression-era readers to remove the romantic scales from their eyes and look at the realities of modern Australia. There has been no progress since the last century.

We know that Tennant was reading Lawson during *Tiburon*'s gestation from letters she wrote to Lewis Rodd while she was on yet another 600-mile walk, this time from Coonabarabran to Brisbane in 1933:

> You know, when you are on the track you cease to think. Your mind feeds itself like an embered fire on charred scraps of book or verses twisted and warped to fit your footsteps. That was the problem with Lawson's poems. He made them up as he walked and beat naturally was more important than phrasing.[41]

While Tennant's analysis of Lawson's poetry might be correct, in that the words are dominated by the rhythm of walking, she also acknowledges that his lyrics and short stories are powerful narratives that settled into the consciousness of Australia and went into the mythmaking around the creation of the modern nation. The outlaws, free spirits and adventurers, their lives

Explosive engagement

forged in dust and almost unendurable hardships, still persist today and form part of the Australian psyche, and Tennant made sure to show, in her characters and descriptions, that she was aware of this legacy. Jim White, the eldest White child, is a classic Lawson hero: taciturn, hardworking, unselfish, part of the land he so assiduously works, but also tragic in that his defence of a woman suffering from domestic violence results in his accidental killing of the violent husband and thus his own unbearable imprisonment.

Where Tennant diverges from her literary predecessors is in her portrayals of Aboriginal people and the landscape. I will first turn to Aborigines, who in early white Australian literature are either given minor, usually comic parts based on stereotypes depicting their drunkenness or laziness, and speaking comic pidgin English; or are mentioned sympathetically as the last of a 'doomed race', similar to early American and Canadian literature; or are ignored completely, the so-called 'Great Silence' of colonial Australian literature.[42] Australian literary critics have argued that white Australian writers' early attempts to obliterate indigenous culture have had a lasting negative effect on modern Australian culture, in that a settler literature can only be authentic if it acknowledges the indigenous peoples who have gone before, even if those people were annihilated as part of settler policy. Thus nineteenth-century North American literature such as Henry Wadsworth Longfellow's 'The Song of Hiawatha' (1855) and James Fenimore Cooper's *The Last of the Mohicans* (1826), despite subscribing to the 'doomed race' theory, at least brought native stories and culture into settler culture, creating a unique nascent culture rather than just a poor facsimile of that of the 'mother country'.[43] Depicting indigenous people as savage, unable to speak English properly or belonging to a distant past also allows the development of the 'powerful myth' of white superiority, and justifies discrimination, ill-treatment and genocide.[44] This 'silence' and stereotyping only began to wane to any great degree in Australia in the 1960s, owing in part to the rise of Aboriginal activism and the publication of literary works by Aboriginal writers.[45] Narratives that address head-on the violence of the European invasion, the attempted extermination of the Aboriginal peoples and the widespread destruction of indigenous ecosystems as land was turned to sheep and wheat farming is even more recent, most of it being written after the 'Mabo' judgement when the Australian courts finally rejected the infamous *terra nullius* declaration in 1992.[46]

Tennant's novel confronted all these issues decades before they circulated commonly in Australian literary production. If we take Lawson's 'The Drover's Wife' again, while there are Aboriginal characters, they are crude and clichéd. 'Black Mary', who comes to help the drover's wife when she is giving birth alone, is 'the whitest "gin" in all the land' and thus an acceptable colour to be giving expert medical care to a white woman.[47] The only speech given to an Aboriginal character is pidgin: 'All right missus – I bring my old woman, she down along a creek.' Finally, a 'stray blackfellow' comes to chop wood for the drover's wife while she goes out to search for a lost cow:

> On her return she was so astonished to see a good heap of wood by the chimney and she gave him an extra fig of tobacco and praised him for not being lazy. He thanked her and left with head erect and chest well out. He was the last of his tribe and a king; but he had built that wood heap hollow.[48]

Lawson's stereotyping works on several levels here. The surprise of the drover's wife that the 'blackfellow' has actually done some

Explosive engagement

work is counterbalanced by Lawson telling the reader that, in fact, the wood heap is hollow: he has cheated her. She pays him in tobacco, again playing to the stereotype of Aborigines' addictions. His leaving with his chest puffed out underlines his subordinate status as needing the praise and approval of a white woman. Finally, 'he was the last of his tribe', a doomed, virtually extinct relic, of more interest to anthropologists than policymakers.

In *Tiburon*, written forty years after 'The Drover's Wife', one of the families camping out at Warning Hill is a mixed-race family, the Willoughbys. Allie Willoughby is Aboriginal, not confined, as many were, to mission settlements, but living among the white down-and-outs. The first thing Tennant tells the reader about her is that, in the eyes of her friend Mary Mulver, 'for all that she was a "dark woman", [Mrs Willoughby] had the softest voice of any of them'.[49] In drawing our attention to the beauty of Allie Willoughby's voice, Tennant is tackling head-on the silence or the corrupted speech that previous Australian writers had condemned Aborigines to. Allie Willoughby speaks slang, to be sure, but it is indistinguishable from the slang of the white travellers. Mary Mulver, who emigrated to Australia from England, has had to reassess her prejudices:

> She had come out from England under the impression that Australia was inhabited by black savages, but her courage had not faltered. After nineteen years of fighting the wilderness she was convinced still that the inhabitants were savages, the only difference being that they were white.[50]

While Allie Willoughby is the victim of domestic abuse at the hands of her drunken husband Ackie, and most of the campers insult her with casual racism, Tennant's harshest criticism is reserved for Emily Claufield, a rich widow and the grandest lady in Tiburon, who lives in a large house with a hideous concrete portico, called, pretentiously, 'Mantana', possibly a – mischievous on Tennant's part – mis-spelling of the Spanish 'mañana' or 'montaña'. Mrs Claufield is a 'tower of strength' in the Country Women's Association of Australia, the equivalent of the British Women's Institute, promoting feminine 'country-mindedness' with bridge games, fundraising tea parties and handicrafts. Mrs Claufield is also president of the Tiburon District Committee for Assisting the Home for Incurables, 'yet another presidency', suggesting that numerous deserving causes benefit from her patronage.[51] Yet when Allie Willoughby knocks on her door to ask for help after her husband has been put off the 'dole' for drunkenness, Mrs Claufield pretends not to be home. When Mrs Willoughby departs empty-handed, Mrs Claufield 'shuddered' and 'rang for the maid. "Elsa," she said, "leave whatever you are doing and go outside and clean the doorbell. Please!"'[52]

Mrs Willoughby is a good mother, nurturing and protecting her young son Wilfred and making sure he does his homework, saving candles so he can write in the evening. Indeed, she is a far better parent than many of the feckless drunks on Warning Hill. Wilfred's barefoot presence also exposes the hypocrisy of the 'White Australia' policy, which influenced domestic policy, particularly the racist Maternity Allowance Bill, passed in 1912, which specifically excluded maternity payments to 'women who are Asiatics or Aboriginal natives'.[53] Wilfred and his mother are as poor as the other families on Warning Hill, but only Wilfred and the White children actually go barefoot: while the White children's mother is dead, Mrs Willoughby, as an Aboriginal woman, cannot claim the allowance. This policy ignored the fact that by the 1920s and 1930s there was a

Explosive engagement

growing number of mixed-race children of Aboriginal mothers and white fathers who usually abandoned their children.[54] The problem of the exploitation of Aboriginal women was so severe that a string of Royal Commissions between 1900 and 1933 concluded that 'Infection with venereal disease is, sooner or later, the fate of most aboriginal women.'[55] It was also noted in the Census of 1935 that while about one third of Aborigines were 'of mixed blood … it should be noted that few half-castes have known fathers'.[56] Wilfred, then, is living testimony that the outrages committed against Aborigines over the previous 150 years are still occurring.

Towards the end of the novel, when the tensions caused by the unemployment strikes, mass meetings and increased levels of violence begin to tear at what little order remains on Warning Hill, and families, homes and social structures begin to dissolve, an interesting scene takes place. In an unusually still and reflective passage, Jim White pauses from his wood cutting and falls into a 'painless daze', contemplating the landscape around him:

> He was on a little plateau that gave him a view for miles and miles over the patchwork slopes of fields: miles and miles of fields with perhaps two trees to an acre. They had all been like Warning Hill once, covered in trees, shaggy with a brown green fur of trees and now they were shaven bare and smooth for the wheat. Warning Hill would be like that some day, not that it would grow anything, but it would be smooth and naked with hardly a tree. It was getting fairly thin now. He wondered did the Hill hate it … Jim began to speculate to himself about the time to come, perhaps, where there would be no wood, no last tree on the flanks of Warning Hill … They say trees attracted the rain. Suppose when there were no trees, there was no rain? What would they do then?[57]

Rebel women between the wars

Here Tennant, in an extraordinarily prescient way, is speculating, through Jim, about how large-scale habitat destruction would disrupt climate patterns, several decades before novelists and other writers began to address anthropogenic climate change in fiction.[58] Yet her interest here is not so much meteorological as mystical. The hills, the trees, the weather have pre-dated white settlers by millennia, yet the settlers with their destructive ways have torn a hole in the fabric of space and time, to unleash as yet unknown horrors: 'naked and bare' earth, the sheep only 'grey dots like stones', lifeless lumps of rock. The settlers are not supposed to be there, and their presence has created an epic wrong.

This strange moment, when Jim, the Lawsonian hero, experiences this 'minute of incredible calm, of passionless sunlight' that was 'almost hurting him with the intensity of its pressure', is so unlike the helter-skelter busyness of the rest of the novel that we must be alert for what comes next. And out of the shadows of a terrified child's mind comes the figure of the 'bunyip', a mythical, swamp-dwelling creature of Aboriginal storytelling tradition, believed by white settlers, up to about the end of the nineteenth century, to have actually existed.[59] The creature was adopted, in attempted indigenisation, by white storytellers as, in the words of short story writer Rosa Praed, 'the one respectable flesh-curdling horror of which Australia can boast. The old world had her tales of ghoul and vampire, or Lorelei, spook and pixie, but Australia has nothing but her Bunyip.'[60] In the scene straight after Jim White's moment of meditation, little Wilfred, Allie Willoughby's son, and therefore the embodiment of the meeting of Aborigine and settler, begins to ask questions about bunyips: 'If a bunyip came, what would you do? … If a bunyip came, say at night, when no one could see it …?'[61] This mysterious megafauna,

Explosive engagement

which lives, according to nineteenth-century storytelling tradition, among the 'swamp oaks and ti-trees ... with the spectral white gums rising like an army of ghosts around you', now represents, argues historian Penny Edmonds, the 'melancholy of the Australian bush and the unspoken spectre of the violent dispossession of the Aboriginal people'.[62] Tennant is using the bunyip in *Tiburon*, not to give permanency and respectability to white settler Australia, but to underline the violence, destruction and environmental degradation of colonialism.

Tennant wrote *Tiburon*, she claims in her memoir, in four months, although its inner gestation had clearly been ongoing since her first 600-mile trek across New South Wales three years earlier.[63] She submitted it under the cryptic pseudonym 'Juren' to *The Bulletin*, which had just launched the S. H. Prior Memorial prize, in honour of a long-standing editor of the magazine, offering £100 for the best entry. The judges were the journalist T. D. Mutch, and the authors Guy Moore, William Stewart Howard, Cecil Mann and Camden Morrisby, all part of bohemian Sydney of the 1930s, and all friends or admirers of Henry Lawson.[64] While the judges 'immediately recognised [*Tiburon*] as the product of a new creative force in Australian writing', the editor of *The Bulletin*, Ken Prior, told Tennant as she autographed his copy that the novel was 'a bad advertisement for Australia'.[65] With the £100 prize money plus a further £50 that *The Bulletin* paid to serialise *Tiburon*, Tennant bought a car for the use of the local branch secretary of the Rural Workers' Union, partly so he could attend meetings in far-flung Methodist halls, and partly to take his cabbages to market. *Tiburon* also launched Tennant into a lifetime of activism through writing, as she followed up her rural novel with its urban cousin, *Foveaux*.[66]

Rebel women between the wars

Foveaux

In January 1936 Lewis Rodd was transferred to Dulwich Hill school in Sydney and so Tennant began her months of research in the slums of the city, taking rooms in distressed families' two-room apartments, sitting on doorsteps shelling peas, and gossiping with the women of the Surry Hills, Redfern and Paddington tenements.

> My room in [Redfern] cost me three-and-six a week, and as a grand mark of esteem it had been newly papered with newspaper for me. The family were just broke, that was all. They had one young boy in gaol and the daughter was the most hopeless case of malnutrition.[67]

Tennant also made contacts at the Child Welfare Department, and attended hearings at the magistrates and children's courts, taking notes like a reporter as she pieced together the chain of events that would lead people from low-paid precarity to prison, squalor, disease and untimely death. The culprits were the absentee slum landlords, an out-of-touch judiciary, economic policies that privileged commerce over human wellbeing, and the self-serving politicians who turned a blind eye to, and even enabled, the exploitation of the weakest. They had been and would continue to be easily recognisable villains from decades of newspaper, magistrates' and public health policy reports on the slums of inner Sydney.[68]

Some critics have accused Tennant of being little more than a documentarist, of producing screeds of plot-driven, superficial characters with little or no inner life, and have suggested that her work contains little artistry. Her reputation suffered particularly through the literary critic H. M. Green's dismissive

Explosive engagement

summary of her work in his monumental *History of Australian Literature* (1961): 'None of Tennant's characters and none of the communities to which they belong stands for anything at all.'[69] Even Tennant's biographer Jane Grant cannot avoid this conclusion in her rather lukewarm assessment of her subject's literary achievements.[70] However, as Tennant's contemporary, the writer and critic Margaret Dick, astutely observed: 'Kylie Tennant, in fact, makes heavy demands on her readers, and unless they are wary they do not even realize the nature of these demands and are left unsatisfied.'[71]

What raises *Foveaux* above being a novel of simple social realism (and there's nothing wrong with that in itself) is the use of time, and its four-part structure representing different phases of the sea – 'Ebb Tide, Full Tide, The Surf, The Rocks' – a metaphor for the submerged inhabitants and their struggles. The novel begins in 1912, the year of Tennant's birth, and ends in the 'present day' of the late 1930s, thus emphasising that it is partly Tennant's personal journey of discovery into 'what makes a slum'. During this quarter-century of rapid change, time rolls back and forth like the tide, revealing as it ebbs the depredations of greed, war and commerce. Tenements are eroded, then thrown back up; country paths become motorised highways; artisans' workshops metamorphose into strange, shiny, production-line factories. The city is shown to be highly mutable, transforming with the currents as the movements of money and power across the globe infect even far-off Sydney. The torn-apart buildings and rubble may be inert but their inhabitants always suffer. As the tide of time rolls back in, the submerged slum dwellers at the foot of Foveaux Hill, the residents of Plug Alley and Ogham Street, either have to scramble to higher ground, or perish.

Rebel women between the wars

The novel opens in 1912 with the Eight-Hour Day Procession, an annual October march celebrating trades unions' victories in securing better working conditions. The bands, banners, jingling horse reins and brightly coloured union floats create an image of optimism and progress, when in fact this is about as good at things will get in Foveaux. Among those watching the parade is Hildebrand Edward Sutton, who lives in the peaceful heights of Upper Foveaux and whose house, the oldest and finest of the quarter, will never be ruffled by the swirling currents below. He discusses the parade with Sam Merrick from the livery stables, who, in an apparently offhand remark, predicts that the procession will be different when the much-vaunted improvements to Lennox Street have been completed. The narrator comments:

> Sam Merrick was right. By the time Lennox Street was gaping into Errol Street in a devastated area of broken houses and torn paving there was a procession streaming the opposite way ... going down the hill to the water side. It was dull, prosaic, khaki-coloured, and the people watching stood on the ruins of the broken houses, on the rubble of the improvements, some of them crying.[72]

The narrative here has slipped through the fabric of chronological time to some unknown point in the future. It could be the First World War that would start calling for young Australian men two years after this point in the novel. This passage is thus an echo of the young Tennant's horrified memories of seeing the khaki-clad soldiers marching to their deaths, quoted at the beginning of this chapter. But Tennant, writing in 1937, and by now a 'militant pacifist', could also be predicting the imminent war to come. The actual date of the book's publication, March 1939, after the Anschluss and the Munich crisis, only reinforces

Explosive engagement

this idea: the 'ruins of the broken houses' could just as easily be bomb damage as roadworks. This flowing back and forth through time, while the overall arc continues steadily forward, creates uncertainty, fluidity, slippage, as if nothing is certain, as indeed, in the late 1930s, even on the opposite side of the world to Europe, nothing was. In this respect Tennant knits Australia's fate, both social and political, with that of Europe, the rubble of Foveaux uncannily chiming with that of Brighton in Graham Greene's *Brighton Rock* (1938): 'Half Paradise Piece had been torn up as if by bomb bursts; the children played about the steep slope of rubble.'[73]

Although dealing with characters pitting their wits, optimism and determination, often with great humour, against the forces of capital, *Foveaux* is ultimately a bleak view of life, and a recognition by Tennant that, although she began writing 'to change the climate of opinion', idealism often ends in disappointment.[74] 'Honest' John Hutchinson, the corrupt local politician, keeps getting elected, and Bill Bross, the slum landlord, gets wealthier in equal and opposite measure to his tenants' desperation. Foveaux's battlers – Linda Montague, Jimmy Rolfe and Bramley Cornish – who try with campaigns, journalism and activism to change the course of events, to alter 'improvement' plans to include model workers' homes among the factories, have little or no agency and are powerless to stem the tide. This gradual waning of optimism can be seen in Tennant's subsequent novels: while her next, *The Battlers* (1941), about itinerant agricultural workers, retains huge reserves of warmth and sympathy for the squalor and misery of her subjects' lives, again she sees no solution for their predicament. *The Battlers* is a parody of the Australian literary tradition of gritty determination against the odds. As one critic noted: 'its outward forms and trappings are there, but its soul is not, for it died somewhere on the road that led from one World War to the next'.⁷⁵ *Ride on Stranger* (1943) is a take-down of the left-wing intellectuals and do-gooding middle-class women who espouse worthy causes, but whose motivations, hypocrisy and hubris result not in helping people but in a dangerous inhumanity. Tennant's recorded view of this time can be read in her popular history *Australia: Her Story* (1953):

> In the twenties, and more so in the thirties, people felt that if they could only grasp some first cause of the whole muddle, they could remedy society and its woes. By the time the Second World War had ploughed up the economic surface ... the sturdy optimism which declared that all you needed was a revolution was replaced by a dejection and a feeling of helplessness, a bewilderment which feels no solution to be adequate.⁷⁶

Foveaux was published in England by Victor Gollancz in March 1939, 'after two years when it drifted neglected. Publishers put their coffee cups on it and forgot it.'⁷⁷ It was mostly well reviewed: Frank Swinnerton compared Tennant's scope to Dickens and the characters to those in Robert Tressell's *Ragged-Trousered Philanthropists* (1914).⁷⁸ In Australia, the Melbourne *Age* described what it thought was a first novel (*Tiburon* was not published in book-form until later) as 'breaking ground in fiction in a way little attempted here before'.⁷⁹ Many critics, however, misunderstood it. The novelist Lettice Cooper, who picked it as one of her novels of the week in her *Yorkshire Post* books column, wrote: 'While there is much to admire in this novel, which is full of humanity and humour ... there is no unifying central theme, no main story, and no great emotional pressure.'⁸⁰ H. M. Green wrote to Tennant to ask what her philosophy was: 'Tolstoy, said H. M. Green, had a philosophy,

Explosive engagement

so had Dostoyevsky. Why not cultivate one?', she reported to a friend. The implication was obvious: in Tennant's novels so far, Green saw no fully coherent artistic vision. Tennant, prickly as ever, responded: 'This was like asking the centipede which leg came after which ... It sounded like growing a moustache to hide my weak mouth.'[81]

The judging of Tennant's work as documentary realism, with hastily sketched characters having little or no inner life, has seen her reputation falter. Tennant was writing at a time when the more obviously experimental modernist novelist Patrick White or the more psychologically exploratory Eleanor Dark had become the 'benchmark of modern fiction'. A binary choice between literary or middlebrow was often made by critics who, for the first time, were dominated by the Australian academic rather than literary establishment.[82] Tennant, rather defensively it seems, declared that she deliberately avoided 'subjective writing like debt or scandal' and had no time for 'introspective books'.[83] While she does indeed avoid extensive introspection, characters such as Paul White in *Tiburon* or Tommy Cornish in *Foveaux* are fully rounded, and it is possible to apprehend their motivations and sensitivities through just a few of Tennant's spare but arrow-sharp brushstrokes. As I hope this brief survey of Tennant's first two novels has shown, it is unwise to dismiss her as a simple realist 'clinging to a documentary tradition', as her own biographer asserted. Her artistic vision was in fact sophisticated and coherent and she created complex, if not immediately visible, meanings and themes in her novels.[84] She certainly made her white readers feel intensely uncomfortable about their privilege, and even their right to be living in Australia at all.

* * *

Rebel women between the wars

Kylie Tennant achieved her goal of becoming a writer-activist by running away: from her family home and her father's control, from her marriage by taking long absences to walk the roads of the Australian interior, from herself as she adopted different personae and, occasionally a different gender, and from the literary modernist fashions of interwar Sydney. She ran away, initially, from motherhood too, deliberately avoiding having children until 1946, by which time, as most critics agree, she had written her best work.[85] She even ran away from the Australian Communist Party, banging on a table during a meeting and accusing the delegates of being 'authoritarian despots and bigots' before resigning.[86] Tennant's strategy thus deliberately excluded any of the kinds of helpful networks, formal or informal, that appear to have helped many though by no means all of the women in this volume. Her success relied greatly on her own strength of character and determination, as well as her talent, which was recognised by the men on the Sydney *Bulletin* whose reading of the manuscript of *Tiburon* – submitted, let us not forget, under the gender-neutral name 'Juren' – helped to launch her writing career. She also ran away from the pigeonholing of her as a woman journalist in order to write what she wanted.

Of course, not all women had the cumulative energy in the combination possessed by Tennant of courage, good education and single-mindedness to take this explosive route. The next chapter will examine what might be described as the direct opposite of Tennant's method of engagement, that of 'hiding in plain sight', taking the path of least resistance, though this also entails risk of a very different kind.

Explosive engagement

Notes

1 Tennant 1939: 98.
2 George Orwell's *The Road to Wigan Pier* (1937) describes the poverty and deprivation of northern England in stark detail.
3 Tennant 2012: 108.
4 Reid 1979: 2–3.
5 Reid 1979: 2.
6 The term 'Gonzo' was originally used to describe the subjective, immersive reportage employed by the American writer Hunter S. Thompson in the 1970s. This kind of immersion in one's subject has, however, a long lineage, with journalists and novelists from Charles Dickens onwards employing it to various degrees.
7 The 'White Australia Policy' (WAP) refers to a set of policies pursued by the newly federated government after 1901, particularly aimed at restricting the numbers of immigrants from Asia. It did, however, bleed into internal domestic policy, for example in excluding women of Asian or Aboriginal origin from maternity allowance payments. This hit Aboriginal women particularly hard as many were kept as unmarried 'wives' by Australian rural workers, and their children were often very poorly nourished. The WAP was gradually dismantled after the Second World War; see Laing 2017.
8 Kylie Tennant papers, National Archives of Australia A6119/283 and 447; 'MP Withdraws "Red" Charge', *Sydney Morning Herald*, 24 September 1952, p. 1. In this newspaper article Tennant claimed she was in the Communist Party for 'one month only'.
9 This dossier is now available to view digitally on the National Archives of Australia website, A6119/283, https://nla.gov.au/nla.obj-234718644/findingaid (accessed 24 May 2020).
10 Tennant 2012.
11 Tennant 2012: 34.
12 Demoor 2016.
13 Demoor 2016: 62.
14 Recording of interview with Kylie Tennant for 'Hazel de Berg Collection', 1967, National Library of Australia, NLA.obj-220868501.
15 Tennant 2012: 7–8.
16 Recording of interview with Kylie Tennant, National Archives of Australia, NAA C100/1227892.

17　Tennant 2012: 42.
18　Tennant 2012: 39–44.
19　Recording of interview with Kylie Tennant for 'Hazel de Berg Collection', 1967, NLA.obj-220868501.
20　On Mansfield's London education and background, see, for example, Snaith 2014: 110–12.
21　Tennant 2012: 33; on Tennant's school achievements, see Tennant 2012: 51.
22　Grant 2006: 6.
23　Recording of interview with Kylie Tennant for 'Women Writers Between the Wars', 1982, NAA C100/1280244.
24　'Woman Author Learnt Art of Sheep Stealing', *Sydney Morning Herald*, 24 April 1939, p. 13.
25　Collett 2007: 130.
26　Recording of interview with Kylie Tennant for 'Hazel de Berg Collection', 1967, NLA.obj-220868501.
27　Tennant 2012: 102.
28　Davies 2007.
29　Various newspaper reports, for example 'Education Report', *The Sun* (Sydney), 28 October 1937, p. 20; 'Back Door Conscription Threatens Australia', *The Labor Daily* (Sydney), 13 June 1938, p. 4; 'Objections to Compulsory Training', *The Advertiser* (Adelaide), 26 October 1938, p. 28.
30　Joannou 1999: 3.
31　Tennant 2012: 74. For an overview of Australian interwar literary politics and culture, and particularly how the tragedy of Gallipoli influenced literary pacifism, see Spittel 2007.
32　Orwell 1937; Priestley 1934.
33　Fishback 2012: 224.
34　Tennant 2012: 78.
35　Recording of interview with Kylie Tennant for 'Briefly Before Bedtime', 1971, NAA C100/1227892.
36　Recording of interview with Kylie Tennant for 'Women Writers Between the Wars', 1982, NAA C100/1280244.
37　Neilson 1926.
38　Tennant 2013: 72.
39　Tennant 2013: 77; in this she is also castigating herself, as she described Coonabarabran on first impressions as a 'filthy hole'. But whereas

Explosive engagement

Jessica Daunt left as soon as she could, Tennant stayed to fight for the bush workers' rights.
40 Tennant 2013: 9.
41 Papers of Kylie Tennant, letter from Tennant to Lewis Rodd (undated), MS 4734, NLA.
42 Brantlinger 2011.
43 Goldie 1989: 13.
44 Miller 2017: 366–8.
45 Brantlinger 2011: 1; Alber 2017.
46 See, for example, Alber 2017; Edmonds 2018; Heiss 2003. The decision in *Mabo* v. *Queensland* and the Native Title Act of 1993 overturned the view that native people were an 'absence' in Australia, not in terms of their persons, but in terms of property rights. This view had persisted since Captain James Cook declared Australia *terra nullius*, belonging to no one, during his 1770 voyage.
47 'Black Mary' may have been the daughter of mixed-race parents. It was common for white men to keep Aboriginal women across Australia.
48 Lawson, Henry (1892), ebook, https://ebooks.adelaide.edu.au/l/lawson/henry/while_the_billy_boils/book2.1.html (accessed 15 August 2019).
49 Tennant 2013: 53.
50 Tennant 2013: 53.
51 Tennant 2013: 305.
52 Tennant 2013: 310.
53 Laing 2017: 224.
54 *Report of the Royal Commission* (1935). The report found that of some 19,000 Aborigines in Western Australia, there were nearly 4,000 'half-castes'; that figure had risen from 1,900 in 1905.
55 Report to the 1933 Royal Commission by Dr Cilento, reported in various Australian newspapers, for example: 'Do White Men Shoot Blacks for Sport?', *Labor Call* (Melbourne), 1 June 1933, p. 9; 'Disease: Blacks and Whites: Startling Evidence Given', *Warwick Daily News* (Queensland), 1 June 1934, p. 2.
56 'Native Women: Position Gone from Bad to Worse', *The West Australian*, 14 July 1936, p. 7.
57 Tennant 2013: 338.
58 See Johns-Putra 2016.

59 See, for example, 'Large Aquatic Animal', *Evening News* (Sydney), 3 September 1872; 'To the Editors of the Sydney Morning Herald', *Sydney Morning Herald*, 13 July 1847; 'Does the Bunyip Exist?', *Clarence and Richmond Examiner*, 15 November 1902; see also Edmonds 2018.
60 Praed 1891: 318.
61 Tennant 2013: 352–3.
62 Praed 1891; Edmonds 2018.
63 Tennant 2012: 101.
64 'S. H. Prior Memorial Prize: Winner Announced', *Sydney Morning Herald*, 7 August 1935, p. 7.
65 Dick 1966: 14; Tennant 2012: 101.
66 Tennant 2012: 101.
67 'Woman Author Learnt Art of Sheep Stealing', *Sydney Morning Herald*, 24 April 1939, p. 13.
68 For example: 'Where the Sun Seldom Shines: Surry Hills Slums: A Terrace of Dugouts', *The Globe and Sunday Times War Pictorial*, 15 July 1916, p. 6; 'Rich Harvest from Slums in Surry Hills', *Tribune*, 28 March 1947, p. 6; 'Factory Ousts Slum', *Sunday Times*, 30 October 1921, p. 3; 'Slum Children's Playgrounds', *The Australian Worker*, 12 July 1939, p. 19.
69 Green 1962: 1010–20.
70 Grant 2006.
71 Dick 1966: 24.
72 Tennant 1939: 23.
73 Greene 2004: 153.
74 Tennant interviewed by Elizabeth Riddell for the Australia Council Archive Film Series, Blackheath, May 1985.
75 Pons 1974: 380.
76 Tennant 1953: 263–4.
77 Tennant 2012: 109.
78 Victor Gollancz publications catalogue, Warwick Modern Records, MSS.318/7/Qu/6a/5.
79 'New Novels', *The Age*, 29 April 1939, p. 11.
80 Cooper 1939.
81 Letter from Tennant to Nettie Palmer, 6 February 1943, quoted in Reid 1979: 52.
82 Sheridan 2012: 1.
83 Letter from Tennant to Doris Chadwick, undated, NLA 6666 undated letters.

Explosive engagement

84 Grant 2006: 60.
85 Tennant had two terminations in the first year of marriage, and her memoir reveals conflict between her writing and the idea of having children (Tennant 2012: 93). Tennant's biographer, Jane Grant, notes the 'marked deceleration' in Tennant's creativity after their first child, their daughter Benison, was born (Grant 2006: 21).
86 Recording of interview with Kylie Tennant for 'Hazel de Berg Collection', 1967, NLA.obj-220868501.

9
Hiding in plain sight

There are two ways of regarding the death penalty. It may be inflicted in the spirit of judicial revenge in accordance with the Mosaic law of an eye for an eye and a tooth for a tooth, and it is impossible to feel in extreme cases of cruel and premeditated murder that such a punishment is too heavy for the crime. There is also the more modern view that fear of death acts as a deterrent. This is certainly true of one class of criminals, robbers and burglars, who have to choose, if surprised, between their safety and their gains. Here it might be supposed that cases of burglary and robbery with violence ending in the death of the victims are more common in countries where there is no capital punishment than there are in those where the burglar knows that if he is disturbed he must either escape and leave his booty or risk his life by stunning and probably killing the intruder. But in practice it has been found that the Netherlands, Scandinavia and Switzerland which have abolished capital punishment ... have in consequence hardly any burglars.[1]

This part of a closely argued editorial on the rights and wrongs of the death penalty is typical of many newspaper and magazine editorials of the spring of 1924. A Private Member's Bill in favour of the abolition of the death penalty in all cases of

Hiding in plain sight

murder and treason was being debated in Parliament, and the new, and first, Labour government had introduced its own Bill on the abolition of the death penalty in some cases of murder. A deputation of progressive organisations, including the Howard League and the Society of Friends, spent an hour and a half with the new Home Secretary Arthur Henderson on 24 March, trying to persuade him of the arguments for abolition. Winds of change were in the air: progressives cheered, and conservatives shivered, then resisted: the *Daily Mail* and *The Times* argued strongly for the retention of capital punishment; the *Manchester Guardian* was more nuanced.[2]

The editorial quoted here, arguing that evidence should be sought from countries where the death penalty had been abolished to see if its deterrent effect could be accurately assessed, might have been read in a liberal progressive journal, the *Nation and Athenaeum*, perhaps, or Lady Rhondda's new feminist paper *Time and Tide*. In fact, the article, 'Capital Punishment', appeared in the 'Editor's Notes' section of the women's weekly society magazine, *The Queen*, a conservative, elite paper for ladies of the so-called 'Upper Ten Thousand', those at the apex of the British class system. While readers of *The Queen* were expected to take a mild interest in general politics, the paper had, up until early 1924, been gently and blandly conservative on all issues. Even this faint suggestion of allowing criminals and housebreakers leniency would have sent a frisson of irritation through boudoirs and living rooms, beautifully upholstered on the advice of magazines like *The Queen*. Other 'Editor's Notes' from this period covered a range of controversial subjects including the beauty and brightness of itinerant travellers' caravans, which although they arrived uninvited on private land (much of it, presumably, owned by the husbands of readers of *The Queen*), should be tolerated because these 'gay nomads' were usually circus entertainers, fat ladies and mermaids, and were less aggressive than other travelling groups such as navvies. Even more extraordinary, considering that much of the readership belonged to the landed gentry and other landowning classes, a strongly worded piece accusing landowners of blocking off public footpaths crossing their land argued that under these circumstances trespass would be justified.[3]

The Queen, classified as a paper and not a magazine, had been launched in 1861 by the astutely entrepreneurial publisher Samuel Beeton.[4] Beeton was keen to take advantage of the popularity of Queen Victoria: a wife and mother of regal womanliness, femininity enthroned, who could influence and humanise, but not direct, the political world. The paper was a huge success, defining 'feminine news' as prioritising information about the court and the doings of débutantes, but also including articles on issues affecting women such as educational campaigns, arts and literature, and, increasingly, fashion and consumer items. While covering political issues that affected women, such as the Poor Law, health and education reforms, it avoided reporting parliamentary affairs, acknowledging in an early issue: 'As our readers are well aware, politics are, by the very nature of the constitution of our journal excluded from its columns.'[5] *The Queen* reported the suffrage debate without openly advocating the right to vote. Most importantly, *The Queen* had been instrumental in establishing the links between women's consumer journalism, advertising and shopping, beginning to direct readers anxious for advice on how to dress their bodies and their homes to specific brands and shops from the late 1880s. From the 1890s,

Hiding in plain sight

dress news became virtually an 'advertorial', and from there it was a short step to complete the circle, with advertisers featuring the endorsement 'as recommended in *The Queen*' in their beautifully illustrated display advertisements.[6]

The Queen was an iconic British women's magazine, the embodiment, as feminist critics see it, of the media industry's age-old collusion in sequestering women and women's interests into a separate domestic sphere.[7] Michelle Elizabeth Tusan picks out *The Queen* in her critique of the women's domestic press, which she describes as an 'important counterpoint to the women's political press … Periodicals that focused on issues relating directly to women's relationships to home and hearth, such as *The Queen* …'[8] Margaret Beetham's groundbreaking *A Magazine of her Own* charts the evolution of the women's magazine and its work in asserting 'the definition of femininity as incompatible with engagement in public affairs', using *The Queen* as her major case study.[9] Women writers during the interwar period would also identify *The Queen* as a major regressive force. Rose Macaulay, in her dystopian novel *What Not* (1919), names the magazines complicit in the authoritarian government's attempts to coerce women into something called mind training, playing on women's vanity and anxiety about marriage to persuade them to undergo a dangerous kind of brainwashing that left many mentally impaired:

> *The Queen*, the *Gentlewoman*, the *Sketch* … had articles on 'Why does a woman look old sooner than a man?', 'Take care of your mind and your complexion will take care of itself', 'Raise yourself to category A, and you enlarge your matrimonial field …'[10]

When the editor's chair became vacant at the beginning of 1924, the paper's owners, the Field Press, also owners of *The*

Field and *Ladies Field*, chose an experienced, respected journalist in Naomi Royde-Smith, who had been the long-serving literary editor of the *Saturday Westminster* (see Chapter 1). For Royde-Smith, however, apart from offering much-needed financial security, it was a strange choice. She was never reticent in expressing in letters her disdain for what she saw as the pampered, vacuous and rich women of the 'smart set'.[11] Her novel *Skin-Deep* (1927), written after she was sacked from the magazine, is a satire on foolish and fashionable ladies unthinkingly following any new trend, and is her harsh judgement on readers of *The Queen*.

Royde-Smith would have been much better suited as literary editor of *The Nation and Athenaeum*, a post that was vacant and that she had been in the running for in February 1923, but Virginia Woolf, who saw Royde-Smith as a rival, had stepped in to make sure her 'foe' did not get it, persuading the board to take her friend, 'poor dear Tom' (T. S. Eliot), as she recorded in her diary.[12] Woolf went to great lengths to prevent Royde-Smith from finding a more suitable position, recording the strings she had pulled and the ears she had bent, and confessing: 'Had I time I could detail my activities and glory in my own importance.' This incident obviously shows Woolf in a poor light, as conniving and mean-spirited, but it also reveals something of the power structures of literary London. Woolf was quite surprised at her ability to persuade both John Maynard Keynes and H. W. Massingham, joint owner and editor of *The Nation* respectively, to do her bidding.[13] In exercising her power, Woolf condemned Royde-Smith to taking a job she was unsuited for.

Hiding in plain sight

The Queen, prior to Royde-Smith's appointment, carried little literary material, dedicating most of its pages to fashion, the court, the house beautiful and photographs of lovely débutantes. While a knowledge of new developments in the arts and literature was essential to a lady's status as leisured and wealthy and a pleasant conversationalist, most of *The Queen*'s cultural content consisted of coverage of the decorative arts: paintings, sculpture, ceramics and contemporary exhibitions. Literary material tended to be devoted to private intellectual pleasures of the novel, or books on gardening, nature and 'feminine' histories of great houses, royalty and the aristocracy. In the early 1920s, only one book was discussed each week on the 'Library Table' page. Royde-Smith's appointment may have indicated that the board of the Field Press wanted to boost *The Queen*'s contemporary cultural coverage in the face of its rival *Vogue*'s repositioning itself, under the editorship of Dorothy Todd, as promoting the modern woman as connoisseur of the artistic avant-garde. The job would certainly have offered, for Royde-Smith, an unmissable opportunity to remake the paper to suit her tastes and interests, as long as she had the freedom and power to be editorially independent. It would soon become clear, however, that this new editorial direction was not what the board wanted at all, and she was sacked just a few months after having taken over.[14]

From the rapidity of Royde-Smith's dismissal, one must infer that the changes she made to the paper were neither approved of nor possibly even fully discussed. She was remaking *The Queen* as a feminist, literary and politically left paper, instituting a fundamental transformation, it seems, to a bastion of the media industry without permission, a strategy that I call 'hiding in plain sight'. The risks of this strategy are plain from Royde-Smith's dramatic early departure. This nonetheless would have been an obvious strategy for the large numbers of women journalists, in the main employed by women's magazines, who wanted to participate in public life, but could only do so on terms dictated by the media industry's concern with making money out of a system that encouraged women to see themselves as passive consumers.

The new sections and themes that Royde-Smith quickly introduced to *The Queen* had much more in common with *Time and Tide*, for which Royde-Smith had been writing since its launch four years earlier, than a fashionable ladies' newspaper. The 'Editor's Notes' page, from which the 'Capital Punishment' article comes, was a wholly new departure introduced when she took over for the 5 March 1924 issue.[15] On the first 'Editor's Notes' page, the editor explained the change in page size from the previous larger pages to a smaller, more compact size. This, readers were told, would be 'more welcome to railway travellers', perhaps a suggestion that times were changing and that *The Queen* was increasingly being read by busy professional women, and not on a chaise longue or an expansive drawing room sofa: in future the paper would be read sitting, rather than reclining.[16] Readers were assured that they need 'have no fear that the change in outward form will be accompanied by any change in the essential characteristics of the paper'. However, Royde-Smith clearly planned to transform *The Queen* before its readers' eyes.

Another new feature that Royde-Smith quickly introduced, 'A Man's Diary' by A. P. Herbert, was an almost exact copy, with respect to the magazines' different genres, of *Time*

Hiding in plain sight

and Tide's tongue-in-cheek 'Our Men's Page', edited by 'Sir Duffer d'Amboring, Bart.' The *Time and Tide* page, introduced in January 1924, offered male readers sartorial advice and fashion tips, and was clearly aimed at sending up the regular 'answers to correspondents' pages of women's magazines (of which one appeared every week in *The Queen*). Sir Duffer, for example, advises an anxious groom to wear accessories 'of deep manganese purple' on his wedding day; to 'an earnest young man' with a quarterly dress allowance of one guinea he advises lining a waistcoat with scraps of silk from handkerchiefs so that it becomes reversible.[17] In *The Queen*'s 'A Man's Diary', Herbert pokes fun at the institutions its readers held dear: the débutante season, Ascot, Wimbledon and all the other society events around which leisured and moneyed women constructed their diaries. On Ascot, Herbert declared that despite the fabulous hats and dresses, 'examine a pageful [*sic*] of society débutantes and you are positively surprised to see a pretty girl'; he announced that there was no difference in beauty between a young woman photographed in the pages of the *Daily Mirror*, 'Miss Hatt of Hackney', and a society girl, 'Miss Jane Tulle chatting to a friend at Sandown', again as presented week in, week out in the pages of *The Queen*.[18] Taken as a whole, the attitude of the 'Diary' urges women to free themselves from the restrictions of the social structures within which they find themselves imprisoned, and to ignore or challenge ideals of feminine beauty. However, sandwiched between page after page of advertisements for corsets, hats and preparations 'to entirely banish lines, wrinkles, hollows' and other 'disfiguring traces on a woman's face', 'The Diary' was an incongruity that must surely have irritated advertisers as well as readers.[19]

Royde-Smith introduced further new sections, one on conversations between well-known men and women of letters, giving women authors an equal footing with men, and one 'devoted entirely to book reviewing, which, without replacing the "Book of the Week" section will afford a more complete guide to current literature than has yet been found in *The Queen*'. The 'Reviews of New Books' page set the new tone of the paper. In Royde-Smith's first official issue, the page carried an item, 'Three Novels by Women', reviewing *Marching On* by Ray Strachey, *Deep Meadows* by Margaret Rivers Larminie and *Lady Susan and Life* by Storm Jameson (this latter receiving a pasting from the reviewer as 'an indiscretion' compared to her more serious novels). In the 19 March issue Royde-Smith gave Ray Strachey a whole page to discuss a biography of Olive Schreiner by her husband; Schreiner's text *Woman and Labour* (1911), a radical call to arms by the women's movement, was again an interesting editorial choice for *The Queen*. As well as increasing the number of theatrical and literary reviews, Royde-Smith introduced more poetry and short stories (including one in an early issue by her lover, Walter de la Mare).[20] The pacifist, feminist and socialist poet Eleanor Farjeon, who had been writing a regular column, 'By Chimaera', in *Time and Tide* since May 1922, became a regular contributor of poetry in *The Queen*.[21] Her poem 'For a cock' aggressively confronts male power and vanity and is clearly aimed at rousing rebellion in its female readers:

> Strutting cock, with swelling chest,
> Stepping on your scaly legs
> Past the warm and busy nest
> Where worried hens lay eggs,
> Why do *you*, I'd like to know,
> Strut and crow and swagger so?[22]

Hiding in plain sight

In July 1924 Royde-Smith published a short story by Dorothy Richardson, 'In the Garden', continuing her interest in promoting innovative writers (see Chapter 1).[23] The story is an important early iteration of Richardson's idea of the 'epiphanic' moment, dramatising how a child discovers her consciousness through her relationship to the natural world.[24] The memory of the garden links, rather like Proust and his famous madeleines, the grown woman's present with her childhood. In the story the child, safe in a garden, stands on the gravel path and watches the bees and the flowers, expecting them to behave like her; but the flowers cannot move or run, and the bees, 'keeping on making dark places in the air as they crossed the path', are not interested in the child. The realisation of her separation and difference from aspects of nature causes such a shock that the child falls on the hard gravel path, the physical pain of the fall blotted out by the deeper emotional pain of the betrayal she feels the flowers have dealt her in their difference. It is a difficult piece of writing and sits oddly in a magazine which in the same issue carried images of débutantes, a report on the International Horse Show, a feature on Samoyed dogs and the *Queen* regular Mrs Charles Peel's 'Fool Proof Recipes'.

Through the summer, Royde-Smith inserted increasing quantities of fiction, including lengthy short stories by Naomi Mitchison, Viola Meynell and the poet Katharine Tynan. It was looking less and less like *The Queen* and more and more like *Time and Tide*, whose owner, Lady Rhondda, was an ubiquitous presence in *The Queen* in published letters and mentions in the Editor's Notes. More seriously, Royde-Smith seemed to be detaching herself from her readers and their concerns. She wrote a lengthy editorial on the need for female architects to plan and build smaller houses for working women and 'servantless' households, and commissioned a lengthy feature by the academic and feminist Theodora Bosanquet on the Federation of University Women, its work and its aims, two topics that would have excited little interest in the *Queen*'s readership.[25] Royde-Smith even started poking fun at her readers' social lives, ridiculing, in the 2 July issue, the Heart of Empire Ball, which according to the prospectus, which she quoted at length and in disbelief, promised a 50-foot-high waterfall tumbling through the Albert Hall:

> I quote the prospectus of this in wonder. [The waterfall] will flow 'not only into the sea below' in which it is to be supposed the dancers will eventually find themselves swimming, but over the organ. It sounds like cruelty to organs, but that only makes the excitement wilder.[26]

Royde-Smith could not last long after that, and she was sacked in September. She recorded in her diary 'Good-bye to the *Queen* for good', and turned to being a full-time novelist, publishing her first novel, *The Tortoiseshell Cat*, the following year.[27] The *Queen*'s board wasted no time in restoring the magazine's previous character: by the end of October, the Editor's Notes and contents page had been replaced by a full-page photograph of a bride or débutante, the 'Man's Diary' had disappeared, and the book and theatrical reviews had reduced from an average of six to two pages per issue. Knitting patterns, banned under Royde-Smith, made a triumphant comeback. The 'New Books' page was, however, retained, although the 'Library Table' page was cut. In the late autumn of 1924 a new editor, Nora Heald, took over, and by 10 December 1924 the new theatre critic, and sister to the editor, was signing her pieces Edith Shackleton (see Chapter 1).

Hiding in plain sight

Stella Martin, 'writing footling little paragraphs' for the women's page

In July 1928 the Bristol *Evening Times and Echo*'s 'Apples of Eve' column was discussing which summer reading books to recommend to its largely female audience. The *Echo*, now long vanished, was a daily Bristol newspaper, the slightly smaller and more popular evening edition of the *Bristol Times and Mirror*, a regional newspaper of enormous physical size, more than twice that of the current *Daily Telegraph*, and dating back to the 1790s. Although not called the 'Woman's Page', the page where 'Apples of Eve' appeared carried domestically focused articles such as 'Poultry Farming for Women', 'New Saucepans for Old' and simple recipes, bounded on all sides by advertisements for department store sales, headache powders, children's food supplements and furniture polish. The summer reading column first establishes that nobody wants to be burdened down on holiday with a lengthy and unachievable reading list, and that probably 'two or three' light novels were the most one could achieve in between swimming, walking and afternoon siestas. After toying with the latest offerings from P. G. Wodehouse and Edgar Wallace as possible contenders, the column plumps for Rose Macaulay's *Keeping Up Appearances*.[28] It's an interesting choice from a female newspaper columnist, as the novel's central theme is the entrapment of a female newspaper columnist who, belittled and stereotyped by the male editors on her paper, is 'imprisoned in a cage of print' and 'doomed ... merely through an accident of sex' to write inane articles such as 'Can Women Have Genius?'[29] The central character, Daisy Simpson, ultimately experiences a shattering breakdown caused by the tensions created between her desire to be a novelist and her financial need to write newspaper articles.

The 'Apples of Eve' column's author was Stella Martin, a young woman who had just turned 21 and who, although sequestered firmly in the women's realm of her paper, took the opportunity to write a series of humorous and gently subversive articles which, at their heart, contained a sustained critique of women's magazines and women's pages in newspapers. Martin, like Daisy Simpson, also wanted to be a novelist, and while she was working at the newspaper she wrote one for a competition.[30] It is possible her editors didn't read her columns too carefully, although she was removed after about eighteen months to become the paper's zoo correspondent while it was engaged in a fight-to-the-death newspaper war.

Helen Estella (Stella) Martin was born at Roodepoort in the South African Transvaal on 18 July 1907, the eldest of four children of John Percival (J. P.) and Nancy Martin. J. P. Martin was a Wesleyan Methodist minister like his father, grandfather, uncles and cousins, and had gone to South Africa as a volunteer missionary.[31] Two days after his eldest daughter's birth, Martin wrote to his sister-in-law:

> I think I can say without prejudice that I have never seen a child with nicer ways ... I have to get ready a paper on 'Modern Socialism' for the Roodepoort Debating Society tomorrow, and really, owing to the events of the past week I have neither the time, nor the inclination to touch it.[32]

It is possible to ascertain here the gentle, mischievous humour that the daughter inherited from her father. J. P. Martin was a writer and storyteller, author of the *Uncle* books, children's

Hiding in plain sight

nonsense stories about a magisterial elephant who wore a purple dressing gown, told initially as bedtime stories to his own children then finally published just before his death in the 1960s. Uncle and his battles with the 'Badfort' crowd, led by 'Beaver Hateman' and his henchman 'Hitmouse', were a constant presence in the Martin children's life. The strange and fantastical narratives wove their magic and created a powerful imaginative world that Stella Martin recalled as being 'more real' than the material world: 'The picture of Uncle's castle Homeward which we had all helped to paint and paste together was bright and vast on the wall of the boys' bedroom.'[33] The family moved to England in 1913 and led the typically peripatetic existence of a Methodist minister's family, until in 1919 J. P. was given a ministry in Camborne, Cornwall. The manse was at the top of a steep hill 'perpetually patrolled by traction engines carrying coal to the mines'. After that point, Uncle started riding about on a traction engine.[34]

At Camborne, the children played in the semi-wild manse garden, described by Martin in her memoir of her father:

> The wide terrace we walked along was edged with dry-stone walls, blossoming with fuchsia and valerian ... we could see our new square house set at the top of a tree-dotted slope of the garden. 'There's a swing,' shouted Grace [Stella's younger sister], 'a big proper swing!' Shouting and laughing we waded through the long grass towards it ... The big windows of our new home looked out onto a dipping, sweeping view of indigo-blue and gold. Fields and woods stretched to a long pale line of sea.[35]

While the Martin children lived a carefree life, with the younger ones performing in plays written by Stella and playing tree-top hide and seek, J. P. found surviving on a Methodist minister's small stipend very difficult, recording in his diary, 'At this time I underwent a good deal of temptation about money ... my financial affairs grew steadily worse.' While the family had the accoutrements of middle-class life – a piano, a wind-up gramophone and plenty of books – J. P. lacked the resources to complete his children's higher education. Stella left school at 16 and trained to be a typist and shorthand writer; Grace trained to be a nurse; John left school at 18 to work in a newspaper advertising department. Only the youngest, Hal, went to university, having won a scholarship at Kingswood,

Figure 14 Stella Martin, c. 1920s

a boarding school for the sons of Methodist ministers in Bath. On several occasions, Martin helped her father out by sending him cheques from the short stories she sold, and when she was offered an apprenticeship at the *Bristol Times and Mirror*, J. P. Martin's diary records simply: 'Stella is to start on the *Bristol Times and Mirror*, Rejoice!'[36]

The paper's offices were in Saint Stephen's Street in a tall, red-brick, Arts and Crafts building (now a backpackers' hostel), with stone mullioned windows and a bridge linking the editorial offices to the printing presses in Leonard's Lane. Stella Martin's first published novel, *Paperchase End* (1934), about a young woman newspaper reporter on the fictional *Ravenport Courier*, was inspired by the real-life *Bristol Times and Mirror*.

> The *Courier* offices, set in the deep channel of Narrow Bridge Street, were deeply shadowed, but the strip of sky between the roof-tops was a faint, austere blue … the corridors had a homely, stretched appearance as if they had often been altered to circle an enlarged room, to make way for a door or an odd step or two … strangers found it the most bewildering office in Ravenport. A multiple whisper seemed to come from behind all the closed doors as she passed them, but the vague, busy sound changed to the confused noise of typewriters, rustling papers, and telephone conversation …[37]

The novel offers insights into the life of a woman provincial newspaper reporter in the late 1920s, the kinds of assignments she was sent to cover, and her feelings of being sidelined into women's subjects: endless weddings and Mothers' Union lectures on subjects such as 'Teaching Children the Value of Truth'.[38] Martin's description of protagonist Susan Calvin's views on the Mothers' Union meeting gives us a fair idea of what she felt about this kind of organisation:

> The rows of women wore creased tweeds and hats trimmed with raffia flowers and [she] guessed that they wove their own skirts on hand looms and were self-consciously involved in the cult of simplicity … A sensible child would dislike most of them, she decided, and lie more than ever.[39]

In the novel women journalists are separated from the men, not only within the different pages of the newspaper, but in the newspaper office itself, in their own small room away from the main newsroom, symbolic of how, as Adrian Bingham comments, sexual difference had become a central organising feature of the whole newspaper operation in the interwar years.[40] The women's room, however, is a protective and nurturing space with an underwater feel, dimly lit by green-shaded lamps, and represents for the three women who occupy it the freedom that comes from the economic independence their jobs provide: for one, to put off an unwanted marriage proposal, for another to leave a disappointing husband, and for a third to allow her to move out of her parents' home which has become toxic after her widowed father has remarried. All three women expect to be able to live in rented flats, not the family home, before they marry, a still unusual departure in the late 1920s, working out their own budgets and paying their own grocery bills. While the economic independence is welcome, the price paid for it is high, in the ruination of the women's writing style and their enforced complicity in providing trivialised or idealised images of femininity for the *Ravenport Courier*. The novel thus represents a rare insight into the conflicting feelings that women engaged in the news industry experienced at a time of rapid circulation rise and the ubiquitous introduction of the newspaper women's page.

Hiding in plain sight

It is through this kind of 'trivialization or condemnation of women in media content' (many of the articles, ironically, written by women) that mainstream newspapers and magazines erect barriers to women's participation in democratic public spheres.[41] As we have seen, journalism did offer literate women a unique opportunity to access the public sphere and to acquire financial independence, even if that access meant submitting to editors' prejudices, producing advertiser-friendly copy for women's magazines and newspaper women's pages. However, once they were ensconced in a newspaper or magazine office, women journalists often swerved the expectations of their role and produced subversively feminist or literary texts from the heart of the consumer journalism machine. Hiding their texts in plain sight, they subtly resisted the market- and advertising-driven media apparatus that sought to create an image of women, as one women's page editor wrote in 1933, 'interested solely in knitting jumpers, in caring for their complexions, in looking after babies, in cooking, in a "good" murder and in silly stories about weddings'.[42]

Of course, there was a wide range of subject matter in women's magazines and newspaper women's pages. Not all articles encouraged consumerism; many were 'service journalism', helping readers navigate the problems of everyday life, born out of the advice articles written for frantic housewives and mothers during the First World War who needed to know how to feed a family on rations, and care for a wounded husband or son.[43] Readers of the *Manchester Guardian*'s women's page, established by Madeline Linford in May 1922, would have read articles by Ray Strachey, Winifred Holtby, Vera Brittain and Francesca Wilson on issues including substandard housing, the development of radio and unchaperoned women being ejected from restaurants. They were still, however, on a separate page and in a separate sphere. Reminiscing on her period as women's page editor of the *Manchester Guardian* in 1963, Linford said of her reader: 'I saw her as an aloof, rigid and highly critical figure, a kind of Big Sister, vigilant for lapses in taste, dignity and literary English.'[44] The reader was also cultured and educated, but expected not to be at work when she read the page, 'sitting down to it with her mid-morning cup of coffee'. At this time the pages of the professional magazine the *Woman Journalist* occasionally carried items regarding this public–domestic dichotomy, but with most contributors emphasising their pride in helping women solve their daily problems. It was 'the special privilege of the woman journalist' to help the housewife manage her duties to husband and home.[45] Some, however, did also argue for a better recognition of the political nature of domesticity. The celebrated contemporary cookery expert Mrs Charles Marshall stated that:

> It will occur to all thinking individuals that upon the well-being of the home depends, largely, the well-being of the nation. The household page, therefore, should be regarded as of importance, and the contents should rank higher, in relation to journalism than the culture of fashion or even of sport.[46]

In Martin's *Paperchase End* and Macaulay's *Keeping Up Appearances*, as well as in a third interwar novel about women's journalism, Rachel Ferguson's *The Brontes Went to Woolworths* (1931), women journalists' role in perpetuating women's absence from the public sphere is problematised. They understand their role in erecting the very barriers that they themselves have struggled hard to overcome, and this understanding induces

Hiding in plain sight

a fracturing of personality (*Keeping Up Appearances*) and physical sickness (*The Brontës Went to Woolworths*).[47] In her memoir Ferguson describes the moment of realisation of what getting married would mean: 'having to be put on an allowance' and bury any dreams 'that the world was mine'.[48] She put off the dreaded day by becoming a freelance journalist, writing 'those would-be controversial articles of the type I've always called Do Women Make The Best Wives?'[49]

The tensions that Martin experienced between earning the money that she and her family needed, and worrying that demotic and trivial newspaper writing would ruin her style, are given dramatic form in the conversations between Susan Calvin and her fiancée John, who acts as her conscience when he admonishes her that writing 'footling little paragraphs' is spoiling her more creative output:

> Half your freshness has gone. I don't see how you can help it. You spend all your time writing conventionally potted writing and even you can't pretend that those woman's page articles are anything but a mass of stupid generalisations … Can't you see that if you absorb unlimited quantities of that cheapness and staleness, and put down ready-made ideas, that you'll soon be incapable of thinking or writing anything else?[50]

Calvin's fiancé specifically criticises the pressure put on her to write about people who advertise their products in the newspaper, thus blurring the lines between journalistic independence and the newspaper's finance department, something that women's page journalists were employed to do, and indeed advised to do in contemporary 'how-to' manuals. The advice quoted below is from Mrs Emilie Peacocke, then women's page editor of the *Daily Telegraph*:

> In this subject [infant and child welfare] we have a feature which possesses a strong human interest, and at the same time has a business end to it. The kingdom of the child is linked up at so many points with the enterprise of the manufacturer and the turn-over of the retailer. Big display spaces for the advertising of infant foods, and other specialities, are associated usually with baby feature articles.[51]

If we read Martin's 'Apples of Eve' columns in this context, we see that below the pleasant chatty tone and feminine subject matter – beauty, marriage, health and fashion – almost every column is, in fact, a criticism of women's journalism and of the deliberate creation of texts that provoke anxiety and often quite irrational behaviour in women readers. Martin's column of 26 October 1928, for example, begins with an anecdote about reading a women's magazine advising her to stop wearing petticoats as they were no longer the fashion. After confessing to not having been aware of this trend, Martin continues:

> Women's magazines combine to make one feel colossally ignorant. They tell one, in the brightest of efficient ways, how to run our homes, children, husbands and faces ... The printed word, somehow has an impressiveness about it, especially if it seems to be written with that passionate sincerity that such subjects as 'wrinkle removing', 'your first mud pack', 'how to pluck eyebrows at home' and 'keep slim by rolling', naturally demand. It seems somehow pathetic to think of hundreds of women feverishly doing all these things.[52]

She then describes a marriage of acquaintances that nearly foundered because the woman, rendered frantic by all the advice on how to be a good wife, started doing odd things such as playing the piano to her husband at breakfast time, and producing overly exotic dishes, when all the husband wanted was a 'plain meat pie', because she was advised to boost his vitamin B intake. In this column and others, Martin is criticising the custom of women's magazines and newspaper women's pages of creating anxiety in women, invoking the idea that their work of becoming the ideal woman is never done, that their lives must be an endless quest for perfection and that they must buy the media and the expensive remedies that the newspapers peddle, creating a vicious circle of anxiety and consumerism that never ends. Other columns by Martin suggested that expensive cosmetics and potions are not worth the money women spend on them; that long walks in the country provide a much more natural shade of rouge than powder; that homemade face masks from oatmeal and orris root work better than shop-bought ones; and that the vogue for adding food supplements to every meal was a waste of time and money (she asks 'How did we manage without them?' in the days before they were invented).[53] She also defended the 'modern girl' from widespread criticism that she was too independent and knowing and was keen to enjoy a career, and attacked the hairdressing industry for one season promoting short shingles and the next a longer style, which meant that the poor bemused female was caught in a constant state of half-up, half-down hair, not sure whether to cut it off or grow it out.[54] While from the 1960s columnists such as the *Observer*'s Katharine Whitehorn made this kind of subversive article fashionable, in the 1920s it was an unusual and brave departure, undermining as it did many of the products advertised on the page Martin was writing for.

In October 1929 the Berry Group-owned *Bristol Times* papers became engaged in a 'newspaper war' with the newly launched Rothermere-owned *Bristol Evening World*, and Stella Martin, possibly as part of the *Times and Mirror*'s efforts to boost sales by becoming more popular, was appointed the *Echo*'s zoo correspondent.[55] It is not clear whether Martin's editors were unhappy with her work, or whether they thought her comic talents would be put to better use in the paper's circulation war with a more downmarket publication. The series of sketches that she wrote observe, with great comic effect, the porcupines, llamas, seals and chimpanzees of Bristol Zoo. The star of the pieces is Judy the elephant, who is engaged in constant, low-level confrontation with her irritable neighbour, the camel White Lady, and who takes up harmonica playing just to annoy the camel. Judy's 'diary' records, in humour worthy of Uncle, 'Great coolness between White Lady and myself, as she said jazz made her head ache. She is incapable of recognising good music.'[56] Despite these efforts, the *Bristol Times and Mirror* closed in January 1932 and hundreds of journalists, sub-editors, printers and other staff were made redundant, bringing an end to Martin's newspaper career. The experience provided inspiration for her novel *Paperchase End*, dedicated 'To those who have known the comradeship and suffering of a newspaper war', and later that year she married long-time family friend Ralph Currey. She continued writing novels, plays and short stories throughout her life (see Appendix).

***

Both Naomi Royde-Smith and Stella Martin found employment and thus financial security within the media structures and publications that perpetuated stereotyped images of women. Each, in their own way, attempted to subvert and alter, from within this edifice constructed to separate women from the world of masculine power, the content of the publications that they worked for. The advantages were not just financial. Royde-Smith must have enjoyed writing her teasing editorials, imagining shocking and annoying her readers; she also made use of her power by commissioning and promoting many of her friends, including A. P. Herbert, Rose Macaulay and Eleanor Farjeon. Her experience also provided valuable material for a later novel. Stella Martin's amusing asides in her 'Apples of Eve' columns also show that she had fun writing them, and all the while she too was gathering material for her first novel. Neither woman lasted very long in this endeavour: Royde-Smith was sacked from *The Queen* less than a year after she took up her post, and Martin was removed from the women's page to become her paper's zoo correspondent. Both strategies reveal that while 'hiding in plain sight' might on the surface be less risky than, say, the direct action of Shiela Grant Duff and Kylie Tennant, it nevertheless carried great risk if one was exposed as being a double agent, as it were, within the fortress.

Notes

1 Royde-Smith 1924.
2 For example, *Daily Mail*, 13 March and 24 March 1924.
3 'Navvies', *The Queen*, 12 March 1924, p. 2; 'The Rights of Way', *The Queen*, 2 April 1924, p. 2.
4 Beeton is probably best known as the husband of Isabella Mary, 'Mrs' Beeton.
5 *The Queen*, LVIII, 1875, p. 105, quoted in Beetham 1996: 92.
6 White 1970: 67; Beetham 1996: 96.
7 It amalgamated with *Harper's Bazaar* in 1970 and was known as *Harper's and Queen*. It has now been rebranded as *Harper's Bazaar*.
8 Tusan 2005: 11.
9 Beetham 1996: 26.
10 Macaulay 2019: 59.

11 Benton 2015: 93.
12 Woolf 1981: 236.
13 Woolf 1981: 236.
14 Benton 2015: 98.
15 Royde-Smith had been working behind the scenes at *The Queen* since January 1924, writing theatre reviews to which her name was appended and the odd editorial, before the changeover was officially announced in March.
16 'To Our Readers', *The Queen*, 5 March 1924, p. 2.
17 *Time and Tide*, 4 January 1924, p. 17.
18 *The Queen*, 2 July 1924, p. 14.
19 *The Queen*, 2 July 1924, pp. 15, 35.
20 Walter de la Mare, 'Epitaph', *The Queen*, 12 March 1924, p. 11.
21 For more details on Farjeon's relationship with *Time and Tide*, see Clay 2018: esp. 42–3.
22 Farjeon 1924.
23 Richardson 1924.
24 This would become Miriam's famous 'bee-memory' in Richardson's novel series *Pilgrimage*.
25 *The Queen*, 13 August 1924, p. 1; *The Queen*, 23 July 1924, p. 20. While *The Queen* had for many years carried a short 'Education Notes' column, its subject matter was normally restricted to news on charitable foundations supported by its readers, and on improving classes in knitting, lace-making and art. *The Queen* did at this time, however, sponsor an annual scholarship to Girton College, Cambridge, underlining its association with elite institutions.
26 *The Queen*, 2 July 1924, p. 1.
27 Diary entry, 29 September 1924, quoted in Benton 2015: 98.
28 Stella Martin, 'Summer Reading', *Bristol Evening Times and Echo*, 27 July 1928, p. 17.
29 Macaulay 1986: 131, 22.
30 Diary of J. P. Martin, 27 July 1929: 'Stella has written a novel for competition and she finished the same the night a few days after her 22nd birthday' (with thanks to James Currey).
31 Martin Currey 2017: 3.
32 Quoted in Martin Currey 2017: 58.
33 Martin Currey 2017: 150–1.
34 Martin Currey 2017: 140.
35 Martin Currey 2017: 141.

Hiding in plain sight

36 Diary of J. P. Martin, with thanks to James Currey.
37 Martin Currey 1934: 15, 18.
38 Martin Currey 1934: 25.
39 Martin Currey 1934: 25–6.
40 Bingham 2004a: 42.
41 Gallagher 2014: 23.
42 Peel 1933: 227. We have already seen how Edith Shackleton and Alison Settle (Chapter 1) and Margaret Lane (Chapter 4) resisted 'woman's page' stereotypes in their writing.
43 Lonsdale 2015.
44 Linford 1963.
45 *Woman Journalist*, July 1925, p. 17.
46 Ibid.; see also Lonsdale 2018.
47 Asked to write a 'bright', thousand-word feature on 'Is the Bank Holiday Girl Naughty?', Deirdre Carne, the protagonist of *The Brontes Went to Woolworths*, asks for 'pencil paper, and a rather large basin' (Ferguson 2009: 17); see also Lonsdale 2018.
48 Ferguson 1958: 118.
49 Ferguson 1958: 163.
50 Martin Currey 1934: 31, 33. As an aside, in giving her protagonist the surname Calvin, Martin, a Methodist, must have been mischievously playing on Methodists' views of Calvinism as an inferior theological proposition, Methodists disagreeing with Calvinists' acceptance of man's utter depravity and lack of any kind of free will.
51 Peacocke 1936: 82.
52 Stella Martin, 'Doing Everything', *Evening Times and Echo*, 26 October 1928, p. 17; 'fat rolling' was claimed to be a method of staying trim, often involving expensive contraptions, and was a favourite subject of women's page writers, for example Lady Kitty Vincent's column, 'Skip and be Slim; Sylph-like at 80', *Daily Express*, 8 July 1926, p. 5.
53 'Powder, Patches and Worse', 15 June 1928; 'The Right Shade of Rouge', 3 August 1928; 'Beauty from the Grocer', 17 August 1928; 'Perfumes and People', 11 May 1928.
54 'Bandages and Lipstick', 7 September 1928; 'More and More Hair', 1 June 1928.
55 The Bristol 'newspaper war' was examined in the *Royal Commission on the Press 1947–1949*, pp. 67–8.
56 Stella Martin (no date; 1930, Stella Martin cuttings book; thanks to James Currey); Martin Currey 2017: 191.

Conclusion

Throughout the course of this book we have seen how different women adopted a wide range of strategies to find an entry into the fastness of the masculine public sphere as it was configured in the 1920s and 1930s. As a useful metaphor I have envisaged the combined power structures ranged against women's entry as a kind of military fortress, operating its own exclusionary strategies to 'repel all boarders', as it were, a common policy of elites. This strategy of defence and exclusion operated at all levels, from the body politic (parliamentarians enacting laws restricting women's ability to work, for example, and thus reducing the employability of a woman engineer such as Claudia Parsons) to the corporate (the editor of *The Times*, the newspaper of the ruling elite, telling Shiela Grant Duff that although he admired women journalists it would be impossible for her to work for the foreign pages of his paper because she was a woman) to the level of individual wielders of power (Kylie Tennant's father refusing to pay her university fees even though he had the resources to do so; Dorothy Pilley's father refusing her permission to become an agricultural worker during the First World War). The counter-strategies adopted by the

Conclusion

women examined here – from joining productive and cooperative networks, to employing artful subterfuge, to embarking on brave or reckless solo missions – are comparable to those adopted by other subjugated or minority groups seeking to overturn entrenched power or merely to share more equally in it. Parallels to the 'non-violent direct action' tactics of, for example, Kylie Tennant or Shiela Grant Duff can be also be seen in climate and nuclear disarmament campaigns.[1] The finding of a 'safe haven' in groups of the same gender or colour, as did Dorothy Pilley and Una Marson, can be seen in the participation strategies of minority ethnic groups.[2] The orchestration of friendly collaboration between different groups to achieve the same end can be seen in the informal and formal friendship and networking strategies of Alison Settle, Edith Shackleton and Leah Manning.[3] The pursuit of access through alternative or informal channels, as adopted by Francesca Wilson in her efforts to be accepted on Quaker humanitarian missions, has been seen in the international women's organisations' peace activities during the First World War and after. Even the mimicking of the characteristics of the dominant group to gain entry, only to subtly work to change it once access has been gained, as did Naomi Royde-Smith at *The Queen* or Stella Martin at the *Bristol Evening Times and Echo*, has been observed in studies of activism and political participation, and is a method that has been shown to be particularly effective where hegemonic power is not only deeply entrenched but particularly active in employing exclusionary strategies.[4]

These women did not have a convenient 'handbook of rebellion' to consult, but instinctively chose one of several possible routes or methods followed by other groups or individuals challenging entrenched power. The precise route – subterfuge, networks, direct action or safe havens – would then be followed according to each woman's particular set of dispositions and goals. Kylie Tennant chose direct action as she was, by her own admission, of a fiery and confrontational disposition. Una Marson instinctively chose one of the most effective methods, that of joining multiple organised networks, as she, facing the double obstacle of gender and colour, had the hardest battle to fight. Margaret Lane chose the easiest and most obvious route available to her: making use of her journalist father's contacts to take her first steps in Fleet Street. Whichever route they eventually pursued, they were busy and resourceful and relentless in working towards their rightful participation in the public sphere. They were also numerous: the 'baker's dozen' of women presented here are just a handful of the thousands of similar women, some mentioned all too briefly in these pages, who were working assiduously at the defences of the fortress.

The more you look, the more you find them, determinedly taking up positions in areas of public life never before occupied by women. Energised by the radical disruption of gender roles during the First World War and by the suffrage victories of 1918 and 1928, women dared to ask for, and take, more opportunities, from becoming JPs and MPs to challenging their husbands for control over the household economy, and over their own fertility in the privacy of the home, or even deciding they did not have to marry at all. It was a hard and often fruitless struggle, with plenty of knockbacks coming from all quarters: Francesca Wilson applying unsuccessfully again and again for a place on Quaker humanitarian missions; Dorothy Pilley finding little appetite among the *grandes dames* of the Ladies' Alpine Club for a women's climbing journal; Claudia Parsons unable to find work as an engineer after qualifying. Even when they had apparently

Conclusion

succeeded, they suffered at the hands of a power structure that resented, threatened and resisted them still. Both Shiela Grant Duff and Margaret Lane were subject to vile sexist innuendo and harassment because they competed with men in the very masculine world of news and newspapers. Una Marson suffered severe mental breakdown partly because of her treatment while at the BBC. Claudia Parsons and another female student, the only females in their cohort, were the only two candidates in their year accused of cheating in their engineering exams, and narrowly avoided expulsion from college. Women journalists were belittled through their papers' undermining their work with diminutive or gendered bylines, and Naomi Royde-Smith was sacked for being too independent. Yet still they spun exquisite and powerful stories, like Scheherazade in the chamber of the murderer-king, making their mark on the public world and ensuring that, slowly, the paths of other women would become less difficult. They did at least see the point of launching a sally, whereas as little as a decade earlier they may well have felt that any efforts would be futile.

Biography as method

I have adopted the biographical approach to examine the details of my subjects' lives to try to grasp at a more slippery truth: what characteristics, attributes and dispositions make it more likely that a member of a minority or subjugated group will make that risky and energy-sapping effort to break out of their dominated position to challenge the forces lined up against them? Where did Claudia Parsons find the courage required to don men's overalls and become one of just three women to enrol on the first post-war diploma in engineering at

Loughborough College in 1919? What psychological stresses in Dorothy Pilley's heart and mind combined to make her reject the marriage proposal of the man she clearly loved, favouring freedom over love (until pursued to the peak of Mount Baker); what strength of nerve convinced Shiela Grant Duff to travel alone into war-torn Spain, and once there, to climb over a wall, at night, during a curfew, into the US Consul's house full of Franco's officers? I have acknowledged the shortcomings of using biography as a method of enquiry but throughout this book we have also seen wherein lies its strengths. When one can drill down into the granular level of detail about a group of women's lives, it becomes possible to piece together the kaleidoscope of their upbringing, personality and the choices they made to focus the image better, and to obtain a clearer picture of individuals' actions and motivations. Thus we can trace a line from Claudia Parsons' childish experiments with plasticine, water and piping, and transgressive bicycle rides, to her taking her place at Loughborough Technical College. We can read, in Dorothy Pilley's diaries and in her journalism, her utter conviction that marriage, even to a man as sensitive and alert to her fears as I. A. Richards, would bring a terrifying curtailment of her love affair with the freedom of the mountains. We can read in Edith Shackleton's PEN letters and union meeting reports that abundantly generous spirit who, having fought her way to the top of her career, enabled others to make connections and advances too. In Shiela Grant Duff's letters to newspaper editors, and in her diaries too, we can read her naturally combative and curious nature, her hatred of injustice and her sense of outrage at being treated as inferior just because of her sex.

We can also find broader shared similarities between the women in this book, while acknowledging the dangers of

Conclusion

generalisation and the limitations of using a selective and necessarily small sample group. However, these findings chime with other studies and may help form the basis of further investigation, particularly in other areas where entrenched power must be challenged and resisted. The first disposition common to all the women in this study, and therefore their most potent weapon, was their education. This is partly because, as acknowledged in the introduction, the biographical approach favours the study of middle-class subjects. It is, however, also a fact that apart from a very few women such as Margaret Bondfield, the Labour MP and trade unionist, working-class women simply did not have the resources in terms of education and financial backing to mount a sustained attack on the obstacles before them at this time.[5] Numerous studies confirm this, showing that the higher a subject's socio-economic status, the more predisposed they are towards political contention, both in the pure politics of standing for election and representing voters, and in being active across a wide range of public organisations in pursuing change.[6] An inclusive society is one that invests in education and social mobility for all of its citizens, and the findings of this study underline this.

While none of the subjects in this book except Shiela Grant Duff came from the 'Upper Ten Thousand' as *Queen* magazine called them, and none came from the elite cultural grouping that benefited Virginia Woolf and the Bloomsbury set, they all came from broadly middle-class backgrounds and had a reasonable school education. Some (Kylie Tennant, Stella Martin, Edith Shackleton and Naomi Royde-Smith) left school before they were 18, and others, such as Dorothy Pilley, attended schools which paid little attention to their pupils' intellectual development.[7] However, some – Francesca Wilson, Margaret

Lane and Shiela Grant Duff – went to university. Others – Leah Manning, Claudia Parsons and Kylie Tennant (briefly) – attended further education and training. Their economic backgrounds were mostly reasonably comfortable, although Alison Settle, Edith Shackleton, Naomi Royde-Smith and Una Marson were only ever able to rely on the money they earned for themselves, and several endured periods of financial struggle. Stella Martin supported herself on her journalist's wage, easing her Methodist minister father's numerous financial worries for a while, until she lost her job in 1931.[8]

Another similarity that half of the women in this book shared was the absence of a father; more than half also, for the duration of the interwar years at least, had no husband, both figures representing one element of the patriarchal structures that could hold women back at this time. We also know from biographical details that in a few cases (Naomi Royde-Smith, Una Marson and Leah Manning), their marriages were not conventional. This lack of a potentially repressive force endowed many of these women with an equal and opposite energy to assert themselves. This might have taken the form of the need to be self-reliant, the provision of a strong female role model in a mother or grandmother, or the freedom to make choices that their fathers or husbands would not have permitted. Another common factor is the absence of children, or a delay in having children at a time when newspapers were encouraging women to help rebuild strong post-war nations by becoming mothers, and when the majority of British adult women married and had children.[9] Only two subjects, Alison Settle and Stella Martin, had children in their twenties and during the period under review. Three others, Shiela Grant Duff, Kylie Tennant and Margaret Lane, had children during or after the Second World

Conclusion

War, all having their first child in their thirties. In 1940 only 18 per cent of British women had not had a child by their 30th birthday (the figures for Australia are comparable); in this study 11 out of 13 (85 per cent) had not had a child by their 30th birthday.[10]

For all the women here, whether they were professional novelists, journalists or biographers, or whether they were enthusiastic amateurs, writing was axiomatic in their construction of self and in the development of their creativity. Growing up during the early days of mass literacy, they certainly benefited from living through a time when, as F. R. Leavis somewhat regretfully declared, 'a deluge of printed matter pours over the world'.[11] As if imbibing the lesson of their suffragist mothers and grandmothers that writing was the one way a woman might begin to be heard outside the domestic sphere, as children they wrote plays, poems and created family newspapers. Writing brought solace to Francesca Wilson during her long, lonely postings across Europe and Russia; for Una Marson, her poetry became a way to process and then react against the racism she experienced in London. For many (Edith Shackleton, Stella Martin, Dorothy Pilley, Naomi Royde-Smith and Alison Settle), writing and journalism provided a ladder out of the domestic sphere, and full or partial economic independence. Being an enthusiastic joiner-inner, whether at school or in adult life – and thus recognising the power of groups with shared goals – also seems to have been common to most, but certainly not all, the women in this study.

Other minor characteristics such as red-headedness (4 out of 13), left-handedness (at least 4 out of 13) and longevity (many women in this study lived far longer than average, and several lived into their nineties) may be more a matter of amusement than any scholarly value (this author being a left-handed redhead). What the biographical approach certainly does provide is a deeply satisfying side to historical study. Who cannot fail to feel a connection with their subject as one reads, in fading scrawl, secret confessions in diaries or powerful emotions in letters? What historian is not thrilled by an echoing resonance down the years of carefully kept menus from special occasions, school reports and dance cards slipped inside personal mementoes or into buff-coloured archive folders labelled unpromisingly 'Miscellany', or by holding the slender ice pick that helped Dorothy Pilley reach the rime-encrusted crest of the Dent Blanche? As one of my subjects here, Margaret Lane, once wrote:

> No biography of any value is possible without a genuine sympathy between writer and subject. Interest is not strong enough, nor amusement, nor psychological curiosity, nor even a strong feeling for a particular period … If you can't feel fond of your subject, let it alone.[12]

Reader, I did feel fond. Indeed, over the course of this book I fell, one by one, for each of the women studied here and wished I could possess even a small portion of their courage and spirit. They were brave pioneers both in their achievements and in their dauntless challenging of unfair authority. They and thousands like them helped to forge a way forward, and we are still, whatever gender, walking in their footsteps. As the biographical approach brings benefits to the scholar, I hope too it brings rewards to the reader, and that the delights of discovering the personal – Alison Settle's charming, weary diary of a single mother; Claudia Parsons merrily selling her clothes at every port she visited to fund her journey around the world; Kylie

Conclusion

Tennant walking 600 miles to escape her father, until her feet were bloody and blistered – help bring an added dimension to the study of this period.

Notes

1 See, for example, Hill 2019; Barr and Drury 2009.
2 See, for example, Ayhan Kaya's work on the political participation strategies of the Circassian diaspora in Turkey (2004).
3 See, for example, Black et al.'s work on collaboration between climate and immigrant justice groups in the US South (2016).
4 Shami Seteney has shown how this method works in large ethnic minorities in the Middle East and the Caucasus (1998).
5 See Chapter 7 for details of Bondfield's career.
6 Milbrath 1960.
7 Shiela Grant Duff was presented to Queen Mary as a debutante in 1931.
8 Martin Currey 2017: 193.
9 Beaumont 2013: 4.
10 www.ons.gov.uk/peoplepopulationandcommunity/birthsdeathsandmarriages/conceptionandfertilityrates/bulletins/childbearingforwomenbornindifferentyearsenglandandwales/2014-12-04 (accessed 6 September 2019).
11 Leavis 1924: 336.
12 Lane 1966: xi.

Appendix: The Second World War and beyond

Grant Duff, Shiela (1913–2004)

Shortly after the Second World War broke out, Grant Duff joined the BBC European Service and became the first editor of the Czech section. At the BBC she met the *Daily Telegraph* foreign correspondent Noel Newsome, who also joined the BBC at the outbreak of war. They married in 1942 and had two children. Throughout the war and after, Grant Duff gave support to Czech journalists and politicians in exile, including the foreign minister Jan Masaryk, who she asked to be godfather to her first child, Penelope. Masaryk was murdered shortly after his return to Prague after the war in the communist coup. After she and Noel Newsome divorced, Grant Duff married Micheal Sokolov, the former white Russian RNVR officer, with whom she had three more children. She and her family moved to Cork where they became farmers.

Published memoir: *The Parting of Ways* (1982).
Published biography: none
Archive resources: archive of Shiela Grant Duff, Bodleian

Appendix

Library, Oxford; journalism in various newspapers and magazines.

Lane, Margaret (1907–94)

Lane continued to write novels, but her best work is in her acclaimed biographies, particularly *Edgar Wallace: The Biography of a Phenomenon* (1938), *The Tale of Beatrix Potter* (1946), *The Bronte Story* (1953) and *Samuel Johnson and his World* (1975). She also wrote regular book reviews for the *Sunday Times* and the *Daily Telegraph*. In 1939 she divorced Bryan Wallace, Edgar Wallace's son, to whom she had been married for five years, and began living with Jack Hastings, 15th Earl of Huntingdon; they married in 1944. They had two daughters, Selina (b. 1945) and Caroline (b. 1946).

Published memoir: none
Published biography: none
Archive resources: St Hugh's College, Oxford; journalism in various newspapers and magazines.

Macaulay, Rose (1881–1958)

Macaulay continued to write novels and non-fiction books and to review prolifically for the *Times Literary Supplement*. The Second World War was a catastrophic period for her. Her sister died of cancer in 1941 and two months later her flat in Northumberland Street, London, was destroyed by a bombing raid, taking with it her books, her 'lost darlings' as she described them in a letter. A year later her lover, Gerald O'Donovan, died. For a while she wrote no more fiction, but she returned to it, writing two of her best-loved novels late in life: *The World*

My Wilderness (1950) and *The Towers of Trebizond* (1956). She was made a Dame in the 1958 New Year's Honours List, just months before she died.

Published memoir: none
Published biography: *Rose Macaulay: A Biography* by Constance Babington-Smith (1972), *Rose Macaulay* by Sarah LeFanu (2003).
Archive resources: Dame Rose Macaulay papers, Wren Library, Trinity College, Cambridge; Naomi Royde-Smith papers, Temple University Libraries, Pennsylvania (letters from Rose Macaulay to Naomi Royde-Smith).

Manning, Leah (1886–1977)

During the Second World War, Manning was the NUT's Evacuation Liaison Officer, and travelled across the country to ensure that there were enough teachers in rural areas to provide education for the influx of children from London and other cities. In 1945 she was selected to represent Labour at the general election, and won a seat in Clement Attlee's post-war Labour landslide. In her second stint as MP, Manning campaigned for better housing for working families and was vocal in support of the New Towns movement and in the building of the National Health Service. She lost her seat in 1950, but campaigned for the rest of her life for a number of progressive causes, particularly women's rights, and, after the introduction of the contraceptive pill, for the right of unmarried women to be given contraceptive advice.

Appendix

Published memoir: *A Life for Education* (1970).
Published biography: *Leah Manning* by Ron Bill and Stan Newens (1991).
Archive resources: Leah Manning papers, Essex County Records Office, Homerton College, Cambridge; journalism in various newspapers and magazines.

Marson, Una (1905–65)

Marson continued as an embattled radio producer on the *Caribbean Voices* programme for the BBC through the Second World War, but throughout this time her mental health deteriorated and she returned to Jamaica in the spring of 1945 for a short research trip and rest. She returned to Britain in December 1945 but went back to Jamaica less than a year later. She continued to write journalism and poetry, publishing several articles in the Jamaican political-literary journal *Public Opinion* and the *Gleaner*. Little is known about her life after 1946, and for much of the time she was battling mental illness. She travelled to America where she lived for about ten years, during which time she married a dentist, Peter Staples, but the marriage lasted less than a year. She continued to work for the Jamaican Save the Children Fund, and her writings often focused on encouraging Caribbean nationalism through literature.

Published memoir: none
Published biography: *The Life of Una Marson 1905–1965* by Delia Jarrett-Macauley (1998).
Archive resources: small collection in the Institute of Jamaica, Kingston; journalism in various newspapers and magazines.

Martin, Stella (1907–94)

Stella Martin married Ralph Currey, also of Methodist upbringing, in 1932; they had two sons, James (b. 1936) and Andrew (b. 1940). Stella Martin Currey, as she was now called, continued writing novels and plays including *The Comfort Tree* (novel, 1946) and *Love and Miss Figgis* (play, 1955). Her most successful publication, however, was her non-fiction *One Woman's Year* (1953), the diary of a 1950s housewife battling with poor food and a small budget. It has become something of a classic among those interested in life in austerity Britain. It contains some extraordinary recipes including the February 'Pancake Pagoda', to celebrate the hens starting to lay eggs again: a mountain of pancakes interlaced with curry, fried vegetables and celery. It has recently been republished by Persephone Books.

Published memoir: partial, she wrote a biography of her father *J. P. Martin: Father of Uncle: A Master in the great English Nonsense tradition* (2017), in which she interweaves tales of family life; it has recently been edited and published by her son, James Currey.
Published biography: none
Archive resources: James Currey private papers; journalism in various newspapers.

Parsons, Claudia (1900–98)

Mid-way through the war, Parsons was taken from the factory floor to work at the Ministry of Labour as a factory inspector with her former fellow student at Loughborough Verena

Appendix

Holmes, where she stayed for the next seven years. Although the pay and status were higher than on the factory floor, she missed her previous employment: 'I longed for my bawdy companions, yearned for the noise of machinery and to be using my hands instead of my yet untutored brain.' She also felt like a 'fish out of water', belonging to 'a despised social class' – not working class, nor professional middle class either. She tried to get other pieces of fiction published after the war, but her files at Chatto only contain letters of rejection after 1941. Although she continued to travel, she did not publish about her adventures again, until her memoir *Century Story* (1995). Parsons stayed at the Ministry of Labour until she was dismissed in 1949, having spent the four post-war years establishing engineering apprenticeships for returning servicemen. She moved back to the family home in Wonersh, Surrey, with her mother and sister Betty, taking sporadic chauffeuring jobs and travelling, when she could, across Europe. She then accidentally fell into china restoration in the days before resin adhesives, the process requiring expert use of diamond drills and wire rivets to hold delicate porcelain together, and she became an expert, with work pouring in as people began to put together the ruins of their homes after the war. She published one further book, *China Mending and Restoration* (1963), and, after a friend left her a large amount of money in her will, she travelled further afield, to Russia, China and, in her late seventies, across the Arabian desert and the Yemen.

Published memoir: *Vagabondage* (1941), *Century Story* (1995).
Published biography: none
Archive resources: Loughborough University; journalism in various newspapers and magazines, particularly the *Woman Engineer*.

Pilley, Dorothy (1894–1986)

Pilley and her husband I. A. Richards lived in China and then the United States from the late 1930s to 1970s while Richards took up chairs at Tsing Hus University in Beijing and at Harvard. They continued climbing together across North America, China and Japan, Pilley completing a long solo journey from China into what was then Burma (present-day Myanmar). Wherever she went, she wrote of her adventures. In Canada on Mount Erebus she wrote: 'We camped that night on a soft green shelf starred with tiny white flowers, a tinkling stream a few yards on one side and a clump of dwarf juniper supplying fuel and bedding on the other. I want no more from Paradise … At Amethyst Lake we met two exploring G. I.s, who casually mentioned V-J Day and the atomic bomb.' In Japan she wrote: 'Down where the water rushes along, real diamond-water so clear it is and sparkling, the granite has set itself into vast horizontal slabs … a procession of six peasant women, old and young they carried immense burdens and slung round them were pails of mushrooms. Our tent seemed so small and camping such a comic thing to do that they roared with laughter. Two of the youngest girls chopped down whole trees and brought them down in their arms. With a smile they were off with their burdens through the shadow of the trees. We slept well that night.' A notoriously feisty conversationalist, she counted among her friends the poets Adrienne Rich and Kathleen Raine and the literary critics Frank and Queenie Leavis. They moved back to Cambridge in 1973 when Richards became professor and honorary fellow at Magdalene College.

Appendix

Published memoir: none
Published biography: no full-length one exists, although she is the subject of her great nephew Dan Richards's book on his experiences of walking in her footsteps, *Climbing Days* (2016).
Archive resources: I. A. Richards papers, Magdalene College Cambridge; Alpine Club Library; journalism in various newspapers and magazines.

Royde-Smith, Naomi (1875–1964)

Throughout the rest of her life Royde-Smith continued her astonishingly creative literary output, writing a dozen more novels after the Second World War, and bringing her total output to 26; her last, *Love and a Birdcage* (1960), was published when she was 85 and practically blind. She also wrote several novellas, collections of short stories and biographies. However, she suffered the fate of many writers without a 'proper job' or private income and her money problems grew increasingly desperate as she grew older. Finally, when she was reduced, at the age of 79, to a bed-sitting room in Winchester, her friend, the writer Eleanor Farjeon, persuaded the Society of Authors in 1954 to pay her a yearly pension initially of £150, rising to £200 in 1958. She remained married to Ernest Milton, fifteen years her junior, but they spent most of the time apart while he pursued his career in films both in London and the United States.

Published memoir: none
Published biography: *Avenging Muse: Naomi Royde-Smith 1875–1964* by Jill Benton (2015).
Archive resources: Naomi Royde-Smith papers, Temple University Libraries, Pennsylvania.

Settle, Alison (1891–1980)

Settle edited the *Observer* women's page throughout the Second World War, and in 1944 was briefly a war correspondent for the newspaper. She considered her war reporting her proudest achievement in journalism, and her sympathetic depictions of the Dutch refugees she met in Holland are particularly fine passages of her writing. Denied a military escort by Field Marshall Montgomery – having been promised one – she had to hitch-hike to the front line in Holland in 1944 after landing in Brussels. Settle was not put off: 'So I stood at the roadside and got picked up – where you get to of course, might be almost anywhere. But gradually I got to Holland in the worst of the fighting and got down to reporting the war.' Settle retired from the *Observer* in 1960, and became a fashion columnist for *The Lady* until 1976.

Published memoir: none
Published biography: none
Archive resources: Brighton Design Archive; Harry Ransom Center (PEN Archives); Women's Library LSE (Women's Press Club); Charles Wakefield Private Collection (diary); journalism in various newspapers and magazines, particularly the *Observer*.

Shackleton, Edith (1885–1976)

Shackleton continued to write book reviews for the *Observer* until 1948, when she moved across to reviewing for *The Lady*, where her sister Nora had just taken over as editor. She remained as chief book reviewer for *The Lady* until Nora retired in 1954, but

Appendix

continued occasionally to contribute until the 1960s. After her brief affair with W. B. Yeats, Shackleton began an affair with the artist Gluck, who moved into Chantry House in Steyning with her, prompting a near-terminal rupture in her relationship with her sister. She is buried in St Andrew's churchyard, Steyning, with her mother and sister. Her brother's name is also inscribed on the gravestone.

Published memoir: none
Published biography: none
Archive resources: Harry Ransom Center (PEN Archives); Beaverbrook papers, House of Commons (*Sunday Express* and *Evening Standard* personnel details); journalism in various newspapers and magazines.

Tennant, Kylie (1912–88)

Tennant continued to write novels, the most critically acclaimed being *The Battlers* (1941), *Ride on, Stranger* (1943), *The Honey Flow* (1956) and *Tell Morning This* (1967). She also wrote several plays and children's stories as well as non-fiction books including *Australia: Her Story: Notes on a Nation* (1953). Tennant also continued her activism, particularly campaigning against nuclear testing and for Aboriginal rights in the 1950s and 1960s. Her Secret Service file mainly contains notes and entries from this period. She had two children, Benison (b. 1946) and John Laurence, 'Bim' (b. 1951). The latter part of Tennant's life was blighted by her son's murder in 1978, and by her husband Lewis Rodd's intense bouts of depression and frequent suicide attempts, one of which resulted in him losing an arm and a foot. Having turned down an OBE twice ('for an old revolutionary there was something faintly ridiculous about symbolically joining the Establishment'), she was awarded, and accepted, the Order of Australia in 1980. A bronze plaque commemorating her life and work is set, alongside those of other stars of the Australian literary firmament, among the paving slabs of Sydney's Circular Quay.

Published memoir: *The Missing Heir* (1986).
Published biography: *Kylie Tennant, A Life* by Jane Grant (2006).
Archive resources: papers of Kylie Tennant, National Library of Australia, National Archives of Australia.

Wilson, Francesca (1888–1981)

Wilson had been back in England working as a schoolteacher during 1939, but shortly after the outbreak of the Second World War she was called up by the Friends and the Polish Relief Fund to report on the conditions of Polish refugees in Eastern Europe. Wilson travelled to Hungary in October 1939. There, as well as helping to find clothing and food for Polish refugees, she helped Czechs fleeing their occupied land to escape westwards. Wilson too had to flee across the border to Romania ahead of the advancing German army in 1940. She then joined the United Nations Relief and Rehabilitation Administration (UNRRA), and arrived in Germany as its principal welfare officer two days after its surrender, working initially to help the victims of Dachau and then working in Czechoslovakia, former Yugoslavia and Austria in 1946. After retiring she lived in Hampstead and then Walberswick, Suffolk, and her niece Elizabeth Horder remembered that she 'always shared her

Appendix

home with refugees from somewhere'. She continued writing, publishing *Aftermath* (1947), about the work of UNRRA, *Strange Island* (1955) and *They Came as Strangers* (1959).

Published memoir: *In the Margins of Chaos* (1944); *They Came as Strangers* is a part-memoir of her encounters with refugees; she partly contributed to *A Life of Service and Adventure* (1995).
Published biography: none
Archive sources: Francesca Wilson papers, Records of the Friends Emergency and War Victims Relief Committee, *Dictionary of Quaker Biography*, all at the Friends Library, Euston; Spanish Medical Aid reports, Marx Memorial Library, London; journalism in various newspapers and magazines, particularly *The Friend*.

Bibliography

Archive sources

Alison Settle diary and private papers, Charles Wakefield (private collection)
Alpine Club Library, London (Dorothy Pilley papers, *Pinnacle* journal)
Archive of British Printing and Publishing, University of Reading (Chatto and Windus archive, George Bell and Sons archive)
Archives of the Trades Union Congress
Beaverbrook papers, House of Commons (BBK)
Brighton University Design Archives (Alison Settle papers)
British Library: British newspaper archives
Bodleian Library, Oxford (archive of Shiela Grant Duff)
Cambridge University Library (Prix Femina-Vie Heureuse committee papers)
Essex County Records Office (Leah Manning papers)
Friends Library, London (Francesca Wilson papers, Quaker records, *The Friend*, *Reconstruction*)
Harry Ransom Center, University of Texas, Austin (English PEN archive)
Imperial War Museum (Tessa Rowntree papers, Virginia Cowles papers, Scottish Women's Hospitals papers)
Institution of Automobile Engineers, London
Institution of Engineering and Technology, London
Institution of Mechanical Engineers (IMechE), London
Loughborough College archives (Claudia Parsons Roll of Graduates, copies of *The Limit* magazine)
Magdalene College Cambridge (I. A. Richards and Dorothy Pilley Richards collection)

Bibliography

National Archives of Australia (Kylie Tennant papers)
National Library of Australia (Kylie Tennant papers)
Penguin Random House Archives (letters and contracts with Margaret Lane)
Private collection of James Currey (Stella Martin papers, newspaper cuttings)
Report of the Royal Commission Appointed to Investigate, Report and Advise Upon Matters in Relation to the Condition and Treatment of Aborigines, b10508 (Perth: Fred. Wm. Simpson, Government Printer, 1935)
Royal Commission on the Press 1947–1949, Cmd. 7700 (London: HMSO, 1949)
St Hugh's College, Oxford (Margaret Lane papers)
Temple University Libraries, Pennsylvania (Naomi Royde-Smith papers)
Warwick Modern Records Centre (NUT papers, Gollancz publishing archive)
West India Royal Commission Report ('The Moyne Report'), Cmd. 6607 (London: HMSO, 1939)
Women's Engineering Society Archive, Institute of Engineering and Technology
Women's Library, LSE

Newspapers and magazines

Age, The (Melbourne)
Alpine Journal, The
Birmingham Post
Bristol Times and Mirror
Bulletin, The (Sydney)
Cheshire Observer
Contemporary Review
Daily Graphic
Daily Mail
Daily News
Daily Sketch
Daily Worker
Deeside Field, The
Dundee Courier
Evening Standard
Friend, The

Bibliography

Friends Quarterly Examiner
Idler, The
Illustrated Sunday Herald
Jamaica Standard
Journal of the Fell and Rock Club
Keys, The
Lady, The
Leeds Mercury
Left Review, The
Life and Letters Today
Limit, The
London Mercury
Manchester Guardian
News Chronicle
Newspaper World
Nursing Mirror and Midwives' Journal
Observer
Oxford Magazine, The
Pinnacle Journal, The
Political Quarterly
Queen, The
Reconstruction
Schoolmaster, The
Spectator
Sunday Express
Sunday Pictorial
Sydney Morning Herald
Time and Tide
Times Literary Supplement
Vote, The
West Australian, The
Western Mail
Woman Engineer, The
Woman Journalist, The
Woman Teacher, The
World's Children, The
Yorkshire Post

Bibliography

Published primary and secondary works

Agate, James (1935), *Ego* (London: Hamish Hamilton).
Alber, Jan (2017), 'Indigeneity and Narrative Strategies: Ideology in Contemporary Non-indigenous Prose Fiction', *Storyworlds: A Journal of Narrative Studies*, 9/1–2, pp. 159–81.
Allen, Charles (2007), *Kipling Sahib: India and the Making of Rudyard Kipling* (London: Abacus).
Allen, Gene (2016), 'Catching up with the Competition: the International Expansion of Associated Press 1920–1945', *Journalism Studies*, 17/6, pp. 747–62.
Alpert, Michael (1984), 'Humanitarianism and Politics in the British Response to the Spanish Civil War, 1936–9', *European History Quarterly*, 14, pp. 423–40.
Anderson, Ben (2011), 'A Liberal Countryside? The Manchester Ramblers' Federation and the "Social Readjustment" of Urban Citizens 1929–1936', *Urban History*, 38, pp. 84–102.
Archibald, David (2012), *The War that Won't Die* (Manchester: Manchester University Press).
Ayers, David (1999), *English Literature of the 1920s* (Edinburgh: Edinburgh University Press).
Baker, Nina (2009), 'More than Pioneers: A Hundred Years of Women at Work in the Scottish Building Industry 1820–1920', *Construction Information Quarterly*, 11/4, pp. 181–5.
Balston, Jenny (1994), *The Story of St Stephen's College* (The Old St Stephenites Society).
Banner, Lois (2009), 'Biography as History', *American Historical Review*, 114/3, pp. 579–86.
Banton, Michael (1955), *'The Coloured Quarter': Negro Immigrants in an English City* (London: Jonathan Cape).
Bar-Yosef, Ofer, and Callender, Jane (2004), 'Dorothy Annie Elizabeth Garrod (1892–1968)', in Cohen and Jukowsky (eds), *Breaking Ground: Pioneer Women Archaeologists* (Ann Arbor, MI: University of Michigan Press), pp. 380–424.
Barclay, Katie (2010), 'Composing the Self: Gender, Subjectivity and Scottish Balladry', *Cultural and Social History*, 7, pp. 337–53.
Barr, Dermot, and Drury, John (2009), 'Activist Identity as a Motivational Resource: Dynamics of (Dis)empowerment at the G8 Direct Actions, Gleneagles 2005', *Social Movement Studies*, 8/3, pp. 243–60.

Bibliography

Beaumont, Caitriona (2013), *Housewives as Citizens: Domesticity and the Women's Movement in England, 1928–64* (Manchester: Manchester University Press).

Beddoe, Deirdre (1989), *Back to Home and Duty: Women Between the Wars 1918–1939* (London: Pandora).

Beetham, Margaret (1996), *A Magazine of her Own? Domesticity and Desire in the Women's Magazine 1880–1914* (London: Routledge).

Belcher, Margaret (1932), *Cape to Cowley via Cairo in a Light Car* (London: Methuen).

Benton, Jill (2015), *Avenging Muse: Naomi Royde-Smith 1875–1964* (Bloomington, IN: Xlibris).

Bill, Ron, and Newens, Stan (1991), *Leah Manning* (Harlow: Leah Manning Trust).

Bingham, Adrian (2004a), *Gender, Modernity and the Popular Press in Inter-war Britain* (Oxford: Oxford University Press).

Bingham, Adrian (2004b), 'An Era of Domesticity? Histories of Women and Gender in Interwar Britain', *Cultural and Social History*, 1/2, pp. 225–33.

Boittin, Jennifer Anne (2014), 'Adventurers and Agents Provocateurs: A German Woman Travelling through French West Africa in the Shadow of War', *Historical Reflections*, 40/1, pp. 111–31.

Bourne, Stephen (2008), *Dr Harold Moody* (London: Southwark Local History Library).

Brantlinger, Patrick (2011), '"Eating Tongues": Australian Colonial Literature and the "Great Silence"', *The Yearbook of English Studies*, 4/2, pp. 125–39.

Bray, Lilian (1924), 'Three Pinnaclers in the Alps', *Pinnacle Journal*, 1/1, pp. pp. 25–9.

Breitenbach, Esther, and Wright, Valerie (2014), 'Women as Active Citizens: Glasgow and Edinburgh c. 1918–1939', *Women's History Review*, 23/3, pp. 401–20.

Bretherton, Eva (1917), 'The Eleventh Hour', *The Quiver*, 52/11, pp. 885–91.

Briganti, Chiara, and Mezei, Kathy (2006), *Domestic Modernism, the Interwar Novel and E. H. Young* (Aldershot: Ashgate).

Brittain, Vera (1987 [1940]), *Testament of Friendship* (London: Virago).

Brittain, Vera (2004 [1933]), *Testament of Youth* (London: Virago).

Brooks, Collin (1998), *Fleet Street, Press Barons and Politics: The Journals of Collin Brooks, 1932–1940*, ed. N. J. Crowson (London: Royal Historical Society).

Bibliography

Bryher (1963), *The Heart to Artemis: A Writer's Memoirs* (London: Collins).
Burke, Thomas (1932), *The Real East End* (London: Constable and Co.).
Bush, Barbara (1999), Imperialism, Race and Resistance: Africa and Britain 1919–1945 (London: Routledge).
Bussey, Gertrude, and Tims, Margaret (1980 [1965]), *Pioneers for Peace: Women's International League for Peace and Freedom 1915–1965* (Geneva: Women's International League for Peace and Freedom).
Cable, James (1979), *The Royal Navy and the Siege of Bilbao* (Cambridge: Cambridge University Press).
Cable, James (1993), 'Naval Humanitarianism', *International Relations*, 11/4, pp. 335–45.
Camboni, Marina (2004), 'Networking Women', in Maria Camboni (ed.), *Networking Women: Subjects, Places, Links Europe-America: Towards a Re-writing of Cultural History 1890–1939* (Rome: Edizioni di Storia e Letteratura), pp. 1–26.
Carey, John (1992), *The Intellectuals and the Masses: Pride and Prejudice amongst the Literary Intelligentsia 1880–1939* (Chicago: Academy Chicago).
Carpenter, Kenneth (2008), 'Harriette Chick and the Problem of Rickets', *The Journal of Nutrition*, 138/5, pp. 827–32.
Chapman, Jane (2020), 'The Struggles and Economic Hardship of Women Working Class Activists, 1918–1923', in Cavanagh and Steel (eds), *Letters to the Editor* (Basingstoke: Palgrave Macmillan), pp. 1–26.
Chatterjee, Choi (2008), '"Odds and Ends of the Russian Revolution," 1917–1920. Gender and American Travel Narratives', *Journal of Women's History*, 20/4, pp. 10–33.
Cixous, Hélène (1981), 'The Laugh of the Medusa', in Elaine Marks and Isabelle de Courtivron (eds), *New French Feminisms: An Anthology* (Brighton: Harvester Press), pp. 245–64.
Clarsen, Georgine (2008), *Eat My Dust: Early Women Motorists* (Baltimore, IN: Johns Hopkins University Press).
Clay, Catherine (2006), 'Re-visiting the Friendship of Vera Brittain and Winifred Holtby: A "Trade" in Work and Desire', *Women's History Review*, 12/2, pp. 309–28.
Clay, Catherine (2012), 'The Woman Journalist 1920–1945', in Maroula Joannou (ed.), *The History of British Women's Writing 1920–1945* (Basingstoke: Palgrave Macmillan), pp. 199–214.
Clay, Catherine (2018), *Time and Tide: The Feminist and Cultural Politics of a Modern Magazine* (Edinburgh: Edinburgh University Press).

Bibliography

Clennett, Margaret (ed.) (2009), *Presumptuous Pinnacle Ladies: A Selection from the Early Journals of Britain's First Women's Rock Climbing Club* (Disley: Millrace).

Cobham, Rhonda, and Collins, Merle (1987), 'Introduction', in Rhonda Cobham and Merle Collins (eds), *Watchers and Seekers: Creative Writing by Black Women in Britain* (London: The Women's Press), pp. 1–7.

Cockburn, Claud (1957), *In Time of Trouble* (London: Readers Union, Rupert Hart-Davis).

Cockett, Richard (1988), *Twilight of Truth: Chamberlain, Appeasement and the Manipulation of the British Press* (London: Weidenfeld and Nicolson).

Collecott, Diana (2004), 'Another Bloomsbury: Women's Networks in Literary London during World War One', in Maria Camboni (ed.), *Networking Women: Subjects, Places, Links Europe-America: Towards a Re-writing of Cultural History 1890–1939* (Rome: Edizioni di Storia e Letteratura), pp. 58–73.

Collett, Anne (2007), 'Review of Jane Grant, *Kylie Tennant: A Life*', *Journal for the Association for the Study of Australian Literature*, 7, pp. 130–4.

Collie, J. Norman (1923), 'Valedictory Address', *Alpine Journal*, 226, pp. 1–5.

Collier, Patrick (2006), *Modernism on Fleet Street* (Aldershot: Ashgate).

Cooper, Lettice (1939), 'Three Women and a Mammoth: England, Australia, Austria and USA: Novels of the Week', *Yorkshire Post*, 15 March, p. 8.

Coser, Ilaria (2017), 'Alison Settle, Editor of British *Vogue* (1926–1935): Habitus and the Acquisition of Cultural, Social and Symbolic Capital in the Private Diaries of Alison Settle', Fashion Theory, 23/1, pp. 85–108, DOI 10.1080/1362704X.2017.1371982.

Cosgrove, Denis (1984), *Symbolic Formation and Symbolic Landscape* (Madison, WI: University of Wisconsin Press).

Court Treatt, Stella (1927), *From Cape to Cairo* (London: George Harrap).

Covi, Giovanna (2004), '"But we not common, we is destant": Una Marson's Transatlantic Connections', in Maria Camboni, (ed.), *Networking Women: Subjects, Places, Links Europe-America: Towards a Re-writing of Cultural History 1890–1939* (Rome: Edizioni di Storia e Letteratura), pp. 413–28.

Cox, Howard, and Mowatt, Simon (2014), *Revolutions from Grub Street: A History of Magazine Publishing in Britain* (Oxford: Oxford University Press).

Currell, Melville (1974), *Political Woman* (London: Croom Helm).

Bibliography

Dark, Sidney (1917), 'Preface', in *Ivan Heald: Hero and Humourist* (London: C. Arthur Pearson), pp. iii–v.

Davies, Thomas Richard (2007), *The Possibilities of Transnational Activism: The Campaign for Disarmament Between the Two World Wars* (Leiden: Martinus Nijhoff).

Davis, Angela (1981), *Women, Race and Class* (London: The Women's Press).

De Havilland, Gladys (1918), *The Woman's Motor Manual* (London: Temple Press).

Dell'Orto, Giovanna (2004), '"Memory and Imagination are the Great Deterrents"; Martha Gellhorn at War as Correspondent and Literary Author', *The Journal of American Culture*, 27/3, pp. 303–14.

Demoor, Marysa (2016), *Their Fair Share: Women, Power and Criticism in the Athenaeum, from Millicent Garett Fawcett to Katharine Mansfield, 1870–1920* (London: Routledge).

DiCenzo, Maria, and Delap, Lucy (2008), 'Transatlantic Print Culture: The Anglo-American Feminist Press and Emerging Modernities', in Ann Ardis and Patrick Collier (eds), *Transatlantic Print Culture, 1880–1940: Emerging Media, Emerging Modernisms* (Basingstoke: Palgrave Macmillan), pp. 48–65.

DiCenzo, Maria, and Eustance, Claire (2018), '"Many More Worlds to Conquer": The Feminist Press Beyond Suffrage', in Catherine Clay et al. (eds), *Women's Periodicals and Print Culture in Britain 1918–1939* (Edinburgh: Edinburgh University Press), pp. 316–32.

Dick, Margaret (1966), *The Novels of Kylie Tennant* (Adelaide: Rigby).

Dilley, Rachel, and Scraton, Sheila Janet (2010), 'Women, Climbing and Serious Leisure', *Leisure Studies*, 29/2, pp. 125–41.

Donnell, Alison (2011a), 'Una Marson and the Fractured Subjects of Modernity: Writing across the Black Atlantic', *Women: a Cultural Review*, 22/4, pp. 345–69.

Donnell, Alison (2011b), 'Introduction', in Alison Donnell (ed.), *Una Marson, Selected Poems* (Leeds: Peepal Tree), pp. 11–31.

Duspati, Teja Varma (2017), 'Going Places: Harriet Martineau's *Letters from Ireland* and the Rise of the Female Foreign Correspondent', *Women's Writing*, 24/2, pp. 207–26.

Edmonds, Penny (2018), 'The Bunyip as Uncanny Rupture: Fabulous Animals, Innocuous Quadrupeds and the Australian Anthropocene', *Australian Humanities Review*, 63 (November), p. 80.

Edy, Carolyn M. (2017), *The Woman War Correspondent, The US Military and the Press 1846–1947* (Lanham MD: Lexington Books).

Bibliography

Eide, Martin, and Knight, Graham (1999), 'Public/Private Service: Service Journalism and the Problems of Everyday Life', *European Journal of Communication*, 14/4, pp. 525–47.

Emery, Mary Lou (2007), *Modernism, the Visual and Afro-Caribbean Literature* (Cambridge: Cambridge University Press).

Englander, David, and O'Day, Rosemary (eds) (1995), *Retrieved Riches: Social Investigation in Britain 1840–1914* (Aldershot: Scolar Press).

Evans, Elizabeth F. (2019), *Threshold Modernism: New Public Women and the Literary Spaces of Imperial London* (Cambridge: Cambridge University Press).

Farjeon, Eleanor (1924), 'For a Cock', *The Queen*, 21 May, p. 11.

Ferguson, Rachel (1958), *We Were Amused* (London: Jonathan Cape).

Ferguson, Rachel (2009 [1931]), *The Brontës Went to Woolworths* (London: Bloomsbury).

Fishback, Price (2012), 'Relief During the Great Depression in Australia and America', *Australian Economic History Review*, 52/3, pp. 221–49.

Fisher, Harriet White (1911), *A Woman's World Tour in a Motor* (Philadelphia: J. B. Lippincott).

Fiske, Susan, and Glick, Peter (1995), 'Ambivalence and Stereotypes Cause Sexual Harassment: A Theory with Implications for Organizational Change', *Journal of Social Issues*, 51/1, pp. 97–115.

Fitzgerald, Louise (2017), 'Still the Last Great Open Secret: Sexual Harassment as Systemic Trauma', *Journal of Trauma and Dissociation*, 18/4, pp. 483–89.

Fort, Adrian (2013), *Nancy: The Story of Lady Astor* (New York: St Martin's Press).

Frances, Raelene (2013), 'Authentic Leaders: Women and Leadership in Australian Unions before World War II', *Labour History*, 104, pp. 9–30.

Franklin, Gerd (1979), 'Margaret, Countess of Huntingdon', *Hampshire Magazine*, 19/11, September, pp. 54–6.

Franks, Suzanne (2013), *Women and Journalism* (London: I. B. Tauris).

Fraser, Nancy (1987), 'What's Critical about Critical Theory? The Case of Habermas and Gender', in Seyla Benhabib and Drucilla Cornell (eds), *Feminism as Critique* (London: Polity Press), pp. 31–56.

Fry, Margery (1938), 'Prisoners in the Balkans', *Manchester Guardian*, 17, 18, 19 February.

Fry, Ruth (1926), *A Quaker Adventure* (London: Nisbet).

Fussell, Paul (1980), *Abroad: British Literary Travelling Between the Wars* (Oxford: Oxford University Press).

Bibliography

Fyrth, Jim (1991), *Women's Voices from the Spanish Civil War* (London: Lawrence and Wishart).

Gallagher, Margaret (2014), 'Media and the Representation of Gender', in Cynthia Carter et al. (eds), *Routledge Companion to Media and Gender* (London: Routledge), pp. 23–31.

Gannon, Franklin Reid (1971), *The British Press and Germany 1936–1939* (Oxford: Clarendon Press).

Gardiner, Juliet (2010), *The Thirties: An Intimate History* (London: Harper Press).

Gearon, Liam (2012), 'Politics, Literature, Education: The Literary Archive in Citizenship – the Case of Poets, Essayists, Novelists (PEN)', *Citizenship Teaching and Learning*, 7/3, pp. 273–91.

Giddings, Robert (1991), 'Introduction', in Robert Giddings (ed.), *Literature and Imperialism* (London: Macmillan), pp. 1–24.

Glew, Helen (2016), *Gender, Rhetoric and Regulation: Women's Work in the Civil Service and the London County Council 1900–1955* (Manchester: Manchester University Press).

Glew, Helen (2018), 'Providing and Taking the *Opportunity*: Women Civil Servants and Feminist Periodical Culture in Interwar Britain', in Catherine Clay et al. (eds), *Women's Periodicals and Print Culture in Britain 1918–1939* (Edinburgh: Edinburgh University Press), pp. 362–73.

Goldie, Terry (1989), *Fear and Temptation: The Image of the Indigene in Canadian, Australian and New Zealand Literatures* (Montreal: McGill-Queens University Press).

Goodman, Joyce (2018), 'Internationalism, Empire, and Peace in the Woman Teacher 1920–1939', in Catherine Clay et al. (eds), *Women's Periodicals and Print Culture in Britain 1918–1939* (Edinburgh: Edinburgh University Press), pp. 348–61.

Gopsill, Tim, and Neale, Greg (2007), *Journalists: 100 Years of the NUJ* (London: Profile Books).

Gorham, Deborah (1992), '"The Friendships of Women": Friendship, Feminism and Achievement in Vera Brittain's Life and Work in the Interwar Decades', *Journal of Women's History*, 3/3, pp. 44–69.

Gorham, Deborah (1996), *Vera Brittain: A Feminist Life* (Oxford: Blackwell).

Gorham, Deborah (2007), 'Review: Catherine Clay. *British Women Writers 1914–1945. Professional Work and Friendship*', *Journal of British Studies*, 46/1, pp. 229–30.

Gottlieb, Julie (2013), '"We were done the moment we gave women the Vote": The Female Franchise Factor and the Munich By-elections, 1938–1939', in Julie Gottlieb and Richard Toye (eds), *The Aftermath*

Bibliography

of Suffrage: Women, Gender and Politics in Britain, 1918–1945 (Basingstoke: Palgrave), pp. 159–80.

Gottlieb, Julie (2014), '"The Women's Movement Took the Wrong Turning": British Feminists, Pacifism and the Politics of Appeasement', *Women's History Review*, 23/3, pp. 441–62.

Gottlieb, Julie (2015), *'Guilty Women': Foreign Policy and Appeasement in Interwar Britain* (Basingstoke: Palgrave).

Gottlieb, Julie, and Stibbe, Matthew (2017), 'Peace at any Price: The Visit of Nazi Women's Leader Gertrud Scholtz-Klink to London in March 1939 and the Response of British Women Activists', *Women's History Review*, 26/2, pp. 173–94.

Gottlieb, Julie, and Toye, Richard (eds) (2013), *The Aftermath of Suffrage: Women, Gender and Politics in Britain, 1918–1945* (Basingstoke: Palgrave).

Grant Duff, Shiela (1935a), 'The Saar at the Polls', *Observer*, 13 January, p. 15.

Grant Duff, Shiela (1935b), 'Saar Minority's Plight', *Observer*, 20 January, p. 15.

Grant Duff, Shiela (1939a), 'How the Coup was Prepared', *Spectator*, 24 March, pp. 475–6.

Grant Duff, Shiela (1939b), 'The Fate of Czechoslovakia', *The Contemporary Review*, May, pp. 552–9.

Grant Duff, Shiela (1976), 'A Very Brief Visit', in Philip Toynbee (ed.), *The Distant Drum: Reflections on the Spanish Civil War* (London: Sidgwick and Jackson), pp. 76–86.

Grant Duff, Shiela (1982), *The Parting of Ways* (London: Peter Owen).

Grant, Jane (2006), *Kylie Tennant: A Life* (Canberra: National Library of Australia).

Green, H. M. (1962), *A History of Australian Literature* (Sydney: Angus and Robertson).

Green, Martin (1976), *Children of the Sun* (New York: Basic Books).

Greene, Graham (1972), *A Sort of Life* (London: Penguin).

Greene, Graham (2004 [1938]), *Brighton Rock* (London: Vintage).

Griffiths, Dennis (2006), *Fleet Street: Five Hundred Years of the Press* (London: British Library).

Grigg, Russell (2002), 'The Origins and Growth of Ragged Schools in Wales, 1847–c. 1900', *History of Education*, 31/3, pp. 227–43.

Guy-Sheftall, Beverly (1999), 'Preface', in Kimberly Springer (ed.), *Still Lifting, Still Climbing: African American Women's Contemporary Activism* (New York: New York University Press), pp. xix–xxiii.

Bibliography

Hall, Mary (1907), *A Woman's Trek from Cape to Cairo* (London: Methuen).

Hammill, Faye (2007), *Women, Celebrity and Literary Culture between the Wars* (Austin, TX: University of Texas Press).

Handlin, Oscar (1979), *Truth in History* (Cambridge, MA: Harvard University Press).

Hankins, Leslie (2004), 'Iris Barry, Writer and Cineaste, Forming Film Culture in London 1924–1926: The *Adelphi*, the *Spectator*, the Film Society and the British *Vogue*', *Modernism/Modernity*, 11/3, pp. 488–515.

Hannam, June, and Hunt, Karen (2002), *Socialist Women: Britain, 1880s to 1920s* (London: Routledge).

Hanscombe, Gillian, and Smyers, Virginia (1987), *Writing for their Lives: The Modernist Women 1910–1940* (London: The Women's Press).

Hansen, Peter (2013), *The Summits of Modern Man: Mountaineering after the Enlightenment* (Cambridge, MA: Harvard University Press).

Harding, Jason (2002), *The Criterion: Cultural Politics and Periodical Networks in Interwar Britain* (Oxford: Oxford University Press).

Harford, Lesbia (1941), *The Poems of Lesbia Harford*, ed. Drusilla Modjeska and Marjorie Pizer (Melbourne: Melbourne University Press).

Harrison, Austin (1915), 'Motherhood the First Duty of Women: Biological Crisis of the Next Decade', *Sunday Pictorial*, 21 March, p. 4.

Harrison, Brian (1986), 'Women in a Men's House: The Women MPs 1919–1945', *The Historical Journal*, 29/3, pp. 623–54.

Harrison, Brian (1987), *Prudent Revolutionaries: Portraits of British Feminism between the Wars* (Oxford: Clarendon Press).

Hassett, Joseph (2010), *W. B. Yeats and the Muses* (Oxford: Oxford University Press).

Hastings, Selina (2014), *The Red Earl: The Extraordinary Life of the 16th Earl of Huntingdon* (London: Bloomsbury).

Heiss, Anita (2003), *Dhuulu-Yala: To Talk Straight: Publishing Indigenous Literature* (Canberra: Aboriginal Studies Press).

Hill, C. J. (1974), 'Great Britain and the Saar Plebiscite of 13 January 1935', *Journal of Contemporary History*, 9/2, pp. 121–42.

Hill, Christopher (2019), 'The Activist as Geographer: Nonviolent Direct Action in Cold War Germany and Postcolonial Ghana 1959–1960', *Journal of Historical Geography*, 4/64, pp. 36–46.

Hinds, Hilary (2009), 'Domestic Disappointments: Feminine Middlebrow Fiction of the Interwar Years', *Home Cultures*, 2/2, pp. 199–211.

Bibliography

Hobusch, Harald (2009), 'A "Triumph of the Will"? Andrew Marton's *Der Dämon des Himalaya* and the National Socialist Need for Heroes', *Sport in History*, 29/4, pp. 623–45.

Hollingworth, Clare (1942), *There's a German Just Behind Me* (London: Secker and Warburg).

Hollingworth, Clare (1990), *Front Line* (London: Jonathan Cape).

Holloway, Gerry (2005), *Women and Work in Britain since 1840* (London: Routledge).

Holtby, Winifred (1971 [1937]), *Letters to a Friend* (Bath: Cedric Chivers).

Holtby, Winifred (1981 [1924]), *The Crowded Street* (London: Virago).

Houssart, Mark (2016), '*The Spanish Earth* (1937): The Circumstances of its Production, the Film and its Reception in the United States and United Kingdom', *Catalan Journal of Communication and Cultural Studies*, 8/1 pp. 113–25.

Howell, Lis, and Singer, Jane (2017), 'Pushy or Princess? Women Experts in British Broadcast News', *Journalism Practice*, 11/9, pp. 1062–78.

Hudson, David (2016), '"A woman so curiously fear-free and venturesome": Eleanor Franklin Egan reporting the Great Russian Famine, 1922', *Women's History Review*, 26/2, pp. 195–212.

Hunt, Karen (2009), 'Rethinking Activism: Lessons from the History of Women's Politics', *Parliamentary Affairs*, 62/2, pp. 211–26.

Innes, S. (2004), 'Constructing Women's Citizenship in the Interwar Period: The Edinburgh Women's Citizenship Association', *Women's History Review*, 13/4, pp. 621–47.

International Council of Women (1966), *Women in a Changing World: The Dynamic History of the International Council of Women since 1888* (London: Routledge and Kegan Paul).

Jackson, Angela (2014), *British Women in the Spanish Civil War* (London: Routledge).

Jackson, Sarah, and Tyler, Rosemary (2014), *Voices from History: East London Suffragettes* (Stroud: The History Press).

Jaffe, Aaron (2005), *Modernism and the Culture of Celebrity* (Cambridge: Cambridge University Press).

Jameson, Storm (1984 [1969]), *Journey from the North, Volume One* (London: Virago).

Jamie, Kathleen (2008), 'A Lone Enraptured Male', *London Review of Books*, 30/5, 6 March, pp. 25–7.

Jarrett-Macauley, Delia (1998), *The Life of Una Marson 1905–65* (Manchester: Manchester University Press).

Bibliography

Joannou, Maroula (1999), 'Introduction', in Maroula Joannou (ed.), *Women Writers of the 1930s: Gender, Politics and History* (Edinburgh: Edinburgh University Press), pp. 1–20.

Johns-Putra, Adeline (2016), 'Climate Change in Literature and Literary Studies: From Cli-Fi, Climate Change Theater and Ecopoetry to Ecocriticism and Climate Change Criticism', *Climate Change*, 7/2, pp. 266–82.

Johnson, Dale (2004), 'Gender and the Construction of Models of Christian Activity: A Case Study', *Church History: Studies in Christianity and Culture*, 73/2, pp. 247–71.

Jones, Helen (2000), *Women in British Public Life 1914–1950: Gender Power and Social Policy* (Harlow: Longman).

Kaya, Ayhan (2004), 'Political Participation Strategies of the Circassian Diaspora in Turkey', *Mediterranean Politics*, 9/2, pp. 221–39.

Kelly, Pat (1921), 'The Pinnacle Club', *Journal of the Fell and Rock Climbing Club*, 5/2, pp. 324–6.

Kennard, Jean (1989), *Vera Brittain and Winifred Holtby: A Working Partnership* (Hanover, NH: University Press of New England).

Kennedy-Epstein, Rowena (2013), 'Introduction', in Muriel Rukeyser, *Savage Coast* (New York: The Feminist Press), pp. vii–xxx.

Kessler-Harris, Alice (2009), 'Why Biography?', *American Historical Review*, 114/3, pp. 625–30.

Killingray, David (1999), 'Race, Faith and Politics: Harold Moody and the League of Coloured People' (inaugural lecture), *Inaugural Lecture Series* (London: Goldsmiths College).

Kipling, Rudyard (2008 [1936]) *Something of Myself* (Ware: Wordsworth Editions).

Knightley, Phillip (2000), *The First Casualty: The War Correspondent as Mythmaker from the Crimea to Kosovo* (London: Prion Books).

Koren, Yehuda, and Negev, Eilat (2011), *First Lady of Fleet Street: The Life, Fortune and Tragedy of Rachel Beer* (London: J. R. Books).

Laband, David, and Lentz, Bernard (1992), 'Self-recruitment in the Legal Profession', *Journal of Labor Economics*, 10/2, pp. 182–201.

Laing, Kate (2017), '"The White Australia Nettle": Women's Internationalism, Peace and the White Australia Policy in the Interwar Years', *History Australia*, 14/2, pp. 218–36.

Lane, Margaret (1927a), 'This Women's Vote', *The Oxford Magazine*, 19 May, pp. 499–500.

Bibliography

Lane, Margaret (1927b), 'Edith Sitwell at the English Club', *The Oxford Magazine*, 9 June, p. 574.

Lane, Margaret (1935), *Faith, Hope and No Charity* (London: Heinemann).

Lane, Margaret (1939 [1938]), *Edgar Wallace: The Biography of a Phenomenon* (New York: Doubleday Doran).

Lane, Margaret (1965), 'Why I Gave up Music', *Punch*, 7 April, pp. 506–8.

Lane, Margaret (1966), *Purely for Pleasure* (London: Hamish Hamilton).

Langhamer, Claire (2000), *Women's Leisure in England 1920–1960* (Manchester: Manchester University Press).

Laracy, Hugh (2013), *Watriama and Co: Further Pacific Islands Portraits* (Canberra: Australian National University Press).

Law, Cheryl (1997), *Suffrage and Power: The Women's Movement 1918–1928* (London: I. B. Tauris).

Lawrence, Jon (2001), 'Contesting the Male Polity: The Suffragettes and the Politics of Disruption in Edwardian Britain', in Amanda Vickery (ed.), *Women, Privilege and Power: British Politics, 1750 to the Present* (Stanford, CA: Stanford University Press), pp. 201–26.

Lawson, Henry (1986 [1892]), 'The Drover's Wife', in *The Penguin Henry Lawson: Short Stories* (London: Penguin), pp. 19–26.

Leavis, F. R. (1924), 'The Relationship of Journalism to Literature', unpublished PhD thesis, University of Cambridge.

Leed, Eric J. (1991), *The Mind of the Traveller: From Gilgamesh to Global Tourism* (New York: Basic Books).

LeFanu, Sarah (2003), *Rose Macaulay* (London: Virago).

LeMahieu, D. L. (1988), *A Culture for Democracy: Mass Communication and the Cultivated Mind Between the Wars* (Oxford: Oxford University Press).

Liddle, Dallas (2009), *The Dynamics of Genre: Journalism and the Practice of Literature in Mid-Victorian Britain* (Charlottesville, VA: University of Virginia Press).

Light, Alison (1991), *Forever England: Femininity, Literature and Conservatism Between the Wars* (London: Routledge).

Linford, Madeline (1963), 'The First Page', *Guardian*, 11 September, p. 11.

Little, Douglas (1988), 'Red Scare 1936: Anti-Bolshevism and the Origins of British Non-Intervention in the Spanish Civil War', *Journal of Contemporary History*, 23, pp. 291–311.

Lonsdale, Sarah (2013), '"We agreed that women were a nuisance in the office, anyway": The Portrayal of Women Journalists in Early Twentieth Century British Fiction', *Journalism Studies*, 14/4, pp. 461–75.

Bibliography

Lonsdale, Sarah (2015), 'Roast Seagull and Other Quaint Bird Dishes: The Development of Features and "Lifestyle" Journalism in British Newspapers during the First World War', *Journalism Studies*, 16/6, pp. 800–15.
Lonsdale, Sarah (2016), *The Journalist in British Fiction and Film: Guarding the Guardians from 1900 to the Present* (London: Bloomsbury Academic).
Lonsdale, Sarah (2018), 'The Sheep and the Goats: Interwar Women Journalists, the Society of Women Journalists and the Woman Journalist', in Catherine Clay et al. (eds), *Women's Periodicals and Print Culture in Britain 1918–1939* (Edinburgh: Edinburgh University Press), pp. 463–76.
Lonsdale, Sarah (2019), 'Introduction', in Rose Macaulay, *What Not* (Bath: Handheld Press), pp. vii–xxv.
Lowe, Sylvia (1933), 'Disillusionment', *The Keys*, 1/2, October 1933, p. 28.
Lowerson, John (1980), 'Battles for the Countryside', in Frank Gloversmith (ed.), *Class Culture and Social Change: A New View of the 1930s* (Sussex: The Harvester Press), pp. 258–80.
Luckett, Richard (1990), 'Introduction', in *Selected Letters of I. A. Richards*, ed. John Constable (Oxford: Clarendon Press), pp. i–xxii.
Macaulay, Rose (1919), *Three Days* (London: Constable).
Macaulay, Rose (1957), 'Coming to London', in John Lehmann (ed.), *Coming to London* (London: Phoenix House), pp. 155–66.
Macaulay, Rose (1986 [1928]), *Keeping Up Appearances* (London: Methuen).
Macaulay, Rose (2011), *Dearest Jean: Rose Macaulay's Letters to a Cousin*, ed. Ferguson Smith (Manchester: Manchester University Press).
Macaulay, Rose (2018 [1926]), *Crewe Train* (London: Virago).
Macaulay, Rose (2019 [1919]), *What Not* (Bath: Handheld Press).
Macdonald, Roderick (1976), 'Introduction', in *The Keys 1933–1955* (New York: Kraus-Thompson), pp. 5–18.
Macdonald, Sheila (1928), 'Kilimanjaro in 1927', *Alpine Journal*, 236, pp. 77–84.
MacKinnon, Catharine (1979), *Sexual Harassment of Working Women: A Case of Sex Discrimination* (New Haven, CT: Yale University Press).
Madden, Cecil (2007), *Starlight Days: The Memoirs of Cecil Madden, the World's First Television Producer*, ed. Jennifer Lewis (London: Trevor Square Publications).
Maddox, Brenda (1999), *George's Ghosts: A New Life of W. B. Yeats* (London: Picador).
Manning, Leah (1935), *What I Saw in Spain* (London: Victor Gollancz).

Bibliography

Manning, Leah (1970), *A Life for Education* (London: Victor Gollancz).
Marrus, Michael (1985), *The Unwanted: European Refugees in the Twentieth Century* (Oxford: Oxford University Press).
Marson, Una (1930), *Tropic Reveries* (Kingston, Jamaica: self-published).
Marson, Una (1933), 'Nigger', *The Keys*, 1/1, July, p. 8.
Marson, Una (1934), 'Social and Political Equality', in *Africa: Peace and Freedom* (London: Women's International League), pp. 18–20.
Marson, Una (1935), 'Education', *The Keys*, 2/3, January–March, p. 53.
Marson, Una (1937), 'Little Brown Girl', in *The Moth and the Star* (Kingston: The Gleaner Co.), pp. 11–13.
Marson, Una (1939), 'The Story of Jamaica', *The Listener*, 27 July, pp. 66–7.
Martin Currey, Stella (1934), *Paperchase End* (Bristol: J. W. Arrowsmith).
Martin Currey, Stella (2017), *J. P. Martin: Father of Uncle*, ed. James Martin Currey (Kibworth Beauchamp: Matador).
Masterman, C. F. G. (1980 [1902]), *From the Abyss: of its inhabitants, by one of them* (New York: Garland).
Matera, Marc (2015), *Black London: The Imperial Metropolis and Decolonization in the Twentieth Century* (Berkeley, CA: University of California Press).
Matless, D. (1990), 'The English Outlook: A Mapping of Leisure, 1918–1939', in Nicholas Alfrey and Stephen Daniels (eds), *Mapping the Landscape: Essays on Art and Cartography* (Nottingham: Nottingham University Press), pp. 28–32.
Maynard, Debra, and Suter, Janita (2009), 'The Challenges of Marketing and Income Generation Training to Support Women in Exercising their Right to Self-reliance in a Refugee Camp Context: A Case Study from the Thai-Burma Border', *Australian Journal of Human Rights*, 15/1, pp. 127–49.
McCarthy, Helen (2014), *Women of the World: The Rise of the Female Diplomat* (London: Bloomsbury).
McDonald, Peter (1997), *British Literary Culture and Publishing Practice 1880–1914* (Cambridge: Cambridge University Press).
McKenna, Stephen (1917), *Sonia: Between Two Worlds* (New York: George Doran).
Milbrath, Lester (1960), 'Predispositions Toward Political Contention', *Western Political Quarterly*, 13/1, pp. 5–18.
Miller, Benjamin (2017), '"Come be off with you": White Spatial Control in the Representation of Aboriginality in Early Australian Drama', *The Journal of Commonwealth Literature*, 52/2, pp. 356–81.

Bibliography

Miller, Carol (1994), 'Geneva – the Key to Equality: Interwar Feminists and the League of Nations', *Women's History Review*, 3/2, pp. 219–45.

Mills, Sara (1993), *Discourses of Difference: An Analysis of Women's Travel Writing and Colonialism* (London: Routledge).

Moore, Aileen (1937), 'The Exodus of the Basque Children', *Nursing Mirror and Midwives' Journal*, 65/1679, 29 May, pp. 192–19.

Moretti, Franco (2000), 'The Slaughterhouse of Literature', *MLQ: Modern Language Quarterly*, 61/1, pp. 207–27.

Morgan, Sue (ed.) (2002), *Women, Religion and Feminism in Britain 1750–1900* (Basingstoke: Palgrave Macmillan).

Mowrer, Edgar Ansel (1970 [1968]), *Triumph and Turmoil: A Personal History of Our Times* (London: George Allen and Unwin).

Mullaney, Marie, and Hilbert, Rosemary (2018), 'Educating Women for Self-reliance and Economic Opportunity: The Strategic Entrepreneurialism of the Katharine Gibbs Schools 1911–1968', *History of Education Quarterly*, 58/1, pp. 68–93.

Mumm, A. L. (1921), 'A History of the Alpine Club', *Alpine Journal*, 223 pp. 1–18.

Munslow, Alan (2003), 'History and Biography: An Editorial Comment', *Rethinking History*, 7/1, pp. 1–11.

Murray, Stella Wolfe (ed.) (1925), *The Poetry of Flight* (London: Heath Cranton).

Nasaw, David (2009), 'Historians and Biography', *American Historical Review*, 114/3, pp. 573–8.

Natchcova, Nora, and Scoheni, Celine (2013), 'The ILO, Feminists and Expert Networks: The Challenges of a Protective Policy 1919–1934', in S. Kott and J. Droux (eds), *Globalising Social Rights: The International Labour Organisation and Beyond* (Basingstoke: Palgrave Macmillan), pp. 49–65.

Neilson, John Shaw (1926), 'Lament for Early Buttercups', *Sydney Morning Herald*, 29 May, p. 11.

Neville, Peter (1999), 'Nevile Henderson and Basil Newton: Two British Envoys in the Czech Crisis 1938', in Igor Lukes and Erik Goldstein (eds), *The Munich Crisis 1938* (London: Frank Cass), pp. 258–75.

Newsome, Penelope (2005), 'Shiela Sokolov Grant (Grant Duff) 1913–2004', obituary, in *Brown Book*, Lady Margaret Hall, Oxford.

O'Brien, Miriam (1931), 'In the Mont Blanc Massif and the Oberland', *Alpine Journal*, 43/243, November, p. 231.

Bibliography

O'Connell, Sean (1998), *The Car in British Society: Class, Gender and Motoring 1896–1939* (Manchester: Manchester University Press).

O'Day, Rosemary (1995), 'Women in Victorian Religion', in David Englander and Rosemary O'Day (eds), *Retrieved Riches: Social Investigation in Britain 1840–1914* (Aldershot: Scolar Press), pp. 339–63.

Oliver, Reggie (1998), *Out of the Woodshed: The Life of Stella Gibbons* (London: Bloomsbury).

Oram, Alison (1992), 'Repressed and Thwarted, or Bearer of the New World? The Spinster in Inter-war Feminist Discourses', *Women's History Review*, 1/3, pp. 413–33.

Orwell, George (1933), *Down and Out in Paris and London*. (London: Victor Gollancz).

Orwell, George (1937), *The Road to Wigan Pier* (London: Victor Gollancz).

Orwell, George (2000 [1938]), *Homage to Catalonia* (London: Penguin).

Parsons, Claudia (1921a), 'Side-lights on the Training of the Would-be Engineer', *The Woman Engineer*, 1/4, March, pp. 66–7.

Parsons, Claudia (1921b), 'To *The Limit*', *The Limit*, 3/3, July, p. 127.

Parsons, Claudia (1922), 'History of a Guileless Student, or, Tossed on the World', *The Limit*, 4/2, April, pp. 75–6.

Parsons, Claudia (1933), 'The Ford Works, Dagenham: Impressions of a Visit', *The Woman Engineer*, 3/4, March, pp. 215–18.

Parsons, Claudia (1935), *Brighter Bondage* (London: Chatto and Windus).

Parsons, Claudia (1941), *Vagabondage* (London: Chatto and Windus).

Parsons, Claudia (1992), *Century Story* (Lewes: The Book Guild).

Parsons, Claudia, with F. H. Curl (1963), *China Mending and Restoration* (London: Faber and Faber).

Parsons, G. M. (1933), *The Dove Pursues* (London: Constable).

Peacocke, Emilie (1936), *Writing for Women* (London: A. & C. Black).

Pedersen, Sarah (2020), 'Speaking as Citizens: Women's Political Correspondence to Scottish Newspapers 1918–28', in Cavanagh and Steel (eds), *Letters to the Editor* (Basingstoke: Palgrave Macmillan), pp. 25–47.

Peel, Mrs Charles (1933), *Life's Enchanted Cup* (London: The Bodley Head).

Pickles, Katie (2001), 'Colonial Counterparts: The First Academic Women in Anglo-Canada, New Zealand and Australia', *Women's History Review*, 10/2, pp. 273–98.

Pilley, D. E. (1920), 'Rain in the Mountains', *Journal of the Fell and Rock Climbing Club*, 5/2, p. 172.

Bibliography

Pilley, D. E. (1921), 'The London Section', *Journal of the Fell and Rock Climbing Club*, 5/3, p. 331.
Pilley, D. E. (1923), 'The North-East arete of the Jungfrau and other Traverses', *Alpine Journal*, 226, pp. 161–80.
Pilley, D. E. (1924), 'Into Spain and Back Again', *Pinnacle Club Journal*, 1, pp. 39–47.
Pilley, D. E. (1931), 'Many Unscaled Peaks in Diamond Mountains', *Japan Advertiser*, 24 June.
Pilley, D. E. (1945), 'Camping in Simon Creek', *Canadian Alpine Journal*, 27, pp. 204–9.
Pilley, Dorothy (1965 [1935]), *Climbing Days* (London: Secker and Warburg).
Plastas, Melinda (2011), *A Band of Noble Women: Racial Politics in the Women's Peace Movement* (Syracuse, NY: Syracuse University Press).
Pons, Xavier (1974), '*The Battlers*: Kylie Tennant and the Australian Tradition', *Australian Literary Studies*, 6/4, pp. 364–80.
Praed, Campbell Rosa (1891), 'The Bunyip', in Mrs Martin Patchett (ed.), *Coo-ee: Tales of Australian Life by Australian Ladies* (London: Griffith, Farran, Okedene and Welsh).
Priestley, J. B. (1934), *English Journey* (London: Heinemann).
Procter, James (2015), 'Una Marson at the BBC', *Small Axe*, 19/3, pp. 1–28.
Raelene, Frances (2013), 'Authentic Leaders: Women and Leadership in Australian Unions before World War II', *Labour History*, 104, pp. 9–30.
Rankin, Nicholas (2004), *Telegram from Guernica* (London: Faber and Faber).
Regan, Lisa (2012), *Winifred Holtby's Social Vision: Members One of Another* (London: Pickering and Chatto).
Reid, Ian (1979), *Fiction and the Great Depression: Australia and New Zealand 1930–1950* (London: Edward Arnold).
Richards, Dan (2016), *Climbing Days* (London: Faber and Faber).
Richardson, Dorothy (1924), 'In the Garden', *The Queen*, 2 July, p. 11.
Riedi, Eliza (2013), 'Imperialist Women and Conservative Activism in Early Twentieth Century Britain: The Political World of Violet Milner', *Women's History Review*, 22/6, pp. 930–53.
Roberts, Sian (2006), '"In the Margins of Chaos": Francesca Wilson and Education for All in the "Teachers" Republic', *History of Education*, 35/6, pp. 653–68.
Roberts, Sian (2011), '"I promised them that I would tell England about them": A Woman Teacher Activist's Life in Popular Humanitarian Education', *Paedagogica Historica*, 47/1–2, pp. 155–72.

Bibliography

Roche, Clare (2013), 'Women Climbers 1850–1900: A Challenge to Male Hegemony?', *Sport in History*, 33/3, pp. 236–59.

Rosenberg, Leah (2001), 'Una Marson's *Pocomania* (1938): Class, Gender and the Pitfalls of Cultural Nationalism', *Essays in Theatre*, 20/1, pp. 27–42.

Ross, Ishbel (1936), *Ladies of the Press: The Story of Women in Journalism by an Insider* (New York: Harper and Brothers).

Royde-Smith, Naomi (1924), 'Capital Punishment', *The Queen*, 12 March, p. 2.

Royde-Smith, Naomi (1926), *The Housemaid* (London: Constable).

Rubery, Matthew (2009), *The Novelty of Newspapers: Victorian Fiction after the Invention of News* (Oxford: Oxford University Press).

Rukeyser, Muriel (1936), 'Barcelona, 1936', *Life and Letters Today*, 15/5, pp. 26–33.

Rukeyser, Muriel (2013), *Savage Coast* (New York: The Feminist Press).

Schaffer, Kay (1989), *Women and the Bush: Forces of Desire in the Australian Cultural Tradition* (Cambridge: Cambridge University Press).

Schreiber, Adele, and Matheison, Margaret (1955), *Journey Towards Freedom: Written for the Golden Jubilee of the International Alliance of Women* (Copenhagen: IAWSEC).

Sebba, Anne (2010), *Battling for News: Women Reporters from the Risorgimento to Tiananmen Square* (London: Faber and Faber).

Seltzer, Andrew (2011), 'Female Salaries and Careers in British Banking 1915–41', *Explorations in Economic History*, 48/4, pp. 461–77.

Selvon, Sam (2006 [1956]), *The Lonely Londoners* (London: Penguin).

Seteney, Shami (1998), 'Circassian Encounters: The Self as Other and the Production of the Homeland in the North Caucasus', *Development and Change*, 29/4, pp. 617–46.

Settle, Alison (1947), 'Journalism Then, Journalism Today', *Women's Press Club Newsletter*, 1/4, May, pp. 3–4.

Settle, Alison (1973a), 'Alison Settle Remembers', *Observer*, 24 June.

Settle, Alison (1973b), 'Alison Settle Remembers', *Observer*, 1 July.

Shackleton, Edith (1922), 'Journalism as a Profession for Women', *Good Housekeeping*, March, pp. 16, 95–6.

Shackleton, Edith (1930), 'Women in Fleet Street', in Michael Pope (ed.), *The Book of Fleet Street* (London: Cassell), pp. 193–202.

Sharp, Evelyn (1910), 'The Women at the Gate', in *Rebel Women* (London: John Lane), pp. 7–19.

Sharpe, Nancie (1934), 'Cardiff's Coloured Population', *The Keys*, 1/3, January, pp. 44–5, 61.

Bibliography

Shaw, Marion (1999), *The Clear Stream: A Life of Winifred Holtby* (London: Virago).
Shepherd, Nan (1938), 'The Colour of Deeside', *The Deeside Field*, 8, pp. 8–12.
Shepherd, Nan (2011 [1977]), *Into the Mountain* (Edinburgh: Canongate).
Sheridan, Susan (2012), 'Sex and the City: New Novels by Women and Middlebrow Culture at Mid-Century', *Australian Literary Studies*, 27/3–4, pp. 1–12.
Simpson, Jacqueline (1991), '"Be bold, but not too bold": Female Courage in Some British and Scandinavian Legends', *Folklore*, 102/1, pp. 16–30.
Sloane, Nan (2018), *The Women in the Room: Labour's Forgotten History* (London: I. B. Tauris).
Smith, Sidonie (2001), *Moving Lives: Twentieth-Century Women's Travel Writing* (Minneapolis, MN: University of Minnesota Press).
Snaith, Anna (2014), *Modernist Voyages: Colonial Women Writers in London 1890–1945* (Cambridge: Cambridge University Press).
Snyder, Carey (2008), *British Fiction and Cross-Cultural Encounters: Ethnographic Modernism from Wells to Woolf* (New York: Palgrave Macmillan).
Solnit, Rebecca (2014 [2001]), *Wanderlust: A History of Walking* (London: Granta).
Souhami, Diana (2013 [1993]), *Gluck: Her Biography* (London: Quercus).
Spittel, Christina (2007), 'Remembering the War: Australian Novelists in the Interwar Years', *Australian Literary Studies*, 23/2, pp. 121–39.
Springer, Kimberly (1999), 'Introduction', in Kimberly Springer (ed.), *Still Lifting, Still Climbing: African American Women's Contemporary Activism* (New York: New York University Press), pp. 1–13.
Stannard, Martin (1978), 'Misleading Cases', *Essays in Criticism*, 28/1, pp. 85–90.
Stark, Freya (1985 [1950]), *Traveller's Prelude* (London: Century).
Stockman, Jan (2017), 'Women, Wars and World Affairs: Recovering Feminist International Relations, 1915–39', *Review of International Studies*, 44/2, pp. 215–35.
Storr, Katherine (2010), *Excluded from the Record: Women, Refugees and Relief 1914–1929* (Bern: Peter Lang).
Stott, Mary (1985), *Before I Go* (London: Virago).
Strachey, Ray (1978 [1928]), *The Cause: A Short History of the Women's Movement in Great Britain* (London: Virago).
Stuckes, Phoebe (2013), 'Daughters', in *Rattle the Hatches: Foyle Young Poets of*

Bibliography

the Year 2013 Winners Anthology, The Poetry Society, https://issuu.com/poetrysociety/docs/foyle_2014_anthol_issuu (accessed 7 May 2020).

Sykes, Reg, and Sykes, Pauline (2001), *One Hundred Years of Rambling 1900 to 2000* (Sheffield: Sheffield Clarion Ramblers).

Tebbutt, Melanie (2006), 'Rambling and Manly Identity in Derbyshire's Dark Peak, 1880s–1920s', *The Historical Journal*, 49/4, pp. 1125–53.

Tennant, Kylie (1939), *Foveaux* (London: Victor Gollancz).

Tennant, Kylie (1941), *The Battlers* (London: Victor Gollancz).

Tennant, Kylie (1943), *Ride on, Stranger* (London: Victor Gollancz).

Tennant, Kylie (1953), *Australia, Her Story. Notes on a Nation* (London: Macmillan).

Tennant, Kylie (2012 [1986]), *The Missing Heir* (Melbourne: Allen and Unwin).

Tennant, Kylie (2013 [1935]), *Tiburon* (Adelaide: Michael Walmer).

Thane, Pat (2001), 'What Difference Did the Vote Make?', in Amanda Vickery (ed.), *Women, Privilege and Power: British Politics 1750 to the Present* (Palo Alto, CA: Stanford University Press), pp. 253–88.

Thane, Pat (2013), 'The Impact of Mass Democracy on British Political Culture 1918–1939', in Julie Gottlieb and Richard Toye (eds), *The Aftermath of Suffrage: Women, Gender and Politics in Britain, 1918–1945* (Basingstoke: Palgrave), pp. 54–69.

Theobald, Marjorie (2000), 'Women, Leadership and Gender Politics in the Interwar Years: The Case of Julia Flynn', *History of Education*, 29/1, pp. 63–77.

Thomas Black, Sara, Milligan, Richard Anthony, and Heynen, Nik (2016), 'Solidarity in Climate Justice/Immigrant Direct Action: Lessons from Movements in the US South', *Journal of Urban and Regional Research*, 40/2, pp. 284–98.

Thompson, Cicely (1989), *Women's Engineering Society 1919 to Present Day* (London: Women's Engineering Society).

Thompson, E. P. (1993), *Witness Against the Beast: William Blake and the Moral Law* (Cambridge: Cambridge University Press).

Tomlinson, Lisa (2017), *The African-Jamaican Aesthetic: Cultural Retention and Transformation Across Borders* (Leiden: Brill).

Tusan, Michelle Elizabeth (2005), *Women Making News: Gender and Journalism in Modern Britain* (Chicago: University of Illinois Press).

Underhill, Miriam (1956), *Give me the Hills* (London: Methuen).

Vaughan, David (1950), *Negro Victory: The Life of Dr Harold Moody* (London: Independent Press).

Bibliography

Vicinus, Martha (1985), *Independent Women: Work and Community for Single Women 1850–1920* (London: Virago).

von Klemperer, Klemens (ed.) (1988), *A Noble Combat: The Letters of Shiela Grant Duff and Adam von Trott zu Solz* (Oxford: Clarendon Press).

Walker, Alice (1997), *Anything We Love Can be Saved* (London: The Women's Press).

Ward, Stephanie (2019), 'Labour Activism and the Political Self in Inter-War Working-Class Women's Politics', *Twentieth Century British History*, 30/1, pp. 29–52.

Waterfield, Lina (1961), *A Castle in Italy* (London: John Murray).

Westaby, D. J. (2012), *Dynamic Network Theory: How Social Networks Influence Goal Pursuit* (Washington, DC: American Psychological Association).

Wheelwright, Julie (1992), *The Fatal Lover: Mata Hari, Women and Espionage* (London: Collins and Brown).

White, Cynthia (1970), *Women's Magazines 1693–1968* (London: Michael Joseph).

White, Winifred (1952), *Hubert Peet*, Quaker Biographies.

White, Winifred (1993), 'Dedicated Work, Difficult Times', *The Friend*, 21 May, p. 659.

Williams, Cicely (1973), *Women on the Rope: The Feminine Share of Mountain Adventure* (London: George Allen and Unwin).

Williams, Raymond (1997), *The Politics of Modernism* (London: Verso).

Wilson, Francesca (1919), 'The Return of the Exiles with a Serb Transport to Belgrade', *Friends Quarterly Examiner*, July, pp. 274–82.

Wilson, Francesca (1920), *Portraits and Sketches of Serbia* (London: Swarthmore Press).

Wilson, Francesca (1923), 'The Women of the New Russia', *Manchester Guardian*, 17 May, p. 6

Wilson, Francesca (1933), 'A German University Town after the Celebrations of May Day', *Birmingham Post*, 16 May.

Wilson, Francesca (1934), 'A Community Experiment', *The Friend*, 28 September, pp. 875–6.

Wilson, Francesca (1937a), 'Listening to the Wireless', *Manchester Guardian*, 24 February, p. 8.

Wilson, Francesca (1937b), 'The Women of Madrid: Dancing in Food Queues', *Manchester Guardian*, 4 May.

Wilson, Francesca (1938), 'Relief Work in Murcia', *The Friend*, 11 February, pp. 109–10.

Bibliography

Wilson, Francesca (1938a), 'A Farm Colony in Spain', *The Friend*, 2 September, pp. 755–6.

Wilson, Francesca (1938b), 'A Children's Camp in Spain', *The Friend*, 25 November, pp. 1038–9.

Wilson, Francesca (1943), 'When Friends Last Worked in Bizerta', *The Friend*, 16 April, p. 261.

Wilson, Francesca (1944), *In the Margins of Chaos* (London: John Murray).

Wilson, Francesca (1945), *Advice to Relief Workers: Based on Personal Experiences in the Field* (London: John Murray and the Friends Relief Service).

Wilson, Francesca (1947), Aftermath: France, Austria, Germany, Yugoslavia 1945 and 1946 (London: Penguin).

Wilson, Francesca (1995), *A Life of Service and Adventure* (privately published).

Wiskemann, Elizabeth (1968), *The Europe I Saw* (London: Collins).

Wolf, James (1991), 'Imperial Integration on Wheels: The Car, the British and the Cape-to Cairo Route', in Robert Giddings (ed.), *Literature and Imperialism* (London: Macmillan), pp. 112–27.

Women's Co-operative Guild (1980 [1915]), *Maternity: Letters from Working Women, collected by the Women's Co-Operative Guild with a preface by the Right Hon. Herbert Samuel M.P.* (New York: Garland).

Women's Engineering Society (1930), *Facilities for Training Women as Engineers* (London: Women's Engineering Society).

Women's International League (1934), *Africa: Peace and Freedom* (London: W.I.L.).

Woolf, Virginia (1981), *The Diary of Virginia Woolf, Volume II (1920–1924)*, ed. Anne Olivier Bell (London: Penguin).

Woolf, Virginia (2006 [1938]), *Three Guineas* (New York: Harcourt).

Young, Michael, and Willmott, Peter (2011 [1957]), *Family and Kinship in East London* (London: Routledge).

Index

Abercrombie, Lascelles 250
Aborigines 281, 313–14
  'doomed race' theory 281–2
  mistreatment of 300, 319
  mixed-race families 300, 315, 317
  terra nullius 314, 329 (n.46)
activism 7
  links to rebelliousness 303
  origins of 7
  women's 2, 9
  writing and 2
Acton, Harold 184
Adelphi 20
Addison, Sir Joseph 161
Agate, James 28
Age, The (Melbourne) 324
Aggrey, James 277
Aid Spain movement 88, 252, 269
Aliens Restriction Order (1919) 254
Alpine Club 113, 115–16
Alpine Club Journal 2, 99, 112
Amalgamated Society of Engineers 228
Amalgamated Union of Shop Assistants, Warehousemen and Clerks 264

American Alpine Journal 114
American Relief Administration 85
Anning Bell, Laura 200
appeasement 151, 165
  British newspapers and 150–1, 162
Association of Hungarian Women Clerks 262
Astor, Nancy 3, 11, 120, 188, 262, 265
  Consultative Committee of Women's Organisations 265
Astor, Waldorf 265
Athenaeum 301
Atholl, Katherine (Duchess of) 165
Attlee, Clement 251
Auden, W. H. 20, 184, 201, 308
Autocar 216

BBC 271–2, 288, 361
  Calling the West Indies 288
'bachelor' women 4
Baldwin, Stanley 156, 251, 269
Ballinger, William 283
Bartlett, Vernon 140, 150

Index

Basque children, escape of (1937) (*see also* Manning, Leah) 251, 267
Bates, H. E. 198, 200
Bayer, Dr Frantisek 14, 162
Beaton, Cecil 42
Beaverbrook, Lord (Max Aitken) 32, 150, 186, 187
Beer, Rachel 187
Beeton, Samuel 334
Belcher, Margaret 238
Bell, Clive 43
Bell, Gertrude 133 (n.72)
Bennett, Arnold 26, 28, 46, 192, 195
Berlin, Isaiah 139, 146
Bilbao, siege of (1937) 267
Binder, Pearl 192, 194
Bingham, Adrian 348
biography as method 12–14, 361
Birmingham Post 61 (n.136), 87, 88
'Black Front' 143, 162
Bloomsbury Group 20, 52
  another/alternative 21, 54 (n.8)
Blumenfeld, Ralph 186, 189
Boer War (1899–1902) 79
Bondfield, Margaret 11, 264, 363
Booth, Catherine 257
Borthwick, Gabrielle 226
Bosanquet, Theodora 342
Boulestin, Marcel 43
Bray, Lilian 2, 114, 120, 121–2, 126
Bretherton, Eva 24
Bristol Evening World 354
Bristol 'Newspaper War' (1929–32) 353–4
Bristol Times and Mirror 343, 347, 353
British Commonwealth League 255, 282, 285
British Women's Patriotic League 101, 103

Brittain, Vera 22, 148–9, 171 (n.44), 296 (n.117), 349
  Dark Tide 25
  friendship with Winifred Holtby 22–6
  Testament of Youth 149
Brooke, Rupert 68
Brown, Curtis 237
Brunhoff, Michel de 41
Bryant, Louise 79
Bryher (Winifred Ellerman) 100–2, 233, 261
Bulletin, The 307, 319, 326
bunyip 318
Burke, Thomas 194
'business woman' 9, 23–4
Bystander, The 223, 232, 237

Cadbury, William 76
Capone, Al 177, 178, 190
Cary, Joyce 198, 200
Census (1911) 32, 252
Census (1931) 33
Chamberlain, Neville 150–1
Chase, Edna Woolman 41, 43
Chatham House 168–9
Chatto and Windus 234–5
  editor Harold Raymond 234, 237
Cheesman, Evelyn 189
Chicago Daily News 140
Chick, Harriette 189
Chilton, Sir Henry 267
Church Terrell, Mary 286
Churchill, Clementine 163
Churchill, Winston 163, 164, 169
Cixous, Hélène 286
Cizek, Professor Franz 84
Clark, Hilda 69, 70, 80
Clifford, Ethel 199, 200
Climbers Club Journal 112
Coal Control Board 264
Cockburn, Claud 139

Index

Colliers Weekly 155
colour bar 253, 276, 284, 285
Common Cause, The 34
Communist Party (Australia) 300, 326
Communist Party (Great Britain) 252
Constantine, Learie 276
Cooper, Lettice 324
Coordinating Committee Against War and Fascism 252
Corbett Ashby, Margery 286
Coronation (George VI, 1937) 267
Cosmopolitan, The (Jamaica) 274
Costelloe, Ray, *see* Strachey, Ray
Council for Promoting Equality of Civil Rights Between White and Coloured Peoples 283
Country Standard 112
Country Women's Association of Australia 316
courage (correct female) 142
Court Treatt, Stella 238
Cowles, Virginia 156, 160
Cox, Katherine 67
Craig, Elizabeth 38
Criterion 20
Cunard, Nancy 261
Czechoslovakia (*see also* Munich Crisis) 161–8
  'Little Entente' 162

Daily Express 15, 30, 103, 105, 106, 150, 179, 186, 187, 189, 190, 231
Daily Graphic 104
Daily Herald 29
Daily Mail 5, 21, 32, 36, 150, 175, 176, 186, 191–3, 202, 204, 214, 333
Daily Mirror 29, 103, 104, 179
Daily News 77, 85, 148

Daily Sketch 77, 107, 108, 179, 183
Daily Telegraph 161, 164, 187, 351
Daily Worker 157
Dalton, Hugh 162, 259
Dane, Clemence 23
Danish Council of Women 262
Dark, Eleanor 325
Dawson, Geoffrey 139, 150
Death Penalty, Bill for Abolition of (1924) 332–3
Deeside Field 112, 117
Delafield, E. M. 20
Depression (Great) 195, 299, 308
  Depression fiction 299
  in Australia and New Zealand 298–9, 308
Devonshire Club 175–6
DiCenzo, Maria 6
Dick, Margaret 321
Dickens, Charles 192, 194
Dixie, Florence 148
domestic service 30, 229
domestic sphere 4
Doolittle, Hilda (H. D.) 54 (n.8), 130 (n.12)
Duff Cooper, Lina 148
Dulac, Edmund 37
Duncan-Jones, E. E. 92

Ebbutt, Norman 148, 151
Eden, Anthony 268
Egan, Eleanor Franklin 85
Egyptian Mail, Cairo 231
Eliot, George 192
Eliot, T. S. 273, 336
Ellis, Richard 269
Eustance, Claire 6
Evening Standard 15, 24, 26, 36
Evening Times and Echo (Bristol) 343

Fabian Society 251
family networks 187–93
Farjeon, Eleanor 23, 340, 355

Index

Fashion Group of Great Britain 38
fathers
  absence of in women's lives 31,
    139, 220, 256, 364
  overbearing/repressive 106–7
Federation of University Women
  (*see also* International
  Federation) 342
Fell and Rock Climbing Club 117
Fellowship of Reconciliation 252
Ferguson, Rachel 350–1
Field, The 336
First World War 4
  Armistice celebrations 102
  Belgian refugees in Britain 27
  Food Control Committees 252
  newspapers launched during 27
  suffrage movement during 34
  women's changing roles during
    4, 28
  women's 'patriotic duty' during
    34–5
  women's work during (*see also*
    'munitions girls') 34, 212
'Fleet Street' as newspaper nexus
  32, 33, 106, 180
Forbes, Stanhope 214
Forchhammer, Henni 73, 263
Ford Works, Dagenham 230
Foreign Affairs 147
foreign correspondence 147
  women's 147–9
Forster, E. M. 177, 199
Friend, The 63, 68, 76–8, 87, 88,
  90–2
Friends of Africa 283
Friends Quarterly Examiner 76, 78, 80
Friends, Society of (*see also*
  Quakers)
  relief missions 76
  Service Council 64, 66, 91
friendship, between women 21–53
Fry, Alice 72

Fry, Elizabeth 257
Fry, Margery 71, 78
Fry, Ruth 70, 71, 78
Fyleman, Rose 52

Gardiner, Juliet 195
Garrod, Dorothy 188
Garvin, J. L. 140, 148, 150, 163
Gellhorn, Martha 155, 169
gender
  'blindness' 7
  pay gap 32–3, 56 (n.29)
General Strike (1926) 252
Gibbons, Stella 36
  Cold Comfort Farm 36–7
Goebbels, Magda 177
Gollancz, Victor 250, 324
Good Housekeeping 21, 132 (n.45)
Gordon Lennox, Victor 150, 162
Gordon, Wilhelmina 188
Grafenberg, Dr Rosie 239
Grant Duff, Adrian 144
Grant Duff, Shiela 10, 14, 136–69,
  217, 220, 221, 358, 359, 361,
  362, 363, 364, 368
  childhood 144–5
  Czechoslovakia 161–8
  editor, Czech Section BBC
    European Service 167
  Europe and the Czechs 166
  marriage to Noel Newsome 167
  Parting of Ways, The 152
  Spanish adventure 151–61
  Times rebuff 139, 147
  undergraduate at Oxford 142,
    145–7
Grant, Jane 321
Graves, Robert 200
Green, Henry Mackenzie 305,
  320, 324–5
Greene, Graham 22, 139, 198,
  201
  Brighton Rock 323

Index

Grier, Linda 146
Guernica, bombing 156, 268

Hadow, Robert 161
Hall, Mary 238
Hall, Radclyffe 200
Hamilton, Cicely 199
Hamilton, Mary Agnes 21
Handlin, Oscar 15
Harford, Lesbia 134 (n.90), 222
Harmsworth, Alfred (*see also* Northcliffe) 179
Harraden, Beatrice 95 (n.62)
Harrison, Austin 28
Harvey, Edmund 69
Haslett, Caroline 212
Hastings, Selina 14, 191
Heald, Ivan 29–31
Heald, Nora 29, 36, 53, 342
   editor of *The Queen* 31, 42
   editor of *The Lady* 31, 42
Hearst, Randolph 189
   newspapers 156
Heart of Empire Ball (1924) 342
Heinemann Publishers 202
Hemingway, Ernest 148
Henderson, Arthur 333
Herbert, A. P. 338–9, 355
Hill, Christopher 138
Hitler, rise of 87, 137–8, 146, 149
Hoare, Sir Samuel 268
Hobhouse, Emily 79, 81, 168
Holtby, Winifred 3, 22, 25, 147, 148, 171 (n.44), 282, 349
   Anderby Wold 25
   The Crowded Street 108
   friendship with Vera Brittain 22–6
Horder, Dr Elizabeth 86
Howard, Brian 184
Hughes, Langston 282
Hulton, Edward 30, 179
hunger marches (1930s) 146

Hunt, Karen 15
Hunt, Violet 199
Hurston, Zora Neale 282
Huxley, Aldous 22, 41, 43

Illustrated Sunday Herald 27, 28, 34
Independent Labour Party 251, 264
Industrial and Commercial Workers Union 283
Institution of Automobile Engineers 225
International African Friends of Abyssinia 255
International Alliance of Women for Suffrage and Equal Citizenship (IAWSEC) 154, 255, 262, 284, 286, 287, 289
International Conference of Women in Science, Industry and Commerce (1925) 228
International Congress of Women (1915) 34
International Council of Nurses 262
International Council of Women 262, 263
International Council of Women of the Darker Races 262
International Federation of University Women 262
International Labour Organisation (ILO) 228
   Night Work Convention 228–9
International Suffrage Alliance (also International Women's Suffrage Alliance) 70, 262
International Suffrage News
Isherwood, Christopher 201, 308
Italian Workers' Union 262
Ivens, Joris 64
   Spanish Earth 63–4

Index

Jamaica Critic 274
James, C. L. R. 276
Jameson, Storm 23, 46, 308, 340
   The Pot Boils 46
Jamie, Kathleen 98
Japan Times 223
Jay, Douglas 145
John, Augustus 41
Johnson, Amy 228, 231
Joint Council to Promote Understanding Between White and Coloured Peoples in Great Britain 283
Jordan, Philip, 268
Journal of the Fell and Rock Climbing Club 112, 117, 128

Katz, Otto 152
Kelly, Pat 118, 120, 123
Kennedy, Margaret 200, 202
Kenyatta, Jomo 276, 282
Keynes, Florence 261
Keynes, John Maynard 336
Keys, The 254, 255, 277–82
Kipling, Rudyard 178, 192, 218
Koestler, Arthur 151
Kubka, Dr Frantisek 162

Labour Party 11, 176
   women's progress in 264
Ladies Alpine Club 121–2
   annual report 121–3
Ladies Field, The 103, 336
   'lady novelist' 193
Lady, The 6, 26, 36–7
Lady's Pictorial 103
Lamb, Dorothy 68
Lane, Allen 164, 165
Lane, Harry George 179, 183, 186
Lane, Margaret 14, 55 (n.10), 175–210, 217, 220, 258, 360, 361, 364, 365, 366, 369
   At Last the Island 202

Capone trial 190
childhood 179–84
Edgar Wallace, Biography of a Phenomenon 203
Faith, Hope and No Charity 184, 194–202
marriage to Jack Hastings 185
Oxford undergraduate 184–6
Larminie, Margaret Rivers 340
Laski, Harold 307
Laughton, Charles 42
Lawson, Henry 305, 307, 310, 312
   'The Drover's Wife' 307, 311–15
Le Blond, Mrs Aubrey 121
League of Coloured Peoples (LCP) 255, 265, 272, 276–7, 286
League of Nations 73, 137, 149, 263, 287
   High Commissioner for Refugees 82
   investigation into trafficking of women and children 73, 263
   Permanent Mandates Commission 73, 263
   Union 148
Leavis, F. R. 20, 365
Leavis, Q. D. 20
Leeds Mercury 35, 268
Leeper, Rex 150–1
Left Book Club 252
Left Review 157
Lehmann, Rosamond 198, 200
Leslie, Henrietta 20, 95 (n.62)
Lewis, C. S. 184
Liaison Committee of Women's International Organisations 262
Life and Letters Today 130 (n.12), 158, 160
Linford, Madeline 80, 85–6, 349–50

Index

literature and journalism, relationship between 192–3
Liverpool Post 128
London Group on African Affairs 283
London Mercury 163
Loughborough Technical College 212, 220, 222, 226
The Limit 222, 224, 225
Lowe, Sylvia 280
Lubbock, Sir John 144
Luckett, Richard 126, 127
Lynd, Sylvia 23, 49, 200, 201

Macaulay, Rose 19–22, 23, 45–52, 199, 335, 343, 350, 355, 369–70
Abbots Verney 20
Casual Commentary, A 49
Crewe Train 46, 49–50
Dangerous Ages 22
friendship with Naomi Royde-Smith 19–22, 25, 45–52
Keeping up Appearances 21, 343, 350
Potterism 45
relationship with Gerald O'Donovan 47, 48
They Went to Portugal 52
Three Days 19
What Not 47, 335
Macdonald, Sheila 114, 116
Madden, Cecil 288
'male equivalence' 188
Mallory, George 115
Malone, Desmond 198
Manchester Guardian 24, 64, 75, 78, 79, 80, 85, 88, 89, 118, 128, 139, 141, 163, 333, 349, 350
'manless climbing' 1, 3, 99, 115, 123
Mannin, Ethel 20
Manning, Leah 10, 220, 250–71, 288–96, 359, 364, 370–1

Basque children 251, 267
childhood 256–8
marriage to Will Manning 260
MP (1931) 251
MP (1945–50) 290 (n.13)
teaching, teacher training 251, 258–61
visit to Spain (1934) 250
What I Saw in Spain 250
Mansfield, Katherine 301, 304
Mare, Walter de la 47, 49, 340
marriage 217
'bar' 8, 39, 59 (n.93), 107, 253
'refusal' 108, 217
Marshall, Mrs Charles 350
Marson, Una 11, 220, 253–6, 257, 262, 265, 271–96, 359, 360, 361, 364, 371
At What a Price 275, 280
childhood 273–4
editorship of *The Keys* 255, 272, 277–82
friendship with Winifred Holtby 282
Jamaica Save the Children 273
journey from Jamaica 271, 275
poetry 254–5, 274
producer at the BBC 272, 288
Martin, J. P. 344–7
Uncle books 345
Martin, Stella 220, 257, 343–55, 359, 363, 364, 365, 372
'Apples of Eve' column 343, 352
childhood 344–7
newspaper apprenticeship 347
One Woman's Year 372
Paperchase End 347–8, 350–1, 354
zoo correspondent 354
Martineau, Harriet 148

Index

'masculine outdoors' 2, 16 (n.4), 98, 111
'masculine public sphere' 5, 8
  conceived as a fortress 5, 8, 358
Massingham, Hugh 161, 336
Maynard, Constance 258
Mew, Charlotte 54 (n.8)
Meynell, Viola, 341
'middlebrow' 21
Middleton Murry, John 301
Miller, Lee 38
Milner, Violet, 147
Milton, Ernest 50
Mitchison, Naomi 251, 341
Mitford, Jessica 89
'mobile' woman 216–17, 237–9
Monroe, Harriet 54 (n.8)
Moody, Dr Harold 276–7
Moore, Aileen 269
Morrison, Herbert 252
Mortimer, Raymond 43
Mosley, Oswald 251
Mothers Union 5, 347
motoring and women 216
mountaineering 98, 111
  as an expression of national virility 98
Mowrer, Edgar Ansel 140, 143, 151–4, 161, 162, 165
Moyne Report (*see also* West India Commission) 284
Mummery, A. L. 115
Munich Agreement/Crisis (*see also* Czechoslovakia) 143, 151, 166, 322
'Munich' by-elections 165
'munitions girls' 212, 214, 229
Murray, Stella Wolfe 35
Murrow, Ed 148

Nansen, Fridtjof 82
Nast, Condé 41, 43
Nation and Athenaeum 333, 336

National Archives of Australia 14
National Association of Labour Teachers 252
National Council of Women 252, 261, 264, 287
National Federation of Class Teachers 251
National Federation of Women Workers 252
National Library of Australia 14
National Review 147
National Union of Journalists 35, 187
National Union of Societies for Equal Citizenship (NUSEC) 5, 265
National Union of Teachers 251, 264
  women presidents 253
National Union of Women's Suffrage Societies 261
Neilson, Shaw 310
networks, professional (*see also* social networks) 32, 33, 37–8
New Fabian Research Group 164
New Statesman 149, 150
New Street Pauper School, Cambridge 260
'New' Woman (1890s) 143
Newberry, Frances 80
News Chronicle 78, 141, 155–6, 166, 268
Newsome, Penelope 142, 161
Newspaper World, The 191
Nicolson, Harold 51, 56 (n.29)
nonconformism 257
Northcliffe, First Lord (*see also* Harmsworth, Alfred) 187
  newspapers 186, 204
Northern Echo 187
Nursing Mirror and Midwives Journal 231, 269

Index

O'Brien, Kate 200
O'Brien (Underhill), Miriam 109, 114, 115
O'Donovan, Gerald 47, 48, 49
O'Faolain, Sean 198, 236
Observer, The 26, 128, 136–7, 140, 143, 150, 161, 162, 163, 169, 187
Ojanguren, Angel, 269
Opportunity 244 (n.4), 246 (n.49)
Orwell, George 158, 194, 198, 273, 308
  Down and Out in Paris and London 299
  Homage to Catalonia 158
  Keep the Aspidistra Flying 198, 201, 202
  Road to Wigan Pier 298
Ould, Herman 45
Outlook 49
Oxford Magazine 184–5, 193

Pankhurst, Christabel 3, 108
Pankhurst, Emmeline 3, 262
parliamentary correspondence (women's) 26, 33
Parsons, Claudia 10, 211–48, 258, 358, 360, 361, 362, 364, 366, 372–3
  Brighter Bondage 223, 234–6
  chauffeur 226, 232–6
  childhood 218
  circumnavigation of the world 236
  engineering training 212–14, 220, 222–6
  Vagabondage 235, 240–2
  WW2 factory inspector 241
Peacocke, Emilie 187, 351
Peel, Mrs Charles 341
Peet, Hubert 77–9, 90
PEN (Poets, Essayists, Novelists) (English) 15, 36, 45, 199

Penguin Specials 165
Perham, Margery 281
Pevsner, Niklaus 87
People's Olympiad, Barcelona (July 1936) 158
Pilley, Dorothy 2, 4, 13, 97 135, 221, 257, 358, 359, 360, 362, 363, 365, 366, 374–5
  Alpine ascents (various) 97, 113–14
  ascent of the Dent Blanche (1928) 5, 99, 127
  childhood 99–101
  Climbing Days 98, 121, 125, 127–8
  early climbs in Wales 102
  editor of *Pinnacle Club Journal* 99, 122–6
  Mount Baker 127
  Pyrenees 124–6
  relationship with I. A. Richards 108, 126–7
Pinnacle Club 118, 120–2
Pinnacle Club Journal (*see also* Pilley, Dorothy) 2, 3, 99, 118–23, 126
Plymouth Brethren 66, 100
Poliakoff, Victor 150
Political Quarterly 163
Pollinger, Laurence 202
Pollitt, Harry 252
Potter, Beatrix 178, 204
Powell, Frank 182
Priestley, J. B. 36, 37, 308
Prior, Ken 319
Prix Femina-Vie Heureuse (Prize) 22, 37, 194–202
Pye, Edith 80

Quiver, The 24
Quakers (*see also* Friends, Society of) 63, 64
  humanitarian activities during WW1 68–9

Index

Quakers (*see also* Friends, Society of) (*cont.*)
 involvement in Spanish Civil War refugee relief 63
Queen, The 21, 26, 333–42

race relations 272
Rackham, Clara 261
Raelene, Frances 222
ragged schools 260
'Raj orphans' 218
rambling 111
 Manchester Ramblers 112
 Sheffield Clarion Ramblers 111
Reconstruction 76, 78–82
Red Cross 82
Rees, Goronwy 139, 140, 145, 146
Restoration of Pre-War Practices Act (1919) 4, 212
Reuters News Agency 137
Rhondda, Viscountess 38, 147, 212, 261, 341
 'whistling' 104
Richards, I. A. (*see also* Pilley, Dorothy) 13, 113, 126–9, 362
Richardson, Dorothy 23, 341
Rickword, Edgell 157
Roberts, Florence 155–7
Rothermere (First Viscount) 150, 187
Rowntree, Arnold 78
Rowntree, Tessa 78, 144
Royal Commission on the Press, 1947–49 357 (n.55)
Royde-Smith, Naomi 19–26, 45–52, 199, 221, 257, 336–42, 354–5, 359, 361, 363, 364, 365, 375
 Double Heart, The 51
 editor of *The Queen* 20, 23, 48, 336–42
 friendship with Rose Macaulay 19, 25–6, 45–52

Housemaid, The 46, 47, 49
 literary editor of the *Saturday Westminster* 20, 21–2
 relationship with Walter de la Mare 47, 48, 49
 Skin-Deep 336
 State of Mind of Mrs Sherwood, The 52
 Tortoishell Cat, The 48, 342
Rucksack Journal 112
Rukeyser, Muriel 158–60
 Savage Coast 159–60
Runciman, Hilda 188
Russell, Audrey 269
Russian famine (1921/22) 84–6

Saar plebiscite (1935) 136–7, 140
Sadleir, Michael 46
Salaman, Peggy 231
Saturday Review 147
Saturday Westminster (*see also* Royde-Smith, Naomi) 336
Schreiner, Olive 213, 340
Scotsman, The 149
Scottish Women's Hospitals 82
Scrutiny 20
Selvon, Sam 272
separatism (as a feminist strategy) 119
Serbian Relief Fund 72
Settle, Alison 26–33, 35, 37–45, 53, 180, 220, 221, 359, 364, 365, 366, 376
 editor of British *Vogue* 26, 38–45
 involvement with PEN 37, 42
 single parenthood 29, 38–43
 war correspondent 44–5
Sex Disqualification (Removal) Act (1919) 16 (n.11)
sexual harassment (in the workplace) 191, 204
Shackleton Heald, Edith 15, 21, 26–45, 53, 156, 179, 220,

Index

342, 359, 362, 363, 364, 365, 376–7
family background 29–31
highest paid woman on Fleet Street 26
involvement with English PEN 36–7
union work 26, 35
Sharp, Evelyn 16 (n.1), 199
Sharpe, Nancie 280
Shaw, Flora (Lady Lugard) 148
Shepherd, Nan 16 (n.3), 111, 117
Shop Assistants' Union 264
Sinclair, May 54 (n.8)
Sitwell, Edith 50, 186
Sitwell, Osbert 43, 50
Six Point Group 131 (n.39), 212
Smith, Stevie 198
social networks (concept) 53, 255–6, 264–5
Socialist League 251
Society of Authors 193
Society of Women Journalists 33, 35
Sokolov, Michail 87
Spanish Civil War (*see also* Grant Duff, Shiela; Wilson, Francesca) 88, 151–61
blockades of Basque ports 155, 167
child refugees in 62–5
humanitarian/medical aid for 88, 155, 252
International Brigades 89
Non-Intervention Agreement 151
nurses volunteering in 89, 231
women's journalism during 154–61
Spectator 163, 164, 236
sports acceptable for women 109
Spurgeon, Caroline 199
Stark, Freya 110, 238
Steer, George 148

Stephens, Pembroke 151
Stephens, Winifred 199
Stevenson, Sir Ralph 268
Stewart, Kilton 242
Stopes, Marie 3
Stott, Mary 187
Strachey, Amabel 200, 201
Strachey, John 252
Strachey, Ray 5, 23, 67, 258, 340, 349
Strasser, Otto 162
strategies of engagement, for women 9–10, 359–60
Strutt, E. L. 114
Studebaker Journal 242
suffrage
movement 2
post-1918 5, 217, 360
press (*see also Common Cause; The Vote*) 32, 34
Sunday Chronicle 30, 179
Sunday Express 31, 105, 107
Sunday Herald (*see also Illustrated Sunday Herald*) 28
Sunday Mirror 104
Sunday Pictorial 27, 28
Sunday Times 141, 156, 187
Swanwick, Helena 3, 11, 147
Swinnerton, Frank 324
Sydney Daily Telegraph 307
Syrett, Netta 200, 201

Tabouis, Genevieve 149, 165
teaching as a profession for women 252–3
Tennant, Kylie 11, 14, 220, 234, 239, 257, 298–331, 358, 359, 360, 363, 364, 377–8
Australia: Her Story 324
Battlers, The 323
childhood 302–4
Foveaux 298, 299, 319–22, 324
immersive, or 'Gonzo' style 299

Index

Tennant, Kylie (*cont.*)
  literary stance 301
  marriage to Charles Lewis Rodd 306
  Missing Heir, The 302
  pacifism 303, 322
  Ride on Stranger 324
  Tiburon 299, 308–19, 326
  walking as escape 300
Thomas, Stella 276
Thompson, Dorothy 114, 123
Thompson, E. P. 12
Time and Tide 21, 26, 38, 45, 49, 128, 147, 149, 229, 333, 338, 340, 341
  'Our Men's Page' 339
Times 139, 148, 150, 168, 333
Times Literary Supplement 52, 128
Todd, Dorothy (*see also Vogue*) 42–3, 337
Townsend Warner, Sylvia 198
Toynbee, Arnold 166
Trades and Labour Councils 251
travellers (women; *see also* 'mobile' woman) 237–9
Tucker, David 278, 279
Tynan, Katharine 341

Ulster Gazette 30
United Nations
  High Commission for Refugees 234
  Relief and Rehabilitation Administration (UNRRA) 91

Vansittart, Robert 150–1
Vogue (British) (*see also* Settle, Alison) 29, 42, 336
Vogue (US) 41
Voigt, Frederick 141, 150
Von Trott, Adam 139, 140, 152
Vote, The 34, 229
Vulliamy, Grace 72

Wallace, Edgar 202, 343
Walrond, Eric 282
Waterfield, Mrs Aubrey, *see* Duff Cooper, Lina
Webb, Beatrice 3
Webb, Mary 307
Weekly Westminster Gazette (*see also* Royde-Smith, Naomi; *Saturday Westminster*) 45
Wells, H. G. 28
West African Students Union 255
West India Committee 288
West India Royal Commission 273, 284
West Indian immigration 276–7, 280
  Tiger Bay, Cardiff 280
West, Rebecca 41, 199
Westfield College 258
Westminster Gazette (*see also Saturday Westminster; Weekly Westminster*) 49, 69
White Australia Policy 11, 287, 300, 316, 327 (n.7)
White, Patrick 301, 325
White Fisher, Harriet 238
Whitehorn, Katherine 353
Wilkinson, Elizabeth 157
Wilkinson, Ellen 3, 149, 250, 268
Wilson, Francesca 10, 53, 62–92, 168, 217, 220, 257, 349, 359, 360, 363, 365, 378–9
  educational philosophy 84
  In the Margins of Chaos 75, 91
  interwar work in Serbia, Austrian and Russia 83–7
  journalism 75, 85–91
  Portraits and Sketches of Serbia 75, 84
  Spanish Civil War work 62, 63–5, 88–92
  student at Cambridge 67–8
  unhappy childhood 66

Index

WWI work in North Africa and Corsica 81
Wilson, Maurice 66, 71, 72, 81
Wilson, Sarah 148
Winthrop-Young, Eleanor 123
Winthrop-Young, Geoffrey 112
Wintringham, Margaret 120, 188
Wiskemann, Elizabeth 149, 151, 169
Wodehouse, P. G. 343
Wolfe, Humbert 50
Woman Engineer 212, 213, 222, 227–32
Woman Journalist 35, 229, 231, 350
Woman Teacher 24, 231, 246 (n.49)
Woman's Leader 227, 229
Woman's Motor Manual 226
Women's Citizens Associations 121
Women's Committee Against War and Fascism 157
Women's Co-operative Guild 264
Women's Emergency Corps 82
Women's Engineering Society 212, 223, 227, 243
Women's Freedom League 35
Women's Institutes 5, 11
Women's International League for Peace and Freedom (WILPF) 11, 72–3, 154, 255, 262, 263, 283, 287
  attitudes towards colonialism 283
  Peace Conference, Zurich (1919) 286
'women's page' in newspapers 32–3, 343–4, 349
Women's Peace Party of America 262
Women's Press Club 37–8
Women's Social and Political Union (WSPU) 261, 262
Woolf, Virginia 2, 3, 8, 11, 20, 43, 55 (n.21), 68, 177, 199, 308
  'Mr Bennett and Mrs Brown' 210 (n.86)
  plotting against Naomi Royde-Smith 336
  Three Guineas 3, 8, 101
Workers Educational Association 224
World Disarmament Conference 262
World Union of Women for International Concord 262
World's Children, The 78
World's Women's Christian Temperance Union 262
World's Young Women's Christian Association 262

Yeats, W. B. 32
Yorkshire Post 180
  books page 324
Young, E. H. 110, 122, 123